Preface

My intention in writing this bool ___ ___ ___ ___ ___ ___ ___ ___ ___ ___sis
of the major contemporary poli___ ___ ___ ___ ___ ___ ___ ___ who
wants to understand politics. I trace their development in context,
to provide a depth of understanding and background.

This book focuses on the driving factors: That is on those things
which determine the structure of government. These are religion, economics, education, and science. But what is behind all of them is the
nature of the human psyche and the relationship between personality
and culture.

published by: Hargrave Publishing
Post Office Box 157,
Carlsborg Washington, 98324–0157

First printing 2000

Library of Congress Catalog Card Number: 99–94283
ISBN 0–9671290–0–X
Recommended Retail Price: U.S. $16.95, Can. $24.95 Softcover

Politics of Change

A Brief History

Dr. Robert N. Crittenden

Hargrave Publishing

Contents

Chapter 1

Classical Foundation

The first four chapters cover the Classical and Early Medieval periods. — During the Victorian era, the practice was to teach only the Classics: They held that everything that one needs to know is contained in them. That is an exaggeration, but many of our basic concepts *do* come from those times.

In particular, this first chapter briefly describes the Classical ideas which define "Western" thought. In trying to give a complete statement, this book must begin at the beginning. Consequently these first chapters give basic material which may be familiar to most people. So, this is covered relatively quickly. But this lays the foundation upon which the later chapters build.

The second chapter gives the Classical origin of "Eastern" thought, and the third shows how these matured in the Middle East to provide many of the World's religions. The fourth chapter covers the early medieval period. That was a time of transition, preparing the way for Western man. Western civilization did not emerge until the Golden Age of France, around 1200 AD.

1.1 Philosophy of Reason

No person has ever had as profound or lasting an effect on the Western World as Aristotle (384–322 BC). He developed the philosophy of reason, which provides the fundamental structure of Western society.

That philosophy was based on the assumption that through reason man can discover the body of physical and social truths known as "Natural Law."[1] These provided the organizing principles of Classical society and,

---

[1]Some of these laws describe physical processes, while others deal with morality, civil law, and the structure of society. To obtain an introduction to Natural Law, Alexander Hamilton's recommended, in 1775, the works of William Blackstone, Hugo Grotius, Samuel de Puffendorf, John Locke, and Charles S. de

later, provided the foundation for America's form of government.[2] They remain an issue today.[3]

The core belief of the Aristotelian school of political thought is that reason is the source of the rights of man, particularly of his freedom.[4] By "freedom" he meant the right to make decisions and take actions within the limits of morality, law and Natural Law.[5] People who reason can perceive those limits and those who also desire a just society and a moral life will act within them of their own free will.[6] Thus, they can achieve true freedom. In contrast, those who do not reason must learn law and morality from those who do. As this latter class of people must live according to rules set by others, they are governed by others and are not free. Aristotle referred to these un–free as "slaves."[7]

Alexander the Great (356–323 BC) learned the philosophy of reason

---

Montesquieu.

[2] Although Natural Law was extensively discussed by the founding fathers, there are relatively few direct references to it in the organic documents of the United States. One is the reference to "the Laws of Nature" found in the Declaration of Independence.

[3] For example, when US Supreme Court Justice Clarence Thomas was going through his confirmation hearings, during the Reagan Administration, he unequivocally stated his belief in "Natural Law ."

A second example is found in the 1996 election campaign. The "Natural Law Party" ran candidates in every state. Their platform was that all the country's problems could be resolved through transcendental meditation. However, that practice is based on inward–looking processes and mystical philosophies rather than outward–looking processes and the philosophy of reason. Their objective appears to have been to confuse the public and discredit Natural Law. The very fact that the Natural Law Party existed and was active national–wide, attests to the issue's importance to current events.

[4] Freedom should not be confused with "license" which is the right to decide or act in any possible way, without restrictions.

[5] The meaning of the English word "liberty" is fairly close to that of "freedom" in this Classical sense. Liberty implies deliberation, that is rational thought. This is an important contemporary concept because according to the Declaration of Independence, governments are instituted among men to secure the rights of life, liberty, and pursuit of happiness. Also, the Preamble to the United States Constitution declares that "securing the blessing of liberty to ourselves and our posterity" was one of the specific purposes for which they formed the government.

[6] Aristotle held that these are man's ultimate goals. But, he, also recognized that there were both virtuous and vicious men and he believed in individual choice and individual responsibility. See his *Nicomanchean Ethics*.

[7] A more contemporary view of slavery was given by John Locke in his *Second Treatise of Government*: "Freedom of man under government is to have a standing rule to live by, common to every one of that society, and made by the legislative power erected in it; at liberty to follow my own will in all things, where the rule prescribes not; and not to be subject to the inconstant, uncertain, unknown, arbitrary will of another man."

Thus, for both Aristotle and Locke, a free person has freedom within the boundaries set by law, whereas a person becomes a slave when he or she is placed under the decision power of another.

from Aristotle, who was his tutor; and spread it across much of what was then the civilized world.[8] His most lasting contribution was the founding of a great library in Alexandria, Egypt, in 330 BC. It drew together nearly a half–million manuscripts, representing much of the world's learning. It remained a nucleus for the spread of Greek culture long after his death.[9]

The philosophy of reason reached its most highly developed Classical form, in the writings of Marcus Tullius Cicero (106–43 BC).[10] He was the last great patriotic leader of the Roman Republic.[11] As the head of their conservative party, he tried to restore and maintain Rome's traditional form of government, in opposition to Julius Caesar.

Cicero followed Aristotle on most things, but the change from Aristotle to Cicero is best illustrated in the view held by the latter that all human beings are naturally equal. In particular, during their republican period, the Roman jurists held, that all authority resided in those individuals who reasoned, and their standard for reason was the practical ability of the individual to manage his own affairs, both public and private.[12]

As Cicero enunciated it, Natural Law has two essential features:

1. It must apply equally to all and grants neither special exemptions nor dispensations.[13]

2. It must be just. Under its classical definition, "justice" is achieved when the practice of the government and the law courts corresponds with the civil heritage of the people. — Classical Rome mostly followed the enlightened practice of allowing the laws to vary, within limits, from province–to–province as the heritages differed. Thus,

---

[8] Alexander's war camp contained not only soldiers but also poets, artists, philosophers, and so on. Thus, he spread Greek thought as he conquered. His empire stretched from Greece into India.

[9] Alexander died young. He drank, not only once but twice, the huge cup of Hercules, and died of that excess.
After Alexander's death, Aristotle, no longer had his protection. Fearing the belligerent ignorance of the Athenians, he went into voluntary exile. He died only a short time afterwards.

[10] Cicero was a Roman. He was educated in Athens and Rhodes, and as a young man gradually advanced through various posts in Rome's government. At the end of his life, he was the leader of their conservative party.

[11] Republic: A form of government where the decision–making power is held by representatives who are elected by the qualified voters and accountable to them.

[12] Aristotle's standard, that the rights of man come from reason, remained the abstract principle, but was difficult to apply in practice. — Who was to decide who the reasoning people might be? Therefore, when Athens formed their republic, they gave suffrage to all competent free Athenian males who were of age. Roman Republic followed much the same course. — They held that the public was composed of "men who are capable of directing and controlling their public as well as their private lives to ends determined by themselves." See Carlyle 1941 his page 11 or Carlyle and Carlyle 1908, page 9.)

[13] As all reasoning people will discover identically the same Laws of Nature, these can not make distinctions among individuals, except those which are based on general principles that apply equally to all.

they attempted to achieve justice throughout their empire, even though it was composed of diverse peoples and cultures.

Cicero lived during the last years of the Roman Republic. He was the leader of the group who killed Julius Caesar in the Senate House, in 44 BC. The next year, Mark Antony's soldiers killed him. That was one of the final acts in the struggle between the conservatives and the monarchists. By then, the struggle had been going on for about one–and–a–half centuries. It had begun during the closing years of their second war with Carthage (218–201 BC).

1.2   Second Punic War

The Carthagian Empire was located in North Africa, west of Egypt. According to legend, it had been founded, around 814 BC, by colonists from the Phoenician city of Tyre.[14] Carthagian society had three classes, strictly divided by race:[15] Phoenicians, Liby–Phoenicians, and native Libyans.

---

[14] The Phoenicians were a branch of the Canaanites, and shared a common language with them.

[15] "Race" means only a group of related people at any of several levels of genetic similarity above that of the basic population. For example, one may speak of the English, Low–Germans, Germans, and Nordics. In this list, "English" is a population or nationality within three levels of race, nested one within the other. No one level is intrinsically "race" more than the others.

A "population" is defined by being freely interbreeding: that is, there are no boundaries preventing marriage among the different parts of a population. Social class is not regarded as a boundary, in this sense, because individuals can move among classes. Conversely, by definition, there are such impediments to intermarriage at the level of race. These may be cultural or geographic. Their effect over the long–term can be seen in the diversity of mankind.

The integrity of the racial concept becomes less defensible as one moves to higher and broader levels. The problem is that all the races of mankind can interbred, and have done so over archeological and historical time–scales. But such mixtures can only occur among peoples who come into contact with each other. Consequently, some parts of a race will interbreed with adjacent races, whereas others will remain geographically isolated and genetically distinct. This lends considerable variety and complexity to the relationships among mankind's various groups which can not be adequately represented simply by blocking peoples together into "races." Therefore, racial designations are more meaningful when they are narrowly defined and become progressively less realistic as the "races" considered become broader and more inclusive.

The highest and broadest races are effectively without meaning, but serve a different social function. — Anthropologist, Dr James Downs, pointed out, in 1971, that "Black," "White," and "Brown/Yellow/Red" are neither race nor social class but the categories in America's traditional caste system.

It was originally based on skin color. — "White" referred to the fair–skinned races, specifically the Nordics and the Alpine Roundheads from the European part of their range; "Brown/Yellow/Red" referred to all the races with lightly pigmented skin, including the Mediterraneans, Alpine Roundheads from the Asiatic part of their range, Orientals, and American Indians; and "Black" lumped to-

The Phoenicians were the aristocracy, while the Libyans were a subject race. Only the Phoenicians held the franchise, had political rights, or could hold elected office or military command.

Carthagian society was purely capitalistic: All of their civil relationships were monetary. A man's life, property, family, rights, ... each had an assigned value. Hence, they treated most of what we regard as crimes as being merely financial transactions.

Their religion was the worship of the ancient deities of the Semitic people.[16] They had a pantheon of Gods and Goddesses, but the main object of their worship was the patron God of the city, the Baal. His worship is described in some detail in the *Old Testament*.[17] They followed primitive religious practices: for example, in the hope of victory, during the Punic Wars, they sacrificed many hundreds of children.

Carthage was in violent contrast against Rome, which, at that time, still strove after the Classical ideal of a just and moral society. These two empires first came into conflict, in 264 BC, over the possession of Sicily and Sardina. That was the First Punic War. It lasted 24 years. In the end, even though Rome's loses were greater, she prevailed because the ruler of Carthage, Hamilcar Barca, sued for peace.

gether all the dark–skinned races, including the Negroes, Negritos, Dark–skinned East Indians, Australian Aborigines, and Oceanians. These categories have been redefined, since then, particularly, since 1960. This can be seen in the definitions used in the US Census. The primary changes were that the Mediterraneans, Latin Americans, and dark–skinned East Indians were redefined as "White," whereas the Australian Aborigines and Oceanians were recognized as categories of their own. — Excepting these latter two groups, these categories are effectively without meaning in terms of biological race.

India was not the only country to have hereditary castes, with their appointed stations in life. As in India, movement between castes in America was not just a matter of money, culture, nor education; a person had to "pass" as a member of a category: that is, the public had to perceive the individual that way. Thus, caste membership was essentially a matter of appearances.

The American caste system was never more than regional. It was prevalent in the Northeast and South, but weak in the Southwest. In particular, the Brown/Yellow/Red caste was generally not recognized there. Individuals who were brought up in the Southwest might not even be aware of these customs from the Eastern United States. — Having grown up in California, during the 1950's and 1960's, I can say that the social divisions which were recognized there tended to reflect the composition of the region, and that prevalent attitude was that people were expected to have self–respect and to present themselves as whatever they were.

[16] The word "Semitic," in the strict sense, refers to a language group: specifically, Akkadian, Arabic, Aramaic, Hebrew, Phoenician, and so on. However, the peoples who speak these languages were also closely related. They form a subgroup of the Mediterranean Race. — The racial groupings which are the most useful for the discussion of history are those which are relatively narrowly defined and coincide with cultural differences. Semitic is one such category.

[17] It is discussed as the religion of the Canaanites: in particular, see Numbers 25, Judges 6, 1 Kings 18, and Hosea 2. Prior to 1200 BC, most of the Semitic peoples followed this religion.

He retired to Spain, where he raised his sons, Hannibal and Hasdrubal to harbor an implacable hatred of Rome and the Roman system. They renewed the contest, in the Roman Province of Spain, in 221 BC. At the opening of this second Punic War, Hannibal took his army from Spain across Southern Gaul. He then crossed the Alps to invade Italy, in 218 BC, while his brother, Hasdrubal, remained behind in Spain with another army. Ten years later, he followed.

Hannibal and Rome had approximately equal military strengths. Neither had been able to entirely overcome the other. But, Rome could never have withstood the strength of Hannibal and Hasdrubal's armies if they combined.

The year that Hasdrubal was expected to arrive (207 BC), Rome sent out approximately 140 thousand soldiers[18] in Italy alone. They were in six armies under the command of two consuls. Cassius Claudius Nero commanded three armies facing Hannibal in Southern Italy, while Marcus Livius prepared, with the other three, to meet Hasdrubal whenever and wherever he emerged from the Alps.

Hasdrubal came down the Po Valley and, after some delay with an unsuccessful siege of the Roman town of Placentia, marched down Italy's Eastern coast, beside the Adriatic Sea. Marcus Livius withdrew before him as he advanced but sent word to the other Consul. Cassius Nero responded by leaving only a small force opposing Hannibal's and took the rest of his men North, by forced marches, to combine with Marcus Livius's men.

When Hasdrubal found that he faced the combined Roman armies, he attempted to withdraw under the cover of night. Unfortunately for Carthage, he marched up the box canyon of the Metaurus River. The next morning, they were trapped by the Romans. Hasbrubal's Gaelic divisions, knowing they were doomed, got drunk. But, he made the best arrangements he could, placing his war elephants in front and his drunken levees behind a steep slope of rubble. There, on that bright early summer morning, jammed between those canyon walls, the two armies met and fought until the smaller one had been slaughtered. — The first Hannibal knew of these events was when his brother's head was thrown into his camp.

That was the Battle of Metaurus. It essentially eliminated Carthage's chance of winning the war, but Hannibal continued operations in Italy for several more years before withdrawing to North Africa.[19]

---

[18] About half were levies from the Provinces.

[19] In 205 BC Rome carried the war to Africa. Slightly later, Hannibal was recalled by Carthage to lead their forces there. The war ended in 201 BC when Carthage sued for peace after losing the Battle of Zama. Rome began the Third Punic War (149–146 BC) when Carthage's power began to recover. It ended with the destruction of Carthage.

1.3 Decline of Rome

We first encounter the moral decay which was associated with Rome's decline, during the closing years of the Second Punic War. — Before Hannibal left Italy, he threw everything he had at them. In 204 BC, they were hard–pressed and desperate. To restore public confidence, the Senate introduced the religious cult of Magna Mater, claiming to have found a prophecy in the Sibylline books[20] that this Goddess would bring them victory.[21]

Magna Mater, or Earth Mother, was an ancient deity of the Mediterranean Region, worshiped in Italy long before Rome was founded.[22] They reintroduced this ancient primitive faith, for their general populace. The worship of Magna Mater promoted the grossest profligacy of manners among the rabble. It would be difficult to exceed the brutality and obscenity of some of their religious ceremonies.

Several other religions were introduced during the years which followed. The Egyptian worship of Isis, was introduced into Rome only a few years after Magna Mater.[23] But it was suppressed in 58 BC, due largely to Cicero's strong objections. He regarded it as a contemptible cult. It was recognized by the Triumvirs, in 43 BC, the same year Cicero was killed. But it was again suppressed, only a few years later, by Augustus. It was finally recognized under Caligula.

These Roman worships of Magna Mater and Isis were only their more prominent new religions. Throughout the period of Roman decay, many mystery religions developed. In particular, during the first century BC, the Neopythagorean movement arose in response to the popularity of this type of religion and also of superstitions and prophesy.[24] This movement continued until the third century AD.

---

[20] The Sibyls were a group of women, in Italy, who had mystical or religious revelations. The Roman government had these duly recorded in the Sibylline books.

[21] See Livy's *History of Rome* XXIX. 14.

[22] She was a deity from the Neolithic garden culture of the Mediterranean region. That culture was matriarchal and Magna Mater was a fertility Goddess. Carroll Quigley pointed out, in 1961, that "Fertility" combined the desires that their wives should produce babies and their gardens abundance

[23] Isis was another earth–based fertility worship of a garden culture. It had originated in Egypt and was associated with the annual vegetative cycle of sprouting, growth, reproduction, and death.

During the fourteenth century BC, the ruler of Egypt, Amenophis IV (1411–1375 BC), conceived of the existence of a monotheic God. However, he was unable to convert the general population to his views due to opposition from the priests. After his reign, the Egyptian court remained monotheic and came to an understanding with the priests: they also admitted an underlying monotheism, but continued to provide the populace with a primitive polytheism.

[24] Neopythagoreanism was not a cohesive philosophy so much as a collection of esoteric knowledge and beliefs for use in building religious myths. It drew together primarily the mystic religious teachings of Pythagoras, Plato, and other philosophers of their general school of thought.

The next landmark in Rome's moral degeneration, following the introduction of Magna Mater, came in about 160 BC when Classical plays were replaced by gladiatorial combats as the entertainment of Rome. The classical play was intended solely to be morally up–lifting and thought–provoking. In contrast, the gladiatorial combats inflamed the lusts of the rabble. At the end of the entertainment, they would rush forth into the streets to be met by swarms of prostitutes. By the time of Nero, the entertainments also included great public orgies.

The economic changes caused by Rome's final victory in the Second Punic War had even more drastic effects. That removed the restraint which Carthage had previously imposed on the expansion of their empire. Thereafter, large numbers of slaves were brought to Rome as a result of her incessant wars of territorial aggrandizement. By the end of their republican period, slaves comprised approximately 40% of the population of Italy. This altered Rome's economy.

Up until about 200 BC the Roman economy had been based on citizen–owned small–farms. Their principle product was wheat and they hauled their produce to market in ox–drawn carts, which was a relatively expensive form of transportation. All the land in the State was taxed, except public land. But, some of the wealthiest patrician families held the public lands in perpetuity and operated them for their personal benefit. Agricultural labor on these large estates was done by slaves. They produced mainly wine and olives which they exported. Shipping around the Mediterranean Sea, largely in slave–rowed galleys, was inexpensive. However it was controlled by the patricians, making the export markets inaccessible to the plebeian farmers. In addition, the provinces often paid tribute in wheat, which was brought to Rome by this same inexpensive means. This gave the State the ability to set the price of wheat and, thereby, control the profitability of the plebeians' farms.

As their empire grew, these factors progressively destroyed Rome's small–farm economy, and replaced it with a slave–based economy serving an export market. The small farms had also been devastated by the Second Punic War and never fully recovered.

Rome offered few other employment opportunities to Roman citizens. They were not a manufacturing society, and the few manufacturers they had employed either skilled artisans or slaves. Consequently, the sons of the poorer Romans usually sought employment in military service. This was available to them, because, the Roman army was only open to Roman citizens. Later, that restriction was relaxed, but only after they were no longer able obtain enough Romans to fill their ranks. Following military service, many of the soldiers remained in the provinces, because economic conditions were better there. — Those who returned to Rome often found their family farms confiscated for unpaid taxes.

A mass of unemployed landless impoverished plebeians and freed slaves accumulated in Rome where they lived on welfare. The State supplied publicly–owned four–story tenements and gave them free food. The conditions of this rabble were poor enough that some of them entered the gladiatorial service. It guaranteed them a violent death, but gave them good living conditions.

Two other practices which contributed to the decline of the Roman population were their high rates of homosexuality and infant exposure, especially of females.

These socio–economic problems were a constant drain on the numbers and composite wealth of Rome's plebeians. Originally, Rome had a sound economy, morality, and social system and this was reflected in a healthy population growth rate of around 1.5% per year. However, these socio-economic problems caused their growth rate to decline. By approximately zero BC, it became negative and their population began to decrease. The patrician families also were affected by these trends.[25]

The Romans were aware of the economic cause of their problems and in 133 B.C. Senator Tiberius Gracchus introduced a program of sweeping agricultural reforms, called the "Gracchan reforms." They distributed over one–third of the publicly–owned land to landless Romans. However the beneficial effects were short–lived and by the time of Cicero, Roman civilization had decayed beyond recovery.

At that time, the pernicious influences of gladiation and the other public entertainments kept the Romans in a constant state of emotional tension and promoted their corruption; they were further led astray by the various new religions; they followed the guidance of priests in determining their views and conduct; and they spent little or no time in quiet reflection. In addition, they lived in State housing and ate the State's bread. By their own standards, they were only worthy of slavery.[26]

With the transformation of Rome from a republic to a dictatorship, in 28 BC, the Roman jurists held that the citizens, although originally the source of all rights, were no longer fit to rule themselves and had transferred their rights to the throne. Thereafter, Imperial Roman law was based on the assumption that the people had only such rights as the monarch granted them.

Despite Rome's debased condition, it was able to continue for another four centuries, because, as her families decreased and died out, their wealth was progressively concentrated among few–and–fewer people. Thus, their population decline maintained their standard–of–living despite their negative net production. — Their economy, during that period, was a system for progressively mining the aggregate wealth of their population.

As Rome's population decline went on unabated, it became difficult

---

[25] We find that of the 20 patrician families in 306 BC, eight had died out by 67 BC and the remaining 12 were gone by the end of another century. The emperors were constantly raising plebeians to the rank of patrician to counteract this.

[26] In the Classical Greek perspective, the rights of man came from reason which led man to a just and moral society; whereas in the Classical Roman perspective the rights of man came from their ability to manage their own public and private affairs to ends determined by themselves. Their general public did not meet either standard.

for them to find Roman youth to fill their legions and tax revenues to support them. Consequently, they adopted a more pacific policy and ceased expanding their territories. But, this reduced their supply of slaves and accelerated their downward spiral. The third century AD was characterized by the complete collapse of their government and economy. They openly became a military dictatorship and the soldiers made and deposed emperors.

1.4   Classical Religions

Religion was the key to Rome's social system. To understand how it worked, we need to understand how they viewed the human psyche. — They thought of men's minds as having three levels below that of the Spirit:[27]

1. The flesh or physical–self receives input from the senses, emotions, and instincts, and performs actions driven by subconscious impulses.

2. Lower–reasoning consists of deductive reason and intuiting,[28] — These processes operate on objects in the mind. These include classifications or facts, laws or rules, perceptions, memories, and emotional content.

3. Higher–reasoning, involves the intellect and intuition. — Some Classical thinkers held that these mental processes communicated with the realm of the Spirit, but, others held that only the intellect did. "Reason" as employed by Aristotle was based primarily on input from the senses, deductive reason, and the intellect.

4. The Realm of the Spirit, where God and pure forms reside. — The Greeks also assumed that the spark of life, which they called the "soul," was a little bit of that Spirit which resided within the individual.

The center of man's religious impulse is the Image of God, which resides within each individual's psyche. Philo Judaeus (circa 20 B.C – 40 AD) may have been the first to discuss it, but many people since that time have also recognized its existence. In particular, both Luther and Calvin held that God had placed His Image in man's minds so that they should be aware of His existence. However, Philo recognized that what people believe to be God differs very widely: For example, he pointed out that the Epicureans made a God of their bellies. Therefore, although the Image

---

[27] This "Classical model for the psyche" was not laid out in detail by any of the Classical authors. John Locke (1632–1704) created this model to explain what they had been thinking. However, he was clearly not the first to do so, as the "stave lattice" from the Nordic Pagan worship of Woden, also, appears to be essentially the same thing. It is illustrated in Figure 4.1.

[28] "Intuiting" is trying out one's feelings on an idea. It differs from "intuition" discussed below, which is knowledge which emerges spontaneously from the subconscious.

of God clearly predisposes mankind to believe in God's existence, it does not describe His nature.

The twentieth century psychiatrist Carl Jung wrote, in 1921, that the Image of God is the archetype for good, that it is the individual's core motivations, what he or she regards as the ultimate objectives or the highest qualities. This definition is essentially adopted here: Then "religion" becomes the mental framework of understanding, belief, and subconscious linkages by which an individual connects his or her Image of God to the real world of existence and the inner realms, to give meaning and value to life.

When religion is viewed in this broad psychological sense, it becomes apparent that a people's religion will establish what constitutes their particular standards of morality, what for them are just laws, and what may be an appropriate form of government for them. Thus, religion provides the natural organizing principles for human society.[29]

Part of the religious need is the individual's need for an affirmation of God. That can be obtained either directly through any of a variety of methods for accessing the psychic interiority or indirectly by experiencing anything which the individual perceives as a sign of God. For example, mystics have religious experiences through meditation; Cicero and, later, Kant saw God in the Truth of reason and the Order of nature; and a present–day tribe in Borneo is said to obtain confirmation of the existence of God when they sight a helicopter, for they believe that the Gods travel in those aircraft. — It is difficult to measure the strength of religious experiences, but, so far as we know, the experiences of all these individuals were equally meaningful. What is religiously meaningful is determined by the individual's motivational goals and what he or she believes.

The Classical philosophers recognized three levels of religion:

1. **Primitive religions** are characteristic of people of the flesh whose dominant mode of mental function is pre–rational:

   People at a primitive level are usually intimately in touch with their psychic interiority, because their primary mental activity resides in the subconscious and is expressed through emotions and intuition; but they are also equally in touch with their physical existence and with nature. According to Spencer and Gillen, in their 1899 study of the aborigines of North America and Northern Australia, these peoples regarded interior mental experiences, such as dreams and memories, as being as real as physical events. But their religious leaders or shamans were at a higher level of mental development. In

---

[29] In her 1944 book, Professor of Religion and Philosophy at Milwaukee–Downer College Louise S. Eby (1901–1948) compared and contrasted what constitutes moral law under each of the major world religions. However, she tended to view religion through rose–colored glasses and she also neglected to include the Almighty Dollar, Science, and Government among the Gods. But, she can not be blamed for that, as they came into wide use in the Soviet Union and the United States only after her time.

particular, they were usually individuals who reasoned. The general tribal members often regarded their words as being prophetic: that is, being of a quality outside of and above their realm of existence, as indeed, they were.

During the Classical and Medieval periods, the bulk of the people may not have been too far from this primitive level. One indication, is the belief, during those times, that the heart was the center of an individual's existence, rather than the head:[30] They were more physical animals than mental beings. This partially explains why ancient primitive faiths, such as the worship of Magna Mater were readily accepted by the Roman masses.

Sexuality apparently played a central role in the Worship of Magna Mater. This can be seen in the initiation ceremony for their priests. It was orgiastic and terminated with their public self–castration. That severed them from sexual emotions and the corresponding parts of their Image of God. In that regard, it placed them outside of that primitive level of existence.

That was their State–sanctioned primitive religion. The significance of Rome's emotionalizing the masses and gratifying their physical lusts was that it fostered a carnally–based Image of God and, thereby, placed the rabble in the hands of this State Church.

2. **Orthodox Faiths** are characteristic of people whose dominant mode of mental activity is based on memory, learned behaviors, and faith or beliefs, combined with intuiting or superficial deductive reasoning, but lacking any deep or comprehensive thought. These were characteristically polytheic religions with anthropomorphic Gods. They include the religions of Roman mythology.

Religions of this general class were practiced by the bulk of the cultured people during Classical times. These individuals were not concerned with abstract ideas; their primary concerns were routine business and social interactions.

There was little division between religion and government during those times. This was further reduced after the fall of the republic. Then, the Caesars had themselves declared Gods and had their statues put in the Temples as objects of worship. The primary function of the priests in these State religions, from the State's viewpoint, was to make their followers accept State policies. The Roman priests were very effective at doing this because the Romans were more religious than we are accustomed to.

The Roman culture ranked piety as the single greatest virtue, almost to the exclusion of all other virtues. Piety is submission to the will

---

[30] This gave a special significance to blood. The Greeks originally regarded the soul as the spark–of–life, and the heart as the site of a person's existence, so they probably regarded blood as being associated with the life–force or soul in some way. The significance of blood pervades Western religion and superstition.

of the Gods. They accepted their beliefs on faith and they consulted the Oracles on the more important questions. Piety inclined the people to accept whatever the priests told them.

Faith opened the doors to their spiritual interiority: The act of accepting faith involves an intellectual sacrifice.[31] Just as some Romans on the primitive level sacrificed their sexuality to enter the priesthood, so did others sacrifice their intellect to enter these mainstream Roman religions. — Faith returns an individual to a childlike condition in which the characters in life are hypostatized. The child's world has security due to responsible kindly parents, and so also does the world of the faithful under the Church. But the world of a child or of the faithful is unreal. One remedy to this problem is to become even more deeply committed to faith by casting away all rational and intellectual thought and grounding belief on the irrational bedrock of the psychic interiority. Thus, faith leads to mysticism and draws towards the primitive.[32] That was the Roman way. But, there was another way, the Classical Greek path, the path of replacing faith with an abstract intellectual religion.

3. **Abstract Intellectual Religions** are characteristic of people whose primary mode of mental activity is rational and intellectual. They characteristically involve an abstract God and are often monotheic. That is because the affirmation of God is obtained through the intellect, which is the mental facility for finding a unified or comprehensive organization: that is, it provides understanding. Like emotions, and intuition, the intellect directly accesses the subconscious and, therefore, can provide the affirmation of God.

The individuals who followed these abstract beliefs did not need the alters of organized religion, they needed only their minds, and good rational and intellectual skills to study nature. Unfortunately, these beliefs can not meet the religious needs of the common man because the affirmation of this God is unobtainable without an intellect. — In all ages, the common man has been almost entirely non-intellectual. That was particularly so, during Classical times, when only a tiny fraction of the population had any education whatsoever.

Mystical Religions use some of the same mental faculties as primitive religions, such as dreams and revelation. But, they were also potentially based on all the mental processes. — The mystical was not always clearly distinguished from the intellectual. — Consequently, some of the people who followed mystic faiths had their general existence at a higher mental level, whereas others did not. The mystics, of course, all viewed themselves as using higher-reasoning processes, but not all the Classical thinkers agreed with them.

---

[31] Carl Jung (1921) added, in his *Psychological Types*, that not every individual has an intellect to sacrifice.

[32] See Carl Jung's, ibid. discussion of Origin and Tertullian.

The minimum that is necessary for a mystic faith to function is for its followers to believe in the intrinsic validity of the mystic experience. — As mysticism does not necessarily have a logical basis, almost any quasi–rational myth could serve as their doctrine, but there were also more sophisticated mystical doctrines such as are found in Hinduism and Buddhism.

During their decadent period, the Romans provided suitable religions for the two lower levels and did everything they could to emotionalize their populace and form their Images of God to the primitive level. People at that level are so easy to control. — The emperor was traditionally their leader. History gives a lengthy record of Rome's Emperors pandering to the crowd's basest nature.[33] His crimes against nature and against men, had the effect of forcing the populace to recognize his special dispensation and elevated status. They also helped to maintain his image in their minds, and focused each individual on him as a powerful psychic entity. — The social result of this was that, whenever He made a demand of the people, they would obey.

The Roman authors wrote for their middle and upper classes. They never tired of relating how tried methods and hard work prevailed over innovation. This promoted orthodoxy and glorified the intellectual sacrifice. But, that sacrifice had a cost for Rome as a society. — They never advanced in science and technology beyond that which they inherited from the Greeks. The Roman perspective can be seen in the architectural works they have left us. Unlike the Greeks who left works of beauty with a delicate balanced form; Roman architecture is characterized by the stolid repetition of a few simple ideas. They wanted their populace to be driven by the subconscious, or to follow on mindless faith, and they were willing to bear the cost of their lack of creativity.

However, the Roman elite, sent their sons to be educated at the Greek academies. There can be little doubt that some of them fully understood the importance of reason and worshiped an abstract monotheic God. They were the masters, the only truly free people in Roman society. Cicero provides the clearest example of a person of that class.

This Roman system worked because it played upon mankind's nature. Under it the individual could do pretty much whatever he or she pleased, within very broad limits, but the individual was controlled through financial pressures and through the alters of his or her religion. This gave Rome's leaders the ability to influence a large enough segment of the Roman populace so that they could direct the public as a whole.[34] This, made decadent Rome a relatively cohesive unit, and although she was no longer capable of conquering any new territories, she was able to hold an empire which was larger and lasted longer than any other before her time.

---

[33] See Seutonius's *Lives of the Seven Caesars.*

[34] As rule–of–thumb, if about a third of the people can be controlled, the rest will follow. But, in Rome's case, the vast majority were controlled.

Chapter 2

Classical Mysticism

The first chapter presented the rational side of Classical culture, whereas this chapter examines the other side. That is their "Eastern" side, as opposed to Aristotle's "Western" orientation. It is called "Eastern" because it can be traced to the Orient: that is, to the lands which lie East of the Mediterranean Sea. In particular, much of it seems to have originated in Persia.

2.1   Persian Religious Heritage

The Persians are descended from the Aryans. They were a northern long-headed people who spoke an Indo–European language.[1] They invaded the Persian plateau from the Northeast, around 1800 BC. At that time, they

---

[1] The peoples of historical interest to Western man were originally of five fundamental types.

The smaller Negrito and the larger and more robust Negroids were the occupants of Africa.

North of them, the Mediterranean region was originally occupied by the southern long–heads. They are also called the "Mediterraneans." They are the brown–skinned race which currently occupies the Middle East and North Africa. However, they originally also occupied much of the coast north of the Mediterranean Sea.

North of them were found the alpine round–heads. They have a short stout stature and skulls which slope back from the brow ridges. They occupied the mountainous regions from France through the Alps, Balkans, Turkish Highlands, Trans–Caucasus Region, and also in a belt from the Balkans across Asia as far as the borders of Mongolia. They were a late arrival, who pushed into Europe from the East. They separated the southern and northern long–headed peoples.

North of them lived the northern long–heads or "Nordics." They were tall, had fine features, and tall vertical foreheads. They were the Celts, Germans, Greeks, Persians, and so on. They are sometimes referred to as "Indo–Europeans," but that really refers to a language group and does not always follow racial lines.

had a cattle–raising culture and their interests centered on their villages
and family life. They had normal families with monogamous adult marriage; and their society was divided into three classes, commonality, nobles,
and priests. The ancient Persian religion was an anthropomorphic polytheism. At the head of their pantheon was Varuna, the sky God, defender of
cosmic order; and Mithrus, the God of light, defender of truth, and enemy
of the forces of darkness.[2]

Zoroasterism: However, Zoroaster, also known as Zarathustra,
converted the Persians to a new religion named after himself. There is
some uncertainty about when he lived, but the current opinion is that he
probably lived during the sixth or seventh century BC. However, he may
have lived as early as the tenth or twelfth centuries BC.

He was Median rather than Persian, so Zoroasterism is often referred to
as the Median religion.[3] When Persia and Media amalgamated politically,
it became the State religion of Persia and was spread by the expansion of
their empire. That began during the late seventh century BC, reached its
peak during the reign of Darius I "the Great" (528–485 BC), and ended
when Alexander the Great conquered Persia in 330 BC.

The expansion of the Persian empire represented more than just the
conquest of one nation over others. It had the general nature of a holy war.
They were spreading what they believed to be the true faith. Although
they were tolerant and did not force their religion upon the nations they
conquered, the nations which were resisting them knew that they were
fighting for both their liberty and their religions.

For example, Plutarch refers to several of Athens' wars as being against
Medism, that is against Zoroasterism. Athens also found it necessary to
use both the death penalty and ostracism[4] to combat the spread of Median beliefs. That was the cause for the execution of several philosophers,
including Socrates; the ostracism of others; and the temporary voluntary
exile of yet more, including both Plato and Aristotle. These great Classical
philosophers were revolutionaries in their time. They were spreading the
bright flame of intellectual thought, which had been ignited by Zoroasterism.

Zoroasterism was probably the most influential religion the world has

---

New races can arise due to adaptation to an extreme environment or by the
crossing of earlier races followed by a period of isolation, until they become genetically stabilized.

Races are constantly appearing, changing, and disappearing. For some examples, the African Bushmen are an Mongoloid–Negrito cross and the Eastern
Baltics are a blond, blue–eyed, round–headed people, representing a cross between the Northern long–heads and the Alpine round–heads. The first group is
of prehistoric origins, whereas the latter emerged entirely within the historical
period.

[2]The Roman Army adopted the worship of Mithrus, during the first century
BC.

[3]Media was in the south–eastern trans–Caucasus region generally along the
western and southern sides of the Caspian Sea.

[4]Ostracism was exile for ten years.

ever known. What made it so, was that it was the first abstract monotheic religion to become successfully established as a State religion. In the Gathas in their sacred book, the *Avesta*, their God, Ahura–Mazda, is referred to as "Mind" or "Good Mind." He is Truth, Goodness, Spirit, and Thought. He is the prime mover, that is the essential existence behind all changes or processes in an otherwise static and lifeless universe. Their principle ritual, the fire sacrifice, symbolized this, for fire, like their God, is a process, without any static material existence.

But, Zoroasterism gradually lost the purity of its initial concept. Some of the adulterations are reputed to have been begun by Zoroaster himself. In particular, in order to account for the existence of evil, he introduced a subordinate Evil Principle, "the Lie," that is Angra Mainyu or Ahriman.[5]

If the ultimate Good, the Image of God, is Truth, as it was for the early Zoroasterans; then its opposite, Evil, or the Devil, is falsehood. But, when Truth is God, the corresponding Evil necessarily plays a subordinate role. That is inherent to the nature of truth. — An idea is "true" only if it exists as a force in nature or accurately describes one; therefore, it is impossible for a "falsehood" to control any phenomenon, for if it did, we would call it "truth." Consequently, when God is Truth, Evil will only be its insubstantial shadow. This is why seeking Truth in Nature is necessarily a wholesome activity.

But, as Zoroasterism aged, the Evil Principle grew until it was the eternal, co–equal twin of the Good Principle. During its later years, some Zorasterians even directly worshiped Evil, to propitiate that powerful deity.

These changes are thought to have been largely due to the Median priests, that is the Magi. At first they opposed Zoroasterism, but later they took it over and introduced into it everything they wanted. These included meditation and communication with spirits. In fact, Mede is the root word of both "meditate" and "medium." They also introduced magic. In fact, Magi is the root word of "magic."

These changes probably reflected a transition from a religion of an agrarian people who focused on truth and the physical world to one of priests who dealt with people and their social and psychic phenomena. With them came Evil, for, although it does not exist in the first realm, that is the realm of Truth and the physical world, it does have essential existence as a psychic or social entity.

Primitive people who can not perceive the abstract, and who may even confuse psychic events with happenings in the physical world, tend to give Evil a physical representation, such as Satan, demons, devils, or unclean Spirits. They may, also, follow superstitious practices to conjure and worship them. During its later years, Zorasterism incorporated many of these kinds of beliefs and practices, but it never wholly lost the abstract concept of Good and Evil.

---

[5] A general the definition of "Evil" is that it is that which opposes God, where "God" is taken in the psychological sense as meaning an individual's ultimate goals or Natural Goals.

Zorasterism flourished for over twelve–hundred years. It was finally replaced by Islam, shortly after 650 AD. Today, it is virtually a dead religion, practiced by only a small number of people in India and Iran.

2.2   Hinduism and Buddhism

From approximately 1800 to 1200 BC, the Aryans continued their invasion from the Iranian plateau into India. There they followed essentially the same way–of–life and religion as their brothers in Persia. Their beliefs are recorded in the Hindu's *Rigveda*. That is the world's oldest living religious scripture and Hinduism is the oldest living world religion. The *Rigveda* was first written down around 1000 BC, but it was, then, already ancient. Parts of it are drawn from the ancient Persian religion, and have similarities to the older Gathas in the Zorasterian *Avesta*.

Early Hinduism, that is Vedic Hinduism, was vigorous and positive. But, the religion became more pessimistic during their Brahmanic period. That was roughly from 800 to 600 BC. At that time, they developed extensive ritual, an unalterable caste system, the beliefs that an individual is trapped in an endless cycle of reincarnation, and that the human caste or animal species an individual is born into depends upon the amount of karma that individual accumulated in his or her previous existence. These ideas are believed to have been introduced by the priest and noble classes to perpetuate their superiority over the commonality.[6]

However, doctrines which developed later said that an individual can rise in this cycle and be united with the Transcendent Spirit by following an ascetic contemplative life–style.

Buddha, that is Siddhartha (563–483 BC), is said to have received his enlightenment in 528 BC. He rejected both asceticism and Brahmatical beliefs and founded Buddhism. The ultimate goal of Buddhism is to escape from the endless cycle of reincarnation. He taught that this can be accomplished through enlightenment, which reunites the individual soul with the Transcendent Spirit.

The contemplative approach, which is part of both Hinduism and Buddhism, reached its peak in the second century BC with Patanjali's *Yoga–Sutras*. That is the seminal book for Classical Yoga.[7]

The Yogis considered there to be a vital connection between the physical realm and the psyche. They believed in clairvoyance, telepathy, telekinesis, and that the mind imposes its structure upon reality. — Although these phenomena have never been demonstrated, the effects of Yoga upon the mind are palpable.

The objective of Yoga is to bring the mind under complete control and also to inhibit the modifications which it imposes on perception and

---

[6]Originally there were four castes: priests, nobles, commoners, and non–Aryans. The latter were the dark–skinned Dravidians, who were the aboriginal people of India.

[7]See I.K. Taimni, 1968.

reality.[8] The Yoga doctrine holds that the individual must pass through seven stages of development. The Sutras warn of the many pitfalls along the way and Carl Jung, also, commented about the risks of meditation.[9] — The proper Yoga practice is done under the direct instruction of a master. There are five major approaches to Yoga:

1. Hatha–Yoga deals mainly with exercises;

2. Karma–Yoga deals with caste duties and is suited to active individuals;

3. Bhakti–Yoga is based on love of God[10] and is suited to affective personalities;

4. Raja–Yoga is what is most widely known a Yoga and is suited to introspective personalities; and

5. Jnana–Yoga is suited to philosophical minds. It stresses nonattachment,[11] thought, and knowledge. According to Johnson 1939, some Yoga masters studied Natural Law. But, the Sutras generally place more emphasis on the intuitive than the intellectual.

These Eastern philosophies have close similarities to beliefs which developed concurrently in Ionian Greece, on the opposite side of the Persian Empire, beginning around 550 BC. At that time, Persia stretched from India to the Mediterranean Sea and had good roads and a regular system of internal communications. However, the similarities between Greek and Indian thought, during that period, may have been as much due to the influence of Persian thought on both as to their influence on each other.

2.3   Milesian Philosophers

The early Greeks were another northern long–headed people. They had displaced the indigenous Mediterranean people during their early migrations, roughly 3000–2000 BC. Other branches of that same migration resulted in the Terremar culture of Italy and the Teutonic peoples along the Danube Valley and into Northern Europe. These cultures were interconnected by a trade route along the Danube River and the Adriatic and Black Seas. That trade also extended throughout the Eastern Mediterranean. In particular, their commerce with Egypt was well established by 2000 BC. This was the Mycenaean civilization which Homer portrayed in his *Iliad* and *Odyssey*. — They had a high culture. For example, around approximately 1600 BC, they adopted a linear script, which replaced their

---

[8] See the second Sutra.
[9] See Jung's *Memories, Dreams, Reflections.*
[10] See the twenty–third Sutra.
[11] See the twelfth Sutra.

older hieroglyphic writing. That allowed the development of an advanced literary style as illustrated by Homer's works.[12]

Around 1200 BC, a second group of northern invaders arrived into the Greek world. They destabilized the region and also introduced an iron–age culture. The resulting wars destroyed the trade route which had interconnected the Nordic, Greek, and Italian cultures. The sack of Troy, in approximately 1184 BC, recorded in Homer's *Iliad*, was part of that conflict. — Troy was the major center for the trade along the Danube River and Black Sea.

The Peoples of the Sea, who broke in waves over the Eastern Mediterranean region, around that time, represented successive migrations out of the Aegean area. Some of these were the fleeing Mycenaean civilization, whereas others were the new group seeking further lands to conquer. However, eventually, the new invaders settled down, and became Classical Greece.

Western thought began, as a unique entity, around 600 BC, in the Ionian Greek trading center of Miletus located on what is today the Mediterranean coast of Turkey, but which was then part of the Persian Empire. There, the practical–minded Greeks encountered the knowledge, technology, and religion of Persia. The result was that the philosophers of Miletus consciously rejected the anthropomorphic Gods of Greek mythology as the agents controlling physical phenomena and sought to replace them with universal truths.

They applied a rational, practical, and positive orientation grounded on physical reality. This approach was passed down to Aristotle, who turned it into an integrated philosophy. They also speculated, quite freely, on the nature of the universe, man, and God, and on applied issues such as the goals of man, the nature of morality, and what might be a desirable structure for civil society.[13]

Anaximander: (611? – 547? BC) was one of these Miletian philosophers. His creation myth was seminal to a great deal of Classical thought. He felt that the universe was originally of one substance, in harmony. He called this primal substance "aperion," which means many

---

[12]Homer lived in the ninth century BC. But his work reflects a literary style which had developed slowly over centuries. His writings drew their material from earlier manuscripts and are thought to have been partial rewrites of them.

[13]When we discuss the ideas of the early Greek philosophers, it soon becomes evident that they were strongly influenced by the structure of their language. Early Greek had a limited vocabulary, tightly defined by explicit definitions. These suggested and allowed certain interpretations, but made others more difficult. This influence was especially strong on Parmenides (circa 475 BC), who felt that all philosophy should be based on the interpretation of the meanings of words. Several other philosophers are know to have followed his suggestion.

But that was only one school of thought. Many of the other Milesian philosophers were more interested in drawing conclusions based on what their senses told them about the world. Nevertheless, they probably all suffered from this fault to some degree. (See, for example, Bertrand Russel, Ludwig Wittgenstein, or Gilbert Ryle of the ordinary–language school of philosophy.)

things all related to the absence of limits. These include infinite, ever-lasting, indefinite, and indistinguishable. In his cosmology, the universe was created by splitting aperion into parts, by segregating it through the formation of limits or boundaries. The four primary parts which were, thus, formed were hot, dry, cold, and wet. However, he reasoned that the primordial substance from which the universe was made, was the union of these and must, therefore, have had all or none of those properties. As he felt that it was impossible to perceive anything like that, he concluded that the primal substance must have been not perceptible and, therefore, that ultimate reality lay in the nonperceptible realm of ideas and the soul.

Pythagoras (584–507 BC), the famous mathematician and religious seer, continued this line of thought, giving it an Eastern orientation.[14] His philosophy had many similarities to Buddhism. In particular, both believed that the Transcendent or Universal Spirit exists, an individual's soul is of the same substance as that Spirit, is immortal, can transmigrate, and is reincarnated. They both also believed that through self-examination, an individual can come closer to the Transcendent Spirit.

"Gnosis" is a critical concept in his ideas. It is a Greek word for knowledge. But the Greek language contains two words for knowledge. One is for the type of knowledge obtained from understanding, for example, of science or mathematics. That is the knowledge associated with reason. Gnosis is the other type of knowledge, the knowledge associated with direct experience. For example, an individual who has met John Smith can say that he "knows" him, in the sense of gnosis; whereas, a person who has studied the writings of John Smith and, therefore, understands his motivations and ideas, would "know" him in the non–gnostic sense.[15]

---

[14] He was born on the Ionian Isle of Samos and was educated in Egypt. He returned briefly to Samos, but soon immigrated to Crotona in Southern Italy. There, he founded a society which was both religious and political. They gained power in that city, until they were ousted by a revolt in which several of their leaders were killed. After that they moved to Metapontum. There they existed until the mid–400's BC. Then they were scattered by another civic movement which rose up against them.

His cosmogony starts with the planting of a finite seed of order in the infinite universe of aperion. About that seed order grows filling an ever–expanding but finite realm. He coined the word "kosmos," for that realm. That word combines the concept of the universe with orderly arrangement and beauty.

He understood the fundamental connection between order and limits. Order arises from laws whether natural, scientific, legal, or otherwise; and laws function by establishing limits. He found order in the world around him, in mathematics, music, and astronomy; and he held that by studying the order of nature man could unite his soul as closely with the divine as it is possible for a mortal to do. His was a mystic and his beliefs were a strange mixture of science and religion. One of the peculiarities was that he held the Earth and Kosmos were living organisms. The Earth was female, Order was male, and the seed of Order created new life, the Kosmos. Thus, his cosmogony myth was similar to sexual reproduction.

[15] In its narrow sense "gnosis" means direct experience of God or of religious or esoteric concepts.

Anyone who has done much mathematics is familiar with gnosis. In particular, algebraic proofs involve constructing a chain of logical steps from known facts to whatever one wishes to prove. But there is also a basic set of theorems[16] which can not be proven by decomposable reason. The individual must see and understand them by direct experience. In the more modern terminology of Immanuel Kant these are called the "a priori" truths, but Pythagoras would have said that they are the truths known by gnosis.

Consider what happens when you solve a difficult mathematical problem. When you begin, you are in the dark, but, nevertheless, you work the equations and think about the problem; then suddenly, "poof," you see the answer. That understanding comes like a flash of light. The process which creates it is not visible to the conscious mind. Pythagorians probably held that it came from the Transcendent Spirit. Therefore, the school of Greek philosophy which dates back to Pythagoras held that as Truth comes from the Spirit and, also, that it is found by seeking inwards. They also turned away from the physical world as they held that the senses should not be trusted, for they can easily be deceived.

Although it might appear to an individual that enlightenment comes from a transcendental source, because it bursts upon consciousness; that same appearance could also be provided by understanding coming from the unconscious mind. In particular, Herman von Helmholtz (1821–1894) showed that the process which results in these events of enlightenment, involves unconscious inferences which occur in the cerebral cortex. The name for this process is the "intellect."

2.4   Unconscious Mental Processes

The intellect is the actively–initiated slow unconscious reasoning process. It is usually highly reliable. For most people it conveys a sense of reality and direct experience. That feeling is heightened when it is combined with support from decomposable reason and sensory input from the physical world. When one looks outwards to the physical world and applies reason to it, to gain an understanding of nature; the mental processes employed are sensing, decomposable reason, and the intellect. If due care is taken to safeguard against the tricks of the senses, this approach can be highly productive. It is the mental process behind the concrete, positive, practical "Western" viewpoint.

But, the intellect is not the only form of unconscious thought. Others are our sense perceptions. They are fast unconscious processes. They also

---

[16] These are the basic theorems A=A; if A=B then B=A; A+B=B+A;.... Technically, this particular set of theorems is not necessarily the only basic set. They can be replaced by any other set of theorems which are reducible be decomposable reason to this set. So, which set is the fundamental one? Obviously, none. All are equally true, but some are easier for humans to experience than others.

have less than perfect reliability, as optical illusions illustrate. Therefore, most people realize that their senses can be deceived and don't perfectly trust what they perceive through just one sense. The feeling of the certainty of physical reality is obtained when input comes from several senses over a range of experiences.

Just as with the sense perceptions, so also with the various other unconscious mental processes: The degree of reality attributed to the products of each process depends upon their reliability. Each individual probably learns, through experience, which mental processes are more trustworthy for themselves and, thus, acquires that conditioning which determines which processes convey the sense of reality, and which do not.

The "Eastern" viewpoint relies on the spontaneous unconscious mental processes of feelings, dreams, the intuition, and religious and psychic experiences.[17] These are arranged in ascending order by the strength of the sense of reality and direct experience which they convey to most people. The higher initiates in the Eastern religions do not necessarily believe them; they just observe and consider them.

Feelings are the gateway to the psychic interior which is open to primitive man or man at the level of the flesh. A person at that level will be immersed in their psychic interiority and often in tune with nature. Symbols and paradigms dominate that level and result in religions of superstition. The thinkers of Classical times generally did not give much credence to these processes nor the associated religions.

They generally regarded dreams as being more reliable. But, their interpretation has always been problematic.

The intuition is the passive subconscious logical process, probably of the right-brain. It is gives holistic understanding, for example, of geometry and physical things. This is Plato's and Pythagoras's gateway to the subconscious mind. It is relatively reliable.

Religious and psychic experiences are a different kind of phenomenon. They bring with them a great deal of emotional energy combined with a sense of direct experience. The property which unites them is that intense sense of reality. As you will see, later on, some people thought that this might be due to a chemical key.

Religious experiences usually convey the existence or presence of God, whereas psychic experiences usually involve what appears to be a communication, whether that be telepathic, from God, or otherwise.

These phenomena are part of the human condition. However, they are rare enough as to be virtually impossible to study among the general population. But, the clinically insane provide a better opportunity. For example, this author knew an individual who suffered from bipolar disorder with rapid cycling who, for more than a week, had a religious experience every afternoon on a routine basis. That implies that these mental processes or the intense sense of reality can be induced by physiological conditions.

---

[17] There are more kinds, of subconscious processes, both active and passive, than are mentioned in this section.

Any thoughtful person will recognize, that the "knowledge" such psychic or religious events convey, is of unknown veracity and, therefore, must be verified or disregarded. Although some of them are as reliable, as the intellect is, others are not.

One can get some impression of the latter kind from the mental aberrations of alcoholics in delirium. They can "see" burning ships, pink elephants, or whatever else emerges from the subconscious. They do not distinguish these visualizations from reality. This kind of phenomenon may account for many "miracles" and "visions."

The fact that these phenomena can be observed in people in a diseased state, confirms both their existence, and that they can be expected among the general population. These types of experiences may also occur in normal healthy individuals, although in many cases they may be the aberrations of a temporary physiological imbalance.

But, whatever they are, they may be expected to leave a strong impression upon affective and non–rational types of people, as well as upon primitive man. — In the wealth of mankind's diversity, there are not only those who believe their personal psychic and religious experiences, but, also, some who believe the other spontaneous unconscious mental processes as well.

Those who seriously follow the mystical path usually refine their ability to use these spontaneous subconscious mental processes. The individual has some control over them, as which one is induced seems to depend upon the process used to induce it. The biblical formula for starting the intellect is, "Seek and you will find." — That is true. If you earnestly seek, study objects in nature, and logically ponder abstract principles, the subconscious processes will be started and enlightenment will, from time–to–time, emerge from the hidden recesses of the mind. — Likewise, Plato and Pythagoras required their students to study geometry. That starts the intuition. The Yoga Sutras give instructions on these methods, and wholesome advice on how to direct contemplation. But, there are also other techniques. These include transcendental meditation, drugs, asceticism, dance, and ritual sex. Some of these probably induce a physiological imbalance and result in mental aberration.

Using these techniques, people delve inwards for the "truth." Among the things which can be found in the inner realm are negative suggestions or "shadows." For example, the social and religious rules forbidding adultery clearly imply that committing adultery is a possibility. So, although the conscious mind might hold that taboo, the unconscious mind may hold its opposite. And, the more strongly society holds a value and the greater the social tension over it, the more likely its shadow is to become implanted in the subconscious and the more likely that is to emerge as a psychic event. As there will always be some people in society who will be swayed by their inner experiences, a counter–culture can be expected to arise whenever the level of tension over an issue is sufficiently high. It, also, follows that the members of such counter–cultures will often have a larger proportion of the mystically–inclined than the general population.

2.5 Culture and Individuation

"Culture" and "counter–culture" usually mean much the same thing throughout most of the world.[18] — Mankind has one dominant set of social values. These include heterosexual love, a regard for life, identification with their own type, male dominance, and what are called "family values." People usually learn these from the maternal care which their mothers instinctively give them as infants, through socializing with their siblings, and through their understanding of some of the rudiments of Natural Law. Young people should also have felt the usual biological urges at puberty, and testosterone would have made the boys assertive and dominant.[19]

There are probably also some instincts and tendencies which are genetically determined, such as the maternal instincts, which are found among all women. However, we must also allow that there may be some inherited differences among the various races and nationalities. Nevertheless, most young people begin life with a very similar set of basic values determined by instinct, physiology, and the conditions of family life.

These provide the goals which an infant holds subconsciously. As he or she matures, other goals and beliefs will be added to them by society until the young child has assembled one of those systems of hypostatized myth by which he or she orders the world.[20] Later, he or she will gradually recognize each goal and belief and replace them with deliberate choices. This last transition usually occurs approximately concurrent with puberty. That is when a child reaches the, so–called, "age of reason." However, a proportion of the population develop more slowly and a few retain child–like beliefs throughout life. Some even remain at the infant stage. These processes of personal development are called "individuation."[21]

Lorna and Raymond Coppinger's, 1982, article on dog breeding provides a clear example of individuation. They identified four stages in the development of dogs between blind, loppy–eared, and round–headed new–borns with their suckling, nuzzling, and litter–mate behaviors and wild–type adult wolves, jackals, or coyotes with their pointy ears, strong muzzles, and carnivorous hunting habits:

---

[18]However, there are a few cultures in which negative values are dominant. The Thugs provide an example.

[19]There is biological evidence that male dominance is the primary pattern among humans. — A study published in *Scientific American*, examined the morphology of the penises of anthropoids, including man. In those species where the female chooses her mate, the males have elaborate penises. Man's simple penis, therefore, indicates that males may have been the decision–makers, among humans, over evolutionary time.

[20]Children will form a system of myths whether or not one is provided. So, one of the valid functions of religion is to provide children with a wholesome integrated system of beliefs.

[21]"Individuation" refers to the differentiation of the individual.

1. Adolescents are adapted to sitting outside the den and exhibit a gradual loosening of the tactile litter–mate behavior. They are wary of novelty and will crouch, yap, or bite in fear, and retreat into the den.

2. Object players are attracted by objects which move and will play with them.

3. Header–stalkers point, stalk, flush, or move to head–off prey.

4. Healers are adapted to following larger prey and focus on their heals.

Dog breeding is primarily neotenous: that is, it is directed at repressing the dog's development so that it retains juvenile behaviors in its adult form. The most juvenile dogs are the Saint Bernards with their loppy ears, rounded heads, and short muzzles. They will not fetch nor play with objects. The sheep–guarding dogs such as the Maremmas and Shar Planinetzs are also at this stage. They become members of flocks, rather than herding them. They are large dogs and serve by defending their flocks from wolves and coyotes. Most breeds of pet dogs, such as hounds, poodles, or spaniels are object players. They are still loppy–eared but have a slightly less rounded head and more pointed muzzle. They are playful, yet quite submissive. The retrievers, too, are at this stage. They are objects players who have been trained to focus on, for example, a duck as a "play" item, the specific playing behavior being to fetch it. Hunting and working dogs, such as the collies and setters are at the third stage. They have longer and more pointed muzzles and some have semi–erect or "tulip" ears. The most advanced domesticated dogs are the Welsh Corgi, Australian Blue Heeler, Samoyed, and Husky. They exhibit healing behavior and are the least submissive. They, also, have pricked–up ears and a strong pointed muzzle closest to that of the adult wild–type.

There is generally a correlation between the stages of behavioral individuation and the corresponding stages of physical development. People show that they intrinsically recognize this, when they trim the tulip ears of a Doberman pincher, which is a third–stage dog, to make it look more adult and, therefore, more dangerous and threatening, like an adult wild–type dog.

Humans, also, are neotenous: Modern man resembles the juveniles and adolescents of his evolutionary ancestors. They were more primitive but more developmentally advanced. In particular, they exhibited stronger brow ridges and a more pronounced nose and jaw in contrast against the softer, flatter, and more rounded features which characterize a baby. And, gray or white hair, which indicates middle or old age in modern man, is the indicator of sexual maturity among the great apes, and presumably was, also, among modern man's ancestors. — In terms of physical characteristics, the Nordic race is the most primitive and developmentally advanced, whereas the Mongoloid is the most advanced and developmentally juvenile. Man's behavioral shift from siblings to independent individuals can also be seen in the differences between cultures: "Eastern" cultures are affective and group–oriented whereas "Western" cultures are based on reason and individualism.

Society too often does not build constructively and positively upon an individual's natural foundation but attempts to prematurely arrest development, reverse it, or retrain the individual to hold other beliefs, even ones diametrically opposed to those which are natural.[22] In particular, the Classical thinkers recognized three levels of development, the infant, child, and adult which corresponded to the three levels of Rome's religions: that is, the primitive, orthodox, and intellectual. So, the Roman's efforts to hold their populace down to the primitive and orthodox levels represented an effort to prematurely arrest their development at the stage of the infant or the child. That can be done fairly readily, because those stages of development are natural to mankind. Nor is that technique limited to the ancient world. — Sir Winston Churchill said, in 1920, that there was a worldwide effort "for the reconstitution of society based on arrested development;" and he went on to say that, "it has been the mainspring of every subversive movement during the nineteenth century."[23]

But, that technique also can cause character change. — When an external force or condition thwarts an individual's nature or development, there is a characteristic reaction: First, oppresion may cause the shadow to be formed and forced into consciousness. Then, the individual may adopt it. That usually occurs when he or she takes an action which is based on it. Therefore, oppressing an individual combined with providing the opportunity for the opposite behavior, may cause the adoption of the shadow. However, if the individual recognizes and rejects the shadow, his or her character will be strengthened.

Similarly, although, mystical and contemplative religions can be morally sound, some people during Classical times felt that they led to corruption and homosexuality. For example, this view can be found in the *Letter of Jude* (7–10), in the *Bible*.[24] It says, in speaking of "Sodom and Gomorrah and the surrounding cities which in the same manner, indulged in sexual immorality and pursued unnatural lust," that, "in the same way these dreamers also defile the flesh, reject authority, and slander the glorious ones. ......these people slander whatever they do not understand, and they are destroyed by those things that, like irrational animals, they know by instinct."[25]

The idea that mysticism is conducive of perversion is not unique to Classical times: It has been the hallmark of that school of thought, in the West, throughout the ages. For example,... Near the beginning of

---

[22] Under the definition that "evil" is that which opposes an individual's natural goals, deliberately perverting a person's goals is clearly an "evil" of a higher order.

[23] Quoted in the *Illustrated Sunday Herald*, London, England, February 8, 1920.

[24] All biblical quotations are drawn from the *New Revised Standard Version with Deuterocanon and Apocrapha*. Thomas Nelson Publ., Nashville, Tenn.

[25] Notice that he also held mysticism to be at the level of the flesh.

the twentieth century, Nesta Webster remarked that:[26] "these deplorable proclivities are peculiarly prevalent among the aspirants to Theosophical knowledge," and concluded that, "the scandals which have taken place among the Theosophists" could be attributed to " the attempt to orientalize Occidentals ... that is to transport Eastern mysticism to the West."

The advice almost universally given to avoid these problems, is that contemplation should be focused on good, positive, or noble objects. When it must be focused on evil, that should be balanced with consideration of the corresponding good, positive, or moral aspects.[27] The failure to do so has predictable consequences.

2.6   Athenian Philosophers

Having seen where the mystical or contemplative approach can lead, and the social beliefs about it, let us examine what happened when it was introduced into Classical Greece.

Socrates (469–399 BC) was only a humble artisan. But, he was also a mystic. In particular, he said that he heard voices, which he took to be those of the Gods. He also said that he had learned many of his beliefs from Aspasia the wife of Pericles. She was a Miletian, beautiful, and the center of a sparkling circle of intellectuals. She advanced Median thought. She was able to do this because her husband, as a military commander, had made great contributions to the State and, consequently, was very influential. For a while, he had complete control of Athens.

Socrates learned and taught the lessons of the Militian philosophers. His approach was to raise doubts about the traditional Athenian core beliefs, by asking leading questions. He did not make concrete suggestions on how to improve conditions, nor did he suggest the proper way to proceed to avoid the pitfalls of contemplation. In the end, Socrates was executed for impiety and for corrupting Athen's youth. His execution is often held up as an example of the belligerent ignorance of the masses. It probably was, in part, but it should also be appreciated that his teaching methods conducted, as they were, in the context of a strong Median influence advancing the contemplative approach, which at that time did not distinguish between mysticism and intellectualism, could not have avoided being a corrupting influence.

Plato (427–347 BC) learned from Socrates and wrote his ideas down.[28]

---

[26] See Webster 1924 pp 306–309.

[27] I can attest to the truth of this, having studied politics. — I found that the contemplation of evil both in general and particular, which was necessary to gain an understanding of current events, had a high personal cost. But, the contemplation of its opposite was restoring. If an individual were not only to study the liberal eastern agenda but to adopt it or practice it, it is difficult to see how that could be other than fatal to his or her sense of personal worth. And shortly after that must follow the sense of personal morality.

[28] He left a large number of writings including a number of letters and at least

His early "dialogues" were probably authentically Socrates' ideas, but gradually he replaced them with his own. Yet, throughout his life, he maintained the practice of attributing his ideas to others. He was a careful man. Following Socrates execution, he went into voluntary exile for ten years.

Plato became distinctly reactionary when he considered the form of an ideal State. This was probably due to his disillusionment with the society and governments of his day. — As a young man, he had entered political life during the rule of the oligarchy of thirty. But, he found that their rule was of poor quality. So, also, did most Athenians. Eventually the citizens of Athens regained control and reconstituted their democracy. They showed consideration for their erst–while rulers. But it was during that period that Socrates was executed and Plato went into voluntary exile. He went to Syracuse, which was a monarchy. So he had, then, lived under all three simple types of government: that is, democracy, oligarchy, and monarchy. He was appalled at the type of men who ran government. He found them ignorant, prejudiced, and unreasoning. From these experiences, he drew the conclusion that mankind was poorly governed by all the types of government which were then in existence.

Later, a more sophisticated body of political philosophy developed. For example, Cicero held that all simple types of government quickly become arbitrary[29] and tyrannical.[30] He preferred a mixed form of government, like the Roman republic, which had institutions representing monarchy, aristocracy, and democracy. The English and American systems provide contemporary examples of the mixed form.[31]

---

twenty–five dialogues. It is from Plato and Aristotle that we know about many of the earlier philosophers.

[29] Arbitrary government is "where a people have men set over them, without their choice or allowance; who have power to govern them, and judge their causes without a rule." This is quoted from John Winthrop, 1644. He was then the vice–governor of the Commonwealth of Massachusetts. This is one of the American historical documents, and provides a definition for "arbitrary" which is essentially that used in the *Declaration of Independence* and later in our system of law. It is fully consistent with the Classical concepts of freedom and slavery. — Thus, an equivalent definition of arbitrary government is that it is one which has enslaved its people.

[30] Tyranny: a government which is unjust in practice.

[31] England has a mixed form with its Monarch, House of Lords, and House of Commons; and the American system with its President, Senate, and House originally was another. But, the method for selecting senators was changed by the seventeenth Constitutional Amendment, ratified in 1912. They had originally been selected by the State legislatures, but that was changed to election by popular vote. That change eliminated the equivalent of the aristocratic element. The founders had thought that the Senate would protect State's rights and, indeed, after that change, they deteriorated. But, that was not the only change, which occurred at that time.

The selection of a mixed form was a deliberate choice by the founding fathers. They were familiar with Classical literature. According to D. S. Luntz, 1988, Classical authors made up 9% of all the citations given by them between 1760

But, Plato's political ideas did not reach that level of sophistication. He thought that the ideal society would be a totalitarian[32] oligarchy ruled by a self–appointing elite. They would completely reform society. This elite would not own any property, themselves, but would have whatever they owned managed by a steward. There would also be a second elite, trained as soldiers. Within these two elites there were to be no marriages; the State would select which couples were to mate, based on a eugenic strategy; and they would raise and educate their children in isolation from their parents. That way, the State would have complete control over their religious and social beliefs. The less fortunate members of society would be tricked or manipulated into accepting their lot and into having no children.

Plato's religious ideas were probably more influential than his thoughts on politics. — His creation myth, was that God is pure Truth, Virtue, and Beauty and resides in the abstract Spiritual realm of ideas and pure concepts. In the beginning, God saw the realm of matter, which was corrupt and lifeless, and desired to put life and spirit into it.[33] Therefore, He mixed spirit and matter and made from that all the pantheon of lessor Gods and the immortal souls of men and animals, endowing them with life, soul, and intelligence. But, He delegated to a lessor God, Demiurgis, the duty of making mortal bodies out of matter. In Plato's *Phaedo* he says that ideas are the source of existence and the physical body is an illusion.[34] Demiurgis made bodies based on perfect patterns which God gave him to follow. He called these perfect patterns "forms."[35] As they reside in the spiritual realm, man can perceive them by looking inwards. — Although Plato delved inwards, he did not follow the shadow but held that man's goal is to pursue the good and moral life and to strive after beauty as contained in the pure forms.

That is as far as Classical mysticism ever went. — Western man was too rational, too firmly attached to the physical world, to ever take mysticism to the limits it was capable of. Its full development came when it was introduced into the Middle East, and acted upon by the rich leaven of the more emotional Eastern mind.

---

and 1805. That is a fairly large proportion given that the *Bible*, which was the source most often cited, makes up only 34% of the citations. The classical authors they cited most were Aristotle, Cato, Cicero, Plato, Plutarch, Tacitus, and Virgil.

[32] Totalitarian: A State which recognizes or allows only one party or way of thought. More generally, any State which practices thought–control over its populace.

[33] Herein lies the fundamental dualism of Platonism: perfect God versus corrupt matter.

[34] But his faith in this concept was not complete, see his *Parmenides* and *Sophist*: he merely suggests it as a probable metaphysics.

[35] The concept of forms had been introduced earlier by Pythagoras.

Chapter 3

Middle Eastern Mixture

Palestine was a melting pot for Classical thought, a bubbling social cauldron which produced several new religions: These include Judaism, Christianity, Gnosticism, and Alchemy. They had a substantial influential on Western man.

3.1 Hebrews

Civilization developed, around the fourth millennia BC, in Sumer, in Southern Mesopotamia. After that, Lower Mesopotania was overrun by successive waves of peoples. Each, generally, adopted and enhanced their culture. The last invasion occurred around 1100–900 BC. Those invaders were nomadic tribesmen who spoke Aramaic, which is one of the Semitic languages. The Chaldeans were one of those tribes. They occupied and settled Lower Mesopotamia, which, thereafter, became known as "Chaldea." Babylon was the center of their civilization.

According to biblical tradition, the Hebrews were originally another nomadic herding people who moved about with their tents and goats among the marginal lands between Mesopotamia and Egypt. That was the same general region as the Aramaic tribes came from, and they are generally thought to have been related, although they spoke a different Semitic language: Specifically, Hebrew, instead of Aramaic. It was similar to Phoenician, Moabite, or the Canaanite language. The origin of the Hebrews is, however, not known with certainty.

Their culture, showed some Greek, Egyptian, and Babylonian influences, but was essentially Semitic. They worshiped Baal and the various other Semitic Gods, but obtained charms and amulets from Egypt. They drew their civil heritage from Mesopotamia.[1] Thus, even at this early date, we find them borrowing customs from other peoples. That was one of the factors which contributed to their becoming a cultural melting–pot.

Palestine had been under Egyptian rule, since the first Battle of Megiddo, in 1479 BC. But, around 1200 BC, as the result of the weakening of Egypt's power, the coastal plain of Palestine was occupied by the Philistines. They were an Aegean People of the Sea. According to biblical tradition, at about that same time, the Hebrews began abandoning their nomadic life–style and settling in the highlands. — However, the evidence from archeological digs in Palestine does not support this. — They reveal no abrupt change in the culture of the Canaanites, at that time, only a continuation of their way–of–life.

3.2   Israelis

According to the biblical account, around 1229–1200 BC, the exodus of the Joseph clans from Egypt, brought the Hebrews a new religion. Specifically, it relates how Moses provided them with Jehovah,[2] who was reputed to have been originally the patron God of Mt. Sinai or Mt. Horeb. They were able to convert Canaan and ten of the tribes of Israel to His worship, by occupying their holy places and alters. These were located in the open air on mountain tops and high ground. Thus, Jehovah replaced each city's or tribe's Baal and became the national God of the Israelis. The two remaining tribes of Israel were converted later, during the reign of King David. — The Hebrews who accepted this religion and occupied Canaan are the "Israelites." They lived, interspersed among the native Canaanites.

At first, they had only tribal governments, but these were gradually replaced by kingdoms. Next, they displaced the Philistines from most of the coastal plain. That process was completed in 933 BC. It established the geographical limits of the Kingdoms of Israel, in the north, and Judaea, in the south. Sumaria was the capitol of Israel and Jerusalem was the capitol of Judaea. Their way–of–life, during this period, may have been as described by the laws found in *Leviticus* chapters 17–21. But, even according to the biblical account, they occasionally reverted to their older Gods. — Except for the biblical account, little is reliably know about this early period, except that several small local kingdoms formed and gradually coalesced.

---

[1] In particular, they learned from them the legal code of Hammurabi. That was a comprehensive system of financial and business law developed by Hammurabi, the King of Babylon from 1955 to 1913 BC.

[2] The name "Jehovah" is of late medieval origin and nothing like it was ever used by the Israelis. It is currently understood to refer to this more archaic form of their God. In the Hebrew literature, He is referred to by the Tetragrammaton, YHWH, which is unpronounceable as it has no vowels. It may have been pronounced Yah–Weh. — They were concealing its pronunciation as they considered the divine name too sacred to write or say aloud.

The historical record becomes much better, around 850 BC, with their adoption of a script alphabet, from the North. Their earlier writings had been in cuneiform, and there were few of them.

Around the mid–eighth century BC, they became monotheic in practice and adopted Jehovah as the International God of Justice.

Not long after that, in 722–705 BC, the Kingdom of Israel was conquered by King Sargon of Assyria. He relocated the ten northern tribes of Israel "in Halah and Habor on the river of Gozan[3] and in the cities of the Medes ... leaving none but the tribe of Judah alone"[4] That was their "Assyrian captivity." Some of them later migrated, in several stages, generally to the North and West. A portion of them are known to have passed through what is, today, Turkey, while others went north through the Caucasus mountains and around the Black Sea; they eventually disappeared into the forests of Europe, in the region generally North and North West of the Black Sea, and off the historical record. But, other groups of them apparently remained approximately where they were or settled along their migration routes. As a body, the "ten lost tribes of Israel" never returned to Palestine.

3.3 Jews

The two remaining tribes lived in the Kingdom of Judaea. They remained independent, for a while longer. The years which followed, during the seventh century BC, were a time of religious innovation for them. They replaced their open air altars with an elaborate temple worship centralized in the temple at Jerusalem. Previously they had felt that the Gods would be most at home on the mountain tops in the open air among the clouds. But after this date their most sacred places were the inner chambers of a great temple in their urban center. These changes reveal a shift from agrarian to urban goals. The process was culminated by Josiah, in 638 BC. After that, their religion was called "Judaism" and they were called "Jews."

Following these changes, the older religious observances lost much of their authority among the people. But, in 621 BC, a "Book of the Laws of Moses" was "found" in the temple of Jerusalem.[5] It discussed how to revive old customs, and became the center of a religious revival. That is generally thought to have been the origin of the fifth book of the *Bible*, *Deuteronomy*.

It probably, also, contained all or parts of *Genesis* and *Exodus*.[6] That

---

[3] The Gozan River is in the Northern part of the Euphrates River Valley.

[4] See 2 Kings 16–18.

[5] See 2 Chronicles 34.8–28 and 2 Kings 22.1–2,

[6] These three books have a similarity in style and content, but differ from the other two books of the *Pentateuch*.

The *Pentateuch* is the first five books of the *Bible*. The Jews call it the *"Torah"*, but that term may, also, refer to the Jewish *Bible* as a whole.

may account for their historical inaccuracies. For example, *Genesis* says that the Hebrews were descended from Abraham who came out of the City of Ur in the Land of the Chaldeans. Ur was located in Southern Mesopotamia. It was one of the ancient cities of Sumer. However, the biblical account would place Abraham in Ur during the times when the Sumerians were the common people of Ur rather than the Chaldeans.[7] The Chaldeans did not set foot in Mesopotamia until roughly seven centuries later. Consequently, it is doubtful whether the biblical stories about the lives of Abraham and his grandsons, Esau and Jacob, among the Chaldeans in Ur have any historical merit. But, the Deuteronomic legends are informative about the views and aspirations of their authors. They are probably "true" in that regard.

One of the key Deuteronomic concepts was the "Divine Covenant." That is a contract between God and a man. Like all contracts it follows a specific format. — God defines the problem and lays out the terms of the agreement. Then come cursings if its articles are broken and blessings if they are adhered to. He then demands a blood sacrifice to signify the man's acceptance of it, and He provides a sign to signify His commitment. The Divine Covenants include those of Noah, Abraham, Moses, and David.

The next major development occurred in 586 BC. That was when the Kingdom of Judah was conquered by Neo–Babylonia and the remaining two tribes of Israel were relocated in Babylon. That was their "Babylonian captivity." After that, the Jews never regained their freedom, except during one brief century.[8]

But, when the Neo–Babylonian Empire fell to the Persians, in 538 BC, the Jews were allowed to return to Palestine. The King of Persia also authorized and financed their rebuilding of the Temple of Jerusalem. However, they had found a home in Babylon, and most of them choose to remain there. It was also during that period that Aramaic replaced Hebrew as the language of the Jews. Their new sense of identity may also account for their claiming, in *Genesis*, to have a Chaldean origin.[9]

Most of the writing and editing on the *Old Testament* was done while they were under foreign rule.[10] The peak of this literary activity occurred

---

[7] According the *Bible*, Abraham lived from about 2167–1991 BC; his son, Isaac, lived from 2066–1886 BC; and his grandson, Jacob, lived from 2006–1859 BC. — Notice their fabulously long lifetimes.

[8] In 538 Neo–Babylonia was conquered by Persia. After that Judah was ruled by Persia (538–332 BC), Greece (332–323 BC), Egypt (323–198 BC), and the Seleucids (198–168 BC). Only after 168 BC did they briefly recover their freedom; first their freedom of religion and later, in 143 BC, their full civil freedom. But, that century was marred by almost continuous civil war. Rome annexed Palestine to reestablish order and ruled it for the next four centuries (63 BC–395 AD). Before the end of that period, the Jews had been expelled from Palestine.

[9] The *Pentatuch's* final edition was not completed until a century later, around 400 BC.

[10] *Saul, David,* and parts of *Samuel* date from around 950 BC; some *Psalms, Proverbs,* and perhaps the *Book of Job* predate 586 BC; *Amos, Hosea, Isaiah, Micah, Jeremiah, Ezekiel, Joshua, Judges, Samuel, Kings* and *Isaiah* 40–55 are

during their Persian and Hellenistic periods. The Persian influence can be seen in the many ideas from Zorasterism which were incorporated into the *Bible*.[11]

The New Covenant was probably the most important concept, dating from that general era. According to the biblical account it began when the prophet Jeremiah prophesied that the Lord would abrogate all previous covenants and put in their place a new one:[12]

> The days are surely coming, says the Lord, when I will make a new covenant with the house of Israel and the house of Judah. It will not be like the covenant that I made with their ancestors when I took them by the hand to bring them out of Egypt — a covenant that they broke, thought I was their husband. says the Lord. But this is the covenant that I will make with the house of Israel after those days. says the Lord: I will put my law within them, and I will write it on their hearts; and I will be their God, and they shall be my people. No longer shall they teach one another, or say to each other, "know the Lord" for they shall all know me, from the least of them to the greatest, says the Lord; for I will forgive their iniquity, and remember their sins no more.

Jeremiah preached from 627 to 586 BC. Those were the last years of the independence of Judaea, and his preaching ended in 586 BC, when Judaea fell. Although, Jeremiah predates Persian and Greek rule, that book of the *Old Testament* was not begun until at least 550 BC, and it was not completed until around 200 BC, approximately a century after the times of Aristotle. So there was ample opportunity for the inclusion of Persian and Greek ideas. — Whatever its true origin is the verse quoted above, *Jeremiah* is the first place where the philosophy of reason is hinted at in Jewish culture, and it has clearly arrived by the time of the Macabees, around 168 BC.

In particular, the *Apocryphal* book, 4 Maccabees, discusses Aristotle's philosophy. Its author states explicitly at its outset that reason is sovereign and leads one to the Law and a virtuous life, and the remainder of that book consists of edifying examples illustrating that point. This viewpoint can, also, can be found throughout the *New Testament*. That is discussed later on.

---

thought to have been written beginning at approximately 550 BC, they were canonized around 200 BC; and *Daniel* dates from around 164 BC. The *Apocrypha* of the *Old Testament* date from about 180 to 100 BC, whereas, *Revelation*, the last book of the *New Testament*, dates from about 95 AD.

[11] According to S.E. Frost, 1943, these include the doctrines of final resurrection and judgment; the belief in a future life in paradise; the Christian and Jewish belief in Satan and their elaborate system of angels and devils; and the prophesy of a Messiah to come —which was, of course, why the three wisemen, who were Magi, came from the East searching for the Messiah.

[12] See Jeremiah 31:31–34.

3.4   Mysticism

Plato arrived about the same time. — Up until the end of their period of foreign rule, there was little or no mysticism in Judaism.[13] It first appeared during the period of the Jewish revolt against the Seleucids, around 168 BC. At that time, we find the Essenes practicing an ascetic monastic contemplative life–style.[14] They focused on purifying themselves, by contemplation, for their final ascent into Heaven. One of the central objects of their contemplation was Jehovah's flying four–wheeled magical throne/chariot, the Merkabah.[15] They ostensively followed the Judaic religious heritage and studied the Hebrew *Bible*, as other Jews did; but they also had sacred books of their own. They believed that most or all aspects of man's life were controlled by predestination and that the experiences of the prophets were mystical rather than literal. Although they were secretive and protected the teachings entrusted to them, they also kept written records. Some of these were among the Dead Sea and Nag Hammadi scrolls.

The Essenes had been among the followers of Judas Maccabaeus, during their revolt against the Selucids. However, following their independence, the Maccabees declared themselves to be not only the rulers, but also the high priests. This displaced the Zadok tribe who had held the high priesthood since the time of Solomon. The Essenes objected to this and removed themselves from the Maccabee's jurisdiction. They established a settlement in Qunram, near the shores of the Dead Sea. There they became open heretics and intrigued against the State.

Later they were associated with the Zealots in their abortive revolt against Roman rule in 66–70 AD. The outcomes of that revolt were that the Temple of Jerusalem was destroyed, and according to the Jewish historian from that period, Josephus, a large part of the Jews were killed or fled and many thousands were taken prisoner.

The Pharisees were another mystical movement from the second century BC. They were a reaction to the Saducees. The latter generally

---

[13] Of course, Judaism was a revealed religion from its very beginning, and the *Bible* records many ancient revelations and prophesies. But, these were attributed to the patriarchs and prophets and recorded in scripture, rather than reflecting the common practice.

[14] They abstained from eating meat, dressed simply in white, and avoided any ornamentation. In some regards their social structure resembled Plato's ideal state. In particular, they held all material wealth in common and appointed a steward to manage it; they did not practice marriage, except for one sub–sect; and their society was divided into three levels: initiates, members, and superiors.

They were described by Philo Judeaus, Pliny the Elder, Josephus, and Herod Antipater. The ascetic practices of some early rabbis are also mentioned in the *Talmud*.

[15] The Merkabah, described in Ezekiel 1, is one of the few references to mysticism found in the *Old Testament*. According to the Jewish Encyclopedia, it was a representation of divine power. It is much more extensively described in the *Zohar* sections Jethro and Bereschith.

representing the ruling class and preferred the strict literal interpretation of Mosaic Law. In contrast, the Pharisees generally represented the educated middle classes: that is, the scribes, lawyers, and money–changers. They wanted something more moderate than the literal interpretation of old doctrines such as "an–eye–for–an–eye."

To this end, they introduced "derash:" that is the homiletic interpretation of the *Bible*, supposedly revealing underlying meanings, but not always logically deducible. That allowed them to represent their new traditions as being "biblical."[16] But, when they departed from the narrow view, they changed many things besides just making the laws more reasonable. — According to Josephus, they adhered to an oral tradition which included a mystical doctrine. And, according to the Biblical account, these did not follow the Law but followed traditions of their own creation.[17] However, the modern opinion is that their traditions probably represented a mixture of traditional Jewish ideas, ones of their own, and Chaldean beliefs.[18]

3.5 Jewish War

The century of Israeli independence, 168–63 BC, saw virtually continuous civil strife. For the history of that period to be understood, it must be recognized that a large proportion of the Jews were, then, at the primitive level; Tacitus said that they were the most superstitious of Rome's subject peoples; and the historical record shows that many of them believed that the events unfolding around them represented prophesy.

One of the central prophesies was contained in the dualistic story of Esau and Jacob. It begins in *Genesis* (25.19) and it continues here–and–there throughout the whole of the *Bible*. According to that story, the descendants of Jacob became the Israelites, including both the houses of Israel and Judah. They were devout, followed the biblical laws, and retained their birthright. In contrast, the descendants of Esau became the Edomites. Edom lay south of Judaea, from the south end of the Dead Sea to the Gulf of Akaba. The story generally gave them a bad character, cast them as the hereditary enemies of Israel,[19] and said that Esau had sold his birthright to Jacob for a potage of red lentils.[20] The story was prophesied to culminate when the Messiah came to give the Israelites their birthright. But, unlike the Christian tradition, in which the reward is found in the after–life, the Jews expected their reward on Earth in the, so–called, "messianic State." There they expected to live according to

---

[16] See "Bible Commentators" in the 1966 *The Standard Jewish Encyclopedia* Doubleday and Co. Garden City NY. pp 311–312.

[17] For example see Mark 7:6–9 and Matthew 23:1–3, 23, and 28.

[18] See the *Jewish Encyclopedia* Vol VI, 1942, page 235.

[19] However, examples can be found in both the *Bible* and in the historical record where these countries were on friendly terms.

[20] This appears to be where the symbol of the red flag of social revolution originated. Edom means "Red."

divinely–inspired Jewish law.[21] — That superimposed a racial conflict, between the Jewish and non–Jewish populations of Palestine, on top of the disputes between the various contending religious doctrines. — The Jewish war was a protracted many–sided affair.

At first the struggle favored the Maccabee party. In particular, John Hyrcanus (135–105 BC), who was the king and high priest, conquered Edom and forced the Edomites to convert to Judaism. Thereafter, they became a part of the Jewish people. However, the fortunes of war favored the other party half–a–century later, in 63 BC, when Rome reestablished order. At that time, Pompey appointed an Israeli ruler and an Edomite Prime Minister, Antipater. There were several changes in government after that, but following the prime minister's death, in 37 BC, Antipater's son, Herod became the King, with Roman support. It was politic for the Romans to support the indigenous but subject race, against their previous masters. However, Judaea did not submit to Herod's rule until Jerusalem fell after six months of siege by the Roman Army. After that, the Edomite faction ruled, under Roman authority, until the Empire collapsed centuries later.

There were several Jewish revolts during those years. It was a time of social instability and turmoil. Josephus wrote about those years that:[22]

> Somehow, indeed, that was a time most fertile in all man-
> ner of wicked practices among the Jews, insomuch that no
> kind of villainy was then left undone; nor could anyone so
> much as devise any bad thing that was new if he wished. So
> deeply were they all infected, both privately and publicly, and
> vied with one another who should run the greatest lengths
> in impiety towards God, and in unjust actions towards their
> neighbors, men in power oppressing the multitude, and the
> multitude earnestly endeavoring to destroy men in power.

The dispute was finally resolved, in 135 AD, by expelling all the Jews from Jerusalem. Most of them moved to Babylon or Galilee.

Babylon, then, became the primary center of Jewish civilization and the Jews became synonymous with the Pharisees. They were the only major sect which survived both the destruction of the Temple in Jerusalem in 70 AD and their expulsion in 135 AD.

Their most important scripture was no longer the Jewish *Bible*, but became the body of legal/religious writings which eventually became the *Talmud*.[23] It represented a compilation of the views of prominent Jew-

---

[21] A defect in the traditional messianic system was that any non–Jew would be a slave. — International justice from the viewpoint of a people who regard themselves as the elect of God and follow a revealed divinely–inspired law amounts to their imposing their laws on others. That is enslavement, in the Classical sense. Later, the *Talmud* and *Cabala*, would be quite specific that slavery was the intent.

[22] Flavius Josephus, *The Jewish War*.

[23] In particular, the *Talmud* says *(Baba Mezia, fol. 33a)*: "Those who devote

ish individuals together with the decisions and opinions of their top theocratic/legal institutions, specifically the Sanhedrin and later the academies. It constituted their religious doctrine. — Throughout that period, the evolving tradition and spirit of the Jewish people was in a constant process of being put into those writings and, thus, being consecrated. The *Talmud* was the final outcome of several centuries of that process. It was completed at the end of the fifth century AD.

Consequently, with the Jew's expulsion from Palestine, Judaism underwent a fundamental change from a religion of place and revealed Law, as contained in the Jewish *Bible*, to one determined by the evolving standards of the people as ruled upon by the leaders of their theocratic/legal institutions.[24] And, as their cultural center was, then, Babylon, their heritage increasingly reflected the traditions, beliefs, and practices of the Babylonians and Chaldeans and departed from the Judeo–Christian tradition.

Their God was no longer the powerful omnipotent creator God of Judeo–Christian tradition, nor the God of the high places and the forces of Nature, but a lessor deity who the *Talmud* says studies the Law and is bound by it. The *Talmud* even relates how, in a few cases, God was overruled by the Rabbis. This represented a new stage in their religious development and a change in what they felt was their appointed station in the grand scheme of things.

This became Rabbinic Judaism, which was the form of Judaism practiced in Western Europe throughout the middle ages. It was not replaced by modern Judaism until the French Enlightenment, at the end of the eighteenth and beginning of the nineteenth centuries. A remnant of it still exists today. We know it as "Orthodox Judaism."

3.6 Christianity

The following interpretation of Christianity may not be familiar, but is of historical significance.

Among the more important things which Jesus did were that he advocated morality as the regulative principle for society instead of the Judaic system of received Law;[25] he proclaimed the doctrine of universality, in-

---

themselves to reading the [Jewish] *Bible* exercise a certain virtue, but not very much; those who study the *Mishnah* [that is the main body of the *Talmud*] exercise virtue for which they will receive a reward; those, however, who take upon themselves to study the *Gemara* [that is the disputations and discussions concerning the *Mishnah*] exercise the highest virtue."

And Sanhedrin 10,3 says: "He who transgresses the words of the scribes sins more gravely than the transgressors of the words of the law."

[24] This may have been the original "progressive" legal/social system.

[25] This can be most clearly seen in a quote from Matthew 22: A lawyer had asked Jesus the question, "Master, which is the great commandment in the law?" to which Jesus answered: "Thou shalt love the Lord thy God with all thy heart, and with all they soul, and with all thy mind. This is the first and great com-

stead of the Judaic concept of the Jews as a chosen people;[26] he ignored
any hidden parts of the Judaic faith; he confronted and renounced Evil;[27]

---

mandment. And the second is like unto it, Thou shalt love they neighbor as
thyself. On these two commandments hang all the law and the prophets."

Love of God may be taken to be the individual's adherence to his or her Image
of God and philosophy. The extension of that attitude of internal consistency to
all aspects of life, constitutes morality in a general sense. But Jesus constrained
morality to a fairly narrow sense, by requiring the consideration of the good or
benefit of others. Thus, Jesus was advocating a society based on morality and
justice.

He swept aside the whole of Jewish ceremonial law, replacing it with the moral
(Mark 7): "Are you so without understanding also? Perceive ye not, that whatsoever from without goeth into the man, it cannot defile him; because it goeth' not
into his heart but into his belly, and goeth out into the draught ... And he said,
That which proceedeth out of a man, that defileth the man. For from within, out
of the heart of men, evil thoughts proceed, fornications, thefts, murders, adul-
teries, covetings, wickednesses, deceit, lasciviousness, an evil eye, railing, pride,
foolishness: all these evil things proceed from within, and defile the man."

Many people say that Love is the Christian God. But, that is not what Jesus
and the Apostles taught. In their doctrine, love of God, self, and others is a
commandment, a rule to live by: specifically, it is the moral imperative. That is
a completely different concept than, God is Love.

[26] Universality is the doctrine that salvation is available to everyone who comes
to an understanding of the religion. Zorasterism appears to have been the first
religion to assert that doctrine, but later abandoned it; Christianity and Islam
adopted it due to the teachings of Jesus; but the Judaic tradition is that the Israelis alone are the "chosen people." — That assumption is clear in the Old Testament, but its full implications were not stated until the later Jewish scriptures.
In particular, the Talmud's tract Sanhedrim and the Zohar's section Vayschlah
state that the Jews alone have souls of like kind with God's and that only they
will be judged and go to Heaven or Hell accordingly, whereas animals, including
non–Jewish people, have an inferior sort of soul and will be summarily condemned
to Hell at the time of the final resurrection and judgment.

But, the bare statement conveys neither how utterly foreign nor how perva-
sive this belief was in the Jewish tradition. Perhaps the following anecdote will
help. — One on this author's neighbors was a woman from Israeli who had been
raised in Conservative Judaism. She also had only a limited command of English. — On being given some food to try, she was concerned that she would
"die" if she violated their dietary Law. So she asked whether it was "Kosher"
or "animal–food." It soon became clear that she thought of the world as being
divided between Jews and animals. She thought that that was how things were
and assumed that everyone else knew it too. — This glimpse of life within the
orthodox Jewish paradigm may give some perspective on the extent to which Jesus's introduction of universality and morality and his disregarding of the dietary
Laws opposed the fundamental assumptions of their every–day lives. It horrified
and scandalized the Jews of his day.

There is one branch of modern Judaism which has accepted universality. That
is the Reconstructionist Judaism of Rabbi Mordecai M. Kaplan. They have
eliminated all references to the "chosen people." (See Kaplan's 1934 book.)

[27] The story of Jesus in the wilderness, appears to relate a mystical or inward
experience brought on by fasting. (See Mathew 4.1 and John 4.1-11. Mark 1.12–
13, and Luke 4.1–13.) Jesus confronted Satan, or the lies within, identified them
as Evil, rejected them, and he went away. Although the story is figurative, it

and he advocated submission to Roman rule and the seeking of a reward in Heaven rather than earthly dominion.

These teachings of Jesus's provided the basis for a new religion. In particular, we see in John 3.16: "For God so loved the world that he gave his only begotten son, so that everyone who believes in him may not perish but may have everlasting life." That statement presents Jesus as the object of worship along, what were then, the conventional lines for an orthodox anthropomorphic faith.

However, Jesus's greatest act, the defining act of the Christian religion, occurred when he implemented the New Covenant at the Last Supper (Luke 22.14–23):[28]

> When the hour came he took his place at the table, and the apostles with him. ...Then he took a cup and after giving thanks he said "Take this and divide it among yourselves; for I tell you that from now on I will not drink of the fruit of the vine until the kingdom of God comes." Then he took a loaf of bread and when he had given thanks, he broke it and gave it to them saying, "This is my body which is given for you. Do this in remembrance of me." And he did the same with the cup after supper saying, "This cup that is poured out for you is the new covenant in my blood."...

His crucifixion provided the blood sacrifice required for a Divine Covenant. That his contemporaries understood this to be the implementation of the New Covenant from Jeremiah is shown in Hebrews 8.1–13:

> Now the main point in what we are saying is this: ...Jesus has now obtained a more excellent ministry, and to that degree he is the mediator of a better covenant, which has been enacted through better promises. For, if that first covenant had been faultless, there would have been no need to look for a second one. [He then repeated, in detail, the new covenant from *Jeremiah* 31.31–34, quoted earlier.]

There is a widespread belief, today, that the New Covenant is either the principle of universality or a general amnesty on sin for those who accept Jesus as a personal savior. There is, however, another historically important interpretation.

In his *Letter to the Galatians*, Paul presents Christianity in the context of the model for individuation: that is, that there are three levels of mental development, infant, child, and adult, and that there are three corresponding levels of religion, primitive, orthodox faith, and intellectual. However, Paul called these three religious levels "flesh, faith, and Spirit." What he

---

clearly gives Jesus's view that Evil resides in the inner realm, that mysticism places the individual in contact with it, but that the individual can identify it as Evil, renounce it, and it will no longer be a problem.

[28] This story is also given in Matthew 26.20–30, Mark 14.17–26, and John 13.21–30.

said in his *Letter to the Galatians*[29] is that the Law of the old covenant was imposed on the Jews during their minority, so that while they were still infants, at the primitive level of the flesh, they would be under the protection of guardians and trustees; but that when they had come of age, they could become children of God through faith in Jesus as Christ. — Those are the first and second levels, the levels of the infant and the child, of the flesh and the faith. Paul said in his opening remarks in his *Letter to the Romans*[30] that he had "received grace and apostleship to bring about the obedience of faith among all the Gentiles." So he does not discuss the third level, much in any of his letters. But, it is clear that he understood that there was a third level, the Spirit, above that of the child[31] and that he regarded that as being God's truth as revealed in nature.[32]

But it was not just Paul who recognized these three levels of development. Jesus also discussed them. In particular, he spoke about the step from the child's world of faith to the adult's estate of reason in the *Gospel of John*:[33] "Philip said, 'Lord show us the Father and we will be satisfied'. Jesus said to him, 'Have I been with you all this time, Philip, and you still do not know me?' " He then presented, for Philip, the anthropomorphic representation of God from his early ministry, that one is saved by faith in Jesus Christ. But to that he added, "And I will ask the Father and he will give you another Advocate to be with you forever. This is the Spirit of truth whom the world can not receive, because it neither sees him nor knows him." — That also shows that Jesus understood that the Jews had not yet reached a level where they could accept an abstract God. This abstract God of the Spirit was the promise of the New Covenant.

Thus, Jesus created an esoteric religion with two levels to serve the two types of people. The first was for the general populace who were at the level of the child, whereas, the second was only for those who were ready to receive it.

Jesus and the Apostles did not view Christianity as separate from Judaism, but as a higher form of it which superseded the old covenants and resolved some of the problems they had caused. Paul said that these were that the Law leads to sin and wrath,[34] for although life according to the Law was not repugnant to God's law, few could live by it. For to live

---

[29] See *Galatians* (3.19–4.7).

[30] See *Romans* (1.5).

[31] This is implied, for example, when he rebukes the Galatians in his *Letter to the Galatians* (3.1–14) for wanting to revert to the Law. He objected to that on the grounds that the Spirit follows from faith, not from the flesh.

[32] For example, he said in his *Letter to the Romans* (1.20), "Ever since the creation of the World, his eternal power and divine nature, invisible though they are, have been understood and seen through the things He has made." And he rebukes the Romans for suppressing God's truth and turning instead to the ways of the flesh, which led them into perversion.

[33] See *John* 14.8 et seq. Or perhaps, John merely attributed a contemporary idea to Jesus. But, either way, that was how Christianity was interpreted during those times.

[34] See *Romans* 4.15.

by the Law was to live at the level of an infant, but an infant's actions are governed by the subconscious, which is where the shadow resides, and the shadow is likely to be the antithesis of the Law.[35] So to live by the Law too often meant being governed by its shadow. — And the harder a person tried to live by the Law, the more its shadow controlled that person's actions. Therefore, Paul concluded,[36] "For this reason, the mind that is set [at that level] is hostile to God; it does not submit to God's law — indeed, it can not."

But, those who accepted Faith in Jesus Christ were not under the Law, their duty was to follow the principles upon which it was based.[37] The faithful, governed by those principles, would dwell upon them and, thus, would exercise their minds on abstract concepts of morality and truth. It follows that their rational faculties would develop and many of them would reach the third level, the level of the adult.[38] The role of the adult is, of course, to live according to an understanding of God's Law in nature, that is according to Natural Law. Thus, Christianity's goal of living according to the Spirit was identical to the Western view of the role of a full citizen in Classical society.

The religion Jesus taught was significantly different in its process, from the orthodox religions of Rome or the Judaism of the Pharisees. Specifically, the Christian way led the faithful to the level of the adult, whereas the Roman way led the faithful to the level of the infant, and so also did the way of the Pharisees. According to the biblical account, the Pharisees, in particular, imposed the Law upon the Jews and, thereby, pushed them down to the primitive level, and they also fostered immorality among them.[39] That is the same general approach as the Romans used. — When Christianity is viewed in this light, it appears as a radical heresy, for it raised the masses rather than arresting their development. Thus, it was directly opposed to the structure of Roman society as it, then, functioned.[40]

The interpretation of Christianity presented in this section is not based solely on the few passages cited; the viewpoint, pervades the *New Testament* and also has continuity with the ideas of those times. Therefore, a strong argument can be put forward that that was the intended message

---

[35] See *Romans* 7.14–24.

[36] See *Romans* 8.7.

[37] For example, see *Romans* 8. In those passages Paul referred to "the Law of the Spirit of Jesus Christ" or "according to the Spirit," by which he is assumed to have meant Natural Law.

[38] See *Romans* 8.1–11.

[39] According to the biblical account, the Pharisees presented the outward appearance of morality and adhered to the Law, but inside were corrupt and evil. (See Mathew 23.25–28, Mark 7) Jesus said to them that (Mathew 23.15): "you make the new convert twice as much a child of Hell as yourselves."

[40] In his sermon on the mount, Jesus warned against false prophets, saying that you shall know good teachings from bad by their fruits, that is by their outcomes. (See Matthew 5:15–20) And, it is argued here, that the principal intended outcome of Jesus's teachings is the estate of reason, with its Law, freedom, and virtue.

of Jesus and the Apostles. At the very least, it was the viewpoint taken by Paul and John.

Admittedly, different interpretations can be obtained by selecting different passages.[41] But this one is one of the two historically most important interpretations of Christianity. — Roughly twelve–hundred years later, it would provide the central ideas of "Western" society, when it emerged during the Golden Age of France.

During the intervening period, the other important interpretation was adopted by the Roman Church. That was the Augustian Tradition. Its roots can be traced to Philo Judaeus and Gnosticism possibly as much as to the *Bible*.

3.7   Philo Judaeus

Philo (circa 20 B.C – 40 AD) was slightly older than Jesus, but contemporary with him. He was the leading Jewish philosopher in Alexandria.[42] He is often said to have been the first philosopher to systematically integrate Classical thought into the Judaic. — He incorporated selected ideas primarily from Plato and Pythagoras, but also from Aristotle and the Stoics, into his work while maintaining its essentially Judaic character.

He was among the first to have identify the Image of God and to discuss the three levels of development. Those were contemporary ideas, during his times.

He held that an individual could achieve knowledge of God either through the mystic contemplative approach of looking inward or through the Aristotelian intellectual approach of studying nature, but he didn't think that an affirmation of God could be obtained through the orthodox approach of faith. That also was the view of his times: In particular, neither the Romans nor the Christians thought of faith as an end in itself; they tended to regard it as a starting point which would lead the individual either to the Flesh or the Spirit.

In two important ways, his philosophy was the antithesis of Christianity. First, he held that mysticism communicated with the spiritual realm. Second, he integrated the Classical into the Judaic, rather than visa–versa.

---

[41] Either some of its authors did not fully understand the role of Christianity in terms of individuation, or were not as careful to put grain among the chaff. — Those were Jesus's instructions on teaching, to lay hints, double–meanings, and short revealing passages on the Spirit in among the instructions on anthropomorphic faith, because not everyone was ready for the message, and also because their political or religious opposition would incorporate lies among the teachings which would be passed down to posterity. (See Mathew 13.1–53.) — The reader or hearer must pick the seeds from the chaff, and determine which seeds are of grain and which are of weeds.

[42] He was from a prominent Jewish family and had received both Hebrew and Classical educations. Alexandria was still, in his time, a nucleus for the spread of Greek culture.

The French historian, M. Matter [43] says that Philo, "wholly attached to the ancient religion of their fathers, resolved to adorn it with the spoils of other systems and to open to Judaism the way to immense conquests." — What he was referring to was the approach, of ruling other peoples by controlling their religions. The first reference to this may be found in *Exodus*, where Moses says his people will become a nation of priests,[44] and its first successful application was when the clans of Joseph mastered the other tribes of Israel and the Canaanites by controlling their shrines and alters. Later *Deuteronomy* would prophesy that Israel's destiny would be to tread upon their enemy's high places.[45]

He also felt that God is illusive: That if He is ever identified, His nature will change. — This leads to a important political technique for causing social change: Specifically, identifying a person's God and occupying and desecrating his alters, will often cause a person to abandon them and seek new goals.

Philo's primary impact was on Christianity. His work contributed to forming a school of thought in Alexandria which, about two centuries later, contributed to the Neoplatonic movement. That eventually became the Augustinian Tradition of the Roman Church. It eclipsed the New Covenant throughout the entire early middle ages, until the philosophy of reason was rediscovered, around 1200 AD. Thus, it captured the alters of Christianity for almost a millennium.

3.8 Gnosticism

The mixing of Eastern, Western, and Jewish cultures is generally recognized as having resulted in the birth of Gnosticism, which is yet another form of religion.[46] It used Platonic mysticism and derash to form quasi-rational mystical doctrines which were the radical antithesis of the most sacred beliefs of other religions.

The invention of Gnosticism is often credited to Simon Magus.[47] He wanted to free people from their enslavement to religion. To that end, he developed a Gnostic theology, and went about preaching it, apparently with substantial success.

Gnosticism spread to Christianity, during the first century.[48] Some of the Gnostic Christians made an earnest attempt convert Christianity to their viewpoint. The Dead Sea and Nag Hammadi scrolls included some

---

[43] M. Matter, 1844 quoted in N. Webster 1924.

[44] See *Exodus* 19.3–8.

[45] See *Deuteronomy* (33.29).

[46] See A. von Harnack (1894) and A.D. Nock (1964).

[47] He became a member of the Christian community and was baptized by John the Baptist. He was also versed in Jewish mysticism, magic, and the Occult. He appears in the *Acts of the Apostles 8.9–24.*. There are also other historical records on him.

[48] See Stephen A Hoeller (1989) and Elaine Pagels (1979).

of the gospels written by this early Gnostic Christian community. They presented themselves as the secret writings of individuals who claimed to have known Christ, John the Baptist, or the Apostles firsthand.[49] They presented these biblical figures as mystical prophets. But, some of them contained enough internal inconsistencies and mistakes in religious philosophy for the Church authorities of the time to conclude that they had been created fraudulently. For example, Irenaeus, the Bishop of Lyons, around 180 AD, complained that the Gnostics kept producing new gospels, which were not authentic. The Gnostic Gospels also often advanced slanders against Jesus and the Apostles.

Although there is considerable variation among Gnostic beliefs, their stereotypic cosmogeny is that in the beginning there was only God and the universe was in perfect harmony. But something happened which caused Good and Evil to separate. The Evil element then created the world and everything in it including mankind. But, for some reason, man's soul had a bit of God in it. Man, therefore, has two possible paths to salvation. The first path is the way of the libertine, who strives to destroy the world, and everything in it, including mankind, and to oppose morality, law, and Natural Law as they are all the work of the Evil God who created and rules the world. The second path is the way of the contemplative, who strives to establish a knowledge (gnosis) of God to, thereby, achieve salvation. In this scheme, God is above Good and Evil. A third level of people, the inner circle of the faith, are united to Him through gnosis. Therefore, they too are above morality. Or, more exactly, being fully informed on the true state of affairs and being in the leadership, they may have promoted the idea that they were above morality and acted accordingly. So, although the contemplative levels of Gnostic religious organizations often had strict moral codes, there is a long history of their innermost circles acting solely for personal gain or political advantage.

Gnostic religious organizations were usually structured this way, in three levels. This provides yet another example of that Classical viewpoint that human development has three stages. But, this time the infant, child, and adult, corresponded to the libertine, contemplative, and member of the inner circle. Each is the antitheses of the corresponding level in Christianity: that is Law, Faith, and Spirit, respectively.

Although the inner circles of these religions were probably fully informed of their true function and objectives, their lower levels were characteristically riddled with superstition. As the Gnostic Religions followed mystic negative theologies, almost all of them recognized the Evil Principle, and many of them tended towards radical dualism: that is where the Good and Evil Principles are equal.

They conjured devils and some of them even directly worshiped Evil.[50]

---

[49] Many of these Gnostic gospels were known to have existed, from historical records, but had been lost. Their loss was largely due to the Roman Church consistently burning them whenever they could.

[50] Despite Rabbinic Judaism's full pantheon of Angles, Devils, and miscella-

They learned many of their magical and demonic rites and practices from the Chaldeans, who they came in contact with after their expulsion from Jerusalem in 135 AD.

The Chaldeans had a sophisticated system of animal and human sacrifice, incantations, astrology, and divination, including divination based on the livers of sacrifice victims. Many of these rites were incorporated into the *Talmud* or retained in oral tradition to be written down centuries later in the *Cabalah*.

Manicheanism was possibly the most important Gnostic faith. It developed during the third century AD. Unlike the other Gnostic faiths, it was a complete religion, intended to stand alone.[51] It had prayer books, hymnals, and all the other usual appurtenances of a religion.

It drew primarily upon Zorasterism, but also upon Christianity and Buddhism. They believed in the division of God into eternal co-equal good and evil principles, in demonology, that Adam and Eve cohabitated with devils, and that mankind arc their offspring. That trapped the good soul in the evil body. But through a system of ethics mankind can avoid evil and the good portion of the soul will be released at death. Among other things these ethics advised the avoidance of sexual intercourse, so that no children would be born, further imprisoning souls in material bodies. That is a radically dualistic doctrine with a hatred for the world and life.

For a short period (241–272 AD), it was the State religion of Parthia. It spread westward across North Africa and eastward into Central Asia. It reached China, and they condemned it as a perverse doctrine, in 732 AD. It may also have been what introduced the Demiurgic creator/trickster figure of Platonic mysticism and the concept of reincarnation into the religion of the natives of the Northeast Coast of Asia and the Northwest coast of North America. There He appears as "Raven." In the fifth century the Huns carried some related doctrines into Eastern Europe, preparing the way for later Gnostic groups.

3.9 Alchemy

Alchemy was yet another religion which originated in Palestine. It appears to have been first practiced by the Gnostic Christians of the second century AD.[52]

---

neous Spirits, they still regarded their religion as "monotheism." The same may also be said about Christianity. — This is primarily a semantic issue: These lessor spiritual beings are not regarded as "Gods," although their nature is divine and fundamentally different from that of any mortal.

[51] The more characteristic pattern of Gnostic faiths was that each existed in association with some specific major religion, whose beliefs they partly used and partly travestized. That is, they had a parasitic relationship to some specific religion.

[52] Alchemy was, also, practiced in the Far East at about the same date. There it was part of Taoism.

It was clearly a product of the mixing of cultures. In particular, we can trace its chemical theories back to the Milesian philosopher, Anaximander. His four primary opposites; gave rise to Aristotle's four elements: water, fire, earth, and air, to which ether was later added. The central concept of Alchemy seems to have been that existence is created through the seperation of opposites.[53]

Like the Yogis, the Alchemists did not believe that the basic building blocks of matter were separated from the psyche and the spirit. Therefore, their experiments involved both mixing chemical ingredients and deep meditation.

During the early middle ages, their aim was usually to turn lead into gold, but during the late middle ages that changed to uniting the soul with the Transcendental Spirit, finding the philosopher's stone, or obtaining eternal life, eternal youth, or enlightenment. But, whatever their quest, the goal served to induce the experimenter to give a high level of commitment to the process. The practical outcome was that practitioner progressively changed his own psyche. That is individuation. That is what Alchemy was about, particularly during the more recent centuries.

Alchemy could either produce change for the good or the bad. The latter is black magic in the real and concrete sense. Ephipius Levi provided the following brief explanation:[54]

> Black magic is really but a combination of sacrileges and murders graduated with a view to the permanent perversion of the human will and the realization in a living man of the monstrous phantom of the fiend . . . . . . hatred of goodness exaggerated to the point of paroxysm.

For example,[55] Gilles de Rais of Brittany (1404–1440) began life gloriously as the companion of Joan of Arc. He rose to become the Marechal of France, but he became involved in Alchemy and expended his vast fortune in that quest. At one point, he offered his soul to Satan in exchange for knowledge and power, in a contract written in his own blood; but no demonic figure appeared to accept his offer. After that he progressed through a series of increasingly horrible acts, ending with the torture and sacrifice of literally hundreds of children, which his agents collected in the French countryside. He was hanged, and burnt in 1440.

---

[53] See Carl Jung's *Mysterium Coniunctionis*, which is probably the most significant modern study of Alchemy.
[54] See Ephipius Levi reprinted in 1969.
[55] This account is drawn from Nesta Webster (1924).

Chapter 4

The Dark Ages

This chapter covers the transitional period which came after the Classical but was not yet Western. It saw a melding together of Classical and Germanic influences. From that mixture, Western man emerged, in the thirteenth century, thereby, beginning the Western epoch of history.

4.1 Roman Church

Rome did not fall without a struggle: They made several attempts to regenerate their society. The most notably of these was due to Emperor Constantine during the fourth century. Specifically, in 312, he adopted Christianity as the official Church of Rome, in a effort to restore morality.

However, despite some successes, he saw that Rome was beyond recovery and, in 330 AD, moved his capitol to the new city, Constantinople, which he had constructed. Later the empire would be divided between Eastern and Western halves. The Eastern Roman Empire remained prosperous and Constantinople stood unconquered for another seven centuries,[1] while Rome continued to decay. It was first sacked in 410 AD by Alaric at the head of a band of German tribesmen.

Before Emperor Constantine, abandoned hope for Rome, he introduced several modifications into the doctrine of the Roman Church to make it compatible with Roman practices and beliefs.[2] The Roman Church's po-

---

[1] It was finally conquered by the Fourth Crusade (1202–1204). That crusade was run by the Knights Templar and was directed against the trade rivals of Venice. The Pope authorized this crusade on the grounds that it would reunite Christianity: that is, it would impose the primacy of the Pope over *his* rival, the Patriarch of Constantinople.

[2] For example, one of the commandments was to keep the Sabbath holy. According to the practice of the early Jews and Christians, the Sabbath was Saturday. But in 321 AD Emperor Constantine and Pope Sylvester changed the

sition on the condition of man, was that mankind are granted souls by
God, that all men are equal in the eyes of God, and that any individual
who believes and performs the expected religious duties, such as baptism
and the other sacraments, will go to Heaven. This is consistent with the
Imperial Roman perspective of faith, piety, and equality below established
authority.

The influence which the Classical pagan religions had on Church doctrine is clearly evident in the views of some of their early leaders. For
example, Jerome (340–420) was an ascetic and influenced monasticism;
and Ambrose of Trier, the Archbishop of Milan, was a Stoic and wrote his
influential *Duties of the Clergy* which is based largely on Cicero.

But the largest Non–Christian influence came from Neoplatonism. That
philosophy was primarily due to Platinus (circa 205–270 AD) and other
philosophers associated with Alexandria. The movement may have had
its beginnings, two centuries earlier, with Philo Judaeus and the Gnostics.
Unlike Neopythagoreanism, it was based on a cohesive philosophy which
shifted the emphasis of thought from the outer world of the senses to the
inner world of introspection: that is, from an Aristotelian to a Platonic
orientation. In particular, Platinus (circa 205–270 AD) regarded the physical world as unreal and saw mystical contemplation of a monotheic God
and asceticism as ends in themselves. The movement was continued by his
disciple Porphyry (232–304 AD).

Saint Augustine (354–430 AD) made a Christianized version of neoplatonism a part of the doctrine of the Roman Church.[3] It became one of
the principle elements of their theology. In particular, he contributed the
doctrines of original sin, predestination, and salvation through grace, all of
which contain a mystical orientation. The Augustinian approach involved
faith and spirituality. He pointed out that in contrast to the Athenian
world or the world of the Macabees, where the will was supreme over the
emotions, sometimes the body does not do what you will, or does what
you do not will. — He lived during a time of great distress, during the
conquest of the North African provinces of the Empire by the German
Tribesmen. People tended to turn inwards and the subconscious strongly
influenced their actions. That helps to explain his orientation.

The next major step came when Boethius (circa 480–524 AD) developed the Augustinian tradition into the mild form of neoplatonism which
dominated Christian theology throughout the early middle ages.[4] Some

---

Christian observance to Sunday, which was consistent with the practice of the
Romans, for whom the Sun was a prominent deity. (see the Codes of Justinian,
lib. 3, title 12, lex. 3.) This change was confirmed in 364 AD by the Council of
Laodicea. That appears to have been a perfectly reasonable action, although it
bothers some people.

[3]He was the Bishop of Hippo in the Roman Province of Numedia, in North
Africa. He had been a Manichean before he was converted to Christianity.

[4]The general nature of that belief was that individual men or animals exist as
physical realities, but that the forms for mankind and the various animal species
preexisted in the mind of God and were used by Him to create these material

neoplatonic concepts were still an accepted part of Christianity even as late as the turn of the nineteenth century. **The early medieval church:** By the seventh century, the Germanic tribes had completed their conquest of the Western Roman Empire. They brought Germanic culture with them but they were gradually becoming Christianized. Pope Gregory I, "the Great," (590–604) played a large part in their conversion.[5] He established alliances between the Roman Church and the Christianized Germanic States of Western Europe. This counterbalanced the power of Constantinople and allowed him to firmly assert Papal supremacy in the West.[6]

That also provided him with an opportunity to set the course of the new social and religious heritage which was then forming out of a mixture of Roman and Germanic customs. He left his mark on the medieval way-of-life. — He followed the Augustianian tradition, and wrote of having had meaningful mystical experiences, and seems to have recognized the positive existence of Evil.[7] His *Dialogues* popularized the belief in angels, demons, devils, relic worship, miracles, the doctrine of purgatory, and the use of allegory.[8] He also encouraged the syncretist[9] approach of introducing pagan customs into Church practices. For example, that is why the Church accepted the Germanic religious symbol, the Christmas tree, and also the spring festival, Easter, which recalls Eastre, the Germanic Goddess of dawn and spring. This provided the rich religious mythology peculiar to the middle ages.[10] The inconsistency which resulted from this also probably impeded the development of a rational doctrine while encouraging the development of belief based on faith and emotions.

In all ages, except for a few short intervals, such as the Golden Age of France and parts of the nineteenth and twentieth centuries, the Roman Church has stood for faith. But, that was not faith in the principles as

---

beings.

[5] He came from a Roman Senatorial family and was the last Pope of the Classical Greco–Roman tradition and the first of the Medieval Western European tradition. He was the largest landowner in Italy and, as such, was a powerful man in his own right. He was the real leader in the war against the Lombards. The Lombards were a Germanic tribe who, at that time, were invading Italy. They eventually settled in Northern Italy. He appointed Governors of cities, directed Generals in war, and administered the funds sent from Constantinople for that purpose.

[6] Innocent I (440–461) may have been the first Pope to assert that Rome had universal jurisdiction, but the Patriarch of Constantinople made an equal claim and had the backing of Constantinople.

[7] For example, he wrote of a vision of radiant darkness brighter than light.

[8] The second Council of Nicea, confirmed these beliefs in 787 AD.

[9] Syncretism is more than just an incorporation of symbols, myths, or compatible beliefs from another religion. It involves the combining of conflicting beliefs into a conglomerate. Thus, syncretistic faiths lack internal consistency. That can lead to a turbulent subconscious.

[10] Syncretism probably facilitated the growth of the Roman Church; because it made their practices more compatible with the native religions and enriched their mythology.

set forth by Jesus and the Apostles. It was an anthropomorphic orthodox faith and often included elaborate ritual and the worship of icons, relics, saints, and so on. That pushed their followers away from reason and down to the level of the flesh and spirituality or froze them at the level of the child.

Pope Gregory also established the Roman Church's view on the structure of government.[11] His theory was that God grants authority to the monarch, who is accountable only to God, but the Roman Church interprets Divine Law and serves as the interface between the monarch and God, through which that accounting occurs. He based this position upon scriptural authority. This was the origin of feudalism. — He followed the Jewish tradition[12] by assuming that all rights are derived from God, based on scriptural authority, and by giving the Pope the role of the High Priest. But, he followed the Roman tradition by recognizing the State as sovereign. Thus, feudalism was a mixture of the Jewish and Roman systems.

4.2   German Heritage

The Germanic heritage was the other major influence on the early medieval way–of–life. The German tribesmen had overrun all of the Western Roman Empire and, after they occupied the land, formed the upper classes and the governments of those regions. So, their heritage provided the basic structure of society to which the Roman customs were added, rather than visa–versa. But, in the end, the mixture was relatively equal.

The original Germanic heritage, was described by Classical authors[13] and also in the ancient chronicles of England.[14] Like all barbaric people,

---

[11] in his Regulat Pastoralis, iii. 41. Libre Moralium in Job XXII 24.

[12] The early Jewish governments described in the *Old Testament* were theocracies.

[13] Tacitus described it and so also did Julius Caesar, briefly, in his commentary on the Gaelic Wars.

[14] Of Western European nations, England is the most Germanic in its social and political heritage. This comes about because, in contrast against the conquest of Western Continental Europe at the fall of the Roman Empire, where the Germanic bands imposed themselves as a new ruling class over a population of romanized serfs; in England, the conquerors, that is the English, cleared the land of all its previous inhabitants and took it for their own.

The English are composed of several low German tribes: the Juts, whose homeland was the Danish Peninsula, that is Jutland; the Angles whose homeland was the provinces of Sleswick and Holstein at the base of the Danish Peninsula and the Island of Helgoland in the North Sea; the Old Saxons, whose homeland was generally the Western regions of Germany; and the Frisians whose homeland was along the Northsea coast and associated islands of Germany and the Lowlands.

Their invasion of the British Isles commenced with the landing of Hengest at Ebbsfleet, in Southern England, in 449 AD. Their initial invasion was the result of pressure from the Huns, whose empire, then, stretched from Persia to Denmark. The English invasion did not end until approximately 615 AD. By then, the Gaelic or Celtic peoples retained only Wales, the Scottish Highlands and Islands,

they had a lust for drink and battle, but they also had the fundamental rudiments of civilization.

The ancient English people lived in small towns jealously guarding their independence. Each town was surrounded by a "Tun" or defensive hedge, from which the modern word "town" is derived. Outside that hedge were the pastures and farmland. Beyond them was the forest which divided the townships from each other. Anyone who came through that forest was expected to blow their horn and come through boldly. Those who crept through were regarded as showing criminal intent.

Each town had a meeting place, often a town green with a large tree under which the residents would gather to conduct the town's business. Any freeman who had a "holding" had a right to vote — Property ownership determined suffrage. The landless man, although no one's slave, wasn't a full member of society. Their society had two classes, Eorls and Ceorls.[15] The former was distinguished by noble blood but there was no distinction before the law.

Officials were elected usually for annual terms. A representative would also be elected to the hundred–court, which was a regional council among the group of allied villages which comprised the tribe or nation. As these countries gradually formed into nations, these elected regional councils gradually evolved into Parliament in England, the Estates General in France, and the Cortes of Spain. The oldest continuous Parliament still in existence is the Allthing of Iceland, which was established in 930 AD.[16] These bodies held ultimate authority.[17]

A war chief might also be elected to lead the nation in times of war. For example, Herman, that is "Armenius" in the Roman literature, the great hero and defender of ancient Germany, was the elected war chief for the Cherusci, a tribe of Old Saxons. He met and overcame the Roman legions under Quintilius Varus on the North side of the Rhine in 9 AD.[18] That battle was of considerable importance as Rome was unable to find enough Roman youth to replace the legions which were slaughtered. For that reason, it forever established the Rhine River as the Northern border of the Roman empire and preserved the German heritage.

Their early legal system was based on a form of trial–by–jury. A man would be accused before his fellow–tribesmen, his kinsfolk served as his sole

---

and Ireland. (Much of this section is based on J. R. Green's 1874 *A short history of the English People.*)

[15] There were also slaves, but never very many.

[16] Iceland was settled by the Vikings shortly after its discovery in 874 AD.

[17] For example, the English crown is hereditary, but Parliament determines the rules of succession. The current rules were established in 1701. They usually follow the succession, but can set it aside, and have done so on several occasions.

[18] This engagement was passed down to us by Tacitus and other Roman historians and is admirably described by Creasy (1876). The historical records even include parts of a discussion between Herman and his brother, who at that time, was serving in a Roman Legion.

judges, and it was by their solemn oath of his innocence or his guilt that he had to stand or fall. If the accusing party didn't like the verdict, then warfare was the sole remedy and kinfolk fought side–by–side in battle. An "outlaw" was not a criminal, per se, but someone who was outside their system of law. It was every man's duty to kill any outlaw he might encounter.[19]

This cultural system must have strongly reinforced that probity of character which the Roman historians said distinguished the ancient Germans from the other barbarians. — The Germans placed great importance upon keeping their word. This also extended to their domestic relationships. The Roman historians commented upon the absence of polygamy and the chastity of their women.

There was a discernible similarity between the Germanic Gods and those of Classical mythology. That may have been due to their common origin and their earlier interconnection by a trade route along the Danube River and the Adriatic and Black Seas. After this trade broke down, around 1200 BC, these peoples went their separate ways. But, cultures only change slowly if they are left to their own devices.[20] Consequently, at the time of Rome's contact with the Germans, more than a thousand years later, German culture still retained a general continuity to early Greek and Roman culture.

The names of the English Gods are recalled to us in the names of the days of the week. In particular, Wednesday is for Woden,[21] the chief God of all the Germanic people, the war–God and guardian of ways and boundaries, the inventor of letters; Thursday is for Thor, the God of thunder, air, storm, and rain; Friday is for Frea, the God of peace and joyful fruitfulness; Saturday is for Saetere; and Tuesday is for the sky God Tiu,[22] Sunday and Monday are named for Sun the Moon. There was also a pantheon of lessor Gods: water–nixies, sprites, shield maidens, and some deified historical figures such as Weland the swordmaker and Herman. The latter's accomplishments were recalled in legend and he was venerated by all the German peoples. For example, in early England, he was held to be the guardian of one of the four great highways: specifically, Irmin–Street.

They had a mythology contained in the poems of their oral tradition which held both their social and religious heritage. Most of it has been lost, but around 800 AD, an Icelandic Christian priest, Saemund, recorded some of it as the *Elder Edda*. They are a collection of poems and songs. They were, later, rewritten as the *Younger Edda* or *Prose Edda* by an

---

[19] This old tradition recognized the principle that a person who is above or outside the law is a common enemy, an arbitrary danger and hazard to everyone.

[20] Ancient cultures which have slowly evolved over millennia, generally have little internal conflict over their basic social values. Consequently, they only change very gradually. Strong conflicts primarily arise when they come into contact with other cultures.

[21] Also called Odin or Wotan

[22] In Norse mythology, Tyr, the son of Odin.

Icelandic historian, Snorri Sturluson (1179–1241).

Woden's, being the God of boundaries, shows the importance which early Germanic civilization placed on that concept. This contributed to their personal freedom. In particular, in the context of property boundaries, the individual was free to manage his land however he wished and the crops and animals he grew upon it were his. He did not have to constantly defend his land nor negotiate land use decisions with his neighbors. These customs freed the individual from those social interactions.

The importance of property ownership to the structure of society was recognized by John Locke and the founding fathers of America. In particular, Thomas Jefferson said that the right of property ownership was the most important individual right and all the others rested upon it.

Freedom is a set of rights established by law or custom which guarantee the individual's right to act within prescribed limits. It is impossible to conceive of a civilization of free people, in which boundaries, in this general sense, are not clearly defined, sanctioned, and supported. The only exception would be the pathological one where there are so few people that they rarely come into contact with each other.

Conversely, people in a society without boundaries, must be deeply and constantly involved in social interactions to obtain or secure any benefits. They must follow, respond to, and manipulate their neighbors or the consensus of the crowd. In that situation, it is most likely that some individual or group would eventually dominate and enslave everyone else. But, even if everyone remained equals, they would still be slaves to each other, as each would be controlled by the others rather than by fixed and equal rules. Thus, a society without boundaries is necessarily a society of slaves.

Similarly, a natural or scientific law establishes a boundary distinguishing that which is true from that which is not. Thus, boundaries are fundamental to the existence of order in both the social and physical realms. This was recognized by several of the early Greek philosophers, including Anaximander and Pythagoras. It is one of the defining concepts of "Western" thought.

 It was also found in the Nordic pagan religion. There it was encapsulated in the rune, Odal. It signifies law, heritage, boundaries, property, home, and liberty.

The runes were the letters which Woden gave to mankind. They were used in common by most of the northern long–headed peoples. According to the *Encyclopedia Britannica*[23] the date of their origin is uncertain. Some historians suggest that they originated as early as 500 BC, but they first appear on archeological artifacts from around 200 AD. There were two runic systems used in Northwestern Europe, one of 16 letters and the other originally of 24, which was later increased to 27. There were also differences between the Anglo–Saxon, Scandinavian, and German versions.

---

[23] 1926 edition.

The runes formed an alphabet, but each character also had an esoteric meaning. The worship of Woden involved the study of their meanings.

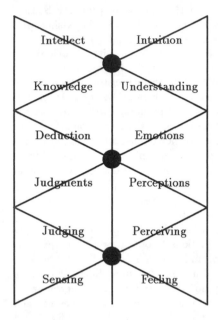

Figure 4.1: Stave Lattice.

The runic characters have some similarity to Greek or Latin letters, but, their exact shapes represent parts of the lattice–like pattern created by nine staves placed on the ground. Three of these staves were placed parallel and vertical, another three were placed across them pointing upwards to the right at thirty degrees, and the last three were placed across them pointing downwards to the right at thirty degrees. This lattice pattern gives the graphical representation of the Classical model for the psyche, or something very close to it. The three nodal points in the center of the lattice represent the three centers of being: that is the ego, lower–self, and higher–self. Each stroke of a rune represents a stave, or a portion of one, and therefore, represents a psychological process.

It follows that each rune, as a collection of strokes or staves, represents a collection of psychological processes.[24] The critical knowledge which is needed to understand the runic system is, therefore, the meaning of each segment of each stave in the lattice.

The figure shown here is partly a conjecture on the part of the author.[25]

---

[24] The positioning of the rune in the lattice is critical to its meaning. For example, consider Odal. It could come from two different positions. In fact, its meaning comes from the upper one, but that is not certain from its structure. Some of the runes have long vertical staves, which show their vertical position. Also, runes can be flipped right–for–left or top–for–bottom. That changes their meaning, but not the alphabetic character.

[25] I am often asked where this came from. — It originated when I diagramed the Myers–Briggs Temperament Test to better understand what it was saying about the structure of the mind. I, then, refined it based on Jung's papers, Philo's work and the *Bible,*, then, on many other things. About, that time, I came across descriptions of Locke's model, which he had constructed with exactly the same intent. The result was that when I encountered the Stave Lattice, I immediately recognized it for what it was. Examination of the runes and the Edda immediately confirmed that. — Thus, I do not claim to have originated this, but to have reverse–engineered it. I believe that there is an original, but it is not widely

The vertical staves[26] and the top and bottom cross–pieces are relatively certain,[27] but the other pieces were filled in to produce an operational model for the psyche and to conform to Jung's work.[28]

Although, it would be nice to fill out this model completely with certainty, in order to better understand what the ancient Nordic people were thinking. Its exact structure is clouded in antiquity, and probably was never more than vague.[29]

Each rune is also associated with a time–of–day, a time of the year a tree, and something specific. For example, the up–arrow, Tyr, is "male-man," the B–rune, Bjarka, is "woman," and so on. Thus, the runes provide

---

known. — I suspect that it reveals too much about various religious mysteries. For example, when I showed this to a Freemason, it produced a marked reaction. So, it must be relatively similar to one of their "secrets." But, the substance of what I am saying is that it can be found throughout much of Western philosophy and religion.

[26] The vertical staves from left to right represent: 1) the left–brained, rational, external, and overt; 2) the central axis of self; and 3) the right–brained, affective, inward, and passive. — They are described in the Edda as explicitly as can be expected of poetry in its description of the three roots of the Ash Tree, Yeggdrasil. Their right–for–left positioning is shown by the rune Bjarka, and any ambiguity as to the nature of the central stave is clarified by the rune Iss, which consists only of that stave.

[27] The top pieces are clearly shown by Algiz, and given in more detail by the eddaic description of the roots of the Ash.

[28] The names assigned to the segments generally follow the Myers–Briggs Temperament Test, which is based on Jung's work. His work may also have been influenced by the Cabalistic model for the psyche. That model is discussed later on, and is related to this one. I have tried to use a common terminology to facilitate comparisons among these models.

The term, "emotions" includes intuiting. The term "thinking" includes deductive reason and judgment: that is the left–brained mental processes excluding the intellect. "Perceiving," as it is used here refers to the process of remembering, generally holistically, what comes filtered through the individual's paradigm. But, people have several different kinds of memory and this model does not have a place for all of them. "Judging" is the process of breaking raw information into classes based on a rule, and then remembering the judgments, the categories, and the rule. Presumably the complete person also remembers the raw information. Also, if judging occurs at this lowest level, the self–image and paradigms must reside there, too, for they provide the rules on which some judgments are made and the paradigms through which perceptions are filtered.

[29] For the purposes of this book, one does not really need to know more than that they had a model for the psyche which was something like this. On the other hand, for the purposes of discussion of what the Classical and Western Authors were thinking and also for considering how the structure of the psyche influences personality and, through it, human society, it is imperative that we have an internally consistent and functional model for the psyche, which is reasonably realistic. Yet, at the same time, it should conform to the originals to the extent possible. — These are the constrains under which this model was assembled. This is no more than a simple and imperfect model. But, it serves well as a single unified model for the Western view of the mind, for the purposes of discussing history and philosophy from antiquity to the present day.

psychological stereotypes.

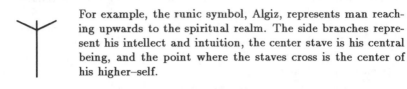

For example, the runic symbol, Algiz, represents man reaching upwards to the spiritual realm. The side branches represent his intellect and intuition, the center stave is his central being, and the point where the staves cross is the center of his higher–self.

For example, Tyr says that that which is uniquely male is centered and has knowledge and understanding.

Bjarka says that that which is uniquely woman is also centered but uses only right–brain processes.

Then, Algiz combined with Tyr might mean "enlightened man." In fact, Madr, is almost exactly these two runes combined and means essentially that. It differs in that it contains the right and left vertical staves instead of the center stave.

Thus, studying the runes begins to reveal what the ancient German peoples were thinking. — It would appear that the goals of the ancient Germanic religion were enlightenment in the Classical sense. Also, their religious leaders were surprisingly sophisticated in their understanding of psychology. They probably inherited that knowledge from the Classical world, where we know this model for the psyche had been applied to religion, during the first century. The runes appear to have been a religious innovation, dating from the second–century. But, the ancient religious tradition of the Northern long–headed peoples probably had a general compatibility with their underlying ideas, dating back to a much earlier period. — This is implied by Patanjali's Yoga Sutras, as they describe a psyche with the essentially the same structure. Likewise, both the Nordic runes and the Sutras are fully consistent with the beliefs of early Zoroasterism and the early Persian religion which came before it. The common factor was, undoubtedly, the Nordic or Aryan mind as it develops under the influences of a civilized society. All these peoples shared that and each knew it independently.[30]

The runes were primarily used for making inscriptions. Predictably, most of the original runic writings are found on tombstones and memorials, called "rune–stones." But, they also appear on various smaller artifacts such as trinkets and talisman. According to Kenneth Meadows, 1996, and many others, they also provided the basis for magic, divination, and

---

[30] That is not intended to suggest that many other peoples did not share it, too. In fact, that is precisely what gives this family of religions their wide appeal.

astrology.[31] That is the weakness of this kind of religion. — It can lead to superstition: that is, to an ignorant veneration of the symbol rather than an understanding of what it signifies. For this reason, the use of runes was suppressed after the North was converted to Christianity.

4.3 Transition to Feudalism

The various nations of Europe did not all make the transition to feudalism at the same time. For the core areas of Western Continental Europe this occurred when Charlemagne (768–814) constructed a uniform system of laws out of Roman and German Law and imposed it throughout his empire, together with Christianity.

After the time of Charlemagne, the Roman Church began the slow process of converting Northern Europe and Scandinavia. They imposed the feudal social structure, on those regions which came under their authority. For example, in 820 AD they sent a mission to Sweden. Later, during the tenth century both Denmark and Sweden used the sword to spread the cross throughout Scandinavia. The areas they conquered were also forced to become vassals. Thus, Scandinavian society came to consist of landed aristocracy and serfs rather than being composed of freemen. The conversion of Scandinavia was complete by the eleventh century.

However, this process of conversion destabilized the region and produced the waves of Vikings which swept forth to conquer.[32] They ended the culturally Germanic era of England. — The first recorded Viking raid on the British Isles occurred at approximately 787 AD. But the most serious onslaught began when the Danes invaded in 832 AD. Their incursions introduced serfage into the parts of England they conquered. In 1017, Canute, the King of Denmark became the King of England, but Anglo–Saxon control was subsequently restored.

However, in 1066, the English lost the Battle of Hastings to the Norman, William the Conqueror. He was descended from a Viking, Hrolf the Ganger, who had conquered Normandy. He and his forces had absorbed the French and Christian culture.[33] Therefore, when William of Normandy conquered England he brought feudalism with him; that was when England made the transition from the culturally Germanic early middle ages to the mixed Germano–Roman culture of the second half of the medieval

---

[31] But, some of his information appears to be drawn from other religions. He appears to have been using Nordic mysticism as a vehicle to promote the Occult. His book was one of the last in a renaissance of Runic Mysticism which occurred during the late 1980's and early 1990's. His statement on his pages 117–118 makes it clear that he adhered some Occult religion. His book provides excellent contemporary examples of syncretism, occupation of alters, and desecration.

[32] There were also a number of other factors involved: population pressure, fashion, desire for plunder, ... But pressure from the Christians was the major factor.

[33] Hrolf was christened Duke Robert of Normandy. He is probably better known under this Christian name.

period. However, this did not represent a change in religion as the English had voluntarily converted to Christianity several centuries earlier, nor was the feudalization as complete as it might have been, because William believed in a strong monarchy and was unwilling to render up England as a fief to the papacy.

At the same time that Scandinavia was being converted, Denmark and West Germany also began spreading Christianity and feudalism eastward by the same means. But military conquest of one nation over another, although it proved adequate to spread Christianity, had limited effectiveness in spreading feudalism. Many of the States which were colonized by this means, retained a more Germanic and republican social heritage and would later become the Protestant States, at the time of the Reformation. that includes Western Germany, Scandinavia, England, and the Low–Countries.

In 1147 the Church changed to a different approach. They put their colonization program under the authority of a religious order, first the Cistercian Order, but later the Teutonic Knights. By 1229, they had extended the feudalized and Christianized region along the Baltic Coast from the Elba River to Finland. These religious orders transferred the land they colonized to the Papacy and received it back as fiefs. This proved to be more effective in creating absolute monarchies.

4.4   Jews in Medieval Europe

The Jews came into Western Europe with feudalism.[34] Their arrival into Continental Western Europe was due to Lois the Pius, the son of Charlemagne. He encouraged them to settle throughout the Holy Roman Empire, in an effort to foster trade and manufacturing. To that end, around 825 AD, he granted them a charter, guaranteeing them protection and freedom of religion.

Their entrance into England was due to William the Conqueror, in 1079.[35] In that case, they were the King's chattel and their lives and possessions were absolutely at his mercy. They lived in separate quarters, or "Jewries," in London, Lincoln, Norwich and Oxford. Like the king's forests, these were not subject to common law. Nor did the Jews have standing in the local courts. But the King established a royal justiciary to deal with their legal problems and contracts.

During the first years of Norman rule in England, the Jews were undeniably beneficial to the nation at large, because their capitalistic practices facilitated economic growth. They, also, introduced building in stone and established schools which taught the Eastern knowledge of science and medicine. For example, there was a Jewish medical school at Oxford and Roger Bacon (1214?–1294) studied medicine under Jewish Rabbis.

---

[34] Spain is one exception: There had been a Jewish community there since Classical times.

[35] The early history of the Jews in England is drawn primarily from J.R. Green, 1874.

Chapter 5

Late Medieval Period

This chapter beings a block of three chapters which cover the
Western period of history.
This chapter of covers the Late Medieval Period: that is from
roughly 1200 to 1529 AD. That age saw the genesis of Western
society.

5.1   Crusades

Beginning in the eleventh century, the Roman Church extended their efforts at conversion to Spain and the Middle East. But, in the end, it was
the Moslems who were the agents of change for the Christian world, rather
than visa–versa.

Mohammed was born in 570 AD. He was a moral and deeply religious man, but everywhere he went he encountered the degeneracy of the
decayed Roman world. He responded by founding an orthodox faith to
restore morality. It combines positive beliefs based on the physical world,
monotheism, an emphasis on wisdom, and simple religious duties which
everyone can achieve. Those duties include striving after goodness. Thus,
the fundamental content of Mohammed's message was very similar to Jesus's, a message which the Western World had, by then, long forgotten.

During Mohammed's life time, Islam did not extend beyond the Arabic
Peninsula. But the year of his death, 632 AD, his successor sent invading armies against the Eastern Roman Empire. They conquered much of
it and then swept across North Africa. In 709, they crossed the Straits
of Gibraltar and in four years were in firm possession of Spain. In 732,
exactly one century after Mohammed's death, they crossed the Pyrenees
and invaded what is today Southwestern France. But, that was the end
of their expansion, for they were decisively defeated at Tours by Charles
Martel, the Duke of the Austrasian Franks. That preserved the heritages

of Western Europe.[1] There followed several crusades first to retake the
Moslem areas of Europe and later to take the Holy Land.[2]

5.2   Golden Age of France

The Crusades resulted in improved communications with the Arab world.[3]
As a result, the philosophy of reason was reintroduced into Western Europe. Aristotle and Cicero, then, were new philosophers for them. And,
as that school of thought was compatible with the German heritage and
gave a new interpretation to Christianity, they had a tremendous impact.
It reignited Western thought and led to the formation of medieval society.

This produced a brilliant culture in Paris, accompanied by a general
material and political progress. That was a golden age, an age of reason.
The period saw an outpouring of French literature, the peak–period for
French Gothic cathedrals,[4] and the founding of the French Universities.[5]

That occurred during the reigns of Phillip II (1180–1223), Louis VIII
(1223–1226), and Louis IX (1226–1270). — Phillip assumed the throne
when he was young, and consequently was not an educated man. But, he
was vigorous in war and laid the foundation for the greatness of France.
Louis VIII only reigned a short time, but Louis IX reigned for forty–four
years. He had been carefully and extensively educated. He completed the
expansion of France, to essentially its present boundaries. But, his greatest
contribution was the high quality of his administration, which secured the
benefits of civilization to his countrymen.

Aristotelianism came into conflict with the Roman Church. The Aristotelian school held that reason allows man to perceive Truth and Order
in the universe.   The religious implications were that that unites man
with God, for Truth and Order is all man can ever reasonably expect to
perceive of God, who is otherwise unknowable.[6] Both sides agreed that

---

[1] At the time of the Battle of Tours, in 732, the Austrasian Franks under
Charles Martel were Christian but their culture was still essentially Germanic.
That battle was before they got feudalized by Charlemagne.
[2] Charlemagne unsuccessfully tried to reconquer Spain. The effort was renewed
around 1050 AD by Aragon and Castile, also without success. But Pisa reconquered Sardinia in 1016, the Normans reconquered Sicily in 1060, and Pisa and
Genoa reconquered Mahdiyah in North Africa in 1087. The first crusade was
in 1095, the second was 1145–1149, the third in 1189–1192; and the fourth in
1202–1204.
[3] After 1087, Genoa controlled transportation in the Western Mediterranean;
in 1118 the Knights Templars were founded to facilitate transportation to the
Holy Land and protect pilgrims; and after 1204 Venice controlled the Aegean
Sea.
[4] Chartes cathedral in 1195, Amiens 1200, and Reims 1210.
[5] The University of Paris was chartered in 1200, and the Sorbonne was endowed
in 1257.
[6] Cicero emphatically argued that the perceptions of order in nature and the
existence of absolute truth are the only signs you should expect from an absolute,
just, and uniform God, the God of Natural Theology. There is no way to know

God was fundamentally unknowable[7] but, the Roman Church then held the existence of God as an article of faith, and did not ascribe the same importance to truth and order. In fact, they believed in a living God who rather than being just and uniform created miracles, granted grace, and so on. Furthermore, there was a difference between the existential viewpoint held by the Aristotelian school that men and things existed in themselves and the essentialist viewpoint held by the Neoplatonic school that men and things only existed in the mind of God, or more moderately, following Boethius, that men and things existed in themselves but that God originally created them from forms in his mind. Thus, there was a conflict between a religion of reason and physical reality and one of faith and spirituality.

France was too powerful and too Christian a nation for the Papacy to suppress the Aristotelian philosophy by force, nor did they want to.[8] Instead, several scholars attempted to rectify the differences. This effort culminated in Thomas Aquinas (1225?–1274?), who integrated these two opposing views in his *Summa Theologia.*

His position was that true reason and true faith must be compatible. He made the philosophy of reason one of the cornerstones of Christian theology and re–examined Church doctrines according to the standards of reason. That resulted in a purification of their beliefs.[9] That is when the Christian Church finally began to follow the new covenant rather than the Augustinian Tradition. They did not, however, exclude the religion of faith based on Jesus's early ministry.

The Church's resolution to maintain this new course became clear, shortly after that, when Meister Eckhart came under censure for practicing mystic Christianity.

There were also civil implications to these religious changes. The new covenant is, of course, the philosophy of reason, and under that system, reason is the source of the rights of man. That implies that Christian governments should have a structure consistent with the fact that all rights reside in the people. In contrast the Augustinian's God was the granter of virtues and benefits including the rights of man: that is, from Him to the Church or to monarchs, from them to the nobility; and so on, eventually to the people. That implies the feudal system. Thus, these two conflicting religious systems led to two fundamentally conflicting structures for civil society, one with rights granted by the people to government and the other

---

more about the essence of what may, or may not, be behind those outward signs.

[7]This was fully consistent with the statements made by Saint Paul about the unknowable nature of God and by Saint Augustine on how God is better known for not being known.

[8]From 1198 to 1276, the Papacy had a long series of excellent and high–minded Popes. So it appears that the wishes of both France and the Papacy were in unison.

[9]In particular, the Fourth Lateran Council, in 1215, made ten decrees moving very significantly in that direction.

with government granting rights to the people.

Thomas Aquinas's position on government was that all authority originally resided in the people but that they had transferred it to the monarch
so long as he or she ruled with justice, where "justice" means in a manner compatible with the Supreme Law of the Land.   Although Western
Europe, at that time, held that all man's laws were beneath Natural Law
and Divine Law, the Supreme Law of the Land was that law which was
accepted by the community. Thus, the people determined the Supreme
Law, not the government nor the Church. The importance of the people
as the source of all power was then the status quo over most of Western
Europe.[10] In fact, representative bodies passed down from the Germanic
heritage were still in existence and later developed, through many changes
and interruptions, into Parliaments, Estates General, Cortes, and so on.

Thomas Aquinas's system became the medieval constitution[11] and governed conduct in Western Europe throughout the remainder of the Medieval period. His position was essentially reiterated in the sixteenth century by Richard Hooker (1554–1600) and Johannes Althusius, with only
slight modifications. It was again essentially reaffirmed at the end of the
seventeenth century by John Locke (1632–1704). At that time, it provided the basis for the constitution of the modern republic of England.
A century later, John Locke's writings were the works most cited when
America's founding fathers were forming the basic principles in the United
States Constitution, although they also drew substantially on the America's practical experience with self–government. Thus, modern Western
society and the American government, in particular, have direct continuity to the medieval society of the golden age and rest, in part, upon the
same foundation.

5.3   Jews in the Late Middle Ages

The golden age was also a time of rapid development for Judaism. In
particular, the Zohar was written down around the end of the thirteenth

---

[10] It can be seen in the thirty–ninth clause of the Magna Carta that no free man
can be taken or imprisoned even by the king except by the legal judgment of his
peers, or by the law of the land. Carlyle (1941) pointed out that this view wasn't
limited to England, but "Indeed we find it asserted by Alfonso IX of Castile and
Leon in 1188, and repeated emphatically by the Cortes of Valladolid in 1299; and
it was laid down in the Assizes of Jerusalem, and by so great a feudal jurist as
Beaumanoir in France, ..."

[11] The social, religious, and legal heritage of a nation is referred to as its "Constitution." This is not a written constitution as the US has.

John Locke argued for a written constitution to prevent people from perverting
the nation's heritage to alter its law or form of government. England did not
accept a written constitution, but, a century later, America did. Then, Noah
Webster (1758–1843) wrote his dictionary to prevent people from changing the
meanings of words to pervert the written constitution.

century. It is part of the *Cabalah*,[12] that is the oral tradition of Judaism. The *Cabalah* has two written parts, the *Sepher Yetzirah* and the *Zohar*. The *Sepher Yetzirah* deals mostly with mysticism, is older, and is esoteric; whereas the *Zohar* is more accessible.

The *Zohar* is usually attributed to the Spanish Jew, Moses de Leon. Among the things it contains is a compilation of magic, drawn from the beliefs of many ancient peoples.

According to Zev Ben Simon Halevi, 1986, it elaborated on the traditional Jewish and Christian mythology. One example is the story of Enoch.[13] — Enoch lived in the earliest times and still remembered his earlier life in heaven. But, he was puzzled as to why Earth and man were incarnated. So, he spent his life contemplating that question. In the end, he was allowed to visit heaven. There he saw that it was structured according to the scheme in Jacob's Ladder, which is discussed below. There were spiritual beings who lived at each of its higher levels, just as men live in physical reality. These were the angels, devils, and spirits. He, also, had an interview with God, in which many secrets were revealed to him. He, then, returned to Earth, where he instructed his people. But, a place was reserved for him in Heaven. That was the vacant seat of Lucifer, highest of the Archangels.[14] That was in the seventh heaven, immediately below God. He was also given the title, "he who bears the name of God."[15] As such, he is the great teacher and communicator to mankind, the source of all esoteric knowledge. He comes to earth from time–to–time to instruct individuals whom God has given a special role. It is he who suspends the Laws of Nature whenever a miracle is necessary to advance some heavenly purpose. The *Cabalah* holds that Enoch was the first human to reach this high position, but they hold that that it is the full potential of any man.[16]

Zev Ben Simon Halevi also described Jacob's Ladder. Its basic unit is a model for the structure of the mind. It provides a psychological/religious system, just as the Classical model for the psyche does, clarifying the relationship between man, God, and the world.

---

[12] Or Kabbalah, spellings vary.

[13] In this tale Cabalism clearly reveals itself as a form of Gnosticism.

[14] According to this myth, Lucifer had fallen because he had refused to recognize that Adam, as a man, and the most perfect image of God, was higher than he.

[15] Several authors say that the Tetragrammaton, YHWH, translates to "I am that I am" and that a man cries "I am" as he enters the seventh heaven.

[16] By "man" they mean, of course, only any Jewish person, but I am uncertain where that distinction arises in this creation myth. Perhaps, it comes from another story in the Cabalah which tells of how Adam and Eve were separated for 130 years and, during that period, cohabitated with various spiritual beings. In particular, Eve cohabitated with Lucifer. (See Zohar, treatise Bereschith.) The twentieth century Rosicrucian Max Heindl stated that the offspring of that union became the most virile segment of mankind, and had divine souls, whereas the rest of humanity had only human parents and the souls of animals. (See Webster 1924.) That might, also, be construed to give them a rightful place in the seventh heaven.

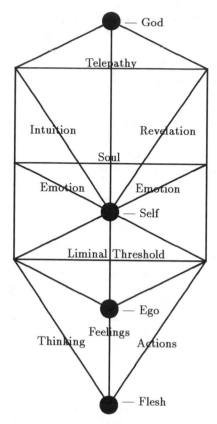

Figure 5.1: Jacob's Ladder.

Jacob's Ladder contains most of the same components as are found in the Classical model for the psyche, but it is structured differently. In particular, it contains the same three vertical paths, although they are flipped right–for–left: The left vertical line is the passive and inward and the right vertical line is the active and outward. There are three centers of human mental activity, the flesh, ego, and higher–self. These are different centers than we have seen before. Specifically, thinking or reason is attributed to the lowest level, the flesh, while the processes of the highest level are active and passive emotions, together with the intuition and revelation, which probably means religious experiences. This model also contains three horizontal cross–connecting lines. The top one of these is transpersonal consciousness, the next is the individual soul, and the third represents the subconscious and semi–conscious processes internal to the mind.

What is shown here is just the basic unit of Jacob's Ladder. The full model is greatly elaborated. Its structure is obtained by chaining together four of these basic units. This describes all the levels of creation, putting them in continuity with the human mind.

Jacob's Ladder is essentially what would be obtained if the central axis of self were oriented horizontally across the Stave Lattice rather than vertically: that is, this model is obtained by introducing a new central axis at a 90 degree clockwise rotation from the central axis in the Stave Lattice. In this new model, the lowest level then corresponds to the external, rational, and left–brained; the middle level becomes the ego; and the higher level corresponds to the affective and right–brained. Its right side faces the physical and becomes the overt and active; while its left side faces the spiritual and becomes the inward and passive.

Jacob's Ladder describes the mental structure of those one–sided individuals who live only in their right–brains: That is, it models the psyche of the affective personality types.

The intuition attaches in its normal position; it is the subconscious logical process which impinges upon the consciousness on the right–brain. But many of these people have no intellect, as there is not place for it in their personality. However, it may possibly act by occasionally producing those bursts of enlightenment which Halevi[17] refers to as "revelation."

In all models for the psyche, the intuition and intellect, if they have one, are assumed to connect the individual to the spiritual realm. For the type of person modeled by Jacob's Ladder, it, therefore, follows that the emotional center will be regarded as the center of "higher self," immediately below the level of the spirit.

Consequently, this type of person will find God by seeking inwards from the center of emotion and feelings. — Seeking the source of emotions necessarily means burrowing into the semi–conscious mind. Thus, this mental structure predisposes the individual towards inwardness, mysticism, and spirituality.

Consider what this model says about conditions in Palestine, during biblical times. The Jews had a very small proportion of "prophets" among them, or so the *Bible* says, and these individuals had "revelations." These were, probably, the individuals who had an intellect, of sorts. This is essentially the condition described by Spencer and Gillen in their, 1899, in their study of the religions of primitive peoples: Most of the people were non–rational except for a few spiritual leaders who had prophetic powers.

Individuals with this type of psyche can be successful in business and usually do not appear different until one has to work with them on some creative activity. — As many of them have no intellect, outside of the purely affective realm, they have no creativity, because they can not form fundamentally new ideas nor new logical concepts. Likewise, they probably can not perceive the pure forms which define beauty. Such people characteristically view knowledge as a collection of facts, which are memorized, and they make decisions based on learned rules or by using intuiting or intuition.

The view on intellectual property held by an individual who never had an idea of his or her own, never will have, and do not recognize other people as having them either is, at best, a system of ethics governing when someone else's idea may be taken as his or her own. In that cultural viewpoint, ideas are common property which come from God. Such people keep their ear to the ground to pick up new ideas and may become very adept at the art of intellectual theft. They may not conscious of the wrong they are committing.

Obviously a people or nation who have a large number of individuals whose mental structures resemble Jacob's Ladder, are not going to be governed by Natural Law, as they are incapable of knowing it by direct experience. The only "truths" they are capable of knowing are socially determined. Such a people are inclined to look to scripture, authority

---

[17] Ibid.

figures, the public mind, their elders, or other peoples for facts, knowledge, and ideas. — This, also, possibly accounts for early Jewish culture's, being very traditional and largely composed of borrowed concepts.

But, if individuals with a psyche as described in Jacob's Ladder lack intellectual creativity, they still can be creative within the affective realm, and their creative energies would be focused there. In addition, like many primitive peoples, the early Jews may not have clearly distinguished objects of the inner realm from physical reality and, as noted above, they probably could not perceive truth and, therefore, regarded it as being socially determined Thus, a picture of *Old Testament* conditions begins to crystallize which helps to explain why such a substantial body of religious myth developed there.

Jacob's Ladder represents the view held by the members of the medieval Jewish community about the structure of their own minds and, it has stood the test of time. Therefore, it should probably be regarded as being as accurate a representation of their psyche as the Classical model was for Western man.[18]

We are fortunate to have inherited this knowledge, of Jacob's Ladder as it provides us with a view into the mind of a person from an Eastern religious and cultural heritage. As it comes from Rabbinic Judaism, which was the original branch of Judaism, coming down from Classical times, and as it was written by a Spanish Saphardic Jew before the mass–migrations of the thirteenth century, it probably represents an irreplaceable insight into the minds of the Jewish people, during biblical times. However, it also transcends the doctrinal and racial boundaries of its origins and applies to other peoples who have a similar heritage.

This author has first–hand experience with the non–rational and affective types. — The University of British Columbia broke some of their larger service courses into sections based on psychological type and, the University of Washington did also, although they were not so explicit about it. — I TAed mathematics and statistics classes composed mostly of nurses. They were university students, so it should go without saying that they were intelligent and could reason. But they preferred not to. — They hated being taught theory; they wanted to be told what to do. Forcing them to think, made them squeal. They said it was painful. I have heard that so often, I believe it is true.

Similarly, one of the things which Halevi pointed out, was that the level of the flesh was regarded by the Jewish community as being "earthly Hell." According to this model, the flesh is the level which provides contact with the rationality and left–brained processes. Consequently, Western society and Western religion, with their outward rational orientation, were inappropriate for this type of person. It would not touch them, except

---

[18] That is excepting the the great elaboration of the spiritual realm found in the full Ladder. None of that is directly connected to any of the three centers of existence for the individual, so its existence is not something which an individual can determine by examining his or her own mind.

through what they regarded as the lowest level, a level which they despised and hated, and which, quite possibly was painful for them. — Absolute theocracy was an appropriate form of society for them; it governed them in a manner compatible with their nature; and it was their tradition.

But, returning to the developments of the late middle ages ... some Christian scholars learned to read Greek, Hebrew, and the other original languages of the scriptures. Some of them read the *Talmud* and, as a result, an increasing circle of people became aware of its contents.

The trouble with the *Talmud* is that it describes the full range of human thought, including some things which would generally be regarded as anti-social or anti-Christian. That made it possible to point to those passages and say, "See, I told you they believe that." — That criticism is unjust: There must necessarily be a corresponding tradition on which parts of their scriptures to believe and which not to.

As a result, towards the end of the thirteenth century, the Jews were tried in many countries of Western Europe for what the *Talmud* contained. In particular, France tried and expelled them in 1242. They were not readmitted in large numbers until 1715–1719. The Papacy also examined them that same year, but after finding them guilty, provided them with a haven. In each of these cases, all the copies of the *Talmud* which could be found were burnt.

They were also expelled from England, but in that case events developed differently. The English upper classes objected to the independent revenue stream they provided the crown. Their lending money on interest provided it with a monopoly on usury. They generated a substantial amount of money, which the King could draw upon whenever he pleased. For example, King John once drew from them an amount equal to the total annual revenue of the realm. This resource provided the Norman kings with the funds necessary to keep their baronage at bay, and provided the Angevin kings with the resources needed to put down revolts and conduct wars.[19] This revenue stream significantly reduced Parliament's control over the royal purse strings.

In contrast, they had increasingly became the objects of popular hatred. The commoners took offense at the Jews privileged position, growing wealth, and religious beliefs and practices. Insults and jeers were often tossed back-and-forth between Jews and commoners, sometimes ending in riots.[20] The crown's protection of the Jews never wavered.

But, due to pressure from Parliament, the King of England was forced to require them to choose between expulsion and renouncing their religion. That occurred in 1290. They were not readmitted to England in large

---

[19] The Norman kings of England were William the Conqueror to Stephen (1066–1154). The Angevins, that is the Plantagenets, begin with Henry I, in 1154, and outlasted the Medieval period.

[20] For example, during Richard's reign (1189–1199) there was a massacre of the Jews of York and during Edward's reign (1272–1307) a Christian religious procession was attacked by the Jews of Oxford as it passed by the walls of their Jewry.

numbers until 1664, under Charles II, and more came to England with William II after 1688.

Although the King of England strictly punished anyone who killed or despoiled them, many Jews probably did not survive their expulsion. In particular, according to Froissart's account, the Jews were burnt throughout all the countries of Western Europe.[21]

That is about all the histories usually tell. The official explanation seems wholly inadequate to motivate the expulsion of peoples, even by the standards of the times. But, the literature dating from that period tells more. — Old Rabbinic Judaism was rife with demonology and magic. Thus, the Jews provided nuclei for the spread of superstition.[22] The result was to test the peoples' faith. For example, a concept which was current, at that time, was that God gives the Devil power so that he can test and strengthen men's souls.[23] That created a need for the Church and State, to combat what the people perceived as the forces of Satan. Thus, the Jews formed what is called, today, a "controlled opposition."

An added advantage of this approach was that the agents who deliberately spread evil beliefs and practices would tend to attract any Christians who drifted towards those ways. Thus, their identity would become known to the authorities. That idea, too, was current.[24]

Thus, the Jews served a vital function for the feudal governments of the early Medieval period. But, the governments of the golden age had diametrically opposite needs. These were to raise every person to the highest possible level so that they could perceive Natural Law and Natural Theology.

The church had fairly good control over the rural populations, but urban heresy was a problem. Saint Francis of Assisi (d. 1226) founded the Gray Friars,[25] specifically to combat anti–clericism in the cities. So, it may be safely said that many of the monarchs would have desired to rid their cities of the Jews, if they understood them to be sources of superstition and anti–Christian sentiments. It is clear from what is recorded of the trials that they did regard them in that light. That may have been what motivated their taking the actions they took. Thus, the expulsion of the Jews can be seen as a consequence of the changes in the governing principles of society which occurred at the golden age.

---

[21] See Froissart's, *Chronicles*.

[22] The Jews were not the only source. There were also the Templars, Gnostics, Alchemists, Venetian traders, and other individuals who traveled to Spain, the Middle East, or Constantinople.

[23] That can be found, for example, in Chaucer's *Canterbury Tales* from that era, in Rabelais' *Gargantua* from around 1500, and many other sources. Chaucer, was in John of Gaunt's household. So, his views may be regarded as having been current in English high society. It is, also, significant that one of his tales retold the book of *Macabees*.

[24] Chaucer gives an example of this technique, but he casts it as being conducted by a member of the clergy.

[25] The Gray Friars were formally incorporated in 1223, but had existed for several years prior to that.

The Jews migrated primarily to Eastern Europe, particularly to Poland and the Ukraine, but smaller numbers also went to the politically fragmented States of Germany.[26]

Podolia, southwest of Kiev, became one of their more important centers. It was inhabited by the descendants of the Khazars. They were a Scythian tribe, one of the Armenoid peoples.[27] The distinctive racial feature of the Scythians is their aquiline nose.[28]

When history first encountered the Khazars, they were a pagan nomadic people, living on the steppes north of the Caucasus Mountains. But, an invasion from the East drove them south through that range. Next, around 590 BC, the Medes drove them back again. After that, they took up residence North of the Black Sea. Around 740 AD, following the leadership of their king, they converted to Judaism. That made them the only Jewish nation of their time and also a large segment, probably the majority, of the worldwide Jewish community, particularly during the tenth century, when their population had become fairly large. However, the government of their country, Khazaria, was destroyed by the Russians in 1016 AD and two centuries later, in 1239, they were overrun by the Mongol army of Balu Khan. Then, they fled to the West and North into the Ukraine and Poland. That is how these regions of Eastern Europe came to be the cradle of Judaism, although these Jews were not Semitic.

The prevalence of the racial characteristics of these non–Semitic peoples among the Jews of Eastern Europe and Germany shows the extent to which they intermarried with those who migrated there from Western Europe. But, intermarriage conflicted with their religious doctrine: In particular, their descendants were excluded from the benefits of their faith, because those are birthrights passed down according to strict rules of de-

---

[26] The Polish king, Casimir III (1333–1370), granted extensive privileges to the Jews in 1334. Many of the other States of that region also gave them charters.

[27] The Armenoids are the subgroup of the round–headed alpines which came from the eastern, or Asiatic, part of their range: specifically from Asia Minor, the Trans–Caucasus region, and a belt stretching from immediately north of the Black and Caspian Seas to the borders of Mongolia.

The Armenoids had contributed to the peoples both of Palestine and Rome at an earlier date. In particular, the Hurrians came from the part of the trans–Caucasus region which is directly north of the Tigris and Euphrates Valleys. The Hittites were their neighbors on the West, and the Medes were on their east. Beginning in the seventeenth century BC the Hurrians and Hittites moved southward into Northern Mesopotamia and Syria, occupied Palestine, and spread westward into Asia Minor. A related group, the Horites, occupied Edom, intermarried with the Edomites, and much later became part of the Jewish nation.

According to Classical tradition going back to Herodotus, the Etruscans, who founded Rome, were Hittites. They came from Lydia on the West Coast of Asia Minor, with its capital in Sardis. They migrated, by sea, to Italy around 900 BC. Although this has not been firmly established, modern authorities generally concur.

[28] An aquiline nose is a nose bent like the beak of a hawk, with its upper bridge in line with the receding foreheads of their round–headed skulls. The ridge of the nose also rarely extends across the forehead.

scent. This created an unstable situation which would lead to change later
on.

In contrast, the Jews who migrated to the Mediterranean countries
generally followed the Saphardic liturgy, which was strict on intermarriage.
They, therefore, remained Semitic.

The last expulsions of Jews from Western Europe involved these Saphardic groups. They were expelled from Spain in 1492 and from Portugal
in 1497. They mostly migrated to the Low Countries. At that time,
those countries were the most unwilling possessions of Spain. They were
predominantly Calvinist and had only recently lost their independence.
After the split between the Protestant and Roman Catholic Worlds, which
occurred only a quarter–century later, in 1529, the religion and liberties of
the Low Countries became one of the most celebrated causes of the almost
continuous wars between Protestants and Catholics which went on for the
next two centuries.

Although the Jews of the Low Countries general opposed the Western
and Christian viewpoints, they feared the Spanish Inquisition.[29] They
often supported either Holland or England and they also got involved in
England's internal disputes, supporting Oliver Cromwell, Charles II, and
William of Orange. Their contributions were mostly expressed in the form
of financing, by the "bankers of Amsterdam." But, this funding came with
strings attached. One of their principle desires was that the disabilities on
the Jews should be removed; but they also promoted capitalism, and sought
legal changes which would help them in their various business ventures.
They had a significant historical impact.

5.4   Albigensian Heresy

The profound changes in religious and social outlook which occurred in the
golden age coincided with the eruption of serious heretical movements.

One of the better known of these was the Albigensian heresy. It occurred in the region around Toulouse, in what is today Southern France.
The movement was based on the teachings of the Cathers. Their doctrine
was Gnostic or Manichean which they combined with the Gnostic Gospel
of John. They came to Southern France from Bulgaria.[30] They were an
offshoot of the Bogomils who had moved to Bulgaria from the Middle East
around 950 AD and by the thirteenth century were distributed throughout
the Balkins.

---

[29]Nesta Webster, 1924, examined many of the primary historical documents
held in the British Museum, and concluded that the Jewish bankers of Amsterdam followed no systematic plan, but seem to have financed any scheme which
promised a good return.

[30]This was the origin of their popular name, "Buggers," which is synonymous
with "homosexuals." They were accused of being addicted to unnatural sex. But
vice of every form was rampant among them. Several of the noblemen even kept
harems.

Macauley, in 1840, says of Albigensian Heresy, "The clergy of the Catholic Church were regarded with loathing and contempt. 'Viler than a priest', 'I would as soon be a priest' became proverbial expressions. The Papacy had lost authority with all classes, from the great feudal princes to the cultivators of the soil." However, this movement was crushed by the Albigensian Crusade, in 1208, under the military leadership the baron of the Île de France, Simon de Montfort.

A second movement emerged as the result of Peter Waldo's hiring some scholars to translate the *Bible* into the regional language, Langue d'oc. He studied it zealously, and concluded that people should live like the early Christians, without personal property. He also rejected the Catholic priesthood. He began a preaching campaign and obtained many converts. In order to suppress this movement the crusade was renewed by Lois VIII, in 1226. In 1229, the Council of Toulouse banned the possession of books of scripture. They only allowed the possession of books of liturgy printed in Latin.

These crusades drenched the region with blood and exterminated their culture. As part of that effort, Pope Gregory IX granted the Dominicans independent authority to investigate heresy, thereby, establishing the Inquisition in the form it retained throughout the remainder of the middle ages.

The Knights Templars[31] were the next important heterodox group to be suppressed. They appear to have followed the Gnostic Gospel of John. This includes an extension of the story of Enoch. — It says that Enoch instructed Jesus in esoteric knowledge during the time he was in Egypt. This completely contradicts the Christian belief in the divine nature of Jesus but presents him as a Gnostic prophet. — Their beliefs apparently included Jacob's Ladder, or an earlier form of it which they referred to it as the "Long Face of God."

They may have learned their Johannism from the Gnostic Moslem cult, the Assassins, who they came into contact with while they were in the Middle East. In 1312, they were prosecuted by the Pope and various Kings for heresy. They were found guilty and were duly suppressed. A few of their leaders were burnt at the stake, which was the customary penalty for serious heresies.

The reason most often given for their suppression was that they had formed a state-within-a-state, had accumulated great wealth, and threatened the stability of France. They had, indeed, become a Power, and this may have been a cause for concern. But, the slanders published by various apologists for the Templars, to the effect that the King of France confiscated their wealth, are not true. The bulk of it was given to another monastic order. The King of France was the original source of their prosecution and he induced the Pope to follow suit. The papal court was then located in Avignon (1305–1378) and was subject to substantial French influence. After that several other countries also prosecuted them. After

---

[31] See Nesta Webster 1924, but many other sources are also available.

their suppression, some of their surviving members appear to have joined the Vehmgerichts[32] and the Rosicrucians.

The Rosicrucians originated contemporary with the suppression of the Templars and continued some of their beliefs and practices.[33] They also may have been initially connected with the Vehmgerichts as their tribunals were referred to as the Rosi–Croix in the literature from those years.

However, the Rosicrucians seem to have been, or to have become, more the product of the spirit of the times than of these other organizations. For example, during the fourteenth and fifteenth centuries, we find them in courtly circles as an association of Alchemists, in contrast against the Templars who were Gnostics but not Alchemists.

Their Alchemical beliefs were Gnostic and included a psychological model, which had some similarities to Jacob's Ladder but others to the Classical Model. In their scheme, as in Cabalism, personal development occurs through a process of conflict and synthesis or "conjunction" between conflicting principles. Three of these pairs of polarities included the sun and moon, the king and queen, and Adam and Eve. Carl Jung discussed them in some detail in his *Mysterium Coniuctionis*. He, also, presented the three stages of Alchemical conjunction as models for the stages of psychological development.

Satanism[34] first appeared during the early fourteenth century. It has been around continuously since then. It is more than just the Gnostic Luciferian doctrine, where Lucifer, the Prince of Light, is worshiped as the true God rather than his dualistic twin, the Christian God. Satanism is the cult of Evil. They worship evil, as Evil, for evil's sake.

One of their central rituals is the black mass. According to Nesta Webster, 1924, citing Huysmans's book *La–bas*, the unleavened bread of the black mass is, by preference, made with the blood of a murdered newly–born baby. — The blood of the very young, being regarded as being especially powerful, because the victim only lived a short span and, therefore, minimally dissipated his or her life–force. — In some cases the infants are abducted, but in others, the female members of the cult, get pregnant to provide these tiny victims.

That is what the literature says of their rituals. Although the religion was practiced in secret, considering the many prosecutions which have occurred over the centuries, the historical evidence is probably reasonably accurate.

The objective of the black mass is the desecration of the Eucharist, which recalls and celebrates the implementation of the new covenant. Thus, Satanism might appear to be focused on enlightened Christianity.

---

[32] The Vehmgerichts were an older secret society which are not of particular importance except that they may have played a role in the Templars and Rosicrucians.

[33] See Nesta Webster, in 1924.

[34] In Italy it goes under the name of "la vecchia religione" or the "old religion."

But, its contemporary form is much the same and, in some cases, focuses on Fundamentalist Christianity. There is also a Jewish form in which the unleavened bread of the Passover is made the same way.

All of these are extreme types of Gnosticism. — The Black Mass could probably be used to travestize any positive religion which is based on a Judeo–Christian heritage or any other heritage in which blood symbolizes life or soul. Participation in such a ritual should cause individuation: Specifically, the participant might later experience difficulty in acting normally in an ordinary Communion or Passover. At the very least, it might change how he or she viewed its significance.

During the middle ages, From the Golden Age through the enlightenment period, Satanists, Occultists, Luciferians, Alchemists, members of non–conformist religious sects, and the followers of the ancient pagan religion of Northern Europe, were actively hunted down and prosecuted for "witchcraft." Witchcraft did, indeed, exist in the sense of that these various religions were practiced. — The witch–hunters usually had the intention of suppressing superstition, but, there were, also, some notorious cases in which they were themselves guided by prejudices and superstitions, possibly only exceeded by their prey.

5.5   Peasant Revolts

The fourteenth and fifteenth centuries, also, saw several rebellions. This was a different phenomenon than the religious heresies.

These revolts highlight the fact that medieval society was not entirely stable. During the early middle ages, the people had been openly held down by force–of–arms. But, during the late middle ages, they had a better social structure, and the people generally willingly followed their rulers. Revolts only occurred when the people lost respect for their rulers or the order of things.

The cause of these problems may lie in a psychological type of person. They see only their own personal needs and their relationships to those nearest them. They do not comprehend abstract concepts nor care about them. Consequently, they are often oblivious to the needs of the general community and have little regard for the structure of society. When conditions get hard for them, they are likely to rise in revolt.

Froissart provided a vivid account of the Jacquerie which erupted in France, in 1358. That was during the Hundred Years War, when things were going badly for them. — It began with a few peasants agreeing on their dissatisfaction with the state of the nation, and blaming the nobility. They went to a local knight's home, killed him, raped and murdered his wife and children, and burnt the house down. Then they went to a second house of a member of the aristocracy and did much the same. Then they went to a third .... Their numbers grew as they went, and they committed progressively worse acts. They picked, as leaders, those individuals who committed the worst atrocities. Later, when they were asked why they did these things, they said they did not know, but they followed what others did. They thought that their troubles would end when they had exterminated all of the nobility. — At first, the nobles fled to places of safety, to walled towns and castles. When they had gathered a strong body of knights together, they slew the peasants by the tens–of–thousands, mowing them down like so many cattle until they were too tired to continue the killing. Thus, the revolt was contained before it spread over all of France.

Two decades later, in 1381, there was another peasant revolt. This was in England.[35] In this case, the common people petitioned the king to end serfage, because they felt that they had been deprived of their natural rights. There was also a radical element among them, but the English commoners mostly did not follow them. The Londoners opened the gates to the masses of commoners who came from over most of Southern England. There followed several days of disorder, but there was no attempt to exterminate the ruling classes. The King granted them what they wanted and they went home: that is, except for the radicals. They remained in London and attempted to start a serious insurrection. They were promptly put down. After that, the King went from village–to–village retracting the promises he had given and executing the ring–leaders. But, as this rebellion was more moderate, so also was the response. — It did not end with a wholesale slaughter.

A revolt in Ghent followed another pattern, although its cause was the same underlying problem. The people of Ghent had developed large guilds which included most of the working men in the city, and they felt a greater loyalty to these guilds than to their duke. So they revolted. When they obtained control, they selected one of their own people as a ruler. He governed them for several years until Ghent was retaken.

There were several other peasant uprisings. One of the worst was the revolt in Estonia, in 1343–1345. In that case, the Danish rulers lost all control of the country. Order was finally restored by the Teutonic Knights, in 1346.

5.6   Decline After the Golden Age

France remained the center of Western civilization for about two centuries. That came to an end when they were completely reduced during their Hundred Years War with England (1338–1453). The critical event was their loss of the Battle of Agincourt in 1415. France was later restored by Louis XI (1461–1483), but in doing so he established the basis for royal absolutism, thereby, ending the medieval constitution. In particular, the last meeting of the Estates–General was in 1469. On that occasion they prayed that in the future the King would rule without them. But a true absolute monarchy was not established in France until 1661, during the

---

[35] The leaders of this rebellion were John Ball, Wat Tyler, and Jack Straw.

rule of Lois XIV.

France was not the only country which had serious problems, during that era. The Hundred Years War was also when the Black Death (1348–1350) reduced the population of Northern Europe by about a third. England's difficulties were due to the protracted dispute between the Houses of Lancaster and York, which culminated in the War of the Roses (1455–1485). That ended their dominance over France.

The Roman Church also underwent changes, during that period. They were disordered by the Great Schism (1378–1417), during which there were two lines of Popes, one in Rome and the other in Avignon. As always, Papal politics were very involved. But, the general trend was that the Popes in Avignon were supported by France and tended to follow their views on religion; whereas, those in Rome was supported by England and the other rivals of France and tended to oppose those views. In the end, the Roman faction prevailed, after the French collapse, in 1415. Over the century which followed, the Roman Church rapidly degenerated into worldliness and corruption

For example, the commission appointed by Henry VIII (b 1499, d. 1547) of England, in 1536, to investigate abuses within the monastic system found that about a third of the religious houses, including the bulk of the larger abbeys, were fairly and decently conducted but the rest were charged with drunkenness, simony, and the foulest and most revolting crimes.[36] This can also be seen in the 95 theses which Martin Luther (1483–1546) nailed to the door of the court church at Whittenberg on 31 October 1517, while, in Switzerland, John Calvin (1509–1564) and Ulrich Zwingli (born 1484) complained of similar things. Historian William Langer says that, "this period marked the nadir of the Papacy viewed from the moral standpoint. Most of the Popes were typical products of the Renaissance, patronizing the arts, living in splendor and luxury, using their position to either aggrandize their families or to strengthen the temporal position of the Church. Of religious leadership there was almost none."

There was also an intellectual decline in Aristotelian thought. It stagnated due to the bickering and obfuscation of the schoolmen. By the time of the Renaissance and Protestant Reformation, it had lost its sparkle. Alchemists and magicians moved into the gap. They provided many of the exciting new ideas of the Renaissance. Alchemy reached its peak during the fourteenth and fifteenth centuries and was primarily practiced among the more educated and courtly circles.

But, medieval society was coming to an end anyway, because enlightenment had led to technological advances. In particular, the invention of the English longbow and later of muskets ended the military supremacy of the mounted knight. The knight with his expensive armor and horse had been the dominant offensive weapon of the middle ages, effectively untouchable by the common man. But, medieval technology was unable to make a full–body suit of armor that could stop a clothyard arrow and

---

[36] See Green 1874.

yet be light enough for general duty.[37] Similarly, the cannon ended the military supremacy of the castle as the dominant defensive weapon of the middle ages. These technological innovations altered the nobility's role and contributed to the end of the three–class society of the medieval world.

The medieval knight's income originally came from plunder and pay in the wars. That made war a social necessity and, indeed, the middle ages saw virtually continuous warfare. As the knights' role in warfare got smaller, they progressively turned to other means for making a living. This led to the rise of manufacturing, trade, and the bourgeois class.

One of the most important factors which caused change at the end of the medieval period was the invention of the movable type printing press in Maintz Germany during the mid–fifteenth century. — In 1476, William Claxton brought one of these presses to London and began operating it under the patronage of King Edward IV. This invention broke the Roman Church's monopoly over learning. Public reading of the newly translated *Bible* became the main public entertainment in many towns and villages both in Europe and on the Continent. This led to Protestantism and spread the new learning.

The medieval way–of–life did not last long after that. The Protestant Reformation, in 1529, marks the end of the medieval period. That rupture between the Roman Catholic and Protestant worlds occurred, when the Roman Catholic party came to the Second Diet in Speier resolved on the reactionary path of strictly enforcing the (1521) Edict of Worms, which forbad all new religious doctrines. They wanted to crush the new learning. The evangelical princes protested. From this came the name "Protestant."

---

[37] Consequently there was a move towards heavier armor, but to save weight, often only the head and torso were protected by a helmet and curass. We find these still in use by some divisions of French heavy cavalry, during the Battle of Waterloo, in 1815.

Chapter 6

English Enlightenment

Christian Enlightenment, began during the Golden Age of France. But, what is called the "Enlightenment Period" extends from the Protestant Reformation, in 1529, to the Battle of Waterloo in 1815.

That was a time of change. The medieval subsistence village was replaced by a bourgoise market economy and, then, by capitalistic industrialized society and the medieval limited monarchies, were replaced by absolute monarchies, and then by modern republics.

The enlightenment period was divided into two halves. This chapter deals with its first half, from 1529 to 1688, that is from the Protestant Reformation to the England's Glorious Revolution. That was when, England went through this transition.

6.1 Machiavelli's Recipe for Change

The most important political development at the beginning of the enlightenment period was Niccolo Machiavelli's (1469–1527) book *The Prince*. It had been published in 1513, sixteen years before the Protestant/Catholic rupture. His principal concern was the moral degeneracy which he found in Italy. He made concrete suggestions on how to make the transition from a morally degenerate medieval society to absolute monarchy. — That is essentially the same transition as Rome made in the first century BC, from its degenerate republic to rule by the Caesars.

He had been involved in an attempt to establish a republic in Florence and had served in a responsible position in that government, as secretary to their council of ten. For his efforts, the Medici, whose rule followed Florence's brief experiment with representative government, tortured him on the rack and, then, exiled him. Machiavelli's experience with representative government had left him disillusioned with both the nobility and the

79

public. He reached the conclusion that an enlightened absolute monarchy was the only way to restore order and virtue to society.

He advanced the theory that a prince is justified in using any means, no matter how unscrupulous, to establish and maintain a strong central government. This included the breaking of promises, the violation of treaties, unjustified wars ... Nor did he regard the Papacy as any other than a secular power.[1] Machiavelli's recipe for establishing absolute monarchy, is first to break the power of the nobility; then to impose the new order upon the people by coercive force and studied cruelty,[2] callously applied and all at once rather than progressively;[3] and finally for the prince to gain the public's affection through equally studied and callous awards of benefits[4] or, better yet, gain their respect through fear.[5]

Spanish Tyranny: Charles V (1500–1558)[6] used Machiavelli's methods to destroy the liberties of Spain. He made the Spanish throne absolute and established the Spanish Inquisition. Therefore, his son, Phillip

---

[1] He cast Caesar Borgia (1475–1507) as the hero in his book. He was the son of Pope Alexander VI (that is, Rodrigo Borgia). Historian William Langer (1940) says that he was a "ruthless, and thoroughly immoral Pope, whose life was a scandal even in the Italy of his times. The main object of his policy was to establish the rule of his family in Central Italy."

[2] For example he wrote: "We must bear in mind that there is nothing more difficult and dangerous, or more doubtful of success, than to introduce a new order of things into a state. For the innovator has as enemies all those who derived advantages from the old order of things, while those who expect to be benefited by the new institutions will be but lukewarm defenders. This indifference arises in part from fear of their adversaries who were favored by the existing laws, and partly from the incredulity of men who have no faith in anything new that is not the result of well–established experience."

[3] He writes "... we may call cruelty well applied (if indeed we may praise evil) when it is committed once from necessity for self–preservation, and afterward not persisted in, but converted as far as possible for the public good. Ill–applied cruelties are those which, though at first but few, yet increase with time rather than cease altogether. ...... Whence it is to be noted that in taking possession of a state the conqueror should well reflect as to the harsh measures which may be necessary, and then execute them at a single blow, so as not to be obliged to renew them every day; and by thus not repeating them, to assure himself of the support of the inhabitants, and to win them over to himself by benefits bestowed."

[4] He recommended that as a prince must, from time–to–time, commit cruelties, he should appoint an official to do that, whereas, he should personally grant all benefits. These should be bestowed one–at–a–time, with much fan–fair, so as to obtain the greatest support from the people. Thus, he would appear magnanimous.

[5] He felt that it is better for a prince to be feared by his people than loved, for he felt that their affection could always be obtained through benefits, but in adverse times, when the benefits ceased, so would their affection. In contrast, a prince who established himself upon fear would be respected by the people in both good and bad times.

[6] He was the king of Spain and the Holy Roman Empire. He was also a reactionary Catholic. He presided over the Diets of Worms and Speier which began the Protestant Reformation.

II (1527–1598), acceded to the Spanish throne as an absolute monarch. However, both Phillip and Charles were bigoted in their Catholicism. — Their greatest desire was to crush all independent thought. Consequently, Spain's government was too repressive. That took a heavy toll from the prosperity and power of the country. — At the time of the Spanish Armada, in 1588, they had a vast empire and were the greatest world power. Had they conquered England, there was little doubt that they would have soon been the masters of all of Europe. But when the Spanish people lost their liberty, they also lost their initiative and, over the next two–and–a–half centuries, during which their government was absolute, Spain progressively declined into an impoverished third–rate Power.

Bourbon Tyranny: About a century after Spain became absolute, Lois XIV (1638–1715) enjoyed a similar position in France. He took the reins of government into his own hands following the death of Cardinal Mazarin (1602–1661). In his case, Richelieu (1585–1642) had previously broken the power of the French nobility, Cardinal Mazarine had suppressed the French Parliament, and the Estates General had been obsolete for two centuries.

However, the French government allowed some liberty of conscience. But, a more important factor was that Louis XIV founded an efficient administrative government and provided many improvements to the infrastructure of France. He promoted private enterprise and labored to make France prosperous. This made the monarchy popular throughout most of the slightly over one century it existed.

Tudor Tyranny: In England the strength of the baronage had already been broken, during the fifteenth century, in the War of the Roses.[7] The result was that the crown rose to almost absolute power and the people had no champion when Henry VIII's Vicar–General, Thomas Cromwell,[8] applied Machiavelli's methods, beginning around 1535. The methods of the English Terror included the Star–Chamber, which was an ecclesiastical court not unlike the courts of the Inquisition.

Henry VIII fulfilled the role of Machiavelli's prince. He was the enlightened benefactor of society, and an enthusiastic supporter of culture, the sciences and, learning. During his youth, his tutor had been the gentle and saintly Thomas More (1478–1535), author of *Utopia*. He had also, at

---

[7]Prior to that, the great barons had been able to raise armies and pursue foreign wars on their own account. For example, in 1386, John of Gaunt, the Duke of Lancaster, raised an army and unsuccessfully made war in Spain, where he had a claim to the throne of Castile through his second wife, Constance, the daughter of Peter the Cruel. But, by the time of Henry VIII, the lords were simply a class of wealthy subjects, incapable as individuals of raising an army.

William Langland (1330? – 1400?) in *Piers Plowman* had portrayed John of Gaunt as a barnyard cat, cruel and selfish but necessary to keep the mice in check. He was referring to the lessor nobility as mice, but it also applied to the king. When the great barons were gone, there was no longer anyone able to restrain him.

[8]Thomas Cromwell (1485–1540), the Earl of Essex, not to be confused with the Lord Protector Oliver Cromwell

one time, been visited by Desiderius Erasmus. Both of these men were enlightenment philosophers of the first rank. Although Erasmus had leveled fierce attacks at the Aristotelian School in Paris, that was for their use of faulty reason. Both he and Thomas More maintained a strong Christian theology based on reason.[9] Thus, Henry VIII was raised in the atmosphere of Christian enlightenment, in the proper sense.

He was a scholar of reasonably good ability and wrote a book refuting Martin Luther. — Both Luther and Calvin had taken a definite stand concerning the Natural knowledge of God. They wished to prevent the development of a rational doctrine on the divine nature which might compete with faith as the basis of religion. They both felt that God should be approached through Jesus Christ as the object of faith revealed in scripture, which they regarded as the revealed word of God. As an enlightenment scholar, Henry was personally opposed to their position.

He later also opposed the Roman Church on both political and religious grounds. At that time the Roman Church was another opponent of enlightenment. They held that religion should be based on faith in the doctrine established by Church tradition and Papal fiat.[10] But their political position was the more pressing matter. By Henry VIII's day, the Church remained as the single major opponent to the power of the crown. He removed it by the Act of Supremacy. That separated the Church from Rome and placed it under the monarch's control.

Thereafter, opposition to absolute monarchy, came only from Parliament, and that was more directed at Thomas Cromwell and specific abuses than at the king. That was politic, because Henry VIII was a popular monarch. Under him, England saw the dawn of a new golden age.

6.2 Conversion of England

Today, England is a Protestant country, but its conversion from Roman Catholicism was slow. Although Henry VIII separated England from Rome on secular matters and suppressed the lessor monasteries, that didn't instantly convert the English. At the accession of Elizabeth I, in 1558, three–fourths of the English were still Roman Catholic. But, by the close of her reign only the North and extreme West of England remained dominantly Catholic, and these were the poorest and most sparsely populated districts during that period.

The Church of England which emerged differed from Lutheranism or Calvinism in that it was the continuation of the tradition of enlightenment begun by Thomas Aquinas, rather than being based on faith in Jesus Christ; and, for the same reason, they differed from the Roman Church, which no longer followed the Thomastian tradition. Thus, the Church of

---

[9] Although Thomas Moore did not agree with Rome on all matters of theology, he was unwilling to renounce the Roman Church in favor of the Church of England, and was beheaded on that account.

[10] Declared by the Council of Trent in 1545.

England was "Protestant" in the sense that they split from the Roman Church and sided with the other Protestants on political issues, but on points of religious doctrine they were as different from the other Protestant denominations as they were from the Roman Catholics.

The English monarchy effectively promoted Protestant beliefs by changing an underlying condition. Specifically, they supported the printing of *Bibles* and also funded schools which taught the new learning. Thus, the English public read the *Bible* for themselves, and reached their own conclusions. As a large part of the doctrine of the Roman Church was not contained in it, but was found in many other sources which were not translated into English, the conclusions the public reached were necessarily Protestant. The crown then respected the wishes of the public by replacing the Catholic priesthood, as they died out, with younger Protestant ministers. They were in a position to do this as the Church of England had been a State Church, since Henry VIII's time. The conversion of England was completed by the Spanish Armada, in 1588. That attempt to conquer England and suppress Protestantism by the sword, was financially supported by the Papacy. Its failure ended virtually all English sympathy for Rome. Thus the conversion of England provides a clear example of both the effectiveness of the indirect approach to changing the culture of a nation and the difficulties with the direct approach.

Machiavelli's recipe is, of course, the direct approach. Clearly it can work if the new heritage is held in place long enough with sufficient force, as was done in Spain. However, this is always unjust as the new order necessarily conflicts with the heritage of the nation, and it is tyrannical for a government to perpetrate an injustice. Consequently, the direct approach creates resistance.

However, if the new order is clearly beneficial to the nation, and does not strongly conflict with the old system, the public may accept the change. That was the case in France, where the introduction of absolute monarchy brought great material advances with no reduction in the people's liberty. But, in Henry VIII's England, even though the material advances were greater, the change to absolute monarchy was opposed, because it meant that the English would lose some rights.

6.3 Skepticism

The next major development occurred during Elizabethan times, when the teachings of the Classical Skeptics came into vogue. This occurred as the result of the translation, in 1562, of the works of Sextus Empiricus, the last great Classical skeptic.[11] The skeptic's viewpoint was that man desires peace of mind, but will never obtain it until he denies all pretense to having any metaphysical or moral knowledge. They described a method for

---

[11] It was reissued in 1569 and 1621. It also contained the positions of all the great Classical skeptics who came before him.

obtaining this condition called, "the principle of equipollence." It states that any given proposition should be balanced against its opposite and each should be treated as equally probable. The individual is, thereby, relieved of having to make a decision between them.

It also included the skeptical tropes. These are the typical ways of setting up contradictions against the positions of the ordinary people. They aim to show, especially, that sense–based perceptions may be misleading. The fundamental difficulty is that perceptions are conditioned by what men are and what they expect. — For example, the leading Natural Theologists undoubtedly had good intellects. Therefore, they saw the comprehensive organization of nature. As they already understood the unknowablility of God except by those outward signs, they perceived His existence. Thus, their perception was conditioned upon their being intellectuals and their notions of God. The skeptical interpretation drawn by Francis Bacon (1561–1626) was that this may explain why they held their beliefs, but it doesn't constitute proof of God's existence.[12]

Francis Bacon was strongly opposed to Aristotelianism and was immensely influential.[13] He headed society away from Natural Theology towards an orthodox religion based on faith. For example, when he was asked by King James I how to improve the general state of learning, he recommended that a deep gulf be maintained between the natural disciplines and theology, because the study of Nature inclines men to believe in Natural theology if they also have a background in theology. This recommendation, which he made four centuries ago, established the custom of separating the sciences from humanities. It is still followed today, although the reason for it has generally been forgotten.

─────────────

[12]More exactly, it did not constitute a proof of the existence of God, as Bacon defined Him. But, it did constitute a proof according to some of the definitions in Natural Theology, discussed later on. — In this it can be seen that Bacon was as much governed by his conditioning as the people he criticized.

Moderate skepticism is healthy when it leads to the critical consideration of the reliability of knowledge. For example, Cicero employed equipollence in his essays *On the Nature of the Gods* and *On Divination* "not to destroy belief, but to give you some conception of the obscurity of the whole matter [about God's existence and essential nature] and of the difficulties involved in attempting to explain it."

However, skepticism carried to its logical conclusion is Nihilism. That is the belief in the impossibility of authentic knowledge. Its destructive influences were not fully reaped until the early twentieth century.

[13]Francis Bacon was a member of high society. He was the son of the Lord Keeper and knew Queen Elizabeth.— It is possible that he may have been her son by Robert Dudley. There is historical evidence that she was pregnant, but it is not known what became of the child. The suggestion most often made by scholars is that her child was adopted by the Bacons, who had the misfortune of a still–born child at about that same time. However, the evidence is not conclusive.

Francis Bacon became a highly acclaimed academic in his own time, and also rose to the highest appointed offices in the land. When he was the Lord Chancellor of England, he advanced absolutism. He was also corrupt and his career in government ended with his impeachment.

Francis Bacon's views on an ideal society are given in his story *New Atlantis*. It contains so many Rosicrucian myths and beliefs, that it is generally regarded as strongly indicating that he was one. That helps to explain his philosophical position and the arts which he employed.[14]

6.4 Commonwealth

Tudor rule ended when Elizabeth I died, in 1603, without an heir. The crown was, then, transferred to the Stuarts, in particular, to James I (1603–1625) then to Charles I (1625–1649). Under them the English Church moved away from enlightenment towards strict orthodoxy and came into dispute with the Puritans and Presbyterians.

Disputes also arose over the power of the crown. The Tudors had greatly increased those powers, resulting in substantial benefits. That included an increased military strength for England. For example, the greatness of England's Navy dates from Elizabeth's reign. But, the Tudors were also adept at defusing the issue of their power, whereas the Stuarts were inflexibly hard–headed. It was not long before they came into conflict with Parliament over that issue. In fact it was Jame's insistence on the royal prerogative to appoint whatever advisors he choose, without the approval of Parliament, that made the Civil War inevitable.

The middle class generally supported Parliament, but the sides were never drawn strictly along class lines. Parliament won and created the Commonwealth.

The Commonwealth (1649–1660) had the appearance of a republic[15] but the power resided in the army, of which Oliver Cromwell was the head. This government tended toward totalitarianism. — One party held control and excluded all other parties from the decision–making process.

The Reformation period was an era of widespread free–thought in religion. It peaked during the Commonwealth. Many short–lived sects arose: the Ranters, Diggers, Muggletonians, Seekers, Anabaptists, Levelers, and a veritable plethora of others. As a group, they were striving for a purer Christianity. But, many of them adopted mysticism, socialism, and a few even dabbled in magic. They tended to adopt beliefs which they thought the first–century Christians followed and they found worthy of emulation.

As a rule, these sects tended to seek inwards. That was the natural direction for a counter–culture when the dominant religions followed either Natural Theology or orthodoxy. As that direction brought them relatively close to Judaic beliefs, and as they may have been largely composed of

---

[14] Thomas More's *Eutopia* is sometimes given a similar billing. But, he was a staunch supporter of enlightened Christianity, and a man of high character. So, although these two books have many similarities, it is difficult to draw the inference further than that.

[15] They had a written Constitution, *The Instrument of Government*; a Lord Protector; a Parliament which sat for three–year terms; and they abolished the House of Lords and the King.

affective types, it is only natural that some of these sects were Judeo–Christian hybrids.

The most important Jewish contributions were egalitarianism and idealistic socialism. These revitalized the older English social traditions, became part of the Puritan's beliefs, and were transplanted to colonial America, where they, later, would contribute to the American heritage.

The Anabaptists were a prime example of a hybrid faith. They were ostensively Christian, but many of their leaders were Jewish. They began as small groups in Switzerland, Germany, and the Netherlands. They were pacifists and also refused to take oaths or participate in civil government. During 1534, encouraged by their growing numbers, they abandoned pacifism and captured the city of Munster. Once they were in control they tried to establish a "New Jerusalem" complete with the community of property and of women. They were quickly and brutally put down. These events gave them a bad name.

The Levelers were an offshoot from them. They were active in England. Their principle goal was the reduction of society to a single class, in preparation for the second coming. But, the Anabaptists also had other offshoots, which desired only to follow a Christian or *Old Testament* lifestyle. Among these were the Memmonites, Hutterites, and Amish. These migrated to the Ukraine and later to the United States and Canada.

These religious splinter groups quickened the religious leaven, set the tone of the times, and led, indirectly to many of the great achievements, such as the settlement of America and literary works, including John Milton's *Paradise Lost*.[16]

This Jewish influence in England was made possible by the financial support which the bankers of Amsterdam gave to Oliver Cromwell. He put a bill before Parliament to allow their admission into England, but it was voted down. Nevertheless, some Jews came to England, at that time, and people overlooked the violation of the law, knowing that Cromwell approved of it.

Quakers: The Society of Friends, commonly known as the Quakers,[17] introduced a sophisticated approach for molding public opinion,

---

[16] Milton is considered by some to have been the second greatest writer of the English language. The quality of his writing is undeniable, but his material does not appeal to the modern reader. For example, his *Paradise Lost* addresses knowledge, reason, and the human will in the Christian context. The modern Christian may not even recognize these as the central issues of Christianity, much less have an absorbing interest in them.

[17] They were one of the non–conformist religious sects from that period. Their congregation met in 1652 in the North of England. That congregation had previously been Seekers. The Seekers were a semi–mystic sect. They were awaiting enlightenment and imagined they would know the truth when they saw it. They were galvanized by George Fox's charismatic speaking. The Quakers expanded rapidly over the next decade largely as the result of his preaching.

George Fox appears to have had a genius for organization. — The Quaker community assumed control over the transmission of their way–of–life to their posterity. In particular, the communities' role in the upbringing and education

which is used today. — They conducted all church business by consensus, that is, by unanimous consent. If there was disagreement on some subject at one business meeting, the decision was postponed to allow the individuals time to search within their souls for the proper solution. As they believed that God was within every man, they felt that it is only necessary to search diligently within one's self, with prayer, to find the correct answer. As the original Quakers, had been Seekers, who, as an article of faith, distrusted their reasoning abilities, they were probably relying on their feelings and intuition. Thus, prayer for them must have been akin to meditation. Given that dissent stopped the entire community, and focused its members upon the dissenters, it produced substantial social pressure for them to conform. That probably produced the level of commitment necessary to open the individual's psychic interiority to change. The situation virtually guaranteed that unanimous consent would eventually be obtained. Thus, the community's decisions were actually being governed by social processes, and these were amenable to control by the Church leaders.

Thomas Hobbes (1588 1679) was the first person to provide a comprehensive modern philosophy for absolute totalitarian government, such as the Commonwealth tended towards. In his theory, the State has complete and absolute sovereignty. It wields power through its organizations and, thereby, provides personal security, civil rights, other things which individuals desire. Thus, individual rights are created and maintained by the State and are derived from it. The individual accepts a social contract from the State to obtain those rights. Alternatively, the State may force its views upon any individual which resists it. Either way the individual plays no role as the source of authority.

He carried the idea of the State as the sole source of authority so far as to assert that good and evil are not fixed things, but change with the needs of the State. He did not allow that there was any content in revealed religious truth nor to Natural Theology, but regarded religion solely as a branch of the State. On matters of doctrine he held that the ruler must have the final word, and that the temporal good must be the decisive consideration.

In his theory, the State has an organic existence:[18] That is, he held that society has an essential existence and functions much like an organism. — It has a public mind which holds the constitution or heritage of the nation and it also has both direct and organic control. Direct control is the chain

---

of Quaker children was at least co–equal to that of the parents. Quaker education involved the careful control of all printed material and the children's seclusion from non–Quakers. Thus, the children were conditioned entirely upon the Quaker perspective. The community also oversaw marriages, the distribution of inheritances, and the care and placement of any Quaker orphans, widows, or invalids.

[18] Wishing to stress this point he entitled his book *Leviathan*, which was how he referred to the State. A Leviathan is a fabulous very large sea monster. Similarly, his other book was *Behemoth*.

of command found in a military organization, on a ship, or in a traditional corporation. In an organism, direct control is exerted through the nervous system.

However, organisms also exert control by providing oxygen and nutrients to some parts of the body but not to others. A society can exert a similar "organic" control over its members by nourishing or supporting people engaged in activities they approve of, but withholding support from those who go a different way. But, this approach of providing carrots will not be effective unless the individuals are in need without them. Therefore, the common people must remain poor. Hobbes never carried his theory to that logical conclusion, but Adam Smith did, a century later.

Hobbes represents a fundamental change from Machiavelli. Machiavelli followed the medieval assumption that people's core motivations were moral and that they would accept tyranny to restore morality. So, his approach was one of relatively straight–forward coercion. But Hobbes followed the modern assumption that the individual is driven by economics and self–interest. So, his approach is to induce them to voluntarily give their consent through organic control. That is, of course, also the indirect approach of social alchemy. Hobbes served as secretary to Francis Bacon for a short period; so one can guess where this influence may have come from. But, it was also the spirit of the times. —The Tudors, Stuarts, and Commonwealth increasingly turned to the indirect approach.

Hobbes thought that Oliver Cromwell might be his ideal ruler, as the Commonwealth was structured somewhat along the lines of his theories. However he outlived Cromwell's rule. With the restoration of Charles II (1660–1685), the crown's view became based on the divine right of kings. Hobbes modified his writings slightly, to be compatible with their views, and they provided him with a small annuity which allowed him to retire.[19]

6.5   Restoration and Revolution

Printing had created the wave of fundamentalism which had led to the Commonwealth. But, its repressive rule was sufficient to dampen the enthusiasm of the English. Furthermore, by then it was a different world, a world where presses and literature were abundant and Spencer and Shakespeare were authors from the past.

Predictably, there was a reaction — the "Restoration" of the Stuarts. That period was bawdy. "Ladies" used course language and pursued light love; while the life of a "gentlemen" was one of continuous raking, dueling, drunkenness, and brawling; and the plays of the period glorified that way of life.

Both Charles II and James II, who followed him, believed in Roman Catholicism and the divine right of kings. Although Charles II intrigued

---

[19] Hobbes had been Charles' tutor, during the royal family's exile in the Low Countries.

and conspired to advance the Roman Church and the power of the crown, he never pushed issues too far. James II, on the other hand, felt that moderation had been the principle defect of his rule.

James did everything wrong, so far as Machiavelli's precepts are concerned. Perhaps he was following some adaptation of Hobbes' ideas. — Specifically, he tyrannized with increasing severity rather than all at once. He never held the respect of the people because of the loose morals of his court; he removed the public's security in their possessions through arbitrary confiscations and the appointment of corrupt and vicious judges; he perpetrated massacres following several risings of the people; he displaced the public from government jobs by giving them to minorities and foreigners; he converted the leading educational institutions, which had been centers of English culture and learning, into Roman Catholic seminaries; and he further offended the public's religious sensibilities by prosecuting the arch–bishop of Canterbury and six leading bishops[20] . . . At the end of only three years, his rule became so intolerable that a group of eminent persons invited William of Orange to take the Crown.

William of Orange was the Head of the Republic of Holland, and was a hero for the Protestants. By his stubborn courage, he had freed that country from the French, who at the time of his accession had controlled virtually all of it. He was also the husband of Mary, the daughter and heir of James II of England.

William came over in a great fleet, landing at Torbay, in Southern England, on November 5, 1688. His army was virtually unopposed, as the English army mostly either disbanded or declared for William. James attempted to flee to France, but was returned by some fishermen who mistook him for an absconding criminal. He was later allowed to leave.[21]

That was the Glorious Revolution. It established a constitutional republic in England. This closed a century–and–a–half of turmoil. That era had witnessed four attempts to establish absolute governments, representing a progression of different approaches. These were the Tudor tyranny, the Stuart tyranny, the Commonwealth, and the Restoration. Excepting the Tudors, who died out, each government was pulled down and replaced until England found, in William, a monarch who frankly admitted that he owed his crown to the people and resolved to protect their rights. He faithfully held to the motto upon his battle flag, "I will maintain the liberties of England and the Protestant religion."

John Locke (1632–1704) was the preeminent seventeenth century political philosopher of the English constitutional republic. He presented a carefully ordered statement of the principles, origin, and structure of

---

[20]The "case of the Seven Bishops" was a great public spectacle. It is one of the few times in English history where the Church of England and English patriotism were fully in unison.

[21]Mary, who was of gentle heart, would not allow her father to be executed. That would have been the wiser course, for he spent the rest of his life making war in the British Isles, with French support. He also thirsted for vengeance against those particular fishermen.

English society.

His work marks the point at which the philosophy of the constitutional republic achieved its modern form. He wrote his *Two Treatises of Government* immediately before England's Glorious Revolution.[22] They influenced the form of the republic of England. However, when the English throne was transferred to the Hanoverian line, in 1702, England reverted to a more authoritarian regime. But, as they retained their representative institutions, they were able to easily return to a republican form of government, during their age of reform, roughly a century-and-a-half later.

But, their reversion to authoritarianism, under the Georges, resulted in the American Revolution. Then, roughly a century after the Glorious Revolution, the founding fathers looked back to John Locke's writings when they considered a form for the US Constitution.[23]

His ideas follow the same general approach as Richard Hooker (1554?–1600). However, he departed from the medieval constitution in that he defended not only the liberty and authority of the community against the ruler,[24] but also the liberty of the individual against the community. Specifically, he denied that the community or State has any absolute or arbitrary authority but asserted that Natural Law is the Supreme Law and, hence, that all rights reside in the individual.

We know John Locke for his political writings, but most of his work was on theology. In religion, he was a moderate skeptic and rationalist. His background is evident in his political works.[25] — Most of his logical arguments commence with either Natural Law or scriptural authority, but he tempered both with common sense.

For example, he began his discussion of property rights with God's grant of the world to Adam and to Noah and his sons, but he then appealed to Natural Law to show that that was actually a grant of the right of appropriation. According to him, unowned property is originally appropriated by the application of labor to it. Its value is derived from that labor, but its price is set in the marketplace. — He was laboring to derive

---

[22] They were previously thought to have been completed just after the revolution, but a newly discovered manuscript places them ten years before. See Peter Laslett's introduction to John Locke: Two Treatises of Government, New American Library, New York.

[23] According to Donald S. Luntz 1988, after the *Bible*, which was always the source most cited, decade–by–decade the authors who America's founders cited most were Locke in the 1770's, Montesquieu and Locke equally in the 1780's, Montesquieu in the 1790's, and Blackstone from 1800 through 1805. Locke addressed fundamental constitutional issues; while Montesquieu's most important contribution was his advice on structure: for example, he recommended the separation and balancing of powers. Blackstone discussed law from a constitutional perspective.

[24] Hooker had reasserted the medieval principle that the law accepted by the community is the supreme law. That is, he held that the community was sovereign.

[25] Most modern Americans will find him excessively biblically oriented. But, he was what would be expected of a conservative intellectual of his times.

a rational system out of the somewhat syncretic heritage of his day.

Similarly, although he believed in Natural Law, he also saw its limitations:[26]

> "There wants an established, settled, known law, received
> and allowed by common consent to be the standard of right
> and wrong, and the common measure to decide all controver-
> sies between them. For though the law of nature be plain and
> intelligible to all rational creatures; yet men, being biased in
> their interest, as well as ignorant for want of study of it, are
> not apt to allow of it as a law binding to them in the applica-
> tion of it to their particular cases."

6.6   Scotland and Ireland

This was the point in history when Scotland and Ireland became part of
the United Kingdom. They were the remnant of the Gaelic culture. The
centers of Gaelic civilization had been conquered by Julius Caesar, long
before, and most of the Gaelic peoples had been become romanized. That
is why little comment has been made on the Gaelic contribution to the
Western heritage: It was effectively gone long before Western civilization
emerged. The exceptions were Wales, Scotland, and Ireland. These were
fringe areas which were semi–isolated or isolated from Europe.

Up until the rule of William and Mary, Scotland was divided among
many small independent principalities, each held by a clan. The High-
landers and Islanders were descended from the indigenous people of the
British Isles, whereas the Scottish Lowlanders were related to the English
and had come in the same migration. These two groups had been in perpetual warfare with each other throughout the millennium they shared
Scotland.

Scotland was not completely isolated from European culture, but the
Highlands and Islands were particularly poor and backward. — Few of
the Scotts were literate; each clan had a bard who maintained their oral
history; and at one of their last battles against the English, the Battle
of Killiecrankie in 1689, history records that one of the Scottish leaders
paused, before the battle, to take off his shoes. They were probably the
only pair in their entire army. Their womenfolk provided the labor and
conducted such limited agriculture as they practiced. They regarded manual labor as being beneath a man's dignity. They were anglers, hunters,
thieves, and pirates, or served in the armies of Europe. At that time,
these customs were so well known to the neighboring peoples that it was
a capitol crime in Northern England and the Scottish Lowlands to wear a
tartan.

William and Mary conquered Scotland not with the sword, but with
the pick and shovel: They built roads. When, that ended their semi-

---

[26] See John Locke's *Civil Government* chapter 9.

isolation, they promptly became full members of Western society, adopted their values, and earned a reputation as an industrious and honest people. The fate of Ireland was entirely different.[27] James II deliberately aggravated the antagonisms between the Irish and the English and used Ireland for his base of operations for the reconquest of England. He was able to take most of Ireland, but failed in the siege of Londonderry, against its citizenry. When the English army arrived, the Irish quickly gave way and were soon conquered. They had offended the English sensibilities and James had even encouraged his soldiers to commit atrocities which violated the standards of warfare as they were then practiced. These things have not been forgotten. — Much of the present antagonism between the Irish and the English can be traced to James II and these events.

The Irish, had a very different culture from that of Europe.[28] When history first encountered them they were a nomadic cattle–raising bronze-age people. During the dry season they grazed their cattle on the rich lowlands, and in the wet season, when these became a morass, they moved onto the moors. They built no permanent structures and practiced no agriculture beyond the planting of potatoes. Those could simply be planted and left. They would build temporary shelters of dry–laid stone or burrow a cavity beneath the roots of a large tree. — The "Irish" castle of Limerick and the town of Waterford had been built by the Danes, and their other large architectural structures were due to the English.

The Irish had many minor "kings." But, beyond that, they had no fixed form of government. The fist–fight was the usual social institution for settling the more serious disputes. Like many nomadic peoples, they did not recognize boundaries nor did they have a fixed system of law. — Everything was governed by oral tradition. One might attribute to this cultural peculiarity, the Irish art of blarney: He who talked the best line, prospered.

Thus, the cultural predisposition of the Irish strongly favored verbal skills. That might be taken to imply a right–brained, feminine, or Eastern mental orientation. But, that would be a wrong conclusion. The incompatible features are that their social structure was not matriarchal, nor were they particularly known for homosexuality, and they characteristically looked outwards rather than inwards.

Irish culture appears to have been a remnant, in relatively pure form, of the culture of the Northern Longheaded peoples from their nomadic period. That period had ended, for some of the Nordic nationalities, shortly after the Aryan and Indo–European migrations three–to–four thousand years ealier. — Their nomadic culture was the precursor to the Western way–of–life and should be contrasted against the matriarchal garden cultures of

---

[27] See Macaulay, T.B. 1848.

[28] There are many historical sources, but one of the more interesting is Froissart's *Chronicles* from the fourteenth century. He recorded the story of a knight who had been captured by them as a pageboy and had been brought up by them.

the Mediterranean peoples, which led to the Eastern heritage.

Any time the Irish were left to themselves, they reverted to their unique way-of-life. But, the other Europeans regarded that as barbarism. Consequently, throughout the centuries, England was constantly conquering and re-reconquering Ireland to restore civilization. For just one example among many, during the early years of Henry VIII's rule, the Pope authorized him to conquer Ireland for the purpose of suppressing the slave and drug trades and to reintroduce Christianity.

The fundamental problem was that Irish culture *was* barbarism, in the strict denotative sense.[29] Imposing civilization upon a people who have not reached that level is difficult. — They do not want it; it is not appropriate for them; and their comprehension of its governing principles is outside the scope of their tradition.

For these reasons, it is hardly surprising that repeated attempts to impose civilization upon them by simple conquest were not effective. Their transition from barbarism required a more concerted effort. That occurred as the result of their following the Roman Church and the English imposing law on them for two centuries, transporting their more turbulent element to the colonies. Today, Ireland, is no longer likely to revert to the extremes of barbarism. The exception is the IRA terrorists. — One must always expect a remnant of the original people and a small conservative element who prefers the ancient tradition. — The Irish who moved to America caused some riots during the mid-nineteenth century, and were prominent in the early union movement and early organized crime, but gradually adopted the cultures they found around them. For all practical purposes, today, a century-and-a-half later, they are fully assimilated.

Rudyard Kipling[30] pointed out that the Thugs were another remnant of that "glorious past of the Aryan people," which some individuals of his times were prone to idealize. — They lived in the jungles of India and Burma: that is, in the fringe areas at the extreme other end of the

---

[29] "Barbarism" is the intermediate condition between a purely animal-existence and civilization. The early nomadic and garden cultures were, therefore, "barbaric" in the exact sense.

Primitive, barbaric, and civilized are the three simple levels of social organization, corresponding to the three stages of mental development in individuation. 0— In this context, a society's recognition of boundaries, in all their ramifications, is an indicator of "civilization."ָ

[30] Those who have only seen only Kipling's *Jungle Books* or *Kim* may wonder why he is held in high regard as a writer. They should read *Stalky and Company*, *The Light that Failed*, or *From Sea to Sea*. Also, although his is generally associated with British India, he married the heir of the Sears fortune and lived in New York, throughout much of his life.

He was cognizant of, at least, the general trend of world-historical developments during his era and occasionally made comments about them. On several occasions, he acted in the capacity of an unofficial British envoy. Some have called him a "British agent," but he was probably just a loyal British citizen, a friendly literary voice, and a member of both British and American high society.

range of the Northern Longheaded peoples. They worshiped the Hindu's dark Goddess, Kali, praised the virtues of theft and murder, and practiced dacoity. The British vigorously suppressed them.

The significance of these cultures is that they were the state of society which Rousseau would admire so much. — They had complete freedom from any fixed law. — This concept became a cornerstone for the philosophers of the French Enlightenment. That is discussed in the next chapter.

6.7   Economic Revolution

The change which occurred in England with the Glorious Revolution was more than just a change in political philosophy, it was also economic. — The economics of the earlier system had been governed by the dictates of morality and often tightly regulated by law, whereas the post–revolutionary economic system was essentially "free": that is it was governed only by the natural economic behavior of the people. These changes had been developing slowly for a long time.

The medieval village had formed a self–sufficient unit. The vast majority of their needs were provided locally and were often paid for in–kind. England was then divided into many small holdings each farmed by a peasant or tenant. The commoners farmed their land and grazed their livestock on the commons; and if they were serfs, rather than freemen, they would also owe feudal dues: that is, they would be required to provide unpaid labor to their lord, to cut his wood, sow and harvest his fields, thresh his grain, and so on.

However, this system slowly changed as feudal labor dues were progressively replaced by cash payments, and the lords began hiring laborers. Manufacturing was also slowly growing in the cities. Still there were only limited opportunities to invest money profitably. So, for the most part, those who had gold stored it. As a result, there was very little cash flow in these early societies.

During the reign of Queen Elizabeth, in the sixteenth century, the growth of the weaving trade, made sheep raising profitable. So many landowners, enclosed fields and turned their tenants out. But, as there were no manufacturing centers which required their labor, they were left to subsist as seasonal agricultural laborers, if they could find any work at all. As a result, throughout the early enlightenment period there were large numbers of able–bodied paupers. To deal with this problem, the government created a system of poor laws, and also created boroughs to stimulate trade,[31] but these were never very successful.

---

[31] Boroughs were trade zones dating from the pre–capitalistic era. Manufacturing and hired labor were legal there. Each borough also sent a representative in Parliament. By the eighteenth and nineteenth centuries, they were obsolete. The representation in Parliament of defunct boroughs was withdrawn, during the reforms of the Gladstone administration, in the late 1800's.

The economic stagnation gradually gave way, as the land was converted to profitable uses. Then small–scale manufacturing in towns grew to serve the rural market. The town's specialization allowed them to provide better and less expensive products than could be produced in the village economies. Thus, economic fluidity, division of labor, and interdependence gradually developed. Towards the end of the seventeenth century, England had become a bourgeois market economy.

Hobbes: Those were the times of Thomas Hobbes and his economic views reflected those conditions. He had abandoned the medieval concept of a just and moral society, in favor of pragmatics, and his political theories were directed, in part, towards the establishment of a capitalistic society. He did not offer any theory of money, nor for the distribution of profits, nor even for the balance of trade; but he provided a rudimentary law of supply and demand[32] and he viewed labor as a commodity.[33] He also regarded the legitimate role of government to include the protection of private enterprise as well as of life and property; and he felt that government had a duty to establish and maintain the conditions necessary for business.[34] He also recognized that the accumulation of capital was essential to the early stages of economic growth and, consequently, concluded that consumption should be taxed rather than wealth or property. He viewed taxes as the legitimate rent paid to the government for providing services.

Locke, in contrast to Hobbes, addressed economics from a moral standpoint rather than visa–versa. He developed theories of property, money supply, and trade. He viewed money as a means of storing value and regarded it as private property. These ideas are consistent with the general theme in his *Second Treatise of Government*. However, there were some inconsistencies in his economic ideas which were, later, pointed out by David Hume. Nevertheless, his ideas provided a starting point for others. He was living at the dawn of the capitalistic era in England, and the economic ideas, of those times, were still fairly crude.

After the Glorious Revolution, in 1688, England saw innovations in banking and finance. In particular, the Bank of England was formed, in 1694, to finance the national debt. They issued paper money based on frac-

---

[32] From Hobbes' *Leviathan*: "The value of all things contracted for, is measured by the appetite of the contractors."

[33] From chapter 15 of his *Leviathan*, "The value or worth of a man, is as of all things, his price: that is to say, so much as would be given for the use of his power, and, therefore, is not absolute, but a thing dependent on the need and judgment of another. ... And as in all things, so in men, not the seller, but the buyer determines the price."

[34] "It belongeth to the Commonwealth, (that is to say to the Sovereign), to appoint in what manner, all kinds of contract between subjects, (as buying, selling, exchanging, borrowing, lending, letting, and taking to hire), are to bee made; and by what words and signs they shall be understood for valid"

tional reserves.[35] This greatly enhanced the circulation of money.[36] The first true stock exchange opened in London, not long afterwards. When stocks provided vehicles for the investment of capital, people took their gold out of storage and invested it. These factors freed the English from their economic stagnation and the period which followed showed an exuberance of creative energy in all fields of endeavor.

At first the stock exchange led to wild speculation as a succession of bubble companies came before the public.[37] But it also provided financing for boni fide ventures.

The British East India Company was the preeminent successful venture of that century. It had been formed, during the reign of Queen Elizabeth I. However, for more than a century it only involved a modest trade and a few warehouses. Its meteoric growth, when it changed from a trading company to a world power, began in 1746, due to the conquests made in India by Robert Clive and the diplomacy of Warren Hastings.[38]

Originally, the English traders in China had labored under the difficulty that although there was a strong demand for Chinese products in Europe, China's domestic industries supplied all of China's needs. There was little demand in China for anything the English could sell them. Without a balancing trade, as large a one–directional transfer of goods as the demand would support could never have been sustained over a long period as it would have drained a large part of the gold from Western Europe and the British Isles. So, the English traders developed a balancing trade. They promoted opium addiction in China. That created a demand for a product which the East India Company could supply from India, where they held a monopoly, thanks to the conquests begun by Robert Clive and Warren Hastings. That trade was the mainstay of the East India Company's revenue and funneled the wealth of China into their coffers.

During the first two decades of the nineteenth century, they illegally imported approximately 5000 chests of opium into China each year. By 1831, that had risen to 19,000 chests and by 1836 to over 30,000 chests.

---

[35] That is, laws allowed them to issue more paper notes than the gold reserves backing them. Notes were easier to use than gold and the fractional reserve system also increased the amount of money in circulation.

[36] The importance of fluidity was appreciated at the time. In particular, John Locke held that the money supply, that is the effective quantity of money in circulation, depended upon its rate of circulation as well as its absolute amount and that the rate of industrial output depended upon the amount of money in circulation.

[37] Each bubble company offered a glowing perspective which engendered wild stock speculation. However, sooner or later the bubble would burst when the company was discovered to have no basis. The South Sea Company was one of the largest and best known bubble companies. See, Charles MacKay's, 1841, book for an entertaining account of the propensity of the public to be swept along by such transitory fads.

[38] See Macaulay, T.B. 1841. The history of these two individuals is well worth reading, and Macaulay was a good writer.

Although, the British East India Company lost its charter as a crown company, in 1833, their line of business was, by then, well established. Attempts by the Emperor of China to oppose it, resulted in two small wars, in 1841–42 and 1857–60, known as the "Opium Wars," to force him to allow the unopposed continuation of the trade.

According to Dr. John Coleman (1994), opium was the basis of most of the great British fortunes and also some of the great American fortunes. But in America, Southern cotton and slaves were other great sources of wealth.[39]

Slavery is as old as mankind. — A primitive man, finding himself more powerful than his neighbors and having no concept of human rights, imposes himself upon them. Thus, we find it among virtually all primitive peoples; but it may disappear as civilization develops, depending upon the prevalent view of the rights of man in the particular society. Slavery is inconsistent with the Christian and Western perspectives and had disappeared from most of Western Europe long before the modern era. For example, although early England allowed slavery during their pre–feudal Germanic period, it was suppressed by William the Conqueror in the eleventh century.

In contrast, it was part of both the Moslem and Jewish heritages.[40] Slavery in Spain dates back to the thirteenth century. Spain had been a center for Jewish culture and learning since Classical times and, until 1492, had been under Moorish rule. Their perspective on slavery became part of Spanish culture as the Christians slowly retook that country from the Moors.[41] The Spanish colonial empire had a slave–economy from its very first years. For example, their first importation of African slaves to the

---

[39]Specifically he says: "Of these the Lehmans are an outstanding example [of a family which drew their fortune from both cotton and opium]. But when it comes to fortunes made solely from the China opium trade, the first names to come to mind are the Astors and the Delanos. President Franklin D. Roosevelt's wife was a Delano."

A sideline of the opium trade was the coolie labor used to construct the Western half of the first American railway to cross the continent. Leland Stanford, who founded Stanford University, was one of that company's major owners. More than 90% of the coolies they hired were opium addicts. Opium effectively enslaved them, as the company could obtain it at a modest price, through their international connections, and resell it to the coolies, thereby, recovering most of their wages. The majority of the coolies didn't return to China but settled in the major cities on the West Coast. This created a flourishing opium trade which continued into the twentieth century, at which time, it was finally outlawed.

[40]The Arabs traditionally had slaves. In their case, the custom arises due to the Koran saying that Jews and Christians should be granted certain rights because they are followers of the book and the earlier prophets. But, people who followed other religions were not entitled to those same considerations. Slavery was clearly part of the Jewish heritage as the messianic State describes a slave–economy.

[41]Langer (1940) says of its beginning, "In the thirteenth century, Barcelona, utilizing the skill of her native sailors and the local (mostly Jewish) capital, and profiting by Italian commercial pioneering, began an extensive slave trade in Moorish prisoners."

West Indies was in 1501. But, by 1574, according to their estimates, there were only 387,000 Black slaves in their entire colonial system, excepting Cuba and Puerto Rico.

The development of the slave trade into a massive industry can be traced to Holland and their disputes with Spain and Portugal. — The Portuguese had been the first European nation to systematically send out explorers to discover the world. Their explorations of the coast of Africa began in 1270 and, by 1487, they had rounded the Cape of Good Hope. As they extended their explorations, they opened trading posts along the coast. These dealt primarily in gold, ivory, and, initially, also in slaves. But the slave trade was prohibited by Prince Henry the Navigator (1394–1460), and it was also periodically suppressed after that date.

But, at the beginning of the seventeenth century, the Dutch Provinces were at war with Spain and Portugal. They commissioned two companies, with independent military and political authority.

The first was the Dutch East India Company, which they founded in 1602. It rapidly displaced the Portuguese from their trade in India and the Spice Islands. As a result, Amsterdam developed into the great center of European trade.

The second was the Dutch West Indies Company, founded in 1621. Their charter gave them a monopoly over trade on the African and American coasts. They seized many Portuguese trading posts on the African coast; made extensive conquests in Brazil; and took the Caribbean Islands of Curacao, Saba, and St. Martin. New York was also, at that time, a Dutch colony.[42] They developed a vigorous trade based on transporting African slaves to the New World.

However, slavery was prohibited in the English colonies.[43] But that changed immediately upon King Charles II's restoration. His return had been financed by the Bankers of Amsterdam. In 1660, he took the throne; in 1661, he legalized the slave trade in the English colonies; in 1663, he granted the charters of Rhode Island and Providence Plantation; and, in 1664, the disabilities on Jews were removed and England seized New York and several Dutch trading posts on the African coast.[44] Over the century which followed, Newport, Rhode Island, developed into the center of the slave trade.

Thus, that industry moved from Amsterdam to Newport.[45] Beginning in 1723, Newport began producing distilled spirits and exporting them to

---

[42] New York was originally called New Amsterdam.

[43] However, there were a few black slaves in Virginia at an earlier date.

[44] The politics of the period are complicated. The slave trade clearly was one of the issues influencing events, but it was only of secondary importance. Other concerns had greater influence. The second Anglo–Dutch War followed in 1665 to 1667. The bankers of Amsterdam soon switched their support to William of Orange. After his government was established, many of the Jews of Amsterdam immigrated to England and New England where they played an important role in their new economic institutions and business ventures.

[45] See Elizabeth Donan 1935.

Africa to be exchanged for slaves. The alcohol industry in the colonies expanded rapidly to meet this demand and soon became an important part of the economics of the region. While, on the other side of the ocean, the slave industry depopulated wide expanses of Africa.

To appreciate the size of the fortunes accumulated and the great difficulty in ending slavery once it had become established, we need only consider the costs involved. When England abolished slavery in all her dominions, in 1833, it cost her 20 million pounds. For comparison, during the peak years of the Napoleonic Wars, in the 1790's, England's national debt rose by 20 million pounds per year, which was then considered "undreamt of." But, the total cost for the four years of the American Civil War, combining both sides, was approximately $10 billion. That was just over twice what it would have cost to purchase the 3.9 million slaves reported in the 1860 census. But, that is so much money that it is unlikely that America would ever have made that transition in any way except by a civil war.

These economic ventures of the eighteenth century, in opium and slaves, this raw capitalism, created a class of nouveau riche, called "Nabobs." In England, Edmund Burke (1729–1797) was highly critical of them. During the early nineteenth century, these excesses were corrected; and by the end of that century, "Nabobs" had became part of popular culture. — They often provided the villains of mystery stories.[46] They were stereotyped as being crass, violent, with a bad liver, and a worse heart.

---

[46] For example, see Arthur Connan Doyle's Sherlock Holmes' story *The Speckled Band*.

Chapter 7

French Enlightenment

The second half of the enlightenment period was from the English Glorious Revolution, in 1688, to the Battle of Waterloo, in 1815. At that time, England had already made the transition to a modern capitalistic republic, but Germany and France were still under the old regime. Their transition took a very different path than England's. — It laid the foundation of modern absolutism.

7.1 Freemasons

The Freemasons were the most important organization of those times. They originated, during the early middle ages, as a stone masons' guild.[1] They were organized in three levels, presumably corresponding to the three levels of individuation: that is the infant, child, and adult. A member was slowly raised from level–to–level as he was found acceptable. With each step he was initiated into new mysteries and made to swear blood oaths of secrecy and obedience. That probably provided an effective means of organization and facilitated training in the art of building in stone.

They operated on a lodge system and their functions were to maintain a monopoly over the building trade and to obtain a favored position for themselves. To that end, they admitted "speculative" members, who were generally individuals of exalted station who had no intention of becoming artisans. They secured the Masons favors from the government including an exemption from the laws restricting fraternal societies. That opened the door for them to become a semi–secret political organization.

Towards the end of the seventeenth century, we find them connected with the Rosicrucians. The Rosicrucians had, by then, come out into the

---

[1] As the art of building in stone was introduced into England by the Jews, the Freemasons certainly did not exist prior to 1079. The earliest evidence of them are their identifying marks cut into the stonework of the York Minster Crypt, dating from around 1190.

open as an association of Alchemists. They practiced magic, in the broad older sense, which included mathematics, physics, chemistry, medicine, pharmacy, and social psychology. But, they were Christian and do not appear to have practiced the occult. Some of them were prominent and highly qualified persons, including Francis Bacon, Robert Fludd, Christopher Wren, and Elias Ashmole. They worked as individuals but kept in touch by letters and an annual meeting, much as modern scientific societies do.

In England, the Alchemists supported the royal cause. That is, they supported the Stuarts, both before and after the Commonwealth. But, when the Glorious Revolution ousted King James II, in 1688, many of the Catholic Freemasons followed him to France. They took the name of "Jacobites." That was also when the Rosicrucians came to an end.[2] — By then, scientific knowledge had superseded magic and scientific investigators no longer needed to hide from persecution. Consequently, the Rosicrucians lost their appeal to educated men.

After the Glorious Revolution, the Freemasons who remained in England were mostly middle class people who were either non–political or supported the government.[3] On June 24, 1717, four London lodges met and reorganized the Masons. This is called the "revival of 1717."[4]

They decided to rewrite their constitution. — The Freemasons had originally been a Christian organization, but two Protestant ministers[5] undertook the task of rewriting their constitution as a Universal Creed, "based on the fatherhood of God and the brotherhood of man — so as to admit men of all religions, nationalities, and stations of life." They drew their religious principles primarily from the *Talmud*.[6]

---

[2] The Rosicrucians have been reconstituted several times since then, but these more recent organizations followed the Occult and don't appear to have had any direct connection to the older organization, except in name.

[3] Nesta Wester 1921, Robison, 1789, and Barruel, 1798, all say that even towards the end of the eighteenth century, the English Freemasons were still composed of sound patriotic individuals.

[4] That was a time of considerable risk for England. — Lewis the Fourteenth of France had died in 1715 and the Regent of France, Alberoni, had promised aid to the Jacobites for a counter–revolution in England. Spain also was threatening. A strong Spanish force landed in Sicily but their Fleet was shortly, thereafter, destroyed by an English fleet in the Straits of Messina; in response, Spain fitted out an armament commanded by the Duke of Ormond to aid a Jacobite uprising in Scotland, but this was wrecked in the Bay of Biscay.

[5] A Presbyterian minister, Dr. James Anderson of Piccadilly, London, and another minister, John T. Desaguliers of Christ Church, Oxford

[6] The quote comes from Stillman, 1905. — The evidence for the use of the *Talmud* comes from various sources, but primarily from Albert Pike, 1871. There is no evidence from that time–period that there was any direct Jewish involvement. However, these London lodges are known to have been pro–Hanoverian and the Hanoverian princes had close connections to the Jewish community, regarding them as their useful servants. So, if there was a political significance to their use of the *Talmud*, it would seem more likely that it was an Hanoverian agenda rather than a Jewish one.

This type of English Freemasonry spread to America during the early colonial period. The first American lodges were formed in Philadelphia, New Hampshire, New Jersey, and New York in 1730 and in Boston, in 1733. Benjamin Franklin was elected Grand Master in Philadelphia in 1734.[7]

Freemasonry is woven all through the American Revolution, on both sides. More than a few of the founding fathers were Freemasons. — It provided a means for organizing men and getting them to work together, cooperatively. Thus, it provides a mechanism which can be used to support almost any cause. — The American Masons supported a constitutional and republican form of government as envisioned by John Locke, whereas the English Masons supported the Hanoverians. The general membership of neither the English nor American Freemasons had much to do with the more radical Continental Freemasons.

7.2   Continental Masonry

The Grand Orient (Paris) was originally composed of Jacobites dedicated to overthrowing the government of England. However, it was taken over by a clique who represented the Duc de Orleans. He became their Grand Master. He aimed at the French throne, and eventually his house achieved that honor.[8]

Scottish Rite Freemasonry was the system used by the Continental Freemasons.[9] In this system a new initiate knows only the person who serves as his sponsor and instructor. He learns various lessons as he progresses through the first six levels. During this learning process he is examined to determine if he will choose to support the organization. To enter the seventh level, he must provide an extensive personal history which included explicit information on his sex-life. This bound him to the organization, which then had power over him.

The number of levels in the Scottish Rite increased over time. These additions occurred by adding new upper levels, based on myths from Eastern Mysticism. As Freemasonry was then based on the *Talmud*, additional levels based on Jewish mysticism[10] could be readily incorporated.[11]

---

[7]Benjamin Franklin (1706–1790) was a Quaker and was politically liberal. Early in his career, in 1727, we find him at the head of a newly formed a "Quaker Party," which was established to oppose a conservative element which had emerged at that time. He was a strong proponent of the consensus process for conducting government. That was, of course, the Quaker heritage, and he is known to have used it early in his career, in a debating club.

[8]the July Monarchy, 1830–1848

[9]It appears to have had nothing to do with Scotland.

[10]According to Nesta Webster (1921), cabalistic magic was the primary source of their "Eastern myths."

[11]The Cabalistic system for individuation has many more levels than the Christian 3–level system. (See Zev Ben Simon Halevi 1986.) Thus, the change from a Christian to a Judaic model prepared the way for the addition of many new degrees to Freemasonry.

The lodge system was the reason to add levels. Any lodge which wanted the new degree had to submit to the leadership of whoever added them.

The principle person who did this was Frederick the Great, the King of Prussia. By this means, he appropriated the Continental Freemasons. He had originally regarded the Freemasons with contempt, but in 1738, while passing through Brunswick, something happened which suddenly changed his mind and, he was admitted into the Hamburg lodge, in a hurried ceremony. Throughout his reign, his interest in Masonry never waned.

Nester Webster pointed out, in 1924, that the famous French satirist, Francois Marie Arouet (1694–1778), better known by his pen name, "Voltaire," appears to have been intimately connected to his involvement in Freemasonry. Specifically, he made his first visit to Prussia just after Frederick acceded to the throne. Soon new degrees, based on the myth of the Templars, were introduced into German Freemasonry and a delegate was sent to France to interest them in these degrees. Between 1740 and 1743, some English lodges, also, added these levels.[12] Frederick used these degrees as a means for extending his authority. By 1746, he was the head of fourteen lodges. The next time Voltaire visited Prussia was in 1750 and the very next year additional degrees were added in Germany and a delegate again was sent to France. They, too, added the new degrees.

The next major event in Freemasonry occurred in 1761. That was the low–point in the seven years war for Prussia, a time when Prussia was so devastated that Frederick could hardly find men nor horses and was carrying poison with which to commit suicide if the Prussian effort should collapse. Yet, that was when he became the head of the Continental Freemasons. The next year, suddenly the Czarina died and Prussia's fortunes changed. — The Freemasons appear to have played a vital part of the miracle of his successes. They provided him with an international espionage network of unequaled quality.

7.3   Frederick the Great

Frederick the Great, more than any other person, was responsible for the social reforms which would transform Europe from decayed feudal States into modern societies.[13] His personality helps to explain what transpired.

---

[12] This resulted in a schism within the English Masons, between the "ancients" who accepted the new levels and the "moderns" who didn't. The two groups weren't reunited until 1813.

[13] See Macaylay's biography on him from the April 1842 issue of the Edinburgh Review. That is a review of Thomas Carlyle's biography of him. According to Nesta Webster, 1924, Carlyle was supported by a Prussian agent to write that. He was decorated by Prussia after its completion. The Prussian government also made many resources available to him, including Frederick's diaries.

Carlyle was a member of the same literary circle as the German romantic poet Johann Wolfgang Goethe, (1749–1832), who was close to Frederick. Some of his

His father, Frederick William I of Prussia, had been overbearing and autocratic. He was prone to kick or cane anyone who came within his reach; and as a strict Lutheran, he didn't allow any frivolities in his children's upbringing or behavior.

In contrast, Frederick was the artistic type and was not inclined to follow his father's beliefs. He questioned his father's religion and preferred playing his flute, reading French literature, and writing French poetry to hunting and drinking beer. On account of these differences, he was beaten and, at one point, his father attempted to strangle him with the cord of a curtain. When Frederick attempted to run away, with another boy, they were caught and sentenced to death. His life was only saved by the intercession of the Emperor of Austria and various other monarchs. But his friend was not so lucky, and Frederick was forced to watch as he was executed. Thereafter, Frederick lived as a prisoner, separated from his father and family. However, his life was then more pleasant, he was better fed, and he could play his flute and pursue his literary interests.

He was a great admirer of Voltaire and entered into a correspondence with him. That began a life-long acquaintance. Noota Webster (1924) concluded that he was probably the guiding light behind Frederick.[14]

In 1733, when Frederick turned 21, he gained his liberty. He served briefly in the army of Prince Eugene, and after that he dedicated part of his time to learning the art of administration. To propitiate his father, he also took a wife who his father suggested. But, the marriage was without love, was childless, and after a short time they separated. Even Maucaulay and Carlyle, his faithful biographers, suggested that Frederick was a homosexual. His homosexual partners are thought to have included Voltaire and Goethe.

Frederick became a master at dissembling. He is said to have been an earnest student of Machiavelli and, in 1739, the year before his coronation, he completed a book, *The Anti-Machiavel*. In it he refuted unjust wars, arbitrary government, rapacity, perfidy,...everything for which he was soon to be known. He sent the manuscript to Voltaire, who got it published.

The next year, in 1740, his father died and he became the King of Prussia. Frederick immediately sent for Voltaire. However, Frederick had changed, he was no longer concerned with frivolous amusements. Before the end of that year, he commenced a war against Austria, by seizing Silesia. He did this without any declaration of war, in flagrant violation of a treaty, and, thereby, cast all of Europe into the War of the Austrian Succession (1740–1748). Frederick didn't even suggest that he had any justification. In his own words:[15] "Ambition, interest, the desire of having people talk about me, carried the day; and I decided for war."

---

letters were preserved and have been reprinted.

[14] In fact, if we look at his early life, there is no one else who could have been, and coincidences make it increasingly obvious throughout their lives.

[15] His memoirs, translated and quoted in Thomas Carlyle's Biography.

After easily taking Silesia, he then, changed sides several times, betraying first one party and, then, another. The deceptive impression which his book had created, helped him to do this: For a long time, the heads of state would not believe that this gentle cultured man could be so cruel and perfidious. Before the war was over, they got a true measure of his personality. By these actions, he won the personal enmity of the monarchs of Austria, France, and Russia. That war ended with the treaty of Aix de Chapelle, leaving him in possession of Silesia.

In 1756, Frederick invaded Saxony to strike against France, Austria, and Russia who were, then, preparing to make war on him. This began the Seven Years War (1756–1763). The death of George III of England deprived him of subsidies and, by the end of 1761, Prussia was reduced to an extremity. Their large cities were destroyed, many of the villages stood empty, and whole districts were left without civil government. Close to a sixth of their population had been killed and it was difficult for him to find soldiers, horses, or supplies. However, he was resolved to die rather than surrender.

But, things suddenly changed, in January 1762, when the Czarina Elizabeth of Russia died. She was succeeded by Czar Peter III, who was a Freemason, a dissipated fop, and an great admirer of Frederick. Although he was deposed, that same year, by his wife, Catherine the Great, the Russian army remained ineffective throughout the remainder of the war.[16] As a result, the war was terminated during February of the next year, 1763. Frederick had won and even retained Silesia.

During the remainder of his life, Frederick completed the Union of German Princes, in 1783; and the League of German Princes, in 1785. These were the first steps toward federating Germany into a single nation under the leadership of Prussia. That was one of the goals of Frederick's foreign policy. Frederick died after a short illness in 1786.

7.4   Silesia

Silesia was the key to Frederick's policy. It was, also, of particular interest to the Jews of Eastern Europe.

Their eastward migration, during the medieval period, had established them in the Ukraine, Podolia, Yedisan, Moldavia, Galicia, and other states in the general region between Poland and Lithuania on the north and the Black Sea on the south. That region was, at that time, mostly under Polish control. But, when the power of Poland declined, around 1654–1668, the Jews migrated westward.[17] They resettled primarily in Silesia and

---

[16] It is notable that Catherine had her own secret society. It was a legion of women who preferred political intrigue to love.

[17] The proximate cause was a Cossack uprising in the Ukraine with Russian aid, in 1654, which was immediately followed by a Swedish invasion of Poland, in 1655–1660; and a second Cossack uprising, in 1672–1676, this time with Turkish aid. The Poles briefly regained some of those areas towards the end of the seventeenth

Moravia. But, Poland was completely overrun by the Russians during the War of the Polish Succession. The Treaty of Vienna, which ended that war, was formed in 1735 and ratified in 1738. It provided for the partitioning of Poland between Russia and Austria. Thus, whereas the Jews had previously been living under Polish rule, which had been favorable to them, they would, henceforth, live under Orthodox Russia, Roman Catholic Austria, or Moslem Turkey all of which were relatively intolerant. So, as of 1738, their leaders would have clearly seen what the future held for them.

But, Prussia, was Silesia's immediate neighbor to the West, and had precisely the conditions they desired: specifically, it had religious freedom and an absolute central government. In that context, it seems likely that some Jewish leaders may have approached Frederick to offer the support of the Jewish community in exchange for his taking and holding Silesia. Alternatively, this could have been an Hanoverian policy and the Jews were merely pawns. — That was 1738, precisely the year when Frederick began exactly the kind of policy that would be expected if he had accepted such an offer.[18]

Consider the chain of events. Frederick's entry into the Freemasons had occurred in 1738, the next year he published his book, and the year after that his father dies and he is crowned. Then, he immediately began the war of the Austrian Succession, aided by the deception created by his book. In addition, a small country might be expected to do some planning before it commenced a war against several Powers of the first rank. The above chain of events leaves the strong impression that he was following a deliberate course of action. It appears to have begun, in 1738, in Brunswick and the Freemasons and Jews were part of it.

7.5 Hasidism

At that time, the Jews still followed Rabbinic Judaism. They were waiting for the Messiah to bring them to the promised land. The religious enthusiasm and the rapid social changes of the previous century led many of them to believe that the messianic age was about to dawn. But, they had been duped by a succession of false Messiahs, during the late seventeenth century. By the early eighteenth century, this had left them depressed as a people. The trend, then, was for them to turn away from the real world towards the realm of mysticism and magic. — The period saw an increase in the number of itinerant Jewish magicians. Some of these were "Ba'al Shems," that is, masters of the arts of cabalistic magic.

Prominent among these was the healer and magician, Yisra'el ben Eli'ezer, know as Ba'al Shem Tov ("Master of the Good Name"). His early history, before 1738, is poorly known. That was the year he began preaching in the Ukraine and Poland.

---

century, but after that their power collapsed due to internal disputes.

[18] This is the simple direct explanation which follows from the historical context, but, the evidence is purely circumstantial.

This was the beginning of Hasidism. He drew his inspiration from the *Zohar*, but his beliefs departed from traditional Judaism by tending towards Pantheism.

Pantheism had been introduced into Western ideas, during the previous century, primarily by Benedict Spinoza (1632–1677). He believed in a heterodox naturalism which derived its animating principle from God. He did his work after the Thirty Years War (1618–1648).

At that time, the Reformation has lost much of its fire and the Lutheran faith had deteriorated into dry formalism and bourgoise respectability. Christian Pietism arose as a religious reaction to this. It was an Evangelical movement in Holland and Germany which stressed personal interior religious experience rather than outward conformity to church dogma. In time, it too, lost its fire.

Then, Ba'al Shem Tov introduced Pantheist and Pietist ideas into Judaism. He disregarded scripture, as Spinoza had done, except that he retained the *Zohar*. He had a happier and more meaningful outlook than Rabbinic Judaism. He stressed the need for joy and enthusiasm in all religious expression. Their religious practices involved ecstatic prayer, song, dance, feasting, and gaiety. He also stressed inwardness and held that evil could be turned to good through mystical processes. Their religious leaders played a special role in mediating that.

More specifically, they held that individual development involved many stages as one progresses up Jacob's Ladder, from one nodal point to another, in a zig–zag path, back–and–forth between the left and right sides.[19] Those two sides represent opposing opposites. When an individual gets stuck at one stage and can no longer progress, conflict from the opposite pole or from evil initiates a subconscious process which results in change. The Rabbi's role is to point the individual in the direction which moves him or her forward, based on the roadmap of the mind provided by Jacob's Ladder.

These beliefs gave the Jews a sense of increased personal dignity and responded to their social and emotional needs. As a result, Hasidism spread rapidly throughout Eastern Europe.[20]

Hasidism may have been what rekindled the Christian Pietist movement in Germany. From there it spread to England. In the end, it gave rise to the Moravian and Methodist Churches. — Thus, although the Jews were physically isolated in their ghettos,[21] they were not unaffected by the developments of their times: They were influenced by them and influenced them.

---

[19] See Halavi for a fairly detailed discussion of each stage.

[20] However, it is no longer widespread there, because their great centers were wiped out by the Nazis. But, before that happened, many of them had immigrated to the United States and Israel. So, that is where most of them live today.

[21] The "ghettos" were the walled in Jewish quarters of the towns, particularly of Germany and Poland. They date from the fifteenth century and were part of the disabilities on the Jews.

7.6 Magic

Although 1738 was when Ba'al Shem Tov began his ministry, he had no known connection to the government of Prussia. However, he was not the only cabalistic magician, and some of the others clearly were connected.[22]

During the late 1730's, Ba'al Shem Hayyim Falk (1708–1782), successfully practiced magic in Brunswick. A few years later, we find him imprisoned in Westphalia, sentenced to be burned for sorcery; but he escaped and arrived, in London, in 1742. Although he was penniless when he arrived there, he soon had considerable wealth. In only a few years, he established himself as the Ba'al Shem of London. During the following two decades he trained a network of other cabalistic magicians.

Joseph Balsamo was one of these. He went by the name of "Cagliostro." He was a Sicilian of Jewish origin but Christian upbringing. As a young man, he became interested in magic and traveled to the Near East where he learned Gnostic religious beliefs. He later obtained additional instruction from Hayyim Falk. After that he became an itinerant magician, traveling about Europe making "cures." After 1782 he formed Egyptian Rite Masonic Lodges and became deeply involved in the French Revolution.

Martines Pasqually, who founded the Cabalistic Jewish sect of the Martinistes, in 1754, in France, also claimed to have been trained by Falk. They, too, were later involved in the French Revolution.

Jacob Frank founded a very similar Jewish sect, the Zoharites,[23] in Eastern Europe, in 1755. They had a large following. His daughter, Eve, succeeded in duping the Queen of Austria, Maria Teressa. On that account, he found it necessary to leave Austria. He resettled near Frankfurt.

There was a host of others. They all had a lot in common: They followed approximately the same beliefs and practices, most of them had been trained by one or another of a small group of Ba'al Shems, and they were mostly later associated with Freemasonry and the French Revolution. Except for Falk, they were not "Jews," according to the Jewish standard, as they were of mixed descent.[24] Their more prominent members also all had abundant wealth whose source could never be found. In particular, that was true of Falk, Cagliostro, Pasqually, Frank, and a few others. But, as they all served Prussian interests, the logical conclusion is that the money may have come from the Prussian treasury.

Falk's escape from jail in Westphalia was particularly suggestive. — How many prisoners awaiting a death penalty escaped and immediately, afterwards, began a lifelong profession serving Prussian interests? Falk's escape has often been cited as a demonstration of his magical power. Indeed, if was, if you allow magic of the Prussian kind, which is the result of

---

[22] This section on the magicians is drawn primarily from Nesta Webster, 1924.

[23] They followed the *Zohar* and renounced the *Talmud*.

[24] Jews of mixed descent were not, then, accepted by either Jews or Gentiles. As a result, they were prone to harbor a grudge against society and were one of the more turbulent elements.

human agency worked behind the scenes.

There was also a connection between the magicians and the Freemasons. The Continental Freemasons were known to have had "concealed superiors" at the very top level of their organization. Nesta Webster (1924) argues that the principle ones were Frederick and Voltaire. But, Falk appears to have been another.

Among a large body of evidence, one of the more interesting statements is found in Gotthold Lessing's, 1777 *Dialogue: Ernst and Falk*. In it he says that Falk was one of the concealed superiors and quotes him as saying that the Rosicrucians had been the concealed superiors before them.[25]

He also attributed to Falk the statement that the ultimate objective of Freemasonry was to create a world–wide federation of nations in which people will all willingly work together for their mutual benefit, without any instruction, as ants do instinctively in an ant heap.[26] Lessing either did not realize that the objectives of the Freemasons and the existence and identity of the concealed superiors were carefully guarded secrets or he did not care.[27] — The printing of his book was banned in Brunswick, where Lessing lived, but it was published in another German State, without his permission, in 1780. He died young, less than a year later.[28]

The Freemasons and magicians gave Prussia the finest espionage service of their time. It was part of the miracle which made Prussia a Power of the first rank, even though by population and wealth she was just barely acknowledged to be of the second. But, this astounding achievement was nothing but an illusion, created with smoke and mirrors, compared to their next move.

7.7   Jewish Enlightenment

This story begins with Gotthold Lessing (1729–1781). He was a relatively obscure German playwright and literary critic. The great objects of his life were the emancipation of the Jews and the enlightenment movement. The first indication of his position is found in his 1749 play, *Die Juden*, in which he pleads for religious and social toleration of the Jews. As the result of that play, in 1754, he met Moses Mendelssohn (1729–1786)[29] who was an orthodox Jew and a promising enlightenment scholar.

---

[25] This implies a concealed Jewish involvement in the revival of 1717, probably serving the House of Hanover.

[26] Francis Bacon's *New Atlantis* contains similar concepts. The hypothesis is often put forward that he was the original founder of the Freemasons. That is supportable, if by "founder" it is meant that he was the first to use them as a political society to advance this distinctive set of beliefs.

That concept became one of the central ideas in the modern liberal agenda.

[27] His wife and child had died tragically only a sort time before.

[28] See Nesta Webster 1924.

[29] He was the grandfather of the composer Felix Mendelssohn. Moses was born in Dessau. His true name was, therefore, Moses Dessau. But he took the Germanized pen name of "Mendelssohn," from the Hebrew ben Mendel (son of Mendel).

The next year he helped Mendelssohn publish his first work. After that, Mendelssohn published a succession of works on religion and philosophy and became the leading figure of the Jewish enlightenment movement. In 1763, Mendelssohn won the prize for the best essay submitted to Frederick the Great's Prussian Academy of the Arts. At that time, Frederick became aware of him and granted him an exemption from the disabilities which otherwise applied to Jews in Prussia. To place that in historical context, 1763 was the year the Seven Years War ended.

During the years 1769–1771, Moses Mendelssohn got involved in an intense dispute with the Swiss theologian, Johann Kasper Lavater. He had publicly challenged Mendelssohn to become a Christian, as he was an enlightened man and Christianity was, then, the religion of reason. It is in Mendelssohn's answer to Lavater that we find the first hints of the modern theory of absolutism.

Its genesis lies in the conflict between the Jewish concept of the messianic State and the Enlightened Christian concepts of Natural Law and Natural Theology. These had previously been thought to be in diametric opposition, but Mendelssohn presented a viewpoint under which they are compatible or, at least, appeared to be.

He thought that the Jews would be accepted by gentile society if they abandoned their ceremonial tradition in favor of Western customs wherever those practices were more reasonable. They could then immerse themselves in Western society. He, also, felt that they should accept the children of intermarriages into their faith. But, he did not abandon the central beliefs of Rabbinic Judaism. In particular, he continued to believe in the prophesy of the messianic State and the Jews as a chosen people. But, he did not look for the Messiah to come, in person, to lead them to the messianic State. Instead, he felt that the Jewish people constituted the Messiah and, therefore, that each of them should assume individual responsibility for bringing it into being. But, he also accepted the concept, from Natural Law, that from reason comes virtue and the right of freedom. So, achieving the messianic State requires that they occupy the alters of reason and displace other peoples and religions from them. They would then be recognized, by the right of reason, as the patriarchs of society and be willingly served. — That is the messianic State obtained by an abuse of Natural Law.

Some of his ideas are shown in a short quote taken from one of Mendelssohn's letters to Lavater:[30]

> Pursuant to the principles of my religion, I am not to seek to convert anyone who is not born according to our laws. This

His father was a poor *Torah* scribe. In 1743, Moses moved to Berlin where he studied enlightenment thought. In 1750 he became a tutor to the children of a Jewish silk manufacturer and was later taken into the business. In 1954 he met Gotthold Lessing, who recognized him as an enlightened Jew and encouraged and subsidized his early work.

[30] Quoted by See Nesta Webster 1924.

proneness to conversion, the origin of which some would fain tack on to the Jewish religion, is, nevertheless, diametrically opposed to it. Our rabbis unanimously teach that the written and oral laws which form conjointly our revealed religion are obligatory on our nation only. "Moses commanded us a law, even an inheritance of the congregation of Jacob." We believe that all other nations of the earth have been directed by God to adhere to the laws of nature and to the religion of the patriarchs. Those who regulate their lives according to the precepts of nature and reason are called virtuous men of other nations and are the children of eternal salvation. Our rabbis are so remote from proselytomania, that they enjoin us to dissuade, by forcible remonstrances, everyone who comes forward to be converted.

What is most obvious and should be puzzling is his assumption that the Law of Nature and the inheritance of Jacob can co–exist. That is incompatible with Christian theology which holds that the old and new covenants are mutually exclusive.[31] The key to understanding his idea seems to be that he did not mean the same thing by the "law of nature" as the Christians did. In particular, his meaning was later taken to be the "iron laws of economic necessity."

The stress of his dispute with Lavater was too much for him and he had a nervous breakdown. He recovered by returning to his orthodox roots. During the remainder of his life, he translated some *Psalms* and the *Pentatuch* into German. He also was involved in a dispute over the right of a synagogue to excommunicate its members. He died in 1786.

7.8   Prussian Absolutism

Others recognized the potential of Mendelssohn's idea and adopted it. It provided the basis for a new philosophy of absolutism. Its obvious flaws, were undoubtedly recognized at the time. But, such defects do not nec-

---

[31] For a fundamentalist, that is so because scripture says that it is so. (See Hebrews 8.13.) But, demonstration requires only slightly more effort under Natural Theology. — It is clear that the benefits of the old covenant require reducing broad classes of mankind to slavery, not because they violated any general law but, because they do not meet the arbitrary standard of a birthright. However, that is repugnant to the first principle of Natural Law that it apply equally to everyone. Likewise, the second principle, that everyone is entitled to justice, is violated as it is unjust to be enslaved without a cause. So, if the new covenant is interpreted as implementing Enlightened Christianity, true faith must be compatible with Natural Law and Reason and, therefore, it follows that the old covenants must be false doctrine.

In addition, the old covenants are of Deuteronomic origin and are, therefore, dubious even by the evidence of the *Bible* itself. Specifically, it strongly implies that they were fabricated in 621 BC.

essarily invalidate a religious or political doctrine, as the historical record shows, in this case.

Prussia supported its further development. This can be clearly seen in their appointments to academic and government positions. There were also corresponding appointments in England.

Gotthold Lessing: Most of Lessing's early works were plays or literary criticism.[32] In 1770, he was appointed librarian to the Duke of Brunswick. That gave him the financial ability to marry.

He continued to work with the circle of enlightened Jews in Berlin, which Mendelssohn was the center of. It became the nucleus for literature promoting Jewish emancipation.[33] The trend in Europe towards that end was primarily due to them. They were also strong supporters of the French Revolution. It was, also, largely due to Lessing's efforts that the Jews were admitted to Freemasonry in 1781.

He also continued his work on enlightenment. In particular, his dialogue *Ernst and Falk* and his essay, *The Education of the Human Race*, both completed in 1777, show stages in the development of his thinking. They are more revealing than his better known play, *Nathan the Wise* which came out in 1781. His philosophical position was that fostering virtue is the purpose of religion and that Freemasonry and the positive religions of Christianity, Judaism, or Islam can effectively do that; but that a higher stage of development is possible in which rational insight, apart from religion, is sufficient to ensure virtue. These ideas were new to Germany, at that time.

But, his wife and son died tragically in childbirth. Shortly afterwards, he gave posterity his *Dialogue: Ernst and Falk*. He died the next year, in 1781.

Johann Goethe's rise to prominence also dates from the early 1770's. In 1770 to 1775, we find him practicing law in Frankfurt. That was when he first became established as a leading writer, and also when he began to move into high society. He had a series of romantic attachments to women and also met Frederick the Great. In 1776, he entered the government of the small Duchy of Weimar, rose quickly to a high station, and was ennobled in 1782.

---

[32]Lessing was the son of a Lutheran pastor. He studied theology and later medicine at the University of Leipzig. At that time he became interested in the theater, and wrote several plays. In 1748, he moved to Berlin, intending to support himself by writing. In 1752, he spent a year at the University of Wittenberg, and received a Master's degree. Then he returned to writing. For a brief time he subsidized a Theater. The works they produced included Goethe's. Thus, during this period of his life, Lessing was in contact with that circle of society. He was also one of the leading figures of the enlightenment in Germany.

[33]They assisted Mendelssohn's friend Christian Wilhelm von Dohrm in publishing his influential book *On the Civil Improvement of the Jews*, in 1781; Manasseh ben Israel's, 1782, book *Vindication of the Jews*, with a preface by Mendelssohn; and they also funded the French Revolutionary leader, Gabriel R. Mirableau's, book which promoted Jewish emancipation and was written in the form of a panegyric on Mendelssohn.

During the 1770's, he also came into close contact with Pietist circles and developed an interest in Alchemical mysticism. That was when he began *Faust*. That is a tragic play written mostly in verse. It is often considered to be the greatest piece of German literature. He worked on it for over six decades, sealing Part II for posthumous publication in 1831. Its theme is the nature of man and the individuation of personality. It is about Alchemy. It provides a chronicle of the evolving understanding of man which was held by that circle of leading scholars which included Lessing, Mendelssohn, Voltaire, Carlyle, Hegel, and so on. It spans the entire period during which they were active: Specifically, he began it just after Mendelssohn's contribution, during the early 1770's, and ended at the close of the Hegelian period.[34] He died in Wiemar in 1832, having lived 83 years.

Immanuel Kant (1724–1804) was appointed professor at Koenigsberg, in 1770, but he did not publish any major works for a decade. He was developing his ideas. Beginning in 1781, he published a major work about every two years until 1797.

His early essay *What is enlightenment?* may be the enlightenment's best manifesto. It established him as an enlightenment philosopher. But his careful examination of the nature of human knowledge and perception, especially in his *Critique of Pure Reason*, published in 1781, eradicated the philosophy of reason, ended the age of enlightenment, and even temporarily terminated the use of the rational approach to religion.

One important question he addressed was whether the existence of God can be proven. He concluded that he could find no infallible means for doing that. The problem lies in the assumption that God has an essential nature. That idea was retained by Thomas Aquinas. It never was compatible with rationality, but any village priest knows that rationality is not compatible with the many of the common people. Faith, anthropomorphism, and some mysticism have to be retained to reach them. It was also part of Christianity as taught by Christ. So, Christianity had never divorced itself from that concept.

Then along came Kant, probably with the intention of destroying Christianity. He saw the essential God as a vulnerable target and obliterated it. From that blow against essentialism, he and his followers concluded that Natural Theology was dead. Scholars objected at the time, but not to much avail, because the State backed Kant and every young aspiring scholar knew that funding came from the State. So despite all the criticism he received, after a few years, when the storm had died down, it was found that the next generation of scholars were mostly Kantians, Neo–Kantians, and the like. That gives the basic tenor of what happened. But that isn't to say that Kant didn't make many valid points.

---

[34] A century later it had a marked influence upon Carl Jung, who was the most important contributor to our modern understanding of psychological types and the development of personality. See his autobiographical work *Memories, Dreams, Reflections* and also his *Mysterium Coniunctionis*.

Moses Mendelssohn called him the "All Destroyer." — The immediate historical impact of Kant's work was to temporarily wipe the philosophical slate clean, creating an opening for the absolutism of Fichte and the transcendentalism of Schelling.[35]

Politically, Kant despised enlightened monarchy, was the enthusiastic supporter of the French Revolution, and did not object to its unnecessary violence and the destruction it caused. He also was a strong supporter of Rousseau. Kant's position on these things would be difficult to understand unless he is viewed in the context of Mendelssohn.

Rousseau: The French philosopher, Jean Jacques Rousseau (1712–1778), had died before Kant began publishing. But his ideas were fully in concert with these developments. One of his central concepts was the "noble savage": that is the idea that the evils of the society were derived from erring cultural institutions and that man, left to his own devices, would express the inherent nobility of his spirit.

A more contemporary view of this was given by Carroll Quigley, in 1961. It was that the mixing of peoples and cultures had resulted in mankind's great advances. He pointed to two examples which we have already seen in this book.

The first was the mixing which occurred when the Aryan and Indo-European migrations brought the pastoral–nomadic Northern longheaded peoples into the Mediterranean region. He felt that that was what caused the great advances of the Classical world. — The more neotenous, affective, and right–brained Mediterreans were predisposed to culture and had formed the early great civilizations; whereas the less neotenous but more rational and left–brained Nordic types tended to be small packs of wolves, living only in small groups, but highly intelligent. The mixing of these two peoples and cultures took the best from each, resulting in Classical civilization.

But the Classical world was gradually strangled by the growth of social organization and religions of an Eastern kind. That cycle ended and the next one began when the Germanic tribes invaded. There followed a long period, the dark ages, during which the old ways and old religion still held sway. And there had been a similar lag between the Aryan invasion and the emerge of Persian and Greek enlightenment, too. But, eventually, in this second case, the mixing of Germanic and Classical elements resulted in the birth of Western civilization. That was the Golden Age of France. After that, Western man was, once again, gradually strangled. By Frederick's day, all that was left was the decayed feudal world he found around him.

But, there was, then, a resurgence of Westernism or Classical liberalism which resulted in the Glorious, American, and French Revolutions. That resulted in renewal which has lasted two centuries. But it, too, has gradually been strangled.

---

[35] Friedrich W. J. von Schelling (1775–1854) had a strong influence on two philosophers who appear later in this book, specifically, Hegel and Keirkegaard. Both of them enthusiastically attended his lectures.

Thus, in Rousseau's time, as today, civilization had reached the end of the cycle and the light of reason was about to be extinguished. So, the great question was then, as it is now, how to achieve renewal or whether that requires the destruction of society.

Rousseau should be viewed in that context: He advocated opening the door to the wolves, that the decayed feudal world might come to an end, that those things which make life worth living might begin again.

Specifically, he held that private property ownership was the first and chief evil, and he extended that concept to renounce all forms of individually held rights.

His doctrine on the rights of man was that man is free, by his nature. That is the opposite of the Classical concept of freedom, In that system, reason sets man free, from the necessity of incessant social interaction, by creating boundaries, order, and civilization. But, Rousseau's concept of freedom consisted of the destruction of that same order and civilization and the return to a nomadic existence, free of boundaries and rules.

In his ideal State, government as we know it would not be necessary, it would be replaced by teachers who manipulate circumstances and appeal to the individual's feelings. Thus, the people would be gently guided down a predetermined path, without most of them ever knowing why they acted as they did. In that State, laws, commands, and prohibitions would not be needed nor given, every individual's behavior would be determined and controlled by social interactions, rather than by any fixed law. Thus, Rousseau's "freedom" was precisely what Classically was called "slavery:" that is to have your actions determined by the arbitrary decisions of other people without any fixed law to live by. Rousseau's interchanging of the names of freedom and slavery was put to a use....

Edward Gibbon wrote, in 1776, that the first Roman Emperor "Augustus was sensible that mankind is governed by names; nor was he deceived in his expectation that the Senate and people would submit to slavery, provided they were respectfully assured that they still enjoyed their ancient freedom."

Gibbon's *The Rise and Fall of the Roman Empire* was published contemporary with these developments in Germany. It was a study of the conditions under which mankind will submit to being ruled. His book was timely and to the point. However, he was considering the English Empire, which was growing rapidly, just then, rather than Prussia's ambitions. But, the Hanoverian Kings of England and Prussia had common interests and Gibbon moved in the same circle as the German thinkers.

Adam Smith (1723–1790) was a professor of moral philosophy at the University of Glasgow. He was *the* philosopher of capitalism. He, too, moved in that circle which included Rousseau, Voltaire, Benjamin Franklin, Edward Gibbon, and the other leading figures of the French Enlightenment, and capitalism was a key element in their scheme to restructure society.

In his (1776) book, *Wealth of Nations*[36], he discussed the meaning of

---

[36] Its full title is, *An Inquiry into the Nature and Causes of the Wealth of*

money and the structure of a society bound together solely by financial relationships.[37]

One of the central questions he examined was, how the wealth created by a man's labor should be distributed. "Wealth" is the improvement or object of value created by labor. What Adam Smith said is that a laborer should be paid what is necessary to sustain him and his family. That is what it cost the laborer to do the work. He called this the "real value" of the labor. Labor is a commodity, with the foregoing real value, which is exchanged for some "nominal value" paid in money. The surplus, that is the difference between the market price of the commodity produced and the nominal value of the labor and raw materials used to produce it, rightfully belongs to the capitalist, because the laborer sells his labor and, therefore, does not own the wealth which that labor creates.

Under his theories, society is divided into capitalists and laborers, with conflicting interests. The capitalist should never pay the laborer more than the real value of his labor, if he means to maximize his own profit. But a more compelling reason for oppressing the working class was that their poverty was essential for maintaining the structure of society, — No individual would sell his labor, if he can avoid it; he would sell the product and, thereby, receive the profit. Also, keeping labor in a condition of need provides an avenue through which organic control can be exercised.

Smith advocated a laissez–faire economy because he felt that unfettered competition would keep wages down to near their real value and also would tend to increase efficiency, specialization, and interdependence. He recognized that the consequences were less than just for the working class, but he felt that that was a necessary evil.

He pointed out that Machiavelli's approach assumed that the people would surrender their rights in exchange for morality and the freedom derived from it. Under that perspective, the State's duty is to try to raise each individual to the level of enlightenment, so that he or she may be free. But Smith was pessimistic. Like Hobbes, before him, he rejected the existence of any true enlightenment, Natural Law, or Natural Theology. Consequently, he also rejected the concept of organizing society around morality and the religion of reason. Instead, he felt that the bulk of humanity would always be governed by their passions. He, therefore, based his system on their lowest common behavior, rather than upon the finest standards of human achievement. His work highlights the change in perspective which occurred at the end of the enlightenment period. He adopted the liberal polity of his times: In particular, he felt that the masses should be released from the strictures of religion and morality to be ruled by their passions and the iron laws of economic necessity, within broad lim-

---

Nations.

[37] His earlier book, *Theory of Moral Sentiments*, published in 1759, is essential to understanding *Wealth of Nations*. It covers much of the philosophy and sociology, He tended not to re–address any issue in his later work which he had already covered in his former.

its set by law. Thus, they could, at least, obtain the benefit of "freedom" in the sense that Rousseau used the word.

He felt that under those conditions, ruthless self–interest would drive society towards maximizing the production of those things which sustain life and that they would, therefore, be laboring for the good of mankind.

Adam Weishaupt,[38] a Bavarian Law Professor, founded the Bavarian Illuminati. That was a secret political organization, led by highly educated and accomplished men.[39] They developed a concrete plan for the radical restructuring of the society and set about implementing it.[40]

The genesis of this secret society began, in 1771, when Weishaupt met a merchant from Denmark named Kolmer.[41] He apparently had spent a number of years in Egypt learning Manichean or Ismaili beliefs. He instructed Adam Wieshaupt in them. Although Wieshaupt held mysticism in contempt, he was willing to exploit these beliefs to build an organization based upon their system. He took five years carefully planning this organization. He founded it in 1776, calling it the Illuminati.

In structure it was much like the Continental Freemasons. Weishaupt regarded the Freemasons as a system for binding men together: that is, for inducing them to accept leadership. Like the Freemasons, the Illuminati

---

[38] During the Protestant Reformation, Bavaria had become Protestant. However, in the years which followed, she returned to the Roman Church without an armed struggle. This was largely due to the Jesuits. They concentrated their efforts on education and soon they controlled all the institutions of higher learning and most of the secondary schools.

Their approach to education was one of rote memorization. They didn't train their pupils to think for themselves. They also exercised the strictest censorship of any written materials, removing anything which they felt contained even a trace of Protestant thought.

Their methods were so oppressive that eventually the Bavarian Elector, removed them from the control of education. In particular, the University of Ingolstadt had been one of the places where their dominance had been complete. The Elector turned its curatorship over to a well known liberal, Baron Johann Adam Ickstatt.

He was then the godfather and guardian of a seven year–old boy, Adam Wieshaupt. Some sources say that he was of partial Jewish origin, but there is not complete agreement on that point. But, whatever his origins may have been, he was raised in a liberal Protestant environment and attended secondary school under the Jesuits. The result was that he developed a profound hatred for them, for the Roman Church, and for Christianity in general.

Later, when he became a professor of law at the University of Ingolstadt he encountered the many defects in the legal and political systems of the decaying feudal states of his day. He also found himself pitted against the Jesuit Professors.

[39] Their members who have been already mentioned included Goethe, Frederick William II who succeeded Frederick, the Duke of Brunswick, Mirableau, and Kant.

[40] This section is drawn especially from works by Abbee Barruell (1798) and Lillie (1894). Dr. John Robison (1798), and Nesta Webster (1921, 1924).

[41] This person seems to have existed, but no one has ever discovered who he was.

had several levels. In the process of progressing up through them, a member revealed detailed information about himself and his family. As this organization sought the sons of wealthy and influential people, they soon held considerable power over society. Their members also became powerful because they followed the custom of advancing their fellow members in their position in the outside world, whenever they could.

According to Stauffer (1918) Their openly stated objectives were opposing religious prejudice and promoting government by the consent of the governed. But, that was Orwellian "double–speak."

Their general tone was more accurately expressed by the French Atheist, Denis Diderot (1713–1784), who wrote: "Men will never be free until the last monarch has been strangled in the entrails of the last priest."[42] — They had a hatred of all Western government and positive religion.

In 1789, Luchet wrote about them:[43] "... learn that there exists a conspiracy in favor of despotism against liberty, of incapacity against talent, of vice against virtue, of ignorance against enlightenment. ... This society aims at governing the world. ... Its object is universal domination."

Later he says, "We do not mean to say that the country where the Illumines reign will cease to exist, but it will fall into such a degree of humiliation that it will no longer count in politics, that the population will diminish, that the inhabitants who resist the inclination to pass into a foreign land will no longer enjoy the happiness of consideration, nor the charms of society, nor the gifts of commerce."

In the Illuminati's private papers they gave five objectives:[44]

1. Abolition of monarchies and all ordered government.

2. Abolition of all established positive religion.

3. Abolition of private property and inheritances.

4. Abolition of patriotism and nationalism.

5. Abolition of family life and the institution of marriage, and their replacement with the communal education for children.

Nesta Webster wrote that Adam Weishaupt's philosophy was so close to Mendelssohn's that she assumed that he had been strongly influenced him. She even suggested that he may have instructed him.

Weishaupt held that once civilization had been obliterated, each patriarch should rule his family, including servants and slaves, according to his perception of nature and reason, under only a global German authority.

---

[42]Denis Diderot was the chief editor of the *Encyclopedie*, developed by the Freemasons. That was their great project, during the early years of Frederick's rule. It was very heavily funded, probably by Prussia. Through it they hoped to influence thought in France. The quote comes from Diderot's, 1877, *Oeuveres Completes*, Paris, Edition Assezat–Tourneaux, Garnier Freres. Vol 9, pp 15–16.

[43]See Webster 1924.

[44]Webster 1921 summarized from papers seized by the Bavarian Government in 1786

Another, slightly different Illuminati plan for the intended form of society was described by the Prussian Baron Jean Baptiste Clootz in his book *La Republique Universelle*. Baron Clootz was an Illuminatus, codename Anacharsis, and according to Nesta Webster (1921), was, also, probably a Prussian agent. She was not alone in that opinion as he was executed, during the French Revolution, by the Commune of Paris, for his internationalist and pro–Prussian views.

Under his system, society was to be a single worldwide socialist nation under German rule. It was to be organized by free agreements between men and women who voluntarily form groups and conduct themselves according to the dictates of reason. All property was to be held in common among them, there was to be no marriage, and their children were to be raised by the community. — This scheme is called "anarchy." The name was coined by the French socialist author, Pierre Joseph Proudhon (1809–1865), recalling Anarchisis, that is Baron Clootz.

They, also, devised a new religion to replace Enlightened Christianity. Philo, that is Baron Von Knigge, wrote about this:[45]

We say then: Jesus wished to introduce no new religion, but only to restore natural religion and reason to their old rights. Thereby he wished to unite men in a great universal association, and through the spread of a wise morality, enlightenment, and the combating of all prejudices to make them capable of governing themselves; so the secret meaning of his teaching was to lead men without revolution to universal liberty and equality. There are many passages in the *Bible* which can be made use of and explained, and so all quarreling between the sects ceases if one can find a reasonable meaning in the teaching of Jesus — be it true or not. As, however, this simple religion was afterwards distorted, so were these teachings imparted to us through Disciplinam Arcani and finally through Freemasonry, and all Masonic hieroglyphics can be explained with this object. Spartacus has collected very good data for this and I have myself added to them. ... and so I have got both degrees ready ...

Later Spartacus, that is Adam Weishaupt, would write:[46]

You cannot imagine what consideration and sensation our Priest's degree is arousing. The most wonderful thing is that great Protestant and reformed theologians who belong to [the Illuminati] still believe that the religious teaching imparted in it contains the true and genuine spirit of the Christian religion. Oh! men, of what cannot you be persuaded? I never thought that I should become the founder of a new religion.

---

[45] See Webster 1924
[46] Ibid.

Those religious leaders probably smiled to see new converts finding the grain among the chaff and holding it to be their own discovery. Little did they realize that, by the "Laws of Nature" they meant only the Iron laws of economic necessity. That is how they interpreted Mendelssohn's idea. Only a little over a decade later, their new religion of reason would be celebrated in Notre Dame Cathedral in Paris, before a prostitute, seated in the bishop's chair as the highest representative of reason.

7.9   French Revolution

The chain of events which eventually led to the French Revolution began when Adam Wieshaupt sought the help of Baron Adolf F.F. Knigge, who held a high position in the Freemasons. They began negotiations for combining those two organizations. In 1782, the Illuminati was restructured with many more steps and then accepted as a higher type of Freemasonry. Thus, they preempted the Masonic organization. The headquarters of Continental (now Illuminized) Freemasonry also was moved to Frankfurt.

That was, then, the center of German finance, controlled by the Rothschilds. — The Rothschild banking house had been founded, in 1743, by Mayer Amschel Rothschild who had a coin business in Frankfurt.[47] His real surname was Bauer. Rothschild means "red shield." Red recalls Edom and they were shielding the great financial Powers they represented. With a few exceptions, those Powers have remained unknown. However, one can make a list of likely candidates based on the policies which the Rothschild Banking House represented. That would suggest the princes of Saxony, Hess, Hanover, Prussia, and probably some other small German States, together with the Hanoverian Dynasty of England, their bankers, and the nabobs. Those were the parties who shared their interests.

Mayer Rothschild did not exhibit any extraordinarily personal wealthy prior to the 1780's. However, he had been successful in his investments. Among these was the fortune which the Elector of Saxony had made through renting Hessian mercenaries to the British to fight against the Americans in their revolution. That ended with the Treaty of Paris in 1782. That was also the year when Mayer Rothschild became allied to the Continental Freemasons.

In 1785, Frederick the Great completed the League of German Princes between Saxony, Hanover, and Prussia. That drew Frankfurt firmly into the Prussian sphere of influence. That year the Rothschilds suddenly showed considerably more wealth and moved into a larger house which they shared with the Schiff family.[48] After 1885, the Illuminated Freema-

---

[47] The principle source for this biography of the Rothschild banks is Eustace Mullins (1993).

[48] Jacob Schiff, born in that house in Frankfurt, emigrated to America and married Theresa Loeb, daughter of Solomon Loeb, the founder of Kuhn–Loeb and Co. which was later to become one of the companies owning the Federal Reserve Bank. As senior partner in Kohn Loeb Co. he entirely financed E. H.

sons, now with ample funding, began a period of rapid growth.

The next year, 1786, held several momentous events. The annual Congress of Continental Freemasons decreed the deaths of Lewis the fourteenth of France and Gustavus III of Sweden (Webster 1924); Frederick the Great died after a short illness; Mendelssohn also died that year; and Bavaria suppressed the Illuminati.[49] Nevertheless, the French Revolution was begun, on schedule, two years later.[50]

Contrary to popular belief, the French Revolution was not supported by the French people. Before it, they were relatively well off and strongly supported their monarchy. It was caused from outside by a coalition which included Prussia and her allied German States, the Illuminists and Jacobins, the Continental Freemasons, the Orleanists, the bankers from Frankfurt, and various opportunists. They all agreed to cause the revolution, and may have agreed to follow the Illuminati's plan,[51] but did not, otherwise, see entirely eye-to-eye. The Revolution saw continuous fighting among them.

During that period and throughout the early nineteenth century, the Revolution was widely held to have been caused by the Illuminated Freemasons. The most important works on the subject, from that period, were probably those by Abbee Barruell and Dr. John Robison, both published in 1798. But, we even find the Duke of Brunswick, who was, then, the head of Continental Freemasonry and an Illuminatus, "issuing a Manesfesto to all the lodges in 1794, declaring that in view of the way in which Masonry had been penetrated by [the Illuminati] the whole Order must be temporarily suppressed." In particular, he wrote:[52]

> They invented the rights of man which it is impossible to
> discover even in the book of Nature, and they urged the people

---

Harriman's railroad empire, Union Pacific, which was largely purchased during the panic of 1857

[49] According to Webster (1924) this suppression resulted from an extraordinary event. An evangelical preacher and emissary for the Illuminati, named Lanze, was struck by lightening during his journey. The authorities found the instructions of the Illuminati on his person. An investigation ensued, the homes of several top Illuminati and the order's offices were raided, providing conclusive proof. The government of Bavaria published these as *The Original Writings of the Order of Illuminati* in 1787.

[50] Many of the original principles had died by then. Voltaire and Rousseau died in 1778, Lessing in 1781, Falk in 1782, and Mendelssohn and Frederick in 1786. Only about half of them were old men.

[51] General instructions on revolutionary technique can be found in *The Protocols of the Elders of Zion*. They first appeared during the late nineteenth century, and were presented as evidence of a Jewish worldwide conspiracy. But, they are generally believed to have been a forgery. Nevertheless, they provide one of the better brief summaries of revolutionary technique, as they were practiced during that period. Nesta Webster (1921) compared them, point-by-point, to quotes from the Illuminati, Haute Vente Romaine, Alliance Sociale Democratique, and other nineteenth century revolutionary organizations, showing their close similarity.

[52] See Webster 1924.

to wrest from their princes the recognition of those supposed rights. The plan they had formed for breaking all social ties and of destroying all order was revealed in all their speeches and acts. They deluged the world with a multitude of publications; they recruited apprentices of every rank and in every position; they deluded the most perspicacious men by falsely alleging different intentions. ... their masters had nothing less in view than the thrones of the earth, and the government of the nations was to be directed by their nocturnal clubs.

This is what has been done and is still being done. But we notice that princes and people are unaware how and by what means this is being accomplished. That is why we say to them in all frankness: The misuse of our Order, the misunderstanding of our secret, has produced all the political and moral troubles with which the world is filled today. ...

The Revolution went through several stages:

1. **Reduce the public's confidence in their government:** They did this by a fraudulent scandal involving the Queen, Maria Antoinette. This was the "Affair of the Necklace." It was made to appear that she had an affair with a Cardinal, thereby, also defaming the Church. Cagliostro was intimately involved in this. Spreading this slander also required control of the press, which they had.

2. **Destroy the economy:.** To do this they placed individuals in critical positions in government to make it ineffective and to promote regulation hampering business. This requires an organized, deliberate, program. In France the organizing agency was the Illumined Freemasons, who formed the Jacobins and then disbanded the Freemasons, in order that it could not be used as the nucleus of a counter-revolution against them. They managed to so reduce the economy that unemployment was widespread, especially among the industrial workers. They also drove the government into debt, from which it was unable to extricate itself, partly because the Masonic representatives blocked reforms. To resolve these problems, the King called the Estates-General, which had been obsolete since before the reign of Loise the fourteenth.

3. **Create an atmosphere of repression:.** They did this by some of their members promoting lawlessness while others called for strict enforcement of law-and-order.

4. **Create a crisis:.** This was done by cornering the grain supply, causing a famine. This was the more annoying to the French citizens as they knew that the shortage had been deliberately contrived, and the government wrangled over rules of order and was ineffective in relieving it.

5. **Spark a revolt and fan it into a general conflagration:.** In France, the revolt opened with the storming of the Bastelle (July 14,

1789). This wasn't a popular action but was done by paid mercenaries imported from Marsailles. To make those events more horrific, they were told to paint their faces to make themselves look frightful and after they took the Bastelle, some of them ate the Swiss guards. These atrocities polarized events. Messengers carried news of them around the countryside together with forged instructions from the king to burn the local larger estates, because they were harboring conspirators. These instructions were faithfully followed by the loyal peasants. This turned over the government.[53]

6. **Gain control of the provisional government and destroy all the vestiges of the old government:.** A series of provisional governments of republican form followed: the National Assembly, the Legislative Assembly, and the Convention. These were republican in form but rife with disputes. At first, they had substantial middle class representation, but they were soon displaced. The king fled, but was caught and brought back early in this period, on April 2, 1791, and he was executed on January 21, 1793. The Jacobins gained control by the middle of this period and then began the Reign of Terror.

7. **Restore the economy by depopulation:.** This occurred under the Jacobins. In particular, Robespierre's plan was to reduce the population of France from 25 millions to either 8 or 16 millions, depending on which source is believed. He said that, "The system of Terror was thus the answer to the problem of unemployment."[54]

However, the moderates broke the power of the more radical Jacobins, and guillotined their leaders, ending the Terror. Therefore, the program of depopulation was incomplete. They only killed about 300,000 people. Contrary to popular belief, only a tiny percent of these were nobility. The vast majority were the unemployed industrial workers and the owners of small businesses and manufactories, that is the middle classes and the people dependent on them.

8. **Establish appointive government:** The directorate was tried first by was unsuccessful. Then they created the Consulate (1799–1804). This system had the appearance of a republic, but was purely

---

[53] The revolutionary sentiment at the end of this stage was well expressed by Trotsky at the Founding Congress of the Communist International (1919, see Ypsilon 1947) "Humanity whose old culture now lies in ruins is facing the danger of complete destruction. There is only one power which can save it — the power of the proletariat. It is the proletariat which must establish real order, the order of Communism. It must end the domination of capitalism, make war impossible, wipe out state Boundaries, transform the whole world into one cooperative commonwealth, and bring about real human brotherhood and freedom." Although stated more than a century after the French Revolution, this is not materially different from the Jacobian's rhetoric.

[54] See Webster 1924.

appointive.[55] According to Langer,[56] the appointees were predominately Jacobins. So, this may have represented the form of government the Illuminated Freemasons were aiming at.

9. **But the Nationalists took over:** The consular system collapsed on May 18, 1804 with the crowning of Napoleon as emperor. This was essentially a coup d' etat. Such take–overs are likely to happen. — When the people are sufficiently oppressed they find the clear message and direct actions of nationalists or fascists appealing.

At the very beginning of the Revolution, in 1792, Prussia had combined with Austria to uphold the monarchy, or so they said. Prussia sent 60,000 men who were regarded as being the finest soldiers in Europe; Austria sent 45,000; a large body of soldiers came from Hess, and these combined with 15,000 French nobility. Their field commander was the Duke of Brunswick. They met the French Revolutionary Army, consisting of about 25,000 raw levees, at Valmy. After an ineffective exchange of artillery, in the fog,[57] the Prussians made a half–hearted attempt to dislodge the French from their position. Frederick William led the Prussian charge, in person. Then, they turned around and marched back to Germany. Creasy (1789) gives an account of the battle. He regarded it as one of the turning points in history. It was the first time the French Revolutionary Army had stood up to an enemy and it gave them heart.

Nesta Webster (1919) gives a different view of what happened. It appears that the crown jewels of France were stolen and used to payoff the Prussians. The question was investigated in Paris, at the time. The evidence was extensive. The testimony included statements from one of the French generals who had been at Valmy and had been at some of the negotiations. Thus, Prussia advanced the revolution and made a huge profit from it. That is what we might expect, given that both Frederick William and the Duke of Brunswick were members of the Illuminated Freemasons.

From that time until 1806, Prussia did not oppose Revolutionary France. The French armies principally fought Austria and her allies. Prussia and

---

[55] This political system which was worked out by Sieyes in conjunction with Napoleon. Napoleon was the first consul (term of 10 years) and was assisted by two other consuls which he appointed (Cambaceres and Lebrun) who served as consultants. Below them was a Senate of 80 individuals who they appointed from nominees presented by the various parts of the government. Appointments were for life. The Senate in turn appointed the members of the two legislative bodies, from lists of nominees elected by the communes. The first body, the Tribunate had 100 members who only discussed proposed legislation but couldn't vote on it, whereas the second body, the Legislative Chamber, had 300 members who voted on legislation but couldn't discuss it. The commune of Paris was run under Babeuvism, which was a precursor to Marxism. Some of the other communes were too.

[56] See Langer 1940.

[57] At this point in the battle, that poet, Goethe went out between the two opposing armies to experience the cannon–fever: that is the effect which having cannon balls flying by has on the emotions. See Creasy, 1879.

France even signed the Treaty of Basel, during March 1795, guaranteeing the secularization of the States north of the Rhine in exchange for granting France the territories on the south bank. Prussia gained influence and power by this treaty, while France gained territory. The French actions generally helped to unify Germany and reduce the power of Prussia's rival, Austria.

Only after the crowning of Napoleon, did Prussia enter into the conflict on the side of the allies (in 1806). However, the Prussian forces had been resting on their fame since Frederick's time and were quickly overwhelmed. But, they improved later on. In particular, Prussian soldiers fought hard under Field Marshal Blucher at the Battle of Waterloo, providing the support which the Duke of Wellington relied upon to bring about the final defeat of Napoleon, on June 18, 1815.

The English had, at first been undecided about whether to support or oppose the Revolution. France was their traditional enemy and many people were, also, glad to see the end of a corrupt monarchy. Edmund Burke was the first to recognize that the Revolution was unlike the English or America Revolutions, but sought to radically reform society. He pointed this out, in 1790, in his *Reflections on the French Revolution.* It swayed public opinion decisively against the Revolution and determined England's course.

Waterloo was not the end of France's troubles. They had a series of revolutions: specifically, in 1830, 1848, and 1871. The Revolution, in 1871, finally ended the French monarchies and began their third Republic (1871–1914).

But, that represented a change only in their national government. The structure of their local governments remained largely as it had been before. — Originally, they had had all the usual representative bodies of a Germanic society, but they had lost these by the time of Lois XIV. At that time, local government was purely administrative. The local intendants, were appointed by various means, which varied widely from town–to–town and region–to–region, except that none of them were elected. They governed and they served the interests of the King. The revolutionary government of 1789, changed this with the stroke of a pen. By decree, they became independent elected bodies. But, the people were not ready for self–rule and all manner of abuse and mismanagement arose. Consequently, in 1795, the national government placed the local officers under the supervision of Paris, although they were still elected. Later, during the Napoleonic period, that too was eliminated and they were appointed by Paris. The situation has varied somewhat since then, with slightly more home–rule under democratic regimes and less under monarchic ones, but it remains essentially the same to this day. Thus, the structure of the part of government nearest to the people was not materially changed despite all their revolutions. — The French remain French: Their heritage has tremendous social inertia.

Chapter 8

Hegelian Period

Modern history is usually considered to begin immediately after the Battle of Waterloo, in 1815. What makes it "modern" instead of "Western" is the inclusion of economics among the primary governing principles of society.

The years between the Battle of Waterloo, in 1815, and the Franco–Prussian War, in 1870–1871, were divided into two distinct parts. The first part was Hegelian. That was from 1815 to 1830. During those years, society was dominated by the philosophy of Hegel, the economics of Richardo, and the political parties of the elite money power. That continued until within a few years of 1830. Then they were emphatically overthrown, all over the world.

8.1   German Idealism

The philosophical movement of German Absolutism peaked after the French Revolution, rather than before it.

Johann Fichte (1762–1814)[1] was the first philosopher who was clearly identified with that movement. As a young man, he had been strongly influenced by Immanuel Kant's works and traveled to Koenigsberg to meet him. Although, he was poorly received, he remained determined to obtain his approval. To that end, he wrote the book *Critique of All Revelation* in which he applied Kant's ethical rule of respect for duty to the interpretation of religion. He also adopted that rule as a central theme in his own philosophy.

---

[1]He was the eldest son of a ribbon maker, in a large family. Under those circumstances he would not ordinarily have been able to attend school much less a university. However, as a boy, he exhibited such an outstanding memory that he was adopted by a German nobleman.

127

Fichte held that the State should control employment, regulate all industries, set all wages, and strictly limit all imports. The individual exists solely to serve the State it imprints whatever views it prefers upon the individual through its control over education. The State is supreme and individuals find freedom in obedience to it.

Kant received his book well and agreed to get it published. Somehow, it first appeared anonymously, in 1792, and the public took it as another work by Kant. This produced considerable public interest and made Fichte's reputation.

This was instrumental to his getting an appointment to a professorship at Jena University.[2] — Fichte was a Freemason, almost certainly was Illuminati, and certainly was promoted by the Illuminati. In particular, Sutton[3] says that Illuminatus, Johann Goethe, pushed for Fichte's appointment to Jena.

He became *the* philosopher of cameralism. That is the idea that the bureaucracy in the service of the State should be a technical and managerial elite. That idea was not new, at that time. It had been adopted by Fredrick William following the Thirty Years War. Conditions were, then, favorable for the State to replace private enterprise. The idea grew in Germany throughout the eighteenth and nineteenth centuries, reaching a high state of perfection in Bismark's time.[4]

Respect for duty was, then, the central organizing principle of German society. Their social classes were organized not as England's were, on a financial basis, into a working class and business owners, but along military lines on the basis of who commanded and who obeyed.

Georg Wilhelm Friedrich Hegel (1770–1831) followed

in Fichte's and Schelling's footsteps. He did most of his work after the French Revolution. That completed the philosophical development begun by Mendelssohn and Kant. It has a nice compact clarity of thought.

He is often given credit as the originator of the "Hegelian dialectic." However, Fichte discussed it before him. Hegel saw it as the mechanism by which the State effects social change. — Life, in his view, was a series

---

[2]At first he drew large audiences at the University of Jena, but his popularity soon waned. The students found him too closed–minded, too radical on the academic topics of government and religion, and too inflexible and stern on issues of student conduct. He was forced to resign in 1799. But, in 1810, he returned to academia when he was appointed the Dean of Philosophy at the University of Berlin. He later became its rector.

[3]See Sutton 1986.

[4]Otto von Bismark was born in 1815. He was appointed Prime Minister of Prussia, in 1862. In 1867, he dictated the first draft of the German Constitution, which, with only a few changes, became the Constitution of the Empire, in 1871. That form of government had democratic institutions, specifically a lower house, the Reichstag and an upper house, the Bundesrat, the but all the power was effectively held by the executive branch, led by the Chancellor and the Emperor. (See Munroe 1938.) Bismark served as Chancellor from 1871 until his resignation, in 1890. That Constitution and form of government continued until the Emperor's abdication at the end of the First World War.

of conflicts, forcing choices, and driving society towards its destiny.

The Hegelian dialectic is a constructive use of the skeptics' principle of equipollence; and it echoes in the Cabalistic view of the role of conflict in learning; but its most likely origin is the Alchemical concept of individuation through the conflict and conjunction of opposites. In this process, "thesis" generates its "antithesis" and out of their conflict arises something new which is neither the thesis nor antithesis. It is called the "synthesis."[5] It is a direct method for causing social change and, therefore, causes public resistance. But the inclusion of the antithesis provides for that resistance and contributes to moving society towards the synthesis. Unmentioned is the elite directing social change by, forcing the conflicts and providing the antithesis, and, thus, defining or delimiting the synthesis.

Hegel took Mendelssohn's concept of the totality of the Jewish race as Messiah to its logical conclusion where the collective Spirit of the People is at once God and the State.[6] He assumed that the people of a nation have a common collective unconsciousness, the Spirit, and also that part of that Spirit resides in the individual as his or her soul. His departure from the usual assumption of the Classical model or Jacob's Ladder is that he assumes that the Spirit is the sum of the souls of the people of the nation. Therefore, it follows that the Image of God is the sum of all the individuals' Images of God for the entire nation. Likewise, the State is the sum of the people and its motivating principle is their collective Image of God.

In this context, morality, which consists of the individual serving his or her Image of God, becomes identical to serving the State.[7] This would be the epitome of freedom, except that it recognizes neither Natural Law

---

[5] For a strict analysis of the dialectic process consider an urn containing black, white, and red beads and a committee which has to select one color of bead. Suppose that one group within the committee prefers black beads, but a second group is opposed to black beads and prefers white beads. Suppose further that each group is sufficiently influential to prevent the other from having its way. The result is that sooner–or–later the committee will settle upon red beads. This example shows exactly what the dialectic process is and how it is utilized: if you secretly favor red beads, then you need to form a group to promote the selection of white beads.

[6] Quoted from Hegel's Philosophical History: "The general principle which manifests itself and becomes an object of consciousness in the State, — the form under which all that the State includes is brought, — is the whole of that cycle of phenomena which constitutes the culture of the nation. But the definite substance that receives the form of universality, and exits in that concrete reality which is the State, — is the Spirit of the People itself. The actual State is animated by this spirit, ...the generic soul pervading all its details." He also says, "God is the unity of the Universal and the individual." and "The conception of God, therefore, constitutes the general basis of a people's character."

[7] Quoted from Hegel's Philosophical History: "But man must also attain a conscious realization of this his Spirit and essential nature, and of his original identity with it. For we said that morality is the identity of the subjective or personal with the universal will. Now the mind must give itself to express consciousness of this; and the focus of this knowledge is religion. Art and Science are only various aspects of the same substantial being."

nor the rights and authority of the individual against the community. Like Fichte, he felt that the State is absolute and demanded absolute obedience.[8]

He also held, as many of the Gnostics did, that the innermost circle, the individuals who determine the future for the State, are above morality.[9] They are not to be held responsible for the historical events they bring to pass, even if they cause the massacre, pillage, and enslavement of peoples for no better reason than a personal whim or monetary gain.[10]

8.2   Modern Judaism

Reform Judaism was founded, in 1818, by a group of Jews in Hamburg. They built a synagogue and began following the teachings of the Jewish enlightenment, particularly, those of Moses Mendelssohn.[11] Their doctrine

---

[8]Quoted from Hegel's *Philosophical History*: "Freedom exists only where Individuality is recognized as having its positive and real existence in the Divine Being."

[9]Quoted from Hegel's *Philosophical History*: "The history of the World occupies a higher ground than that on which morality has properly its position; which is personal character, — the conscience of individuals, — their particular will and mode of action; these have a value, imputation, reward or punishment proper to themselves. What the absolute aim of Spirit requires and accomplishes, — what Providence does, — transcends the obligations, and the liability to imputation and the ascription of good or bad motives, which attach to individuality in virtue of its social relations.... in revolutions, both parties generally stand within the limits of transient and corruptible existence. Consequently, it is only a formal rectitude — deserted by the living Spirit and by God — which those who stand upon ancient right and order maintain. The deeds of great men, who are the individuals of the World's History, thus appear not only justified in view of that intrinsic result of which they were not conscious, but also by the point of view occupied by the secular moralist. But looked at from this point, moral claims which are irrelevant, must not be brought into collision with World–Historical deeds and their accomplishment. The litany of private virtues — modesty, humility, philanthropy, and forbearance — must not be raised against them."

[10]This was a recognized issue at that time and was discussed during the trials before Parliament of Robert Clive, in 1772, and Warren Hastings, in 1786. They were charged with having violated the principles of morality and Natural Law. It was recognized that ordinary laws are made for ordinary people and do not cover the crimes of those great personages who cause world historical events. In the end, it was ruled that their great contributions atoned for their offenses. However, the Frenchmen, Labourdonnais, Dupleix, and Lally were found guilty under similar charges in France. Labourdonnais was imprisoned, Dupleix was dispossessed, and Lally was executed. These five individuals were responsible for the conquest India. That was begun by France and completed by England. They had conducted unjust wars, broken agreements, committed judicial murders, and literally sold entire nations into slavery.

[11]Of course, Mendelssohn wrote a great deal more than just that letter to Lavater. Most of his religious writing is under his Jewish name, Moses Dessau. There were also other Jewish enlightenment writers. Unfórtunately, Jewish religious literature is not readily available, as their custom is to conceal their alters.

included abandoning their belief in a personal Messiah; replacing Him with the Jewish people as the Messiah; replacing the Law with reason; abandoning their ceremonial, dress, and dietary laws in favor of the Western practice, whenever it is more reasonable; and allowing the offspring of intermarriages to become members of their religion.[12]

This represented a tremendous advance for them. Rabbinic Judaism had been based on faith and mysticism and was full of superstition, so, the founding of Reform Judaism, represented their abandoning that path and taking their first tentative steps towards reason.

In 1824, a Reform Judaic synagogue was founded in Charleston, South Carolina. After that, it spread rapidly throughout the United States, but it grew more slowly in the Old World. Today, it is the mainstream of Judaism. The vast majority of the branches of modern Judaism trace their roots either to it or to Hassidism. The exception is the relatively small orthodox community.

There have been several offshoots from Reform Judaism. In particular, Conservative Judaism was formed in 1845 in Germany. They felt that Reform Judaism had gone too far. So, they restored many parts of the Law, including those on diet, dress, and family purity. — They followed scriptural precepts and Rabbinic law if these were "responsive to the modern requirements of Jewish life."[13]

The nineteenth century, was a time of rising Jewish "racial" consciousness. It manifested itself in the form of Zionism:[14] that is the movement to establish a Jewish homeland. Like all Jewish politics from that period, their movement was theocratic and their hope was messianic. They made concrete proposals to the British government in the 1850's and 1870's to establish a Jewish State in the Holy Land under English protection. But, none of these movements gained any substantial following among the Jewish masses. However, this changed in 1896 when the Viennese journalist, Theodore Herzl (1860–1904), took over the project.

That was the dawn of the age of anti–semiticism which culminated with the Nazis. At that time, there was a growing belief in the existence of a global Jewish conspiracy. The election of anti–semitic candidates in Vienna and Lower Austria, in 1895, convinced Herzl that the Jews would not be allowed to immerse themselves in Western society. So, he began advocating Zionism. He gained the support of the Rhodes–Milner political

---

[12] Many authors have commented upon a possible connection between Freemasonry, modern Judaism, and the Hanoverian and Prussian foreign policies. Some suggest that Judaism was the motive force behind all of this, whereas, others hold that they were the products of Hanoverian and Prussian policies. The latter interpretation would appear to provide the best explanation, but the evidence is far from conclusive. However, irrespective of what their origins may have been, these various groups soon became a polycentric movement.

[13] See *The Book of Jewish Knowledge.*

[14] See "Zionism" *Encyclopedia Britannica* thirteenth edition, 1926. Most of the material on Zionism is drawn from that article.

organization, and in 1902, the British government offered them the Sinai Peninsula and, in 1903, the 6000 square mile Nasin Gishiu Plateau in East Africa. Although these regions were uninhabited and lay in or near regions traditionally occupied by Jewish tribes, they rejected both offers. They were inconsistent with their religious mission.— They wanted the Holy Land, as described in the scriptural prophesies of the messianic State.

But, Palestine was not uninhabited nor was the Ottoman Empire likely to release control of it. So, they settled down to wait. — The changes came with the First World War. On November 2, 1917, Britain declared their intention to make Palestine a national homeland for the Jews,[15] and a month later the British army took Jerusalem. When the First World War was over, the region was assigned to Great Britain. They allowed extensive Jewish immigration and, as a result, civil unrest grew between the Jewish and Arab populations. In 1947, the British referred the problem to the United Nations. They partitioned Palestine, thereby, creating the modern State of Israel.

Modern Jewish history provides some excellent illustrations of historical processes. One phenominon it exhibits is historical cycles. In particular, they had a two-hundred year cycle. That is the same length as China's dynastic cycle. And, in fact, they are essentially the same phenomenon.

Whenever a new dynasty conquered China, they would begin a period of good government which would last for about three generations. This comes about because the sons and grandsons of the dynasty's founder would be raised under the conditions of a military camp. This would give them a high standard of morality and a practical outlook. But, their descendants would be raised in the seraglio. There they would learn faction and vice. Then, the quality of government would progressively decline. That would last, on the average, seven generations, until a new dynasty would overthrow them, thus, ending that cycle and beginning the next one.

The Jewish historical cycle begins when they are expelled from one country and find a new place to live. They bring financial institutions and capital to their new home, and a period of growth and prosperity follows. That lasts about three generations,[16] as the sons and grandsons would benefit from the hard lessons the original settlers learned at the time of their expulsion. They would know better than to take advantage of their new hosts. But, that social memory dies away and the initial burst of prosperity which resulted from their financial institutions overcoming the scarcity of capital, ends too. Then, there follows a long period during which their the community becomes better established and increasingly ethnocentric. One of the factors contributing to this is that their children are educated within their own community. During this period they gradually gather together wealth and gain position through working cooperatively.[17] Even-

---

[15] That was the Balfour Declaration.

[16] That is the period throughout which the people in the community have a living memory of its founders.

[17] As a minority they are pushed together as a group and, therefore, tend to

tually they rise to positions of power in the community at large and they may try to impose their culture on the host nation: in particular, the may try to implement a messianic State or level society in preparation for one. Some time during this final stage, the indigenous people rise up and expel them, ending that cycle and beginning the next one.

This cycle repeated itself again–and–again in European history and it even happened in Classical times in the Middle East.[18] One clear example is the Jewish experience in England from their arrival in 1079 to their expulsion in 1290. Another is their experience in Germany from Prussia's conquest of Silesia, in 1740, to the holocaust, ending in 1945.

Up to that time, no country had found a completely satisfactory method for resolving the conflict of cultures which drove the cycle. So, the issue of the age was to find a "final solution." Israel was the English version. Their moving to Israel should have broken the cycle, for their social conditions, there, are fundamentally different. — They were no longer a small group, like a dynasty, which comes into a host country, but a nation unto themselves on their own land, occupied by their own people. That has different dynamics. Thus, the Jewish historical cycle, with its perpetual recurrence of pogroms and holocausts, need never occur again.

When Israel became a nation their concerns and conditions suddenly changed. As a State, they had to deal with all the same issues as any other State must deal with, including all the psychological types in their public and all their attendant predispositions and conflicts; whereas as a religious organization, their leadership represented a fairly narrow segment of their population and were concerned largely with maintaining their heritage and culture. So, with their becoming a State, there naturally was a marked change in perspective, although it took a while for the various political parties to sort themselves out. The half–century which followed saw rapid progress.

To begin with, the Jews who moved to Israel were not all of the same mind as they had been before. Many of them had learned from the holocaust the injustice of a messianic State. — Nazi Germany was explicitly messianic, but, in that case, the Germans were the chosen people rather than the Jews. Consequently, many of them repudiated the messianic concept. — That was the origin of Reconstructionist Judaism and it also accounts for the large number of emigrants to Israel, after the Second World War, who sought a purely secular State. This shows that they, as a people, had gained an understanding of the first principle of Natural Law, that it applies equally to everyone.[19]

---

work as one, for their mutual benefit and their ethnic and religious customs promote and support this.

[18] The *1980 Jewish Almanac* lists 34 instances of their expulsion. Many of them followed this pattern.

[19] Of course, there still remains a range of opinion among Israelis. The dispute between their messianic and secular views is one of the leading political issues in Israel, today. This is essentially a conservative–versus–liberal dispute: The messianic viewpoint is conservative, as that group looks back to scripture and

Later, during the 1990's, Israel would allow the Palestinians the right to exist as a community, and to self–rule, according to their own laws and customs. That shows evidence that the Israelis, as a people, had also learned the second principle: that is, that all people are entitled to justice. But, what is most noteworthy is that they are practicing "justice" in the Western sense.

Thus, a significant proportion of them, as a people, had absorbed the basic principles of enlightenment. This provides a remarkable example of learning in the public mind. That took only approximately half a century, which is extraordinarily rapid for such a fundamental change. For comparison, it took France three revolutions and roughly a century to abandon monarchy, and that was only a change on the national level, leaving local government as it was. These examples illustrate how very resilient the heritage of a people can be.[20] And, both of these are examples of rapid change, caused by wars. In contrast, fundamental changes may take as many millennia if a people are left to themselves.[21]

The worldwide rise in Fundamentalism, over the last few decades, has affected Judaism as well as Christianity and Islam. Unfortunately, those Jews who return to their roots may return to the messianic concepts. If that trend remains unchecked, it would reverse the progress which they have made. But, this has not gone unrecognized by the Israeli government. For example, in the mid–1980's, Martin D. Kahane's Kach Party,[22] was banned in Israel for its racist anti–Arab sentiments. Thus, it appears that their conservative trend may be confined.

A conservative reaction, such as his party represented, can be expected after any period of change. That is not necessarily bad. — Lenin said that causing change is like driving a nail. You strike it and it moves forward until it comes to a stop. Then, you draw the hammer back. The back–stroke is as important as the forward. It is a time to readjust your aim. Then, each time you strike the nail, it advances a little further.

The back–stroke can, also, be used constructively: In particular, that is the time during which the "old tradition" can be redefined, as people

---

ethnic tradition to define what constitutes "justice." In contrast, their liberals look forward and are governed by understanding. — The names "conservative" and "liberal" are reversed, due to their old tradition being Eastern rather than Western. — These issues are occasionally covered in broadcasts of international news and even were discussed in *Time Magazine*, during 1998.

[20] Individuals, of course, learn more rapidly. But, those who do usually simply leave their original community rather than altering it. Thus, individual learning may have little influence over the heritage of a people.

[21] Thus, unless changes in a people's tradition are caused, they effectively do not happen. — That provides a general–purpose justification for causing world–historical events.

A corollary is that if the structure of society can be so altered that changes occur with little effort, then war will not be necessary. Thus, world–peace is seen to be contingent upon continuous–change.

[22] He was a US Citizen by birth and the founder of the ethnocentric Jewish Defense League.

rediscover it.

For example, an attempt was made during America's Republican Revolution, of the early 1990's,[23] to spread the beliefs that the early American colonists had learned their democratic form of government from the Iroquois and that the right of freedom was a grant from God. That this was attempted shows that someone felt that America's conservative community was almost completely ignorant of the origin and basis of our form of government.[24] The way this was done was that a "conservative" leader on the national level enunciated these ideas and they were, then, picked up and parroted by leaders at the local level. Many of these local leaders were simply ignorant, but, others were concealed activists who had entered the conservative community to cause change. The masses knew no better and unquestioningly accepted whatever their leaders told them. — This illustrates how easily a network might exploit a conservative reaction.

In contrast against the Jewish community in Israel. American Jews were not subject to the same cultural learning experiences and remained a minority. However, many of them have learned by immersion in American society.[25] The effects of this are marked. For example, Dr. Lilienthal estimated, in 1965, that of the 5.5 million American Jews only 1.25 million were members of their various zionist political organizations.[26] Thus, as Aaron Zelman stated, in 1989, the Jewish activist "is a minority within a minority."[27] However, they are probably the best organized of any minority group.

---

[23] This was the conservative reaction to President Clinton's policies.

[24] That was not a bad assumption, as these beliefs were objected to by only a tiny fraction of that community.

[25] Public education was probably one of the main contributing factors.

[26] Thus, they represent approximately 23% of their population. We know from Jacob's Ladder that what Jung called the non–rational types were traditionally dominant among the Jewish people. Also, their religious and social heritages were suited to those types. Therefore, they might be expected to be a larger proportion of the Jewish population than among Americans in general. Their numbers are probably, also, enlarged by Jews of other types who join them on account of their effectiveness as organizations.

For comparison, the religious right is the corresponding phenomenon in the general American public. They represent approximately 11–15% of it, and the writing style of their literature clearly reveals that the non–rational types are prominent among them. So, finding that roughly a quarter of American Jews are actively involved in extremist groups is consistent with what might expected if they predominately represent those same types.

Given the nature of mankind, such groups will arise. It is helpful to understand why this occurs, as it provides some insight into what they can and can not be expected to do and how best to deal with them.

This should, also, serve to illustrate the importance of the change which occurred when Israel became a State rather than being a political and religious movement. — Previously they were led by essentially this segment of their population, whereas afterwards they became the conservative wing of the political spectrum and government represented the majority.

[27] Cited by Weiland 1994.

America, also, has another significant departure from the conditions
which drove the Jewish historical cycle. That is that, whereas, the Jews
traditionally were a body of capitalists who formed an isolated community
within a non–capitalistic host country, the United States is a capitalistic country. So, when one considers the "Jews" as a functional group in
America, with regard to the Jewish historical cycle, they should probably
be identified as that financial elite which isolates itself from society and
works, to some degree, for their mutual benefit. That better describes
the liberal Eastern Establishment. And, they are about two–thirds non–
Jewish. Their cycle may have begun during the period of 1789–1815: that
is, between the signing of the US Constitution and the dawn of the modern
era. Approximately two centuries later, at the beginning of the twenty-
first century, they are said to possess about 80% of the world's wealth.
And the riot in Seattle, in December 1999, was about the World Trade
Organization's plans to establish what amounts to a worldwide messianic
State. Thus, their cycle is nearing completion. — But, the "Jews" in this
case are no longer the same group of people.

Many of the original Jews have merged to varying degrees into the general population. One ramification of this is the emergence of what might
be called "Judeo–Christian Fundamentalism." — Today, a significant segment of Fundamentalist Christianity are these Jewish–Christian hybrids.
It is among them that one most often finds the belief that the rights–of–
man are a grant from God. That is the old–fashioned Jewish viewpoint.
But, they mix that with the Christian and American heritage, and sometimes obtain some surprising results. One of these is that although one
might, expect them to support one–world absolute government, they are a
significant segment of the right–wing.

It is generally not appreciated the extent to which World War I ended
the connection between the Jews and Germany. After that, the Germany,
which probably founded them, and which they served whether willingly
or involuntarily, no longer existed. The unfortunate outcomes of that war
made the Second World War necessary. But with the holocaust, that entire
era of Jewish history came to an end. What followed afterwards was a new
àge, and there is reason to hope that this can be not just the beginning of
yet another cycle, but the dawn of something different.

8.3   Classical Economics

David Ricardo (1772–1823) was the great economist of the Hegelian
period, and possibly also the most influential economist of modern times.
He extended Adam Smith's work and developed most of the body of classical economic theory.[28] His work was accepted in England during the first

---

[28] He was born in London, descended from Sephardic Jews on both sides. However, his marriage, to an English Quaker, violated the tenants of their faith and
resulted in his being disowned from his family and their religion. However, he
was supported by a prominent firm of London stockbrokers and soon made a

half of the nineteenth century. John Keynes wrote that "Ricardo conquered England as completely as the Holy Inquisition conquered Spain."[29]

A pamphlet which Ricardo published, in 1810, on the price of gold, was well received by the public, reaching a fourth edition by 1811. As a result, he became accepted as an economist and began participating in government. Later he gained a seat in Parliament, representing a rotted Irish borough. He soon became intimately acquainted with James Mill (1773–1836) and Thomas R. Malthus (1766–1834).

James Mill acted as his mentor, helping him develop his understanding of economics and improve his writing skills. Mill was the author of *Elements of Political Economy* and various other works. However, he was also a notorious liberal. — He was an Atheist and, also, held unorthodox views on sex and marriage. He wrote several tracts on woman's liberation, and had even spent a night in jail, in 1789, for distributing birth control literature among London's poor. Throughout most of his life he was a clerk at the British East India Company.

Thomas Malthus was, then, regarded as the leading economist in London. He influenced Richardo's ideas. He is best known for his work on population growth rates. In particular, he showed that natural populations will expand until they become limited by some resource. Richardo applied this concept to wages and the theory of distribution, reaching the conclusion that the population of laborers would always expand until their wages declined to their real value. But in this case, the "real value" was that which allowed labor to replace itself on the average. That is such a low rate of pay that widespread poverty would cause sufficiently high mortality rates to balance their birthrate. This was different from Adam Smith's definition, which assumed a decent standard of living. This view resulted in the fundamental pessimism of the Classical school of economics: They held that, in the end, nothing could raise the working class out of their squalor.

These economic ideas set the tone of the early nineteenth century. They determined public policies and were also implemented by the great banking houses.

The Rothschild Banking House had emerged from the French Revolution as the dominant financial Power of the nineteenth century. In fact, nineteenth century literature often referred to their times as the "Age of Rothschild."

Mayer A. Rothschild had five sons who he sent to manage various banks throughout Europe and the British Isles. Nathan Mayer Rothschild was the one who went to England. His rise to wealth and power came

---

large fortune on the commodities and foreign exchange markets. In 1799, he read Adam Smith's *Wealth of Nations* and greatly admired it. After that time, economics became a consuming interest for him. Some successful investments allowed him to retire from the brokerage business, thereafter, he devoted his time to economics and public affairs, for the rest of his life. He died suddenly, in 1823, from an ear infection.

[29] See Keynes 1936.

as a result of the Battle of Waterloo in 1815. He created a run on the stock market based on a false impression of the outcome of that battle.[30] His brothers held similar positions in the other banks of Europe and even in America. In particular, America's national bank was the First United States Bank, chartered from 1791–1811. It was backed by James D. Rothschild of Paris.[31] He was also the principle backer of the next national bank, the Second US Bank.

Nathan Rothschild's stratagem of creating a run on the stock market was a crude way to take large profits. A much more sophisticated and cleaner method had just become available.— In 1796 the French mathematician/astronomer Pierre Simon Laplace[32] invented the Laplace transformation. This advance in mathematics provided the means by which equations describing the dynamics of economic systems could be solved.[33]

The first true economic crash and depression of industrial society oc-

---

[30] He had been with the allies at that battle. When it was clear that the allies were going to win, he hurried back to the London exchange. There was a storm in the English Channel and he had to pay a high fee to get a fisherman to take him across. The next morning he was in his place at the exchange, selling bonds and securities as fast as possible. That included consuls, or shares in the Bank of England. This created a run because the other brokers knew he had been at the battle, and assumed that he knew the outcome. Rothschild however, had agents who quietly bought up these financial instruments. In a single day he made a million pounds sterling. That is the origin of his fortune. It also placed him in a controlling position in the Bank of England.

David Richardo also made a large profit at that time. That was what allowed him to retire from his stock brokerage and concentrate on public life and economics.

[31] That was right in the middle of their Revolutionary period. The First Bank was a national bank which managed the US accounts. It was strongly supported by Alexander Hamilton but vehemently opposed by Thomas Jefferson. Alexander Hamilton also later supported the formation of the Second US Bank. It existed until the renewal of its charter was vetoed by President Jackson, in 1832.

[32] The Laplace transformation was his most important contribution, but at the time he was best known for having been the first to apply Lagrangian and Hamiltonian dynamics to the orbits of the planets. Immanuel Kant had shown, only shortly before, the planetary orbits would decay until the planets fell back into the sun. But that is incorrect as it is based on Newtonian dynamics which are inadequate to solve "three body problems" such as planetary orbits.

He was more than just a great mathematician/scientist. He became a member of the French Senate, in 1799, and was its Vice–President, in 1805. That was during their Consular Period. The Vice–President of the Senate was the fifth highest position in France. As most of the appointees in that administration were Jacobins, it seems likely that he was one too.

[33] That is, they could be solved provided the underlying relationships could be accurately described. That is the more difficult problem as the structure of society and the value of money depend upon the aggregate behavior of the people. These interactions were not very well understood before the contributions made by John Keynes, during the first three decades of the twentieth century. Prior to that date, economists concentrated primarily on micro–economic scales where the structure of society was fixed.

curred in America in 1819.[34] [35] President Monroe's administration didn't know what to do about it. Nor did anyone else. In fact, the event led to the, 1820, Ricardo–Malthus debate on the possibility of a general glut in the market. — The American economy eventually recovered naturally; but, a second panic occurred ten years later, in 1829. By that time, some people in financial circles were beginning to understand how economic systems functioned. The Rothschild Banking House put that knowledge to use in 1837, when they produced the first artificially–induced crash. More exactly, as the economy is cyclic, it would have crashed anyway. They just precipitated it, so that it crashed at a known date.

The opportunities to profit from economic panics were not fully exploited during this first trial of the method. However, over the two decades which followed, the Rothschild banking house established a group of representatives to exploit the crashes which occurred at regular intervals throughout the remainder of the century.[36]

8.4 Tycoons of American Industry

Morgan:[37] The J.P. Morgan Company began in the slave trade as George Peabody and Company.[38]

This trade was very lucrative and, in 1835, George Peabody opened an investment establishment in London. There he met Baron Nathan Mayer Rothschild, who became his financial backer. The arrangement was highly successful.

Their American agent was Beebe, Morgan, and Company. — George Peabody was impressed by Junius Morgan and, in 1854, invited him to

---

[34] See Baird and Baird 1944.

[35] The stock market crashes caused by balloon companies during the eighteenth century weren't the same type of phenomenon.

Economic depressions occur when the technological capacity to overproduce is combined with the credit to finance it. Over–production gluts the market, reducing prices and resulting in lay–offs. The loss of employment reduces the consumer's buying power, further reducing demand for the products. However, the economy eventually recovers when the products are no longer in over–supply. Then industrial capacity is rebuilt and the cycle repeats itself. Nineteenth century America had economic depressions or panics about every ten years.

This discussion assumes a constant money supply. However, if the amount of money in circulation is altered, by altering credit, then the dynamics of the economy can be changed. In particular, crashes can be precipitated by abruptly contracting credit, or a crash can be forestalled by increasing the amount of credit. Thus, the timing of a crash can be controlled. That makes it exploitable.

[36] The House of Rothschild is known to have precipitated the economic crashes of 1837, 1857, 1873, 1893, and 1907. Regarding the specifics of these events see Eustace Mullins 1993.

[37] The following account is drawn primarily from Eustace Mullens (1993).

[38] George Peabody (1795–1869) operated the Georgetown, D.C., slave market under the corporation of Peabody, Riggs, and Company from 1814 until 1835.

become his partner in George Peabody and Company. As he was, at that time, an elderly man without heirs, he was giving his business to Junius Morgan, John Pierpont Morgan's father.

They obtained substantial profits during the Civil War and Reconstruction Period.[39] But, they generally made their largest profits on the financial panics, which had been artificially induced. For example, Rothschild advanced Peabody and Company $5 million to withstand the panic of 1857. In the financial panic of 1873, J.P. Morgan bought the Northern Pacific Railroad.[40] In later panics J.P. Morgan Co. bought several other railroads and eventually, in 1967, these became Burlington Northern Railroad.[41]

The settlement of the Pacific Northwest is intimately related to these railroads. In order to encourage the construction of a transcontinental railroad along a Northern route, from Lake Superior to the Puget Sound. To provide them with the needed lumber, the US government granted Northern Pacific a sector alternately on either side of their rail lines along their entire route.[42]

This land was specifically intended to be held by the railroads only for five years after the completion of the railroad. They were required to build and maintain roads on these lands and they were to be sold to settlers for homesteads or, if the railroad failed, they were to be sold in public auction. However, they managed to avoid this. They still retain some of this land although they sold much of it to other large companies.[43] There

---

[39] According to Gustavus Myers biography of George Peabody, they represented England which supported the Confederacy. They inflated the American currency largely through their Company, to their very substantial profit. Also, according to the New York Times, Oct 31, 1866, Peabody and Company profited from Southern reconstruction (carpetbaggers) after that war.
In 1864, the Morgans opened a new business, Dabney, Morgan, and Company, which handled the Peabody account and continued his relationship with Rothschild. In 1895, they changed their name to J.P. Morgan and Company.

[40] Its principle owner had been Jay Cooke and Company, the largest American banking house of its day. They failed in that panic.

[41] In the panic of 1893, Northern Pacific absorbed Great Northern Railroad owned by James Hill, another very wealthy independent American. However, in 1896 the Supreme Court ruled this merger to be an illegal constraint on trade; the two railroads set up joint ownership instead. In 1901 they bought the Chicago, Burlington, and Quincy line and in the process of doing so caused a stock market crash. They again attempted to create a holding company for the three railroads, but were overruled in the courts. In 1920 the transportation act exempted railroads from the Sherman Anti–trust Act and they finally merged, in 1967, forming Burlington Northern Railroad.

[42] The Northern Pacific Land Grant Act of 1864 and another in 1870.

[43] According to Jensen et al. 1995 they sold 900,000 acres in Washington State to Weyerhaeuser Co., in 1899; 1,000,000 acres in Montana to Amalgamated Copper Co (later Anaconda), in 1907; 670,000 to Champion International, in 1972, who resold some of these lands to Plum Creek; and additional land in Idaho was sold to Weyerhaeuser which they transferred to Potlatch and Boise Payetter (later Boise Cascade).

have been numerous US congressional investigations and court cases on this issue. It would appear that these railroad grant lands are still within the public domain and under the power of the US Congress to demand their appropriate disposal or return.[44] In 1980, Burlington Northern Railroad divided into a railroad and a holding company, Burlington Resources, for the remaining grant land.

This issue is directly connected to contemporary Washington State politics. For example, ex–Governor Dan Evans is on the board of Directors of Burlington Resources; ex–Governor Booth Gardner is the stepson of the single largest stockholder of Weyerhaeuser Company, Norton Clapp (now deceased); and these two companies are the two most influential political interests in Washington State. And they also have had an influence on the national level. They may be maintaining their positions of power to ensure their continued control over the grant lands, without which they would be nothing at all.

J.P. Morgan was also involved in several insurance companies, bought US Steel for \$480 million in 1900, and was involved with several banks. In particular, the meeting at which the Federal Reserve Bank was first proposed was held in J.P. Morgan's hunting lodge on Jekyll Island and he was intimately involved with the drafting of the Federal Reserve Act and became one of the largest owners of the Federal Reserve Bank.[45] However, people were surprised to find that, at the time of his death, his fortune was modest. — He had been acting as the agent of the Rothschild banking system.

Rockefeller: John Davison Rockefeller, the founder of the Rockefeller fortune, was born July 8, 1839, in a rented cottage outside Richford in New York State.[46]

After his graduation from highschool, in Cleveland, Ohio, in 1855, he briefly attended Flosom Commercial College to learn bookkeeping. His

---

[44] See Northern Pacific Land Grant Hearings before the House Committee on Public Lands (1924), The Senate Committee on Public Lands and Surveys (1924), and the Joint Committee on Investigation of Northern Pacific Land Grants(1925–28), US v. Northern Pacific (1940) 311 U.S. 317 and settlement U.S. v. Northern Pacific (1941) 41 F. Supp. 287 which was not approved by Congress. Many of the relevant documents are reprinted in Jensen et al. 1995 who go into the history of these lands in considerable detail.

[45] See Mullins 1993.

[46] His mother, Eliza Davison, was a devout Baptist, daughter of a prosperous farmer, and a homemaker. His father, William Avery Rockefeller, was a traveling salesman, a confidence artist who passed himself off as a physician, "Dr. Livingston," to sell a patent medicine for cancer, which was mostly composed of morphine. John D. Rockefeller's father spent most of his time away from home, on the road, or with his other wife (he was a bigamist), Margaret Allen, who lived in a small town in Ontario.

In 1853, the Rockefellers moved to Cleveland, Ohio, which was at that time a hub of trade and commerce. John D. was enrolled in Central High School there. There he met Celestia Spelman who was later to become his wife.

first job was in a commission house.[47] They arranged transportation for dry goods and also did some wholesale buying and selling. In 1859, he left them and opened a commission house with a partner.[48]

Following the discovery of oil in Ohio, during 1859, they slowly became involved in the oil industry, but only in its refining and transportation not in its production. The business prospered but his partnership ended in 1865, not on good terms. This was the result of his partner's opposition to the company's continually increasing debt, which they were using to finance expansion. John D. Rockefeller took new partners and that same year he initiated trade in kerosene to China.

In 1870, he formed Standard Oil of Ohio. Ten years later, they had monopolized nine–tenths of the oil refining business in that state. In 1882 he formed a trust and a year later centralized control of between two–thirds and three–fourths of the national oil business in Standard Oil of New Jersey. Standard Oil controlled the oil industry through their monopolistic control over transportation, a control they couldn't have obtained without the aid of Jacob Schiff.[49]

In 1891 William Rockefeller, brother and partner of John D. Rockefeller in his oil company, bought into National City Bank which, thereafter, became the principle bank for the Standard Oil account. It was derived from the First US Bank and about a century later became the largest single owner of stock in the Federal Reserve.[50] In 1955, they merged with JP Morgan's First National Bank. Together they owned about a quarter of the shares of the Federal Reserve. According to Mullins 1993, since that date, they have been its controlling block. Spanish American War, in 1898, was sponsored almost entirely by $200 million in bonds offered by National City Bank.[51] The press called that war "National City Bank's War."

Carnegie:[52] Andrew Carnegie was born on November 25, 1835 in Dunfermline, Scotland.[53] However, economic times became progressively

---

[47] Hewitt and Tuttle

[48] Maurice B. Clark

[49] He represented Kuhn–Loeb Company, who financed most of E H Harriman's Rail Empire (Union Pacific), with backing from the House of Rothschild. His largest railway purchases occurred during the economic panic of 1857. Harriman's attempted hostile takeover of Morgan's Northern Pacific caused the economic panic of 1901. (see Mullins 1993).

[50] Specifically, National City Bank had been founded, in 1812, in the same rooms that the First US Bank had occupied until its charter had expired. The owners and directors of National City Bank were mostly the same as of The Bank of the United States. When the Federal Reserve was formed, John D. and William Rockefeller and James Stillman, an inlaw of theirs, formed its National Bank of New York group. They owned the largest single block of stock in the Federal Reserve.

[51] These were sponsored by Frank Vanderlip, President McKinley's assistant secretary of the Treasury (1897–1901). He later became the president of that Bank (1909–1919).

[52] The following account is drawn from Joseph F. Wall's (1970) and John S. Bowman's (1989) biographies of Andrew Carnegie.

[53] He was the first son of William Carnegie and Margaret Morrison Carnegie.

harder for them. Consequently, in 1848 they emigrated to Pennsylvania, near Pittsburgh. There Andrew's father and he worked in a weaving mill while his mother worked for a cobbler. Andrew moved on to work in a bobbin factory, a telegraph company, and then for the Pennsylvania Railroad. He worked as an assistant to a manager, Thomas A. Scott. In 1859 when Mr. Scott was promoted to Vice President of the Railroad, Andrew Carnegie was appointed the Superintendent of the Western Division.

At that time, he made some successful investments, including buying a farm in an oil producing region of Pennsylvania. During the Civil War, which began 1861, he had responsibility for the telegraph and railroad operations in the Washington DC region.

In 1866, he traveled to London where he obtained financial backing from Junius Morgan. With this behind him, his businesses and personal wealth expanded meteorically. He invested in several new inventions. One was iron railroad bridges another was the sleeping car, originally invented by Theodore Woodruff. These ideas were great successes.

In 1868, he amalgamated his sleeping car company with the Pullman Company, and provided sleeping cars for the Union Pacific Railroad; in 1870, he focused his attention on the Iron and Steel Industry; and, by 1873, he was constructing the most modern steel industry of the day, based on the Bessemer process. He profited by the financial crashes of 1873 and 1893. By 1890, Carnegie's company was the dominant steel producer in America. In January 1900, he sold the business to J.P. Morgan for $480 million. This was the origin of US Steel.[54]

Weyerhaeuser: Frederick Weyerhaeuser emigrated to the United States from Germany and settled in Rock Island Illinois, in 1856. He was then a teenager and is said not to have had any notable personal wealth. He worked at a saw mill for one year. But, the next year he profited from the

---

They lived in a single room above the workroom where his father made his living operating a handloom to make damask linen tablecloths and napkins. His grandfathers had also been of humble station; one was a weaver, the other a shoemaker. Although this family had only modest means, they were far from ignorant. They were well-versed in the political and religious issues of the day. One of his grandfathers had even been a lecturer and writer during his spare time.

Andrew's father was a Swedenborgian. That was a nineteenth century religious sect which believed in direct communication between this world and God and incorporated Northern mysticism. Cagliostro met with them during the French Revolution. He claimed to have a deeper understanding of their doctrines than they had themselves (Webster 1921). That may have been the truth, as he had been trained by masters of Freemasonry, Cabalistic magic, and Gnosticism, whereas the Swedenborgian's beliefs were probably assembled out of partially understood bits and pieces borrowed from various religions.

Andrew's mother was a Unitarian. It was during this era that American Unitarianism was influenced by Ralph W. Emerson towards German idealism.

[54] Carnegie's share of the transaction was $226 million, which left his personal fortune at around $300 million, making him, then, the wealthiest man in America. The interest on this fortune was more than he could spend, and he established a trust to dispose of the surplus through "philanthropic" gifts.

economic panic of 1857 and became the owner of a saw mill. He developed that into a thriving business.[55] As the West was settled, the numerous Weyerhaeusers, their inlaws, and their lumber businesses spread with it. His eldest son, John Phillip Weyerhaeuser took over the original saw mill. It was his children who eventually ran their operation in Washington State.

Transportation was an important issue for Weyerhaeuser Co. because it was necessary to get their products to the eastern markets. The movement of Weyerhaeuser Company to Washington State was contemporary with the planning of the Panama Canal. In 1899, Weyerhaeuser purchased 900,000 acres of railroad grant land in Washington State from Northern Pacific Railroad for $6.5 million.[56] They subsequently expanded by buying more land in Washington State.[57] Apparently, a large part of that land was originally homesteads.[58]

Weyerhaeuser Company bought out independent saw mills during the Great Depression, and profited from both World Wars. After the Second World War, they began diversifying. By 1957, Weyerhauser was ranked among the top 100 companies worldwide in number of employees, sales, and assets. By 1973, it was the largest private owner of timberland both worldwide and in Washington State and it was second in sales among timber companies.[59] They remain closely connected to world banking.

---

[55] He married Sarah Elizabeth Bloedel, they had seven children. He died in 1914 having accumulated a fortune valued at $30 million.

[56] At that time the railroad was jointly operated by James Hill and J.P. Morgan. When James Hill died in 1917, Frederick Weyerhaeuser took his place on the board of Great Northern Railroad.

[57] By 1905 the company owned 1.5 million acres valued at $9.5 million and by 1916 it owned 2,013,404 acres valued at $28.9 million (See Multinational Corporations Group, 1975.)

[58] Several local publications on Washington history relate how a citizen would claim acreage under the land donation act and then immediately transfer it to Weyerhaeuser Company Agents in exchange for a small cash payment. There, apparently, was also some pressure on homesteaders to sell out.

[59] International Paper sold $2.31 billion, whereas Weyerhaeuser sold $2.30 billion.

Chapter 9

Post–Hegelian Period

The post–Hegelian period lasted from roughly 1830 to 1870. In America it was expressed as the anti–Masonic movement and Jacksonian democracy; in England, it was their Age of Reform; while in France, it was their July Monarchy.

The leading economist of that period was John Stuart Mill and there were a variety of post–Hegelian religions. Most people would regard these as strange, but, they contributed several important concepts which influence public policy today.

9.1 Anti–Masonic Movement

Both Presidents Washington and Adams knew that the Illuminated Freemasons were the source of the problems in France.[1] Although President Washington was a Freemason, he came out at the head of a force of 13,000 troops to overwhelm the Whiskey Rebellion, in 1795, which he believed to have been instigated by the Illuminated Freemasons. Furthermore, fully understanding the difference between a republic and a democracy, he expressed the view that the young democratic societies should be exterminated.[2]

In 1798, President Adams, passed the Alien and Sedition Acts specifically to combat the Masonic threat. But as the Illuminati/Masonic conspiracy in New England never developed into anything serious, the Alien

---

[1] For example, President Washington wrote in 1798 (from a letter to Rev. G.W. Snyder quoted from Still 1993) "It was not my intention to doubt that, the Doctrines of the Illuminati, and the principles of Jacobinism had not spread to the United States. On the contrary, no one is more truly satisfied of this fact than I am. The idea that I meant to convey, was, that I did not believe that the Lodges of Freemasons in this Country had, as Societies, endeavored to propagate the diabolical tenants of the first, or pernicious principles of the latter."

[2] See Beard and Beard 1944, page 168.

and Sedition Act was soon repealed and the Freemasons of New England regained much of their good reputation.

The greatest blow to American Freemasonry came in 1826, with the publication of Captain William Morgan's book revealing the inner secrets of the craft. That same year he was murdered by three Freemasons for revealing those secrets. They would have murdered his publisher too, but he escaped during the hot pursuit of the kidnappers and their captives by a group of outraged citizens. The story received national news coverage. This all but ended Freemasonry in America. — In 1826 there were reputed to have been approximately 50,000 American Freemasons, but by 1830 there were only about 5,000. Their membership did not recover until after they were reformed, during the 1870's.

Anti–Masonic laws were passed at the State level[3] and an Anti–Masonic Political Party was formed on the national level.[4]

President Andrew Jackson got elected, in 1829, by riding the crest of the anti–Masonic movement. His inauguration party was the victory celebration of the common man over the elite; his supporters even stood, in their muddy boots, on the fine couches and chairs of the White House. During his term in office, power was shifted to the majority: restrictions on suffrage were removed, property qualifications for office were abolished, terms of office were limited, and the number of appointed offices were drastically reduced.

The end of Jackson's second term in office, marks when the financial Powers first tried to control the opinion the a nation, through the manipulation of credit. The particular issue in dispute was the Second US Bank. That was a national bank, like the Federal Reserve. President Jackson was opposed to it and had vetoed the renewal of its charter, in 1832. He then transferred the US funds to State banks. This provided local financing and resulted in a period of vibrant economic growth, from 1833–1836.

According to a banker, Henry Clews, writing in 1888, in response to the closing of the Second Bank, the House of Rothschild engineered the panic of 1837.[5] That panic coincided with the presidential election. The establishment of a Third US Bank was one of the leading campaign issues. It was supported by the Whigs and opposed by the Republicans. The

---

[3] For a few examples, in 1829, the New York State Legislature launched an investigation of Freemasonry; Vermont and New Hampshire passed laws banning many of the Masonic Oaths; and, in 1834, the Massachusetts legislature also called for an investigation.

[4] As a young man, Millard Fillmore, who was later the thirteenth President, joined that party in 1828 (Still 1990). That party, innovated the use of a national convention for nominating candidates.

[5] Specifically, the Bank of England, which was then synonymous with the Baron Nathan Mayer Rothschild, refused to accept or discount any bonds or securities based in the United States. This caused a temporary stoppage in the issuance of any further stocks or bonds within the US and, hence, caused an abrupt contraction of credit. The result was the financial panic of 1837 with the ruin of many US businesses and individuals (Mullins 1993).

Republicans won, so a Third US Bank was not formed until the Federal Reserve System was established in the twentieth century.

Although the Jacksonian period represented a victory for the common citizen, According to Alexis de Toqueville, in his famous book, *Democracy in America*,[6] during this first bloom of democratic government, once popular opinion was established minority opinions were no longer tolerated. On this issue he concluded, "I know no country in which there is so little independence of mind and real freedom of discussion as in America."

Deism was one of the victims of this intolerance.[7] It had been prominent throughout much of the enlightenment period and was followed by many of the leading scientists and philosophers. However, it was a superficial doctrine which may have served more to satisfy the public so that these scientists and philosophers could continue their work unmolested.

Its doctrine was that God made the world but, thereafter, retired to the status of God–emeritus, and let his creation run itself according to the laws of nature. However, the public associated it with Illuminism and the French Enlightenment. — It seems that Adam Weishaupt, Voltaire, and several others of that circle had been Dieists. Among the American founding fathers so, also, were Thomas Jefferson and Tom Paine.

The Jacksonian period and the remainder of the nineteenth century was a time of evangelical gospel preaching. Karl Marx recognized that this led the people away from enlightenment towards faith and spirituality. In particular, in his early writings prior to 1848, he wrote that this had effectively Judaized American Christianity.

The Unitarians were another group who changed during this period. They trace their origins to the Arian heresy of the late Roman period. The Arians held that Jesus was a prophet during his lifetime whereas the Roman Church believed he was always divine. Emperor Constantine tried unsuccessfully to resolve the conflict between these two sects. It was finally settled, in 325, by the Council of Nicea. They ruled in favor of the Roman Church and the Arian beliefs were suppressed.

That led to the development of the doctrine of the Holy Trinity of Father, Son, and Holy Ghost as the three faces of one God. This encapsulates the Christian concept of God as viewed by each of the three stages of individuation.[8] The idea is attributed to Athanasius (died 373), who was at the Council of Nicea. It was officially recognized by the Council of Constantinople in 381. The current form of the "Nicean Creed" is, however, of more recent origin, representing the gradual theological developments of the early Middle Ages.

---

[6]He was a young French nobleman, but saw that the French monarchy was crumbling and popular government would soon replace it. He, therefore, came to America ostensibly to study our prison system, but actually to see how popular government functioned in practice. It is an insightful book which remains surprisingly relevant, today.

[7]See Larrabee, 1944.

[8]Admittedly, If you ask ten Americans today what the meaning of the Trinity may be, you may well get nine different answers.

An anti–Trinitarian heresy was begun by a Spaniard, Michael Servetus, during the sixteenth century. In his book, *On the Errors of the Trinity*, he asserted his belief in monotheism and stated that the Trinity was not mentioned anywhere in the *Bible*, but was solely a product of the Roman Church. — What he said is literally true, as it was never mentioned by name. But, the concept clearly has Biblical support: This can be seen in the repeated references to the Father for the infant, the Son for the child, and the Spirit for the adult.

Michael Servetus evaded the Inquisition and fled from Spain only to be captured, tried, and burnt at the stake, in 1553, in Geneva, under the authority of John Calvin, with his knowledge and consent. However, his beliefs took root in Poland and by the eighteenth century had spread to England and Colonial America, That was the origin of the Unitarians.

During the anti–Masonic era, the Unitarian beliefs changed, largely due to the influence of Ralph Waldo Emerson. Then, they adopted transcendental and German idealist doctrines.[9] They have maintained a liberal orientation, ever since.

Mormons: The Church of the Latter Day Saints, that is, the Mormons, were another product of the Anti–Masonic era.[10] Joseph Smith jr., the founder of the Mormon religion and co–author of the *Book of Mormon* was a Freemason and he borrowed some things from Freemasonry when he created the Mormon faith. Like Freemasonry, a new initiate passes through several levels as his or her faith develops. At each stage, there is an initiation ceremony where the individual forms a personal covenant to live according to the teachings of Jesus.

They have more of those than other denominations, because their *Book of Mormon* contains His teachings in the New World, where they believe He had a ministry following His death in Palestine.

Joseph Smith was born in Sharnon, Vermont on December 23, 1805. While he was a boy, his family moved to New York State. He was literate but not much more than that. He had a third–grade education and spent most of his youth in heavy manual labor. As a fourteen year–old lad, he had his first religious experience. He said that Jesus Christ appeared to him and gave him specific information. However, his best known religious experience is supposed to have occurred on his birthday, in 1823. He said that the Angel Moroni appeared to him and revealed the location of some golden plates which were inscribed with a religious history and also a miraculous searstone with which he could decipher them. This resulted in the *Book of Mormon*, which was written by him and his brother. It was printed in 1829–30, just three years after Captain Morgan's murder. The *Book of Mormon* was a remarkable achievement for a person of Joseph Smith's background, but the great masters of Victorian literature made

---

[9]see *The American Historical Dictionary*, James T. Adams (ed.)] Charles Scribners and Sons, NY 345 p.

[10] As their origin is post–Reformation, they do not regard themselves as Protestant, but as "Christian."

light of his writing style.[11]

Their religion appears to be Christianity interpreted primarily in the light of the *Old Testament* and Christ's early ministry. They believe in a living God, who periodically communicates to the leaders of the faith.[12] The heads of the faith followed suit by running an absolute theocracy whenever they had the opportunity. Their intention is to recreate the system of government described in the *Old Testament*.[13] — An individual who believes in a "living God" might well support such a form of government. In that context, it makes sense.

Briefly, the history of the Mormons is that a number of people were converted to Mormonism; they were run out of various communities; Joseph Smith and his brother were shot by a mob in Carthage, Illinois, in 1844; and the Mormons eventually migrated to Utah where, for a short time, they operated an absolute theocracy. But, their subjects didn't like it any better than any other Western person ever has. Most of the abuses which arose involved property and business, but the best publicized were their use of terrorism to maintain the influence of their church and their occasional habit of stealing women from passing wagon trains to support their practice of polygamy. To suppress these activities, according to Rudyard Kipling, who visited Salt Lake City during the late 1800's, the US military stationed an artillery base on the heights overlooking Salt Lake City. However it was not too long before Utah was absorbed into the United States.

Although their early history is colorful, with time they learned moder-

---

[11] For example, in *From Sea to Sea* (1889) Rudyard Kipling says the following about the *Book of Mormon*:

> Very sincerely did I sympathize with the inspired brothers as I waded through their joint production. As a humble fellow–worker in the field of fiction, I know what it is to get good names for ones characters. But Joseph and Hirum were harder beset than I ever had been; and bolder men too boot. They created Teancum and Coriantumy, Pahoran, Kiskumen, and Gadianton, and other priceless names the memory doesn't hold; but of geography they wisely steered clear, and were astutely vague as to the locality of places, because you see they were by no means certain what lay in the next county to their own. They marched and counter–marched blood thirsty armies across their pages; and added new and amazing chapters to the records of the New Testament, and reorganized the heavens and the earth as it is always lawful to do in print. But they could not achieve style, and it was foolish of them to let into their weird mosaic pieces of the genuine Bible whenever the laboring pen dropped from its toilsome parody of a sentence or two of vile, bad English of downright penny dreadfulism. "And Moses said unto the people of Israel: 'Great Scott. What are you doing?' " There is no sentence in the Book of Mormon word for word like the foregoing; but the general tone is not widely different.

[12] That is the ninth item in their Articles of Faith.
[13] That is the sixth item of their Articles of Faith.

ation and settled down to being a Fundamentalist Christian religion.[14] In that regard, they appear to fulfill the religious needs of their congregation and, their method of initiation seems to be more effective in gaining the adhesion of their congregation to their beliefs than is found in most other denominations.

9.2   England's Age of Reform

Events similar to the Jacksonian Revolution also occurred in England. — Following the Battle of Waterloo, there were formidable riots due to the dissatisfaction of the poorer classes. England was then the greatest world Power, but the common Englishman was poorly fed, poorly clothed, poorly housed, and not represented in Parliament. These riots were mostly over parliamentary reform and oppressive laws, such as the corn laws.[15] As a result, the party in power made a few adjustments to reduce the hardships, but they stalwartly refused to make any fundamental changes.[16]

By 1830, the (conservative) Tory government, had been in power continuously for over half–a–century.[17] They represented the elite money interest. However, the death of King George IV required a general election, and they were replaced by the (liberal) Whigs. An age of reform followed (1830–1885). In 1831, suffrage was enlarged; in 1833, both slavery and the British East Indian Company[18] were abolished; and, in 1867, suffrage was once again enlarged, this time in a far more sweeping manner. From 1868 until 1885, the Prime Minister's seat alternated between two good men, (liberal) William Gladstone and (conservative) Benjamin Disraeli. They rolled back the policies of the money interest and restored morality and virtue as the guiding principles of government.

---

[14] They believe that all the *Bible* and *Book of Mormon* are the word of God, so far as they are correctly translated. That is the eighth item of their Articles of Faith.

Some people who claim to be familiar with their beliefs say that their higher levels follow a doctrine which is quite different than the Fundamentalist Christian image they present outwardly to the world. They describe it as the cabalistic system where at the seventh level, men are Gods. — But, that could be desecration, which is something the Mormons are vulnerable to as they conceal their alters. — Judged on the whole, from the outside, their behavior appears more Christian than some mainstream denominations.

It should also be noted that there are many splinter groups off the Mormons.

[15] These laws prohibited the importation of grain, to protect the domestic farmers. Importation was only allowed once famine prices were reached. This was not popular with the, all too often, literally hungry public. Another problem was that the change from a war economy resulted in widespread unemployment.

[16] They were an elite–driven society operating under the economic theories of Richardo.

[17] That is since 1770 except for one brief interval.

[18] That is the East India Company was abolished as a crown company. It continued to operate as a business.

The money interest was also expelled from power in France, by the July Monarchy (1830–1848). Thus, the viewpoints of the Hegelian era were resoundingly rejected in France, England, and America around 1830. Hegel died the next year. But, it was not long before new philosophies stepped into the gap.

9.3 Post–Hegelian Economics

John Stuart Mill (1806–1873) was the leading economist of the Post–Hegelian era.[19] He had been born into that literary circle which then included Thomas Carlyle, Johann Goethe, David Ricardo, his father, that is James Mill, and others. His father had provided him with an excellent and rigorous education, and, at the age of seventeen, he joined him at the East India Company, as a junior clerk. By the time he retired in 1858, he had risen to the post of Chief Examiner.

However, his father's autocratic ways had instilled in him a regard for freedom. He objected both to traditional Western values and to liberal orthodoxy.[20] Thus, he was reacting to the forces of the preceding

---

[19] His most important work was probably his 1848 *Principles of Political Economy* and his best known is probably his, 1859, essay *On Liberty*

[20] Quoted from his 1859 *On Liberty*:

> Reflecting persons perceived that when society is itself the tyrant
> — society collectively over the separate individuals who compose it
> — its means of tyrannizing are not restricted to the acts which it
> may do by the hands of its political functionaries. Society can and
> does execute its own mandates; and if it issues wrong mandates in-
> stead of right, or any mandates at all in things with which it ought
> not to meddle, it practices a social tyranny more formidable than
> many kinds of political oppression, since, though not usually upheld
> by such extreme penalties, it leaves fewer means of escape, pene-
> trating much more deeply into the details of life, and enslaving the
> soul itself. Protection, therefore, against the tyranny of the magis-
> trate is not enough: there needs protection against the tyranny of
> the prevailing opinion and feeling; against the tendency of society
> to impose, by other means than civil penalties, its own ideas and
> practices as rules of conduct on those who dissent from them; to
> fetter the development, and, if possible, prevent the formation, of
> any individuality not in harmony with its ways, and compels all
> characters to fashion themselves upon the model of its own. There
> is a limit to the legitimate interference of collective opinion with
> individual independence; and to find that limit, and maintain it
> against encroachment, is as indispensable to a good condition of
> human affairs, as protection against political despotism."

According to Hayek, in 1944, he drew his inspiration from Johann Goethe and William von Humboldt. Also, he says that Lord Morley "in his *Recollections* speaks of the "acknowledged point" that the main argument of the essay *On Liberty* "was not original but came from Germany." — Mill's rather moderate liberality may have reflected the actual position of the German leaders. In particular, both Frederick William II and Bismark were known to have been fairly

generation. He formed a synthesis which reflected the post–Hegelian era.

Although he is known as a champion of personal liberty, he was also the head accountant for the worldwide opium trade. This seeming dichotomy appears to have followed the intellectual tradition of Malthus, who, in fact, taught for many years at the college run by the British East India Company. Specifically, Mill's activities advanced good for the fitter classes, while subjecting the less fortunate to evil. Thus, he was promoting a process of social evolution. But, the East India Company had difficulty promoting opium use in England. — The working classes would have none of it. — So, Mill provided an alternative economic plan which was less evil but, also, allowed less personal freedom.

He followed Ricardo quite closely on economics, but he departed from him on three important details:

1. Instead of considering the early period of capitalism, with its rapid growth but limited capital; he considered a mature economy.

2. He criticized Ricardo's work for being based on equilibrium conditions, whereas, real–world economics were dynamic, naturally oscillatory and, also are constantly changing due to innovations. That meant that the working class was not necessarily trapped in poverty by their reproductive rate. He recommended that by practicing restraint they could retain some personal savings. That would allow them to rise above the conditions of squalor and obtain a measure of freedom.

3. He observed that although the costs of production are determined by the rules of nature and economics, once wealth is produced it can be distributed however the parties might prefer: that is, there is a Natural Law of production but not of distribution. Thus, he questioned the principle of private ownership, in particular, the workman's ownership of his own labor which he either may or may not choose to sell to a capitalist. This concept of ownership is a fundamental principle from the English Constitution, which Ricardo had not questioned, but which socialists of Mill's time, such as Karl Marx, did.[21]

He was acknowledged to be the great economist of the Victorian era. He is often said to have passed on the torch to Alfred Marshall (1842–1924), who founded the economics program at Cambridge, in 1903. But, that leaves a quarter–century gap, which people try to ignore. During those years, a significant segment of the liberal establishment was guided by the economic theories of Karl Marx. He was an economist of the first rank, although he was not from the same line of intellectual descent. More will be said about his ideas, later on.

Alfred Marshall advanced the discipline from the stage of political economy, based on religious and philosophical principles, to a science, based on

moderate. Their support for radicals such as Hegel and Marx may have served to oppose conservatism and move society towards a middle ground.

[21] His work was published the year after the *The Communist Manifesto.*

social psychology. His "monitarist" theory of economics, generally moved back from the position of Mill towards that of Richardo, but he did not view people as being driven entirely by economics. He held that they were also motivated by social approbation, a desire for distinction, and a need to provide skillful behavior and creativity. Thus, he had a more human viewpoint: He treated men as men, rather than as animals.

His connection to the liberal establishment can be seen in his having been the staff economist for the Royal Colonial Society, which was in the Rothschilds' sphere of influence. In addition, he spent many of his summer vacations in Austria where he did much of his writing on economics. There he associated with the Rothschilds' Viennese School of Economics. — They became a center for monitarist theory, based partly on his ideas.

The two most important figures among Marshall's students were Arthur C. Piegou (1877–1959), who founded welfare economics, and John. M. Keynes (1883–1946), who founded macro economics. Shortly after Marshall's death, the torch was passed to John Keynes. Less than a decade later, his theories would be used by President F.D. Roosevelt to relieve the Great Depression and they were, later, revived by President Reagan, during the 1980's.

Thus, Smith–Ricardo–Mill–Marx–Marshall–Keynes was the line of leading establishment economists. They were the individuals who guided public policy on economics throughout the entire nineteenth and most of the twentieth centuries.

9.4   Post–Hegelian Religions

Existentialism was the most important Christian movement of those times. Its revolves about metaphysics, the study of being: that is the study of existence or the continuous self–propagating process of becoming. These issues date back to Aristotle and Zoroaster.

Aristotle had been impartial on them and had only drawn those conclusions about the nature of God which he could deduce from observing the physical world. He and Cicero had regarded God as the unknowable essential entity behind His outward signs. Those are truth and order. God's sole function in their scheme was to maintain them. But, if their existence was self–propagating, the existence or non–existence of this hidden essential God becomes irrelevant. He could, at any time, be equivalently replaced by His sole function, the Divine Act of Being.[22]

Deposing, thus, of the essential God and adopting a purely Existential viewpoint represents a theological shift to an abstract God. That would have made Aristotle's theology very close to ancient Zoroasterism, in which God is Truth and Being. Alfred North Whitehead (1861–1947) recognized

---

[22] In a sense, being is the same as truth. — Consider the definition of truth: it is that which is a force in nature; or, more simply, it is that which is; alternatively, it is that which is continuously becoming.

the irrelevance of the essential God to Aristotle's scheme and suggested that his inclusion of Him, at all, may have been motivated by a desire to avoid the fate of Socrates.

Thomas Aquinas also retained the anthropomorphic and essential God of Judeo–Christian tradition as well as the abstract God. Of course, that was perfectly defensible in the Christian tradition, for it allowed Christianity to meet the needs of those large segments of the population who can not relate to abstract concepts: that is, the faithful, the children of God who are not yet ready to receive the Spirit. When they are ready and discover the grain among the chaff, they take it for their own, as their own discovery, although it was put there to be found. Yet, the difference between discovery and having the Law imposed upon them, is all the difference between a positive and a negative process, and leads to positive and negative outcomes accordingly. So, obviously, the essential God had to be retained in Christianity, or it would not have been that staged progression of personal development which *is* Christianity.

Similarly, James Collins pointed out, in 1959, that Spinoza, Leibnitz, Descartes, and other rationalist theologians from the English enlightenment period had identified the "theory of a true idea as expressing the real structure and dynamic thrust of the divine essence." But, they maintained that the proof of God's existence progresses from the "known real essence of God to the necessarily entailed real truth of His existence." Thus, they recognized the knowable existence of the existential God, and tried to provide a rational justification for the old Judeo–Christian concept of an essential and/or anthropomorphic God. But, without much success.

That is how things stood until Immanual Kant implemented Moses Mendelssohn's scheme to reverse the relative positions of Christianity and Judaism. He attacked the essential God. That was a weak point in Christian theology. — It was not there for those at the rational stage of development and could not withstand close examination.

Kant mostly left the existential portions of Christian theology alone. Later, Schelling would criticize that as not being emotionally fulfilling. He introduced Spirituality, Pantheism and Naturalism in fill the gap. Thus, one arrives at Judaism or something much like it. — That was the intention.

Hegel's synthesis of Kant and Schelling was a religion of pure Spirit based on a Spirituality of the collective unconscious.

It was at that point that Existentialism came upon the scene. Their task was the reconstruction of religion from the remains of Christian theology. The Existentialists followed a wide variety of approaches which ranged from Atheism to Christian Existentialism.

Soren Kierkegaard (1813–1855), a Danish philosopher, was the leading figure among the Christian Existentialists. He was younger than Hegel, but contemporary with him and, like him, had attended Schelling's lectures. Later he would be followed by the American psychologist William James (1842–1910), who would bring existentialism into the twentieth century, where it became incorporated into progressive education.

The Christian Existentialists accepted the existence of physical things and they restored the Christian myths and the essential God through acts of faith.[23] They grounded their religion on faith as a defense against rationalism, which they felt had allowed the German philosophers to destroy Christianity. — Soren Kierkegaard never criticized Natural Theology, he just despaired of being able to get the populace to follow the Christian path to it, in the face of Kant's criticism.

Kierkegaard held that truth can only be communicated indirectly as true understanding only arises from experience. Due to this belief, the Existentialists found it inconsistent to present any cohesive philosophy, or to directly state anything of importance.[24]

He also put forward the idea that all significant truths are subjective: that is, those which most impinge upon man are socially determined. Therefore, they can not be stated explicitly, even if one wanted to, because they are not always the same. Also, forcing the reader to infer everything of importance from vague statements provided an effective defense against the occupation and desecration of alters, because no one could be entirely certain of exactly what they were.

Thus, Kierkegaard was reconstructing Christianity, using a variation on the theme of Jesus's explanation of why one should teach through parables, as given in *Matthew* 13.1–53. — He did not deviate from the Christian path nor change the outcome, but he provided a new pre-rational stepping stone and camouflage for the final state, whatever that might be.

John S. Mill also made a contribution to religious thought. — His father had been a vehement Atheist, and consequently he had been raised completely without religion. However, he felt that God had been deposed without due cause. So, he restored Him.

He saw a danger to personal freedom both in the omnipotent Christian God and in Hegel's in Absolute Spirit. So, the God he installed had only limited powers. He felt that this would defend the individual against all-powerful deities.[25]

---

[23] William James supported belief through faith and followed it himself, but Soren Kierkegaard felt that the freedom obtained by remaining in reality was better, although some people, needed to accept myths on faith.

[24] This defined a new literary style and led to some excellent creative works, such as Albert Camus' *The Stranger*. But, it didn't improve the clarity of Soren Kierkegaard's technical writing on philosophy nor William James' on psychology.

[25] Notice that this is similar to "freedom" in the sense of Rousseau. It contrasts against "freedom" in the Western sense, which is obtained through recognition of Natural Law: that is of universal and invariant Truth.

William James[26] was strongly influenced by John S. Mill.[27] Consequently, he adopted a finite God who had only limited powers. Like Mill, he hoped to assert individual freedom by denying the power and scope of any given truth or law of nature.

His achieved this by adopting pluralism: that is the belief that there were many different essential realities, some dependent on each other, but others partially or wholly independent. Truth differed among them: In particular it differed among individuals. Thus, under his system there could be no single overweening Spirit of the People nor any omnipotent God.

In the long–run, the importance of the Existentialists was that they contributed the concepts of pluralism, socially determined truth, and education by experience. These were passed by William James to John Dewey who incorporated them into progressive education. They remain part of of political programs and education policies today.

Contemporary with the development of Existentialism, Auguste Comte and Ludwig Freuerbach laid out the premises of Atheistic Humanism.

Auguste Comte (1798–1857) called his version of Humanistic Atheism, "Positivism." Its central concept is the idea of progressive change: that is, the directed evolution of a people's beliefs much as Hegel envisioned.[28] As a young man, John S. Mill had admired his scheme, but, by 1859, he recognized that his "social system, as unfolded in his *Systeme de Politique Positive*, aims at establishing (though by moral more than by legal appliances) a despotism of society over the individual, surpassing anything contemplated in the political ideal of the most rigid disciplinarian among the ancient philosophers."

Comte's philosophical contribution was also somewhat erratic. — The death of his sweetheart, after he had only known her for a single year, had

---

[26] William James was an interesting character. His father had been a wealthy eccentric who believed in a mixture of Swedenborgianism and Transcendentalism — a living transcendental God, who could be approached through Nordic mysticism, and who had created the Universe through the Truth of His thought. This filled his young son, William, with a fear that God might, as the result of an irrational thought, destroy all creation.

His father provided William and his brother with an education consisting of travel interrupted by short stays in many private schools, both in the United States and abroad, and exposure to the many accomplished men who were his father's house guests. William finished his education by studying under the German professor of the psychology of societal change, William Wundt.

He became an influential psychiatrist and philosopher. But, the effects of this unusual mode of education can be seen in he works and viewpoint. — He reacted to it. He denied mysticism, determinism, transcendentalism, an infinite God, and even the existence of a unified organization in Nature.

[27] William James was in that same elite circle of people. Some of the letters between James and Mill still exist.

[28] The earliest record of progressivism was with the Pharisees. Consequently, it was part of the Jewish heritage, which had a strong influence on the French Enlightenment.

a strong impact upon him. After that, he developed his philosophy into a full religion with rites and practices resembling the Roman Church's, but without Christianity. He incorporated the memory of his sweetheart by making her a veritable saint. In 1881, the Positivist Church was officially established in Brazil with headquarters in Rio de Janeiro. It still functions today. The motto "Order and Progress," which appears on the Brazilian flag, was Comte's maxim.

Positivism was extended by a variety of other philosophers, including Herbert Spencer (1820–1903) and Bertrand Russell (1872–1970).[29] It was also applied by Harvard Law School Dean Christopher C. Langdell (1826–1906) to the law, producing the legal doctrine of "positivism" and "case law." These are of substantial significance and more will be said about them later on.

Ludwig Feuerbach (1804–1872)[30] felt that Hegel's contribution to religion was that he had humanized God, but by retaining Absolute Spirit, Hegel had failed to take the final logical step, of reducing everything superhuman to man.[31] Feuerbach held that the doctrine of God's existence is the product of man's psychological drives: that is, that man's perception of God or Absolute Spirit merely objectifies human aspirations, and that religion is the process of making divinity out of one's own essential being and then humbling one's self before it. For him, God was merely the symbolic expression of man's wishes, and man, himself, is the proper object for worship rather than an externalized God. He held that once man recognized the real significance of religion, he could dispense with God and devote himself to developing his own potentialities. He was trying to remove God and yet retain a religious attitude which would induce men to strive toward self–improvement and a just and moral life.

Karl Marx had been born in Treves, Prussia, the son of a relatively wealthy lawyer, descended from a long line of rabbis. He was well educated, accomplished, a poet, playwright, and philosopher. He attended the University of Berlin and received a degree in philosophy from Jena. He was considered to have been the brightest of the young left–wing Hegelians, but he was unable to find a teaching position because he was too radical.

His father had converted to Christianity, so Karl had originally been a Christian. But during his senior year in High School he became a Satanist.[32] However, this appears to have merely been a youthful stage.

---

[29] Charles Darwin's theory of evolution got appropriated by this philosophy. They have often been used it as a justification for their beliefs. However, biological evolution is not directed change. Mill's scheme of providing the forces of social evolution, was closer to the biological process.

[30] Freuerbach presented his ideas in four works published between 1839 and 1843.

[31] Quoted from his *Grundsatze der philosophy der Zukunft*: "If, therefore, the old [Hegelian] philosophy said:'only the rational is true and actual', then contrariwise the new philosophy says 'only the human is true and actual'. For only the human is rational; man the measure of reason ... The absolute to man is his own nature."

[32] This is sometimes attributed to the influence of Moses Hess, who Marx called

According to Friedrich Engles, Ludwig Freuerbach, provided Karl with the guidance he needed towards Naturalistic Humanism.[33]

He essentially adopted Feuerbach's theology. Both Feuerbach and Hegel were firmly grounded upon the Classical/Christian perspective. They had been concerned with morality, justice, in exactly the same sense as the Christian and Stoic theologians. Karl Marx, however, replaced that with the paradigm of capitalism.[34] — This should be recognized as being that new religion of reason based only on the iron law of economics, which Mendelssohn hinted at, Weishaupt and Knigge first designed, and which was celebrated in Notre Dame during the Revolution of 1789.

He held that religious spirit was nourished by the inhumane conditions of capitalistic society and that it was an expression of man's desire to find peace in a realm free from everyday miseries. Thus, he held that man engages in religious estrangement from reality and the worship of God as a protest against social tyranny. He felt that existence of religion called for the revolutionary transformation of society.[35]

Friedrich Nietzsche: (1844–1900): The trend towards Atheism and Nihilism, continued throughout the nineteenth century. This happened especially in Germany, where it reach a climax when Nietzsche proclaimed God's death in his 1883 book, *Thus Spake Zarathustra.*

He followed Hegel in considering the State as God.[36] But, there is a fundamental problem with that concept. — The State is an institution created by men to implement the social order implied by their dominant concepts of morality. And, morality consists of the individual's adherence to his or her personal Image of God and religion. So, the act of reversing the roles of man and the State as the source of morality, which is what is done when the State becomes God, is, therefore, necessarily hostile to the human conscience.[37]

In the case of imposing the God–State of German Absolutism on a population who follow enlightened Christianity, the beliefs which it would

---

a "communist Rabbi." He made significant contributions to atheistic humanism, contemporary with these others.

[33] See Engles 1888 book *Ludwig Freuerbach and the Outcomes of Classical German Philosophy.*

[34] Communism lies entirely within the Capitalistic paradigm as Smith and Ricardo enunciated it.

[35] "The abolition of religion, as the illusory happiness of men, is a demand for their real happiness. The call to abandon their illusions about their condition is a call to abandon a condition which requires illusions. ... The immediate task is to unmask human alienation in its secular form, now that it has been unmasked in its sacred form [by Freuerbach and Marx]. Thus, the criticism of heaven transforms itself into the criticism of earth, the criticism of religion into the criticism of law, and the criticism of theology into the criticism of politics." Quoted from Karl Marx's *Toward a critique of the Hegelian philosophy of right.*

[36] This view that God is dead and the State has taken his place, is also widely held among the Jewish community. In that case, God is the Jewish people as the Messiah or Israel as their State. See James Jaffe 1968.

[37] These ideas come from James Collins, 1959.

be necessary for the individual to lose are the core beliefs which define the Western or Christian moral system. They include the existence of Absolute Truth and the validity of reason and human understanding. In fact, that was specifically part of Nietzsche's scheme. He held that one can not speak about "the" truth, only about socially determined truths, and these are revisable and confined to human projects. Thus, the God–State was antithetical to all positive religion and the particular form which Nietzsche presented was antithetical to enlightened Christianity, in particular.

When we consider the large following these philosophies obtained in nineteenth century Germany, it should be remembered that they came from a different heritage than France, England, or America. In particular, Germany had been mostly Lutheran or Calvinist, which emphatically rejected Natural Theology, and after a progression of viewpoints had arrived at German Idealism. By the dawn of the twentieth century, they were, as a people, strongly opposed to individualism, personal freedom, democracy, and capitalism. Their lives, the structure of their government,[38] and even their social classes revolved about the individual's duty to the State. The individual existed only to serve the State. — They referred to this as the "heroic" viewpoint.

According to F.A. Hayek, in 1944, extreme collectivism, such as this, leads to a definite system of morals, although these are so different that he doubted whether they could be called "morals." — He observed that a collectivist system is driven by two central concerns, the need for a commonly accepted set of goals for the group and the desire to give to the group all possible power to achieve those ends. He felt that out of this there grew a system of collectivist ethics, which had no fixed rules except that the end justifies the means. He concluded that, "there is literally nothing which the consistent collectivist must not be prepared to do if it serves the 'good of the whole,' because the 'good of the whole' is to him the only criterion of what ought to be done."

9.5 Communism

Modern Communism, also, came to the fore during the Post–Hegelian era. It is the economic theory which goes with Naturalistic Humanism. Although its origins can be traced into antiquity,[39] it first became a modern reality with the commune of Paris, during the French Revolution of 1789.

---

[38] All public policy decisions were made by officials and all individuals were either employed by the State or their conditions of work and wage were set by the State.

[39] By the second century AD, a Jewish Gnostic community, the Carpocracians, had arrived at essentially the same social beliefs as the modern communists; during the middle ages many of the monastic societies held goods in common; and during the enlightenment period various Protestant groups experimented with socialism.

But, for many people, modern communism began, in 1844, when Friedrich Engels (1820–1895) visited England to study the social effects of industrialization. He wrote his findings in *The Condition of the Working Class in England.* — Slightly over one–fourth of that book consists of quotes from Thomas Carlyle especially from his *Chartism* (1839) and *Past and Present* (1843).[40]

Thomas Carlyle (1795–1881)[41] was possibly the most influential literary figure of that period[42] and he was in communication with most of the other liberal thinkers of his times. That included John Stuart Mill, Johann Goethe, Ralph Waldo Emerson, John Ruskin, and others.[43]

He watched Manchester industrialize and in *Past and Present* he expressed how it changed. It produced deplorable conditions, rancorous discontent among the working classes, and increasing disrespect for their temporal and spiritual superiors. — In this can be seen the unraveling of the very fabric of Western society, because it was the people's respect for the order of things which held it together on a daily basis.

Karl Marx (1818–1883) extended Engels' work, making the alienation of labor a cornerstone for their theory of communism. In 1847, he and Engels co–authored a short pamphlet entitled *The Communist Manifesto.* Its ten planks are:

1. Abolition of property in land;

2. A heavy progressive or graduated income tax;

3. Abolition of the right of inheritance;

4. Confiscation of property of all emigrants and rebels;

5. Centralization of credit in the hands of the state, by means of a national bank with State capitol and an exclusive monopoly;

6. Centralization of the means of communication and transportation in the hands of the state;

7. Extension of factories and instruments of production owned by the state, the bringing into cultivation of waste lands, and the improvement of the soil generally in accordance with a common plan;

8. Equal liability of all to labor. Establishment of industrial armies, especially for agriculture;

---

[40] Notice that all of their bemoaning of the poor conditions of the working man was written after the liberal establishment had been expelled from power, and the age of reform was well on its way towards resolving the problem.

[41] He had been raised in a subsistence economy in Northern Scotland; he was educated at the University of Edinburgh, showing marked skill in mathematics; and, as a young man, he had moved to London.

[42] He is often cited as one of the originators both of modern Communism and of National Socialism.

[43] His correspondence has mostly been preserved, collected, and published. It provides a window into the views of his times.

9. Combination of agricultural and manufacturing industries, and the gradual abolition of the distinction between town and county by a more equitable distribution of the population over the country;

10. Free education of all children in public schools. Abolition of children's factory labor in its present form. Combination of education with industrial production, etc., etc.

Eight of its planks dealt with controlling wealth, in the broad sense which includes not only money but also products, land, and labor. Their substance is an approach for tying the worker down to the real value of his or her labor. The other two planks dealt with controlling the constitution of the nation through control over education and communication.

The Communist Manifesto was a statement and justification for Babeuvism.[44] — Francis Noel Babeuf (1762–1797) had been the philosophical leader of the Paris commune after Baron Clootz was executed. His scheme for State Socialism was also followed during their second revolution, in 1848. It was in preparation for that event that Marx and Engles wrote their manifesto.

Marxist communism is an ultimate form of industrial capitalism where the State controls labor. Lenin wrote truthfully, in 1918, that their system was "State capitalism."[45]

Why, then, would it appeal to the alienated worker, if it is only a more extreme form of capitalism? The answer is that the worker was trapped by poverty and ignorance within the capitalistic paradigm and sees only the class–struggle. The old Natural Law and religious standards no longer held any meaning for him, and capitalism made sure that the worker had no opportunity but to accept the common lot. The genius of Karl Marx was that he deliberately wrote his philosophy from entirely within the confines of that narrow and blinkered sphere.

During the late 1800's, the most effective communist organization was the International Working Man's Association: that is, the First Internationale. Its first meeting was held in London during September 1864.[46] Marx was not the only intriguer who introduced himself into the Internationale. Soon it became a mixture of communists, socialists, Freemasons, Illuminists, and individuals from the various other secret societies.

Michel Bakunin (1814–1876), the anarchist, was originally among them. But, the anarchists split from the Marxists, left the Internationale, and formed the Jura Federation[47] and the Alliance Sociale Democratique.

---

[44] Nesta Webster (1921) says that "Babeuvisme and Bolshevism are identical," with the exception that the former was not internationalist.

[45] See Lenin (that is Vladimir Ilitch Oulianoff or Ulianov) 1918. "The Chief Task of Our Times." published by the Workers Socialist Federation. 12 p.

[46] It began to be organized around 1862 as a working man's association interested in improving their lot. However, people seeking violent revolution gradually infiltrated it. Karl Marx didn't immediately take a leading role but got appointed to the committee drawing up their rules and statues.

[47] The Jura Federation moved its offices to New York and then to Philadephia. It closed after only four years.

Bakunin wrote, in 1869, that, by then, the Internationale was effectively under the control of Prussia and their bankers.

It was partly responsible for inducing France to disarm, as a gesture of World Peace, only two years before she was involved in the disastrous Franco–Prussian War (1870–1875). These events benefited Prussia and were supported by them. In particular, Karl Marx wrote in a letter to Engels, dated August 3, 1870, that Bismarck had paid him 10,000 English Pounds to promote Prussian interests in that war.[48]

Following Napoleon III's capitulation to the Germans at Sedan, revolt broke out in Paris under the red flag of social revolution, during March 1871. However, unlike the earlier Paris communes, this time, the anarchists gained control. Their leader was Michel Bachunin who, by then, was an anti–Babeuvist and an anti–Marxist.

His system was based on the permanent abolition of the State and of all organized religions. He advocated the violent destruction of all civilization. But, after that was accomplished, society was to be reorganized along the lines set out by the Illuminati, as described by Baron Clootz. — Proudhon had followed that school of thought and Bachunin's ideas were derived from his. They were emphatically democratic, in contrast against Marxism which was based on dictatorship.

However, the Bachunin's commune failed to retain control of Paris because the National Guards expelled them. Consequently, the Third Republic of France (1870–1914) was established instead.

9.6   Italian Unification

When Adam Weishaupt died, in 1830, at the age of 82, the leadership of the Illuminati passed to the Italians: specifically to Guiseppe Mazzini. They worked to bring about the unification of Italy.

1849–1870 was the period of Italian unification. Up until that time, Italy had been broken into many small states. Some were under the control of foreign powers, most notably France and Austria. Italy was eventually united by the Italian patriot, General Guiseppe Garibaldi. He was not a member of these secret societies, but obtained some financial backing from them. The conflict was long and involved. The final victory came when France withdraw her troops in view of the Franco–Prussian War.

Throughout the first half of the nineteenth century, Germany, too, had been struggling towards unification. That also was culminated, in 1871, as a side–effect of the Franco–Prussian War. Thus, the results of that conflict were that Italy was united, Germany was united, and France became a republic. That finally achieved the ambitions of Frederick the Great almost a century after his death.

The Illuminated Freemasons ran the government of Italy for most of the remainder of that century. They formed the triple alliance with Austria

---

[48] See Nesta Webster, 1921

and Germany and built a large army and the world's third largest navy, all officered by Freemasons. But these armed forces were more luxurious than effective. — This was shown, in 1896, when Italy attempted to make Ethiopia a colonial possession. The Ethiopians slaughtered their Army. That disaster overturned the Italian government. Nor were Italy's statesmen, during that period, any better than their soldiers. — They refused to come to Austria's aid in a minor conflict in Eastern Europe, but did not fail to demand their share of the spoils; and later, in World War I, they would betray their allies in exchange for part of Dalmatia.

The cultural effects of their experiences in Africa provide a good introduction to Italian culture. — Unlike the British who wrote poems in praise of the natives when they chewed up their columns in the Sudan, the Italians responded in the spirit of vendetta. Even today, many an ethnic Italian will tell you that Ethiopians are the lowest form of human life and a peculiarly Italian insult is to speak of someone's Ethiopian grandmother. — The traditional Italian despises Ethiopians because he feels that their successful defense of their homeland affected the honor of his ancestors and by the customs of vendetta, the right to obtain revenge is hereditary. The insult of, having a Ethiopian grandmother, touches the traditional Italian because he knows that although he may not literally have a Ethiopian grandmother, some of his ancestors had similar origins.[49] Thus, gradually a hatred of Ethiopians grew among them until it became a national prejudice. — Italians are not a people of reason, they are a people of feelings and emotions.

Nor, strictly speaking are they a people, they are an aggregate of peoples who share a culture and a language. They traditionally identify with their extended family rather than with their nation. Likewise, traditional marriages occur primarily within those families. Thus, the family is their

---

[49] The Ethiopians are of mixed Negroid and Mediterranean stocks and so, also, is the modern Italian. Only the proportions differ. — Probably, only a small part of the ancestors of the modern Italian were Classical Romans. The indigenous Mediterranean people had been displaced only from the north of Italy by the early invasions of Nordic and round-headed peoples, or stayed where they were but became a subject race, and the same was, also, true for the invasions which happened after the Roman era. It, also, should be recalled that about 40% of the Roman population were slaves during their imperial period. In addition, the percentage of slaves was much higher in Southern Italy, which was mostly given over to large plantations. Many of the slaves came from the Middle East and North Africa, as that was where the bulk of the Roman Empire was located. Palestine and Carthage, in particular, had been seriously depopulated following their wars and revolts. Those captives became slaves. Consequently, the modern Italian has a substantial contribution from the Mediterranean race, particularly in the south. However, the woolly hair and full lips of the modern Italian attest to the fact that the Romans also had large numbers of black slaves. Those features are racial characteristics of the Negroid. In contrast, both the Mediterranean and European races are straight-haired and thin lipped. Of course, the Italians did have some Nordic and Alpine Round-headed ancestors, but, their contribution is substantial only in the north. The Italians recognize this in their saying that, "Africa starts south of Napoli."

basic social and genetic unit instead of a nationality or population. That is why races which invaded Italy more than a thousand years ago have not mixed uniformly throughout the peninsula.

The institution of the family also makes Italy much more heterogeneous than most other nations in terms of their customs and beliefs. Thus, although the Italian customs described here may be the dominant ones, there are also significant departures from them. In particular, Italy has one of the largest communist parties of any European country.

Italian families are often matriarchal and appear to have been so more–or–less continuously back into the neolithic period.

Matriarchal societies are characteristically violent and emotional. The best example may come from Western Samoa. They are matriarchal and are, also, one of the most violent of contemporary human societies. So much so, in fact, that their traffic code says that in the event of an accident, the first duty of every individual is to leave the scene. Otherwise, murders often occur, even over minor traffic incidents.

The root cause of the high level of violence in matriarchal societies is more than just thwarted male–dominance.[50]

Consider the psyche of a man when he is fighting. — The center of his existence shifts from the focused rational/analytical left–brain to a more diffuse consciousness which allows him to be simultaneously aware of all the events which are transpiring around him and his mental processes become more based on learned behavior, trained reflexes which allow the lightning–fast strike and parry which is so vitally important. There is, at the same time, a focus on motor skills and a corresponding physiological mechanism, implemented by stress, shunts blood to the major muscle groups. That, also, sharply reduces the blood supply to selected regions of the brain, leading to an altered state of consciousness in which pain can not be felt and some experience an intense desire to cause harm or pain and a pure joy of destruction. That is "berserkism."

The mental orientation which has just been described is much like the normal mental attitude of woman, except that they do not exhibit berserkism.[51] They also tend to be verbally–oriented rather than action–oriented. Otherwise, the mental processes which are characteristically woman, may correspond to the fighting–response in men.

One wonders if something similar to a mild form of berserkism can not, also, be found in the ordinary behavior of women. Indeed, based on stereotypes, some women seem to enjoy interfering with a man's work, or destroying the products of his labors, while others seem to derive almost a

---

[50] In the Arab and Persian cultures there is a widespread belief that thwarted male dominance is the root cause of homosexuality. That may come as a surprise to those Americans who regard Arab cultures as an extreme form of patriarchy. — Although Arab women traditionally are veiled, they rule the home. The men rule only in the outside world. Thus, most Arab cultures are matriarchal in their families, which is that part of life closest to the heart. They, also, have high rates of homosexuality.

[51] The female psyche is described later on in the section on typology.

sexual pleasure from being bad, and when a group of women or girls gather together, it is not long before they are squabbling over some nonsense or other. Thus, our cultural perception of woman hints at a mild form of this same behavior pattern.

A society, such as a matriarchal society, which forces men to adopt the female mental attitude and which also has a high level of stress, is likely to result in their exhibiting some of the characteristics of fighting or feminine behavior.

For example, Italian culture is matriarchal and operates at a high level of stress. Predictably, Italian men exhibit emotion, verbalization, social interaction, posturing, cruelty, and sometimes violence and reduced rationality. But, this is fully integrated into their social institutions. — When a group of Italian men sit down together, for example, after a day's work over a bottle of wine and some sausage. They do not talk congenially of things which interest them or of the events of the day. Their social interaction is characteristically confrontational, consisting largely of insults and attempts to cheat, provoke, or harm each other. In any other culture, this would lead to serious consequences, but to the Italian, screaming insults at each other may be an enjoyable social interaction. This is how they choose to spend their leisure time. And, as this is how men have acted under the Italian cultural institutions over the long–term, these behaviors have come to be what Italians regard as the model for masculinity.

But, the reverse process might, also, be functioning. — An individual who seriously contemplates or glorifies evil, meaning the joy of negativity and destruction, has assumed the mental attitude of the berserk, which is a right–brained orientation. If, in addition, this attitude is assumed in the context of contemplation or social interaction, rather than in overt action, the individual has assumed something relatively close to the feminine mental orientation. Therefore, other feminine feelings and behaviors might be exhibited, too.

Notice that these factors might also apply to the impact of mystical and contemplative religion or counter–cultural political thought. This provides a possible explanation for the fact, mentioned earlier, that these types of doctrines, in all ages, have been associated with high rates of homosexuality.

Predictably, some Italian men act like women: There has always been a high rate of homosexuality among them. But, the same can be said of virtually any group of Mediterraneans. With only a few exceptions, their traditions are derived from garden cultures and are wholly or partially matriarchal. This feminizing influence may contribute to their high rates of homosexuality.

But, the Mediterranean races are, also, more neotenous than the races of Northern Europe. And, as the more neotenous is usually the more egalitarian, and the indiscriminate bisexuality which was the common form of homosexuality during Classical times is markedly that way, too, these races may have a natural psychological predisposition towards that. Likewise, their neoteny might be expected to, also, give a tendency towards a more affective, verbal, and symbolic orientation: That is a child–like mind.

However, one should expect that peoples and cultures which have been subject to these influences over the long–term, might show some adaption to them, so that their men could better perform their normal social and biological functions under these conditions.

The Italian family also has another difference. — Whereas, infidelity is unacceptable in the Northern European cultural heritages and will usually terminate a relationship between a man and a woman, the English ridicule the French for their laxity in these matters and, the difference between them is equal to that between the French and the Italians: Italian husbands are notoriously unfaithful. They, also, characteristically are not the providers in the family. That role is usually filled by the sons, under the leadership of their mother. Thus, their family structure is completely different from that found in Northern European cultures and, so also, are their views on sex and marriage.

La Vecchia Religione[52] is natural to this type of culture.[53] As that is a negative or destructive religion, the Roman Church has a clear role in its suppression. But, their strict orthodoxy and doctrinal intolerance may often serve to bring out the shadow.

The Roman Church, also, suppresses the next transition in individuation. — To them, religion means spirituality and faith: particularly, faith. They grind that into the members of their congregations so hard that even highly educated Roman Catholics are singularly hard to convince that intellectual religion can even exist. Thus, the Roman Church can be seen as being completely compatible with traditional Italian cultural institutions.

The Mafia was one of the results of the instability and changes associated with the Napoleonic wars and the unification of Italy. Specifically,[54] in 1812, at the request of England, Ferdinand IV granted Sicily a Constitution. This released large numbers of armed retainers who had previously been in the service of the Sicilian feudal nobility. They soon formed into bands of brigands. Ferdinand was unable to suppress them, so he organized them into a rural militia. It was not long before they had established a reign of terror. They subsequently spread throughout Sicily and Italy.[55]

---

[52] That is the Italian name for Satanism.

[53] This applies, potentially, to all the derivatives of the Mediterranean garden cultures. The Israelites are a counter–example, as they were a Mediterranean people. But, they were a pastoral society rather than a garden culture. — Pastoral societies require different virtues and, thus, have different Gods: Specifically, the Sheppard or herdsman must be true to his commitments to his flock, brave in defending them from wolves or robbers, and single–mindedly persevering in searching for the lost lamb or calf. These are characteristics of the male psyche and, so far as I know, all pastoral cultures are patriarchal. (The idea of the importance of a pastoral versus a garden existence is due to Carroll Quigley, 1961.)

[54] See *Encyclopedia Britannica*, 1926 edn. There are other explanations for the origin of the Mafia.

[55] These events illustrate that although an absolute monarch can create a repub-

As a social institution the Mafia represented a conservative reaction to the changes which were, then, occurring in Italy: that is, they supported Italy's old traditions. Specifically, they followed the code of vendetta, were strongly group or family oriented, and were based on the Italian concept of manliness.

It should be apparent that Italian culture is fundamentally non–Western. It is of interest because social changes occurring in the United States are creating matriarchy. Thus, something like Italian culture may be what the future holds for America.

In Italy, the Mazzinists had been connected to the Illuminati and the outcome of Italian unification resembled Adam Weishaupt's scheme for the ideal State. — He had suggested using the family as the primary social organization of the people; but, Baron Clootz had replaced the family with voluntary associations as that was more consistent with the viewpoint held in the Commune of Paris. Next, the Mazzinists tried to establish the Freemasons as the grassroots organization of the people, but Italy mostly became a democracy with the people organized into extended families, partially networked by the Mafia.[56] That approximates the Illuminiti's original scheme.

One of the alternative explanations for the origin of the Mafia is that the Mazzinists refined and modified it, making it into what it is today.[57] That might appear likely as the Mafia was a pre–existing institution which had a structure of society fully compatible with the general outline of their scheme. But, there is a huge defect with that theory: The Mafia were strongly pro–Church, whereas the Mazzinists were virulently anti–Christian.

The Freemasonic government of unified Italy attempted to suppress the Mafia, during the 1890's. This resulted in some of them moving to the United States. In particular, the murder of David Hennessy, the Chief of Police in New Orleans, in 1890, was one of the first Mafia crimes in America. Soon they would form loose allegiances with the other criminal elements in America as well as with those members of the liberal Eastern establishment who ran the opium trade. Perhaps, that is where they began to be drawn into their camp.

During the inter–war period, Bonito Mussolini's primary focus was the suppression of communism. But, he also suppressed the Mafia. In revenge, they cooperated cordially with the US Army in their invasions of Sicily and

---

lic by fiat, that does not change the people. And the adoption of enlightenment as a religious doctrine by the Jews, in 1818, provides a second example.

At that time, it was generally supposed that making such a transition was simply a matter of revolution or decree. It had, indeed, appeared that way in the case of the Glorious Revolution. But, on closer examination those changes represented the English reverting to something closer to their tradition, rather than their moving towards something new.

[56] Of course, there were also several other social organizations at the grass–roots level, such as the Freemasons, Communist Party, and so on.

[57] See *Encyclopedia Britannica*, 1926 edn.

Italy, during World War II. That resulted in their becoming re–established in Italy. They are certainly present there today, whereas, one never hears of Italian Freemasons.

Their affinity to the Roman Church probably continued to make them incompatibility with the liberal agenda, until the Roman Church became aligned due to the changes which occurred at the Vatican II council, during the early 1960's. After that, they should have potentially become completely compatible. More will be said about these changes, later on.

Moving to current events in America ... In addition to their usual activities, the Mafia are also found as consulting companies holding lucrative contracts and as middle management positions in government. — They have the organization and connections. But, they do not appear to be the drivers of programs, merely functionaries. They also have a reputation for being more competent than the other networks which currently infest government.

Chapter 10

Progressive Education

The next two chapters cover the period from the Franco–Prussian War through World War I. The outcomes of this period were that most of the republics and monarchies of the Western world were replaced with free or socialist democracies.

With the dawn of the modern age, economics had been introduced as a governing principle of society, side–by–side with religion. But, during this period, science and education would take religion's place beside economics.

Alfred Whitehead pointed out that Enlightened Christianity had evolved into science. In addition, prior to public education, Christianity was the main institution for raising the people to reason and teaching them the accumulated knowledge of Western man. So, when science took–over reason and public education took–over the transmission of learning, religion no longer had a central role to play. That was to be the dawn of a godless scientific era. At least, that was the intention.

However, at this time, education came to be of considerable importance. It is the topic of this chapter.

10.1 German Approach to Education

Frederick the Great had used his power, as an absolute dictator, to tightly control the government, army, and education. He was vigilant, suspicious, and strict in those quarters. But, he felt that that this made his position sufficiently secure that he could grant his subjects freedom of speech, freedom of the press, and freedom of religion.[1]

By Frederick's time, they had reduced their approach to a system. — To insure that the students would obtain the full benefit of their education,

---

[1]See Maccauley's biography of him.

Frederick strictly limited their allowance, by law. The extremes of hunger, cold, poor housing, and social isolation, tended to limit university education to those individuals who had a sincere commitment to improving themselves. Want and their zeal for self–improvement often led to their reexamining their beliefs. In the end, only those students who bent in the desire direction were allowed to advance. But, they were never told what that direction might be.[2]

Such guidance as the students received came through the control of information. At that time, that was already a well–established educational method, long used by the Jesuits. Frederick improved upon it by limiting which universities students could attend and restricting their travel. A student could go nowhere except the designated University town, unless he obtained a permit. Thus, the students worked in a controlled environment with only selected materials. They developed their views based almost exclusively upon the writings of their professors and the audience they wrote for was that same academic community. These conditions tended to make them adhere, with great loyalty, to the views of their particular philosophical school. Each generation advanced their predecessor's views in a clear line of intellectual descent, generation–after–generation.

The State exerted its control over their views through their control over the professors. Every individual who aspired to become a university professor was expected to develop a new philosophy and put it forth in a multivolume set. They either received an appointment or not based upon it. These appointments were either directly under State control or were made by the majority vote of the academic faculty of the university, But that came to much the same thing, as the universities relied on State funding. Thus, the State controlled the culture taught at its universities and, through them, the beliefs of their common people.

During the late eighteenth and early nineteenth centuries, the leaders of Prussia wanted better control over the cultures of their people and, also, those of their neighboring countries. The first progress in this direction came when several scholars developed philosophies of culture.[3] But, it soon became apparent that a better understanding of social psychology was needed before this could be achieved. So, the next major step was the founding of the science of psychology.

Credit for the notion that psychology is a science independent from philosophy or physiology is usually given to the German philosopher, Johann Friedrich Herbart (1776–1841). He wrote two books which were influential in establishing that field.[4] However, a half–century earlier, another German philosopher, Johann Nicolaus Tetens (1738–1805), had argued for the same thing.

---

[2] In dealing with new ideas, the ruling elite would not necessarily know what the right direction was. So, they raised a crop of academics and selected those they thought were the best among them.

[3] See Johann Gottfried Herder (1744–1803), Wilhelm von Humboldt (1767–1835), and Friedrich Von Savigney (1779–1861).

[4] That is, *A Textbook of Psychology* (1816) and *Psychology as a Science* (1824)

The first major contribution which incorporated the new science of psychology into the philosophy of culture was made by William Wundt (1832–1920).[5] His views were Hegelian, but strictly rational. In 1875, just after the Franco–Prussian War, he was appointed to the chair of the Department of Philosophy at the University of Leipzig. He taught there until 1917, during World War I. During, that period he developed a scientifically–based philosophy of culture and wrote a ten–volume set on it.[6] He completed its last volume in 1920, the year of his death, after the Germany he served had ceased to exist. According to Sutton, in 1993, it is still studied by those interesting in molding the political and social heritage of a nation.

That was also the general era during which the techniques of brainwashing originated.[7] The best known research on this was that done by the Russian physiologist, Ian Pavlov (1849–1936). Besides the better–known parts of his study on dogs, in which he conditioned them by providing food and ringing bells, he also experimented with brain surgery, chemicals, and starvation. But, he found that the most effective approach involved repeatedly breaking and retraining the subject.

When this approach is applied to people, the subject is broken through a combination of deprivation and conflict. Then, he or she is retrained with new beliefs or a new personality. The transfer of loyalty occurs when the individual acts or makes decisions based on the new values. Each time this process is repeated, it becomes easier to break and retrain the individual. Eventually, he or she will be rendered into a lump of clay, to be molded at will.

---

[5] He was born in Mannheim, the son and grandson of Lutheran pastors. His father was Maximilian Wundt and his grandfather was Kirchenrat Karl Wundt (1744–1784). His Grandfather is the more interesting personality as he was also a professor of history at Heidelberg University, and had been in the leadership of the Bavarian Illuminati. His code name in the Illuminati was "Raphael." (See Antony Sutton 1986 citing Richard van Dulman 1977.)

William received an MD from the University of Heidelberg, in 1855, but rather than becoming a practicing physician, he went to the University of Berlin for a PhD in psychology. The next year, 1856, he became severely ill, close to death for several weeks. During that time of crisis, he developed his philosophical views.

In 1857, he received an appointment to be a professor of physiology at the University of Heidelberg. He taught there for seventeen years. During that period he conducted studies in psychology, using an inflexible experimentalism, to examine responses to stimuli.

[6] His *Volkerpsychologie* contains two volumes on language, three on myth and religion, one on art, two on society, one on law, and one on culture and history.

[7] For the history and methods of brainwashing see Edward Hunter 1971. — Two techniques are involved: "Brainwashing" which is the substitution of externally determined beliefs for the subjects original beliefs, and "Mind Change" which is the transfer of loyalty from the latter to the former.

10.2   Early Internationalist Education

Immediately after the Franco–Prussian War, Prussia founded academic programs abroad, which applied the German system of education. — Throughout the four decades, from 1875 to 1917, Dr. Wundt and his students studied and developed methods for causing societal change while the internationalist universities tested and applied them.

The internationalist education programs are called "internationalist," because internationalism was traditionally their key lesson. — An individual's national identity distinguishes that person from others of different origins and heritages. In contrast, internationalism, requires that the individual identify with humanity rather than with any single people. But, that establishes no distinctions and, therefore, is a nullity. Thus, accepting internationalism as a personal belief begins the process of breaking–down the individual.

The aim was not just to destroy nationalism, but to destroy the self–image, what Kurt Lewin called the "person." — So, whatever the student valued became a target, with the goal of destroying all of his or her original goals, values, beliefs, and identity until there was nothing left. This caused the student to regress to the infant state of development.

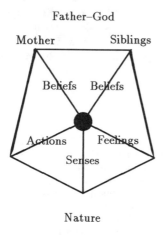

Father–God

Mother   Siblings

Beliefs   Beliefs

Actions   Feelings

Senses

Nature

Figure 10.1: Pentagram.

The infant mind can be diagramed using a pentagram. The infant has only one center of being, the self. Above the infant's world is the vague Father–God spiritual realm, below it is nature, to the left is the external and overt, and to the right is the internal and emotional. The infant's actions are impulsive as he or she has no reasoning skills. His or her actions are governed by beliefs and learned behaviors. These are externally determined either by the authoritarian parent–figure or the egalitarian group of siblings.

Several models for the infant mind existed during that era.[8] The pentagram also may have been a model for the infant psyche. One of the

---

[8] Jacob's Ladder provides a model for the infant psyche: Specifically, the infant is at the level of the ego. However, that model is not appropriate for discussing the development and education of an individual with a Western psyche.

Likewise, Alchemy was, then, the state–of–the–art for directing the processes of individuation and deindividuation but, it used archaic symbols which unnecessarily complicate the issue. So, I do not use it either.

arguments for suspecting this is that the Occult is the religion of the primitive level. Therefore, one would expect that a model for the infant mind would be central to their symbols, as the pentagram is. But, whatever the case may be, it provides a convenient diagram for purposes of discussion.

We speak of the lowest level of the Classical Model as the level of the infant. However, the infant mind is at an undifferentiated state which has yet to develop the two higher centers of being and all their related mental processes. Nor does the infant mind probably have the more refined mental processes of the lower level seen the Classical model. Therefore, an accurate representation of the psyche of an infant requires a simplified model, which is not exactly a sub-set of the model for the adult, but is connected to it developmentally.

Like most mammals, the very young human infant exhibits collectivism because he or she does not distinguish the self from anything else. And, having little or no means for forming beliefs himself or herself, the infant's views are probably either inherited or externally determined. In the latter case the dominant external influences in the infant's rather simple world are his or her parents and group of siblings. That leads to the two dominant modes of the infantile mentality: specifically, parent-based or left-brained authoritarian collectivism and sibling-based or right-brained egalitarian collectivism. Thus, one has a bipolarity, which is probably natural to mankind. Therefore, it follows that adults may exhibit it, if they regress, or never advanced much above this level in the first place.

This bipolarity is timeless. For example, it was discussed by Hayek, in 1944, with regard to the conflict between the Nazis and the Communists, and it can, also, be found in the conflict between Rome and Babylon discussed in *Revelation.* — The latter case is in some ways the better example, as there is evidence that mass-man was, then, predominately at the primitive level.

In terms of the Classical model for the psyche, what internationalist education does is drive the individual down from the level of higher reasoning to the level of the infant and the flesh. The result would be an egocentric personality, except that the individual either regresses naturally to the more infant-like collectivist behaviors, or arrives there as the result of having his or her identity shattered. But, that identity is necessary for judging, which is the left-brained mental process of the infant level. The absence of an identity, therefore, predisposes the individual to right brained processes. He or she, then, uses and develops them and reindividuates into an affective personality.

Now consider the impact of internationalist education on a person with a personality as described in Jacob's Ladder. ... In that case, the locus of the ego is held to be the level of the infant. So, destroying the student's identity necessarily drives his or her psyche to a higher level and facilitates the formation of that affective type of personality which is held, in that system, to be "higher reasoning." — It is not necessary for an individual who begins with this type of psyche to be driven down to the infant level. He or she can simply be educated and develops to the desired form naturally.

The intended outcome of internationalist education was an affective personality, but the production of an infantile mentality was probably an acceptable alternative. Either type was fully consistent with the Prussian foreign policy. — They wanted to alter the Western peoples so that they would not only accept an absolute State, but would intensely desire one and want nothing else. As was discussed earlier, people with a psyche as described in Jacob's Ladder are so disposed. For the same reasons, so, also, are individuals at the level of the infant.

At that time, most of the States of Western Europe were nation–States and either republics or monarchies. Those structures for society are fully compatible with Western man's strong self–image, because in republics the people self–govern, whereas, in monarchies they tend to identify with the person of the ruler.

But, the long–term goal of the internationalist agenda was to replace individualism and nation–States with collectivism and an absolute global government. And, of course, there is rhetoric supporting these changes. — One of the more common arguments which the internationalists present against nation–States is that they are prone to territorial wars.[9]

Nation–States, also, have national cultures. And, because having a culture usually means having values which define "good" and "bad," they can exhibit intolerance and provincialism. But, even in Roman times, people were enlightened enough to recognize and respect other cultures. Then, a person was considered to be "good" or "bad" according to the values of his or her own people, within the broad guidelines established by reason and Natural Law. That leads to the rich and diverse mosaic which is the highest form of Western civilization. And, although they recognized their own kind and others, that does not mean they discriminated against the latter, as to do so would be most uncivilized and contrary to the principles of Natural Law. Thus, a well developed personal identity and understanding of the Western system implies the equitable treatment of others, rather than the opposite as the internationalists would tell us.

But, that is precisely what the Prussians did not want, because under a Western system the peoples of the world have rights. They wanted them to be slaves. So, they strove to make the people unreasoning, emotional, or infantile and also to erase all cultures, values, and distinctions.

---

[9] A nation's territorial claims become part of an individual's self–image. According to White, in 1968 and 1969, this process is similar to territoriality in animals and about half the wars in the first seven decades of the twentieth century were due to overlapping and conflicting territorial claims. This kind of conflict is difficult to resolve, as the territorial identity lies deep in the human psyche, at an non–rational level. — One justification commonly given for internationalist education is that it produces individuals who do not recognize borders and, thus, is not subject to these conflicts. Of course, an alternative approach would be to raise the people to the level of reason. But, that conflicts with the other objectives of internationalist education.

One of the common approaches for internationalist education is to bring the students into contact with a wide range of other kinds of people, and if possible, to isolate them from their own kind. The former provides an opportunity for them to form new social allegiances, while the latter creates stress.

Social isolation produces similar psychological conditions to imprisonment.[10] In particular, a prisoner is subjected to two kind of penalties: The first and most obvious is the deprivation of his or her decision–power over the simple decisions of daily life; and, the second is isolation from society. The Classical Greeks and some American Indian Tribes used only the second as a penalty for serious crimes, in their sentence of "ostracism."

This stress is called "cognitive dissidence," in the educational literature. It is considered, by some, to be necessary for social learning.[11]

The schools may also strive to enhance the educational experience by removing from the students as many of the decisions over their lives, as they can. They usually, also, promote group housing, group activities, international mixing, and cross–cultural education. These foster conditions of life not unlike those of an infant or prisoner and, also, provide opportunities for the student's new values to be adopted in practice.

But, internationalist education is not the only way to achieve these ends. Another is to introduce into a nation many different kinds of peoples. — Individuals learn to get along with others who are not of their own group, but they often have little feeling for them. And, when people with significant differences are forced together, that usually does not lead to their uniting: First, they try to find a common ground where they can live–and–let–live, but if that fails, the outcome is often conflict and alienation.

A country which has so many different kinds of people that it is difficult to find sufficient numbers of any one type to form the basic social infrastructure, will characteristically suffer from a mild faceless form of chronic alienation in which people have no identity nor form any deep social bonds. That is characteristic of Americans. They are egalitarian and form friendships easily, but these are shallow.

This phenomenon was mentioned by Alexis de Tocqueville several decades before the Franco–Prussian War.[12] That is a very remarkable book

---

[10] Some of the most insightful writings on internationalism come from individuals who have studied prison systems. In particular, see de Toqueville, Zimbardo 1969, and Zimbardo et al 1982.

[11] The theory of cognitive dissidence (See Festinger 1962.) holds that learning occurs as the result of conflict, and that there is an optimum amount of stress for learning. (See Hebb 1966, Luft 1970, Moore 1972, Hamkins 1974, Cross 1976, Kirby 1979, or McCarthy 1980.) However, that level is only appropriate in some circumstances: For example, an absence of stress is essential to the clearest thought, whereas, a much higher level of stress is used in brainwashing to break the individual. (See Sargent 1957.) — This approach is best for emotional or religious development, not traditional educational goals. Its origin can be traced back to the *Cabalah* in which evil serves a role in teaching.

[12] See the concluding chapter of De Toqueville's *Democracy in America*, entitled, "What sort of despotism democratic nations have to fear."

which remains surprisingly relevant. He describes a century–and–a–half ago exactly the same things we see today. He was the first to recognize a new type of tyrrany. — It consisted of all men being equal and alike, without sense of community beyond family and immediate friends, nor of country. They are engaged in seeking after the "petty and paltry pleasures with which they glut their lives." The government is far above them and of immense power. It is "absolute, minute, regular, provident, and mild," directing everything and providing whatever is needed or desired. It assumes almost a parental authority except that, rather than preparing the children for life, it keeps them in a state of repressed development. He concluded, that their aim was to gently remove all decisions from the people until they were reduced to a "flock of timid and industrious animals, of which the government is the Sheppard." With remarkable insight, he questioned whether that left anything to make life worth living.

According to Paul Mantoux,[13] the Ecole Libre des Sciences Politiques of the University of Paris was the first internationalist educational program founded outside of Germany. It was founded, in 1871, to advance the study of social sciences for the control of public opinion.

The first university to introduce international education and the German educational methods into America was Johns Hopkins. It was founded only three years later, in 1874.[14] The first President of John Hopkins University was Daniel C. Gillman. He had done his graduate work at the University of Berlin.[15] After his return to the United States he served as the librarian at Yale until 1872. The intention apparently had initially been to make Berkeley the first American University in their program of internationalism and Mr. Gillman had been appointed its first president. But he was there for only a brief period (1872–1874) because of strong grass roots opposition.[16] He felt that Johns Hopkins provided a better opportunity to plant the German system in America and, therefore, went there instead. He served as their president from 1875 to 1901.

His most important actions as president of Johns Hopkins University were to hire faculty, which he did personally. Among them were G. Stanley Hall. He had been the first American student to study under William Wundt at Leipzig.[17] He chaired their Department of Psychology and Ped-

---

[13] He wrote the preface to John Harley's (1931) definitive book on Higher Education.

[14] Johns Hopkins left his fortune to found a University bearing his name.

[15] He was a Yale graduate. Dr. Sutton (1993) says that his graduate study at the University of Berlin was under professors von Ritter and Trendelenberg. Von Ritter was a right–wing Hegelian but Trendelenberg taught Natural Law.

[16] During that time, in California, there was a hotbed of grassroots opposition to federalism. Gilman had sought the position at Johns Hopkins because, in his own words, regarding the University of California, "I feel that we are building a superior structure but it rests over a powder mill which may blow it up any day. All these conditions fill me with perplexity."

[17] Other American students of Wundt include J. McKeen Cattel, who became a professor at Columbia University; E.W. Scripture, who became a professor at Yale University; E.B. Titchener, who became a professor at Cornell University,

agogy.

10.3 Progressive Education

John Dewey (1857–1952) received one of the first doctorates granted by Johns Hopkins University. The direction of his graduate study was initiated by George Sylvester Morris's suggestion that he study Hegel.[18] Dewey's dissertation was on the psychology of Immanuel Kant, viewed from the perspective of a mixture of Hegelian philosophy and Wundtian psychology.

In 1884, John Dewey got an appointment to the University of Michigan. While he was there, he was influenced by William James' treatise, *Principles of Psychology*. James' recognized the roles of both the affective and rational parts of the human psyche and also held the pluralist viewpoint, which he inherited from Mill, that social truths or laws of nature may have only a limited or local influence and may vary according to a person's type, condition, and needs. Dewey adopted these viewpoints from James, thereby, loosening the shackles of the strict logical determinism which he had inherited from Wundt and Hegel. That established Dewey's characteristic system-of-belief which he held for the rest of his life.[19]

Dewey created "progressive education" by incorporating knowledge of the new science of psychology into the German approach to education. It targeted the students' affective side, and accommodated differences among students.

He viewed formal education as only the first stage of a life-long process, used to control the masses. And, he felt that the State should be run through psychological manipulation of public meetings, committees, elected officials, and so on.[20]

Together with Professor Frederick J.E. Woodbridge at Columbia University, he also developed a religion which was compatible with his general outlook. It is called "American Naturalism." It is a pluralistic scientific Atheism. It continues into the present day under the leadership of John H. Randall, Earnst Negel, and Justus Buchler, the chairman of the Department of Philosophy at Columbia University.

---

but who was critical of Wundt's approach; H. Gale, who became a professor at Minnesota University; G.T.W. Patrick who became a professor at Iowa University; and Charles H. Judd, who became a professor at University of Chicago. See Sutton 1986.

[18] Dr. Morris was at that time the chair of the department of psychology at the University of Michigan. He was spending his leave at Johns Hopkins. He also had received his Phd at the University of Berlin under Dr. Trendelenberg.

[19] In 1894 John Dewey went to the University of Chicago which Rockefeller had founded only four years earlier. In 1902 he became the director of their newly founded School of Education (again with Rockefeller funds). Finally he resigned from that position in 1904 and went to Columbia University where he remained until he retired in 1930.

[20] See Dewey 1899, 1909, 1935.

10.4   Typology

John Dewey's pluralistic viewpoint on education is based on a major advance in psychology which occurred roughly contemporary with his work. It was the scientific description of psychological types.

Their existence had been recognized much earlier. — They were one of the central issues of Alchemy and they were also defined by Jacob's ladder and the Classical Model for the Psyche. Thus, typology was essentially part of religion.

The first real break–throughs came just before the First World War, and Jung's theory of type was published just after it, in 1923.

Carl Jung was the single most important contributor to typology.[21] He observed that people have distinct personalities with which they are born. — The identification of those personality types is called the "typological problem," and the description of the process of development and maturing of personality is called "individuation." — According to C.A. Meier[22], one of Jung's students, after 1913 he focused his research on the problems of typology and individuation.[23] His motivation was to find a method for restoring meaning into people's lives. His approach was to reform the structure of their personalities and deeply held beliefs. — That is both individuation and religion, because according to him, "God" is the center of a person's motivational structure and "religion" is the framework through which it gives meaning and value to life.

He developed his typological system by observing and describing the types of people he encountered in his clinical practice. His publications consist of descriptions of distinct types of people.[24] In 1962, a mother–daughter team, I. Myers and E. Briggs, converted these into a cohesive system and a quantitative test for categorizing people. The result was the Myer–Briggs temperament test[25]. — That system is based on four variables with the individual receiving a score on each. For purposes of popular discussion, each variable is divided among three possible levels, a first type, a second type, or in between. The four variables are:

1. I/E: Introvert versus Extrovert — An introvert is someone who is worn down by contact with people, but is revitalized by being alone. An extrovert is the opposite. Most Americans are introverts.

---

[21] He was born in Switzerland in 1875. His grandfather was a medical doctor and professor at the University of Basel and his father was a Protestant minister. Dr. Jung was educated in Basel, was employed as a lecturer in Zurich, and worked for many years in the Zurich mental hospital. He was one of the leading clinical psychiatrists, in one of the world's finest mental hospitals. He died in 1961.

[22] Soul and Body: Essays on the Theories of C.G. Jung, (1986) Lapis Press, Santa Monica, CA. 242 p

[23] for a collection of his contributions see V. de Laszlo's (1990) The Basic writings of Jung. Princeton Univ. Press. 561 p.

[24] For Jung's theory of types see his 1923 *Psychological Types*.

[25] See L. J. Stricker and J Ross 1962. A description and evaluation of the Myer Briggs type indicator Educational Testing Service Res. Bull pp 62–6 Princeton NJ

2. S/N: Sensation versus Intuition — This variable describes how an individual gathers data: whether the individual primarily gathers data from the physical world through his or her senses or whether he or she seeks inwards. Thus, "intuition," here, also includes the intellect.

3. T/F Thinking versus Feeling — This variable describes the relative importance to the individual of conscious thought versus emotions and feelings. Which is the individual's dominant mode of psychic activity? For example, a feeling person may prefer to do a little intuiting instead of deductive reason.

4. P/J Perceiving versus Judging — This describes how a person treats information from the senses. A "judging" person pigeonholes or categorizes what he or she encounters in nature according to some rule or model, and treats them according to their category; In contrast, a "perceiving" individual remembers the perceptions, that is the raw data as it comes to them filtered through their senses and paradigms.

Thus, each individual is one of 81 different psychological types.[26] The types are named by combining the letters for the categories of the four variables.

Jung's system represented the state–of–the–art during the late nineteenth and early twentieth centuries. Specifically, introversion and extroversion had just, then, been demonstrated to be psychological types and the three remaining variables were drawn from the Classical model for the psyche, Jacob's Ladder, or possibly some related model from Alchemy.[27]

The processes described by his categorization system only come from the levels of the ego and the physical self: that is the lower two levels. — By using the I/S variable for an inward versus an outward orientation, rather than being more specific about the nature of the higher mental processes, his system could apply to either the Classical Model for the Psyche or Jacob's Ladder. Thus, it is inclusive of both of these major groups of psychological types.

The Myer–Briggs system does a remarkably good job at breaking people into groups according to their philosophical and religious predispositions. — In some instances it has been shown to correctly classify people more than 90% of the time.[28] And, because it is based upon the Classics and religion, the types it delineates can be readily connected to the

---

[26] However, the more recent versions of that test exclude the in–between type (X). In that case, there are 16 different possible types.

[27] In his autobiography, Carl Jung comments on how Faust's work had been influential for him. He also studied the works of the Alchemists, was versed in the Classics, and was a Gnostic. So, he may well have been familiar with all of these models.

[28] It was used in California's schools for counseling for two decades beginning in the 1960's. Its accuracy in predicting job placement was in the mid–90% range. Of course, counseling had raised that percentage above what it was naturally. But, this still shows that Myers–Briggs typology accounts for a large component of behavior.

major philosophies, religions, and political doctrines. Thus, they delineate the natural constituencies in religion and political outlook, and they go a long ways towards explaining the dynamics of historical and political processes. Presumably, these were the differences among students which Dewey wished to incorporate into progressive education and which thinkers like William James wanted to allow for in pluralistic religion.

That also provided the basis for a new philosophy of culture. — It said that an individual inherited a personality type which largely established which political philosophy and religion were natural for him or her. Cultural change, therefore, came to be regarded as an issue of genetic change in populations. Therefore, political programs of that era often included eugenic policies. This orientation was clearly in evidence, during the period of the two World Wars.

There are also several tests for determining learning styles. These are of more recent origin, but are discussed here because they simplify the explanation of social and political processes. The Canfield Learning Style Inventory and the Productivity Environmental Preference Survey are two examples of these tests.

Field–Dependence: One of the more important learning–style variables is field–independence versus field–dependence:[29] Stereotypical, this is the difference between abstract thinkers and people whose ideas are always in context. In teaching, the field–independents need to be taught the underlying theory and prefer to work alone. They are better analytical problem solvers. In contrast, the second type, the field–dependents, must be told what to do and have it put into context. They also need a higher level of social support. But they function better in collaborative learning and group processes. [30]

Field dependence appears to involve dysfunction in the processes of symbolization. In particular, they are unable to isolate the parts from the whole. For example, an extreme field dependent may do well in trigonometry or geometry, because these involve real concrete objects. They can fully understand that a side of some particular triangle might have a length of 5. But, you will lose them when you make a statement from algebra such as, "let us call the length of that side "A" and think of triangles in general." Conceptually, what that does is take some of the properties of that particular triangle, but not all of them. — They can not make that step. They are obligately holistic thinkers.

These are the people who see and relate only to the people, relationships, and conditions they directly encounter. They are oblivious to the impacts on the larger community and incredulous that anyone would be motivated by an abstract concept. They not only do not see it, but in extreme cases they can not see it. This is probably the class of people who caused the peasant revolts of the late middle ages and the proletarian movements of modern times. They may not be the majority, but they are

---

[29] The role of this variable was studied by Herman Witkin.
[30] See Robert M. Smith (1982)

a large segment of the population.

Religion has an entirely different meaning for this class of people. Orthodoxy or Fundamentalism suite them. They could, perhaps, find meaning in mysticism if there were symbols floating in their subconscious minds. But, an abstract God is inconceivable to them.

And, what can morality mean to people who can not separate abstract principles from social interactions? It can only mean adherence to fixed rules. — Thus, with this one trait comes a wholly different outlook on life.

Simultaneous versus sequential learners: Another learning–style variable describes how people process information. Some people must understand each individual piece of information they encounter before going on to the next, whereas other people remember several un-understood facts until they get enough information to see the big picture. The former type of person, who processes information one–at–a–time, is called a sequential learner or linear–thinker whereas the latter type, is called a simultaneous learner. Approximately 90% of the American population are sequential learners.

An extreme sequential learner can not read the law, with all its clauses and big words, and, therefore, they can be deceived by adept writing. In particular, it is possible to write a sentence which means one thing to them, and quite another to the ten percent who are simultaneous learners. If you know to look for this writing style, you will find it. — John Dewey was good enough at it that some of his speeches were playful and sprightly.

This also is part of what defines "popular writing." — Mass man can neither comprehend nor appreciate the Victorian masters, whose sentences may stretch out for several hundred words, with the grammar perfectly matching the structure of the ideas and a rich vocabulary lending them tone and style. Give them Hemingway, with his limited vocabulary, simple sentences, and ideas to match.

Sex Differences: Women and men's minds perform the same functions, but do them differently, often with different parts of the brain. In particular, men tend to preferentially use the logically–oriented left–hemisphere. This gives them a better ability to focus their attention on a single issue. In contrast, women tend to use the right–hemisphere and also a larger region of their brains at any given time. This gives them a better ability to track several things simultaneously.

Women are also better at detecting emotions in others. In addition, recent studies indicate that melancholy feelings activate about eight–times as many neurons in women as in men, and women's sense of sadness or loss is usually due to personal relationships rather than work–related issues, whereas men are the opposite.

Women tend to be more oriented towards communication whereas men are more action–oriented. And, women often regard language as symbolism, whereas a men views it as a tool for communication.

Women also have more acute senses, better memories, and are more intuitive; whereas men have better physical–spatial and logical abilities.

And, sexual pleasure occurs in entirely different parts of the brain for the two sexes.

Overall, women are more neotenous than men: that is, they are more juvenile in their physical characteristics and that can also be seen in their mental orientation. Specifically, they are more socially oriented, more affective, and more right–brained. In addition, their verbal orientation is characteristic of the adolescent and their symbolic use of language is characteristic of the infant. Both show a tendency to be more governed by beliefs, paradigms, and culture. Predictably, they more often join religions of orthodoxy, faith, spiritualism, and inwardness than men do.

All of this merely confirms what each of us already knows, that men and women are different.

10.5   Implementation

The great foundations helped to get progressive and internationalist education implemented in America. According to John Harley, the Carnegie Endowment and the Rockefeller Foundation agreed to partition their effort in education so that their programs did not duplicate each other. The Carnegie Endowment took international and higher education, while the Rockefeller Foundation concentrated on primary and secondary school education within the United States.

Higher Education: Several planning organizations for higher education were also founded just before World War I.[31] Their intention in founding them before the Great War, was that they should be in place after it, to oversee education. That would be the primary mechanism for controlling the populace of the Western World once perpetual peace had been established.

The move to implement this scheme occurred, in 1926, when Madame Curie proposed to the League of Nations that the International Institute for Intellectual Cooperation should be founded to coordinate these organizations. France donated two million francs to construct a building to house it. However, that plan came to an end when the League of Nations foundered.

But that didn't stop the organizations involved. Several of them met in Berlin, in 1928 and again in 1929, for the purpose of founding such a centralized coordinating agency.[32] As the result of their efforts, by 1931,

---

[31] In 1910 the Carnegie Endowment for International Peace, the World Peace Foundation, and the Rockefeller Foundation were founded; in 1911, European center of the Carnegie Endowment for International Peace was founded; in 1914 the Institute for International Education was founded; and in 1925 The John Simon Guggenheim Memorial Foundation was founded. These were all major funders of the internationalist program in higher education.

[32] The institutions represented include The University of Paris, London School, Williamstown Institute of Politics, Geneva International Universitare des Sciences, Hauts Estudes Internationale, Institute of Pacific Relations (Honolulu),

fourteen universities had internationalist programs in America.[33] These programs remain active to this day. For example, the first Internationalist program in Washington State was the Henry M. Jackson Institute of International Studies which began as a small department, in 1910, but, which has grown considerably since that time.[34] It remains active and its internationalist program has spread to the entire university. In particular, during 1992, Carol Eastman, the Dean of the Graduate School, was appointed to, also, be the University of Washington's Vice Provost in charge of their international program. She indicated[35] that the entire graduate program at the University of Washington would soon become directed toward internationalism. A draft mission statement which was developed at that time shows that "internationalism" still means much the same as it always has.

Secondary School Education: In the United States, prior

to the twentieth century, secondary school education was provided mostly by the private sector. Where there were public high schools at all, they were run by local governments. In order to develop America's educational system into a means for controlling the populace, the first step was, therefore, to provide a government–run school system under centralized control.

To that end, the General Education Board was established, in 1902, by John D. Rockefeller and an Act of Congress. Its mandate gave public authorization and some federal funding for this primarily privately funded and privately operated organization. John Rockefeller's commitment to this project was substantial. He donated approximately $50 million to it during its first ten years. That leveraged a far greater amount of State funds.

---

the Council on Foreign Relations, and the Royal Institute on International Affairs.

They held a second meeting the following year, in London, and appointed officers. an executive committee, consisting of (chair) Sir William Beveridge, the director of the London School; Dr. Earle B. Babcock of the Carnegie Endowment; and several professors from the other institutions. At this second meeting the Carnegie Endowment (Paris) was also represented in addition to all the other aforementioned groups. (See Harley 1931.)

[33] Those listed by John E. Harley (1931) were: Georgetown University, George Washington University, Harvard Law, John Hopkins University, Louisiana State University, Pomona and Claremont Colleges, Stanford University, University of Chicago, University of Colorado at Denver, University of Georgia, University of Idaho, University of Southern California, University of Virginia, and the University of Washington.

[34] It was renamed after Senator Jackson, in 1983. By 1993, it had 36 full time faculty members but if joint appointments are included, it had about 100 faculty; it had 481 students; and a budget of $3.8 million. Hammer and Chapman, in 1993, say that the school runs six federally funded national resource centers to provide training and continuing education for teachers, business people and the public. In comparison, Columbia University has seven such centers and the University of California has six; the Universities of Wisconsin and Indiana , five each; Cornell, Stanford, and Michigan, four each.

[35] In an address to the Discovery Institute, May 6, 1993.

In 1905, Georgia became the first State to establish a Statewide public school system. They provided public taxation to fund their system of High Schools. Soon many other States followed the same course. That is how the public school system came into being in the United States. According to Beard and Beard, as of 1880, there were only 800 high schools in the US, whereas, by 1910, there were over ten–thousand.

Having created the school system, by 1910, the next step was to introduce progressive education into it. That began immediately after the Great War, during the 1920's; by the 1930's those methods were used throughout America.[36] They were a failure in terms of traditional educational goals.[37] However, neither did they succeed in teaching a new Spirit to the American People which would induce them to accept being governed. We even find John Dewey using his presidential address to the Progressive Education Association, in 1928, to criticize his fellow educators for "destroying better than they built."

Although the acceptance of Government as the provider of education was a major change in public opinion, the outcry against progressive education, grew, until those methods were terminated in America. The pivotal event which brought it to an end, was the publication, in 1940, of Augustin Rudd's book, *Bending the Twig.*

The General Education Board continued to exist into the 1950's and never stopped promoting the use of these methods. Their effort was taken over by the Carnegie Foundation, in the early 1960's, leading to the implementation of its contemporary form under a new name, "Outcome Based Education."

According to Rudd, these methods were also introduced into the Soviet Union. By the 1930's, they had produced a generation of Russian youth who could not read, write, nor do arithmetic, but formed violent gangs who roamed the countryside stealing, raping, and murdering. As a result, Soviet schools restored "traditional education" under centralized control. They taught basic skills but were also designed for indoctrination.

---

[36] For example, see Rugg's *Building of America* series of textbooks which were being used during that era.

[37] That was to be expected, given their background and origin. — A half–a–century earlier John Mill had regarded public education as a vehicle for State controlled social change and advised against it.

Chapter 11

Crisis in Capitalism

This chapter covers the political and economic developments leading to World War I.

11.1 Marxism

The events leading up to World War I were driven by a developing socio–economic crisis.

Throughout the nineteenth century, the investment bankers had assisted the industrialists in building vast business empires, as we saw in the previous chapter. They used them as a farmer uses crops. They invested in them, let them grow, harvested them during the financial crashes, and resold them later when the economy recovered.

As, Karl Marx pointed out, in his great work, *Das Kapital*,[1] this system must eventually collapse. Marx was an economist of the first rank and had studied all the other economists. He foresaw, that Marxist communism would replace it. And, indeed, it would have, had other factors not intervened. — The crux of the matter was that some industries had gotten big enough to self–finance. That removed them from control by the bankers. But, what was more important was that once they had established monopolies, they escaped for the cycle of boom–and–bust. At first they used their monopolistic power to keep wages down. However, that soon resulted in great strikes.

Organized labor was the other pole of that dialectic. — As Carlyle, Engles, Marx and others had observed, the shift to capitalism alienated the working classes. The intended function of society is to provide liberty, a reasonable opportunity to obtain happiness, and a chance to live long enough and well enough to replace yourself and get your children well

---

[1]Its first volume was published just before his death, in 1883, and the other three volumes were published later by Engles.

enough along that they have a reasonable chance of doing likewise. All "Western" societies have similar objectives. A failure to perform these functions for a class of people can be expected to produce their alienation. — Smith, Richardo, and Malthus had admitted that capitalism, as it was then practiced, did not provide these benefits to the common worker and the improvements, under Mill's scheme, were only limited.

But, man is a social creature, so when he rejects the existing order of society, he generally replaces it with another. — The alienated worker of communist theory was most definitely field–dependent. They characteristically respected only those of their own social class, particularly those with whom they worked on a daily basis, and were generally oblivious to the needs of the larger community. Indeed, most working men's associations seem to have followed that pattern, throughout history.

Proudhon appears to have been the first to have recognized the potential of these organizations. He suggested that workers' groups should run all industry and that no other form of government was needed nor desired. That was part of his system of "anarchy." The split between anarchy and Babeufism developed into an intense rivalry at the time of the Franco–Prussian War. After that, Georges Sorel picked up the fallen standard of anarchy, this time under the name of "syndicalism." That was the beginning of the union movement.

The general strike and industrial sabotage were the syndicalists' great weapons of social warfare. They believed that a general strike would bring society to a halt and the people to destroy what remained of it.[2] After that, a new order could be established.[3] Those were the sentiments of the leaders of the union movement. They show the extent to which a death struggle had developed between labor and industry.

In several of the larger strikes in the United States, towards the end of the century, private, State, or Federal troops were brought in to coerce the workers. That effectively imposed Marxist communism,[4] which was precisely where society was, then, headed.

But, it was not too long before labor realized the political power of their numbers and ended industry's use of direct coercion. They got legislation through Congress allowing unions and restricting monopolies.

When industry could no longer keep wages down, they switched to using their power to prevent over–production and impose control prices. This allowed them to raise prices to meet union demands. As they provided vital services which affected all segments of the economy, by raising their prices they could raise the cost of living and, thereby, keep wages at near their real value. By this means they could protect their profits and maintain the structure of society. However, price controls only pitted

---

[2]See Sorel's *Reflexions sur la Violence*.

[3]The approach has been tried in several nations. But it has not been as effective as they hoped. — The anarchist revolutionaries have a hatred for society. If all people were like them, things might transpire as they suggest, but the general public does not feel the same way.

[4]Notice that Marxism was what industry imposed in opposition to Anarchism.

industry against the consumer who, like labor, had strength in numbers. Soon price fixing was prohibited, too.

Thus, by the end of the nineteenth century, the structure of capitalistic society had broken down: that is, it no longer functioned as it previously had and had largely escaped elite control.

In response, the elites founded several institutions to study economics. One was the London School of Economics and Political Sciences which was founded specifically "to the study of economic questions endeavoring to prepare the public mind for the broad changes which, in their view, must be effected if social peace is to be preserved." It remains a world center for internationalism and economic research, to this day. Another was the Institute for Weltwirtschaft founded at the University of Keil, Germany. Also, various universities created Departments of Economics. For example, this was when Marshall founded that department at Cambridge.

11.2 Rhodes–Milner Organizations

But, this crisis had not developed entirely of its own accord. It was being pushed by social revolutionaries. There were several contending political organizations but, one leading one. To find its origins we need to go back to just after the Franco–Prussian War.

From 1868 to 1885, England's Prime Ministers had alternated between two good men, William Gladstone (liberal) and Benjamin Disraeli (conservative). However, in 1885, approximately a decade after the Franco–Prussian War, the conservative ministry passed to Lord Salisbury and then, in 1902, to Arthur Balfour.[5] These conservative administrations can be decisively connected to the network of political societies formed, about that same time, by Cecil Rhodes.

Cecil Rhodes had attended Oxford University where he was greatly influenced by Professor John Ruskin, who held the fine arts chair. Ruskin's importance stems from his ability to consider most aspects of life from a moral perspective. His essay, *The Seven Lamps of Architecture* is particularly good, and his *Sesames and Lilies* is a refined statement of Benjamin Franklin's concept of "virtuous revolution."

The substance of that latter work is that war is good for art. The reason for this is that it exterminates the riff–raff and parasites, focuses men's attention on the real and concrete, and involves them in direct action to provide a solution. Thus, war is strongly Westernizing and morally uplifting. Consequently, it reawakens the perception of Natural Law and pure forms and a period of artistic creativity invariably follows afterwards.[6]

---

[5]Except that Lord Rosebury was Prime Minister for a single year and Mr. Gladstone for two (1892–1894).

[6]That is it follows traditional war. Modern gorilla warfare, in contrast, tends to focus the individual on the social and political and, therefore, is demoralizing and destructive to art, morality, and creativity.

Rhodes gave the outward appearance of having dedicated his life and fortune to an endeavor Ruskin had suggested. That was to unite the English peoples[7] into one union, and then to spread English culture worldwide. His plan was based on a type of internationalist collectivism, called "Fabian socialism"[8] It had continuity to the German school of thought.

However, the organization he founded ended up seeking the opposite end. In particular, the final outcome of the Bolshevik Revolution, was to virtually eliminate their "English" or Western element. This came about due to their programs of genocide which targeted intellectuals, Christians, and ethnic Russians. They killed approximately 68 millions.

Rhodes resources and accomplishments weren't modest. Quigley (1966) says that with the help of Lord Rothschild and Alfred Beit he was able to monopolize the diamond industry of South Africa as De Beers Consolidated Mines. He was Prime Minister of Cape Colony, South Africa, from 1890 through 1896; and, as a measure of his importance, Rhodesia bears his name. Although Rhodes' personal annual income must have been in excess of a million pounds sterling, he was often overdrawn on account of the political programs he advanced.

The history of the founding of Cecil Rhode's political organization was described by Carroll Quigley. — He was given access to the records of these societies. He felt that they had made such an important contribution to history, that they should not be kept secret. He wrote his 1966 book *Hope and Tragedy* about them. Much of its content had already been reported by revisionist historians, but it is the magnum opus on that topic. It received a cold reception from the establishment. However, Bill Clinton paid tribute to him during the 1992 Democratic National Convention. — According to him, on January 5, 1891, Cecil Rhodes and a British journalist, William T. Stead, formed a semi–secret society to advance their objectives. It was organized, with three levels. It had an executive committee,[9] an inner circle of the initiated and an outer circle. The outer circle was initially known as the "circle of helpers" but, later, was organized by Lord Milner as the Round Table organization.

Rhodes willed the bulk of his fortune to Lord Rothschild to be used for the further development of that society.[10] After his death, in 1902, his estate gave the society a substantial revenue. With his resources added to those of the House of Rothschild, the financial resources behind this

---

[7]That, of course, included the British Commonwealth and America, but, it could, also, have included Denmark, Russia, and parts of Germany, Austria, and France: That is, all the Low German peoples. — These were the peoples who had embraced enlightenment.

[8]See *The Open Conspiracy* by their main spokesman, H.G. Wells. Other writers for the movement were Edward Bellamy and George, B. Shaw. Beatrice and Sydney J. Webb were the main contributors of their ideas.

[9]The leader of this society was Cecil Rhodes, and its executive committee included William Stead, Reginald Baliol Brett (Lord Esher), and Lord Alfred Milner.

[10]See Rotberg 1988.

movement were vast.

These organizations operated behind a facade of morality. They held up Ruskin and widely quoted him, they participated in social programs to help the English working class,[11] they endowed university chairs,[12] and founded scholarly programs.[13] Between these various programs they probably felt that they had a sufficient presence in the English academic community to exert an influence over English culture.

According to Carrol Quigley,[14] from 1897 to 1905, Alfred Milner, who at that time was the Governor–general and High Commissioner of South Africa, recruited young men from Oxford and Toynbee Hall. He placed them in influential positions in government and international banking. They became the dominant influence in England's politics up to 1939. Quigley said that they were responsible for planning the Jameson raid of 1895 which resulted in the Boer War in South Africa (1899–1902).

Between 1909 and 1913, they formed semisecret groups known as Round Tables, in the British Commonwealth and the United States. At that time, they were involved in planning the First World War. That was within their capability as they had significant influence over the governments of Germany, England, America, France, and Italy.

During the late 1800's all of these nations were preparing for war. For example, Germany had imposed a special war tax and had enlarged the Kiel Canal, so that their warships could not be bottled up in the Baltic. But, more specifically, as of 1905, they had drafted their war plans: that is the Schieffen Plan.

America, too, was ready for war. President McKinley had built a large modern navy but was reluctant to depart from the isolationist tradition which George Washington had begun. But, political forces pushed him so strongly that he changed his policy, although reluctantly. America developed a dispute with Spain over the civil liberties of the Cubans. Although Spain acquiesced to all of America's demands, that was not enough to avert war. The US Legislature was suspicious of the Administration's intentions and required Cuban freedom as part of their declaration of war, but they hadn't foreseen that the American Navy would conquer two other Spanish possessions, Puerto Rico and the Philippines. So, with that act, America acquired two colonies and became a belligerent international Power.

Theodore Roosevelt was McKinley's vice–president, in his second term, and followed him into office when he was assassinated, almost immediately after his re–election, in 1901. According to the Beards,[15] the Republicans

---

[11] for example, Settlement House and Hull House.

[12] for example, including the Beit chairs at Oxford, the Montague Burton Chair at Oxford, the Rhodes Chair at London University, the Stevenson Chair at Chatham House, and the Wilson Chair at Aberystwyth. As these chairs were endowed by them and they selected who would occupy them, they guaranteed that the philosophies and views they desired would be advanced.

[13] The best know of these are the Rhodes Scholarships.

[14] See Quigley 1966.

[15] See *The Beards' Basic History of the United States*. Also, see Foster R.

were prepared to pursue active imperialism the moment Roosevelt took office. Roosevelt's connection to the Rhodes–Milner organizations is clearly visible in his choice of Secretary of State, Elihu Root, who was in JP Morgan's sphere of influence and was the founder of the Roundtable of New York.[16] Thus, America positioned herself for the opening of World War I.

That war probably would have begun in 1906, if slavery had not been discovered in South Africa. That caused the fall of the Balfour ministry. Consequently, the war was postponed until the Rhodes–Milner group got back into control of the British government, with Lloyd George's war administration (1917–1919).

Herbert Hoover, who would later be a US President, was deeply involved in that slavery issue.

The following brief sketch is drawn from to J. Hamill, 1931.— Herbert Hoover was a Quaker by birth. He was orphaned as a boy and brought up by an uncle, a con artist who ran a fraudulent land company in Oregon. That was his first experience in business. After that was detected and came to an end, he attended Stanford University, earning a degree in geology. He then briefly held several jobs in California before obtaining a permanent position as a field agent for a mining company in Australia. They were a bubble company, defrauding their investors. Later, he was involved in takings in China. He is known to have also carried out a number of mining promotions in various parts of the world in which he showed a brutal disregard for the miners. — For example, in one report he stated that paying compensation for deaths in the mines was more economical than buying more timbers. — His panegyrists euphemistically referred to this as his "globe trotting career." He was rewarded with a directorship in one of the principle Rothschild enterprises, the Rio Tinto Mines in Spain and Bolivia.

Beginning in 1902, Hoover's Chinese Engineering and Mining Company provided approximately 200,000 Chinese slaves to South African mines. Some of them had been fraudulently induced to sign on as contract labor, while others were simply shanghaied. They were shipped to South Africa in aging tramp steamers at about 2000 men per ship. In the mines, their wages were a bare subsistence and they were housed in guarded fenced compounds. Within the compound, 20 men lived in each 27 X 19 foot hut, sleeping on wooden shelves, two to a shelf. The Chinese were forbidden from accepting other work in South Africa but many tried to escape.

In 1904, this system of slavery became known in England and was soon the leading campaign issue in the Parliamentary elections. Following the fall of the Conservative ministry of Arthur Balfour, on Dec 4, 1905, the new liberal government ordered the repatriation of the slaves.[17]

Dullas, 1954. He was in the inner circles and gives an account of the personalities involved.

[16] See Schulzinger 1984 and Quigley 1960.

[17] However, about 50,000 of them were sold to South West Africa instead.

11.3 American Monetary Policy

Had the war begun, in 1906, America would have played only a minor part. It was, then, primarily a European affair, which would probably have principally benefited Great Britain. But, during its nine year postponement, America took steps so that she would not only take a leading role, but shift the center of Power from Europe to America.[18]

One of the changes to prepare for those events was the creation of a great mechanism of finance. The first step in this was the economic crash of 1907, during Theodore Roosevelt's administration (1901–1909). It was caused by an abrupt contraction of credit. The American public was acutely aware of its cause and called for reform of the American currency. They wanted a system which would be immune to artificially induced crashes. The Roosevelt administration passed the Aldrich–Vreeland Act of 1908, which created a national monetary commission to study the issue. They submitted their report, in 1912, at the end of President William Taft's administration (1909–1913) [19]

During Taft's campaign for re–election for a second term, Theodore Roosevelt, although previously a Republican, like Taft, ran as a third party candidate. Both parties, then, had bills for the creation of a central bank: the Republican bill was the Aldrich Plan, while the Democratic bill was the Federal Reserve Act. They were virtually identical except in name. When it became evident that the Democrats would control both Houses of Congress, Roosevelt entered the race, insuring a Democratic Presidency and the quick passage of the Federal Reserve Act.[20]

President Woodrow Wilson (1913–1921) was an academic. He had received one of the first doctorates from Johns Hopkins University, only slightly after John Dewey. After graduating, he became the president of Princeton University, Governor of New Jersey, and, then, President of the United States.

His administration came in with a bang: as the Democrats controlled the House, Senate, and White House, they immediately passed the Federal Reserve Act of 1913. This transferred to the Federal Reserve Bank Congress's right to issue, control, and print the US currency. That bank is part of an international banking cartel and isn't a part of the US

---

[18] According to Baird's Basic History and Norman Dodd's report on the activities of the Carnegie Foundation, from his investigations of them in the Reece Commission, Andrew Carnegie had been active in opposing America's imperialistic schemes, up until 1908. But, that year, his foundation began a policy which would ensure America's entry into the war.

[19] Taft was politically much akin to McKinley. His actions were pro–banker and militarist, but he was not enthusiastically in support of these things. (See Dullas's 1954 *America's Rise to World Power*.

[20] According to Mullins, 1993, the directors of Kuhn Loeb Co. were the primary backers of all three candidates.

Government.[21] However, that apparently is legal.[22]

At the time the Federal Reserve Act was passed, the revenue from tariffs had been adequate to finance the needs of the federal government. But, an income tax would soon be needed to finance the war.

The Federal Reserve System provided a mechanism for accessing American capital. This mechanism for finance was extended to all the countries involved in the First World War. America became the leading lender for the War, but many of the loans were arrainged through London.

Specifically, most of the member banks of the Federal Reserve are also member banks of the Bank of England or are connected through affiliates. As the head of London's Morgan Grenfell acknowledged that, the American banking system brought the credit, capital, and skills which made London the great center of international finance it became. This was due to their connection to the Federal Reserve Board which created a mechanism by which they could back huge loans with the American money supply. What allows this is the ability of the Federal Reserve Board to create dollars when necessary.[23]

America's rise to Power dates from then. In population and industrial strength, at the commencement of the war, she was the equal of France, Germany, Austria, or Russia; whereas in its aftermath, she had risen to the equal of England, who was then the greatest world Power. That rise was due partly to America's financial system.

---

[21] As a federal judge stated in the case of Lewis v. US (680 F 2nd 1239, 1241, 1982), "The Federal Reserve Banks are privately owned locally controlled corporations."

[22] Chief Justice John Marshall ruled in 1819, in the case of McCulloch vs. Maryland, regarding the contested legality of the Second US Bank, that the Federal Government had the power to establish a National Bank. This is because the regulation of money is one of the enumerated powers of Congress but the Constitution does not narrowly constrain what form their action may take.

In contrast, the US currency is defined as being gold or silver coin. (Article 1 section 10). This issue was not left to the discretion of Congress. The founding fathers debated this issue a length. They admired the stability of the Spanish dollar, which was based on gold and wished to follow their example. So even though Federal Reserve Notes say on them, "this note is legal tender for all debts public and private," Federal Reserve Notes aren't redeemable in gold an silver and, therefore, aren't legal tender. What they are is a loan of credit.

The Federal Government gives a bond to the Federal Reserve Bank. The Federal Reserve then issues notes based on it and charges interest on that loan. Thus, the money supply, that is the total amount of Federal Reserve Notes in circulation, is directly related to the US debt: Specifically, the notes are drawn against a portion of that debt. The greater the debt, the greater the money supply, and the higher the total interest paid by the US to the privately–owned Federal Reserve Bank. A large part of the income tax goes to pay the interest on that money.

[23] See McRae and Cairncross 1963.

11.4 Bolshevik Revolution

The revolution in Russia occurred in the middle of World War I, and was an integral part of the overall plan. There had been revolutionary agitation in Russia since the early 1800's. Serfage and absolute monarchy were the key issues, but there was no widespread discontent among the Russian people. Like the French Revolution, the forces for change in Russia did not originate from within. The principle parties behind it appear to have been the Rhodes–Milner organization, Wall Street, and Germany.

The final revolt began when Nicolai Trotsky (that is Lev Davidovitch Bronstein) organized the Bolsheviks in New York City, with financial backing from Wall Street.

The single largest contributor to the Bolshevik Revolution was Jacob Schiff of Kuhn–Loeb.[24] He contributed an estimated $20 million, according to his grandson, Jacob Schiff,[25]

Kuhn Loeb appears to have been centrally involved in World War I. In addition to Jacob Schiff, Paul Warburg, one of their partners, had been involved in formulating the Federal Reserve Act. While, his brother Max Warburg of the Rothschild subsidiary, M.M. Warburg, was the personal Banker for Kaiser Wilhelm. He orchestrated their war build up and, later, he was the negotiator for Germany in the peace conference of 1918–1919.

Trotsky sailed from New York on the S.S. Christiana on March 27, 1917. That was during World War I, less than a week before America entered the war. The Canadians jailed Trotsky and his men when his ship stopped in Nova Scotia. Canada did not want to send revolutionaries against their ally, Russia. However, Woodrow Wilson's chief advisor, Colonel House[26] negotiated their release. By then, America had entered the war, but Trotsky was even provided with an American passport.

On April 16, 1917, Vladimir Lenin, who was in exile in Switzerland, was allowed to travel through war–time Germany in a sealed train with 159 other Bolshevik revolutionaries. Germany, also, provided them with a large quantity of gold. There is strong evidence that Lenin was a paid German agent,[27] whereas Trotsky represented American interests.

---

[24] An address he delivered, in 1910, before the New York Free Synagogue reveals that he was a religious extremist. "'Hear, Oh Israel, the Lord our God is the only God' has a living meaning, who carries within him the conviction that the day will come, and labors to bring it nearer when the Unity of God and the brotherhood of man will be universally recognized, is a Jew." (See Rabbi Stephen Samuel Wise 1910, p8, quoted by Weiland, 1994.)

[25] See New York Journal/American 3 Feb 1949. quoted by Still, in 1990.

[26] Edward Mandell House, was a self–avowed communist: specifically, he stated in his book *Philip Dru: Administrator* that he was working for "socialism as dreamed of by Karl Marx." That book is a fictionalized plan for creating a One–World–Government.

He was the son of a Rothschild agent in Texas who had been active in Texas politics. As he had attended the grammar school associated with Johns Hopkins' University, he knew the elitist programs since childhood.

[27] See Webster 1921.

The Bolshevik's first attempt to seize power, during July 16–18, 1917, failed, but on a second try, on November 6, they took the government offices and the Winter Palace. This disrupted the Russian fight against Germany, as Germany had intended. They signed a treaty with them on March 3, 1918. — The Bolshevik Revolution was the final achievement of the Prussian system, in which they used the International Jewish community as a weapon against their enemies.[28]

Thereafter, civil war ensued in Russia (1918–1920).[29] At the beginning, there were several rival factions, but these gradually sorted themselves out, leaving the Bolsheviks in command. Lenin was their leader and Trotsky and Stalin served as his Field Marshals.

The original Bolsheviks who came with Lenin and Trotsky were predominately international Jews. However, Lenin soon realized that to succeed, the revolution had to become a Russian revolution. Joseph Stalin[30] played a central role in making the necessary concessions to Russian ethnicity. As a result, much of the Czar's Army came over to their side. They saw in the Bolsheviks a vehicle to restore the greatness of Russia. This union transformed Jewish International Bolshevism into Russian National Bolshevism and, also, established the Jewish–Russian or red–brown composition of the USSR's government, which lasted until 1952.[31]

In June 1918, British troops landed in Murmansk to prevent military stores from falling into the hands of Germany and immediately began supporting a puppet government. France, Japan, and America also sent troops. However, the British declined to oppose the Bolsheviks and withdrew; the French betrayed the Czarists as the price of their own free retreat;[32] while the Americans supplied the Bolsheviks.[33] The American forces were sent without Congressional approval solely on President Wilson's order and went into action to keep the Trans–Siberian Railroad from

---

[28] They were well–connected in the Jewish community and had intimate knowledge of their ethnic and religious sensitivities. Consequently, by contriving circumstances designed to exploit these, they could expect to raise a body of men from among them, whenever they needed one. These were predominantly political or religious extremists and probably generally came from the non–rational psychological types. Such people form a small percentage of any population and there were 12–16 million Jews, worldwide, during that general era. By these means, they were able to raise about 500 men to follow Lenin and Trotsky.

[29] The methods used in the Bolshevik Revolution are admitted to have been copied from the French Revolution. See Nesta Webster 1921.

[30] Stalin was a Georgian of Christian origin and upbringing. Georgia was a small nation in the Caucasus Region. It had been independent until about 50 years before the revolution and, at that time, still retained much of its independent spirit. However, Stalin was chauvinistically pro–Russian. He had become a Marxist when he was still a schoolboy and was an active revolutionary from that time onwards. In his private life, he was a family man and lived modestly, almost ascetically.

[31] The momentous events of 1952 are discussed later on.

[32] But the Bolsheviks broke their agreements and murdered the French Generals and many of their troops.

[33] See Modlhammer *Moscow's Hand in the Far East*.

Japanese control.

The Japanese consistently and firmly opposed communism and fought an orderly retreat eastward across Asia. They eventually evacuated Vladivostok, during October 1922. But, they continued to fight communism in China until their collapse at the end of the Second World War.

If Wilson's support for the Bolsheviks was not already clear, it became so in his fourteen points for the peace treaty of Versailles, which closed World War I. Specifically, his sixth point prohibited any international intervention in Russia, to allow her "an unhampered and unembarrassed opportunity for the independent determination of her own political development and national policy."

Stalin did not agitate to rise in the Communist Party until after Lenin had a stroke, in 1922. — That was the same year that the USSR was formally formed. — After Lenin's death, in 1924, he became the General Secretary of the Party; and, after Trotsky's murder, in 1928, he took command. Thus, Lenin was their leader during their revolution and Stalin led them after the USSR was formed.

The Soviet government is government by committee. In fact, "soviet" is the Russian word for committee. According to their 1918 Constitution, each factory or workshop had a soviet, and so also did each rural village or commune. The citizens elected representatives to their local soviets. The local soviets elected representatives to the Provincial Soviet and they elected delegates to the All Soviet Congress. The urban workers were given more seats in this than the peasants, as they were considered more reliable. There was also a Union (Federal) government which consisted of a Union Congress, a Central Committee, a Presidium, and a Union Council of Commissars. Their members were elected by the lower bodies. The virtue of this form of government was that it was so cumbersome that responsibility got lost between the Local Soviets and the Central Committee. Consequently, Russia enjoyed a measure of local control and the people obtained some self–determination.

In 1936, Stalin introduced a new Constitution which was far more democratic in structure and also guaranteed personal rights. It simplified the structure of their government so that there were only local, regional, and provincial councils, a Supreme Council, and a Presidium, with all except the Presidium elected directly by the people, with universal suffrage and secret ballots. This was more efficient and, therefore, more dictatorial. It put an end to any local control.

Thus, Soviet government was a form of democracy. But, as Edmund Burke once said, the structure of government "reaches but a little way." It is the spirit of the government which establishes the distinction between democracy and dictatorship. — Modern dictatorships do not abridge the voting rights of the public. They merely make sure that the public votes right. One of the surest signs of a dictatorship is the elimination of opposition parties and the soviets were quick to do that.[34] But, their greatest

---

[34] These ideas were due to William Bennett Munro, 1938.

achievement may have been their use of their control over information, which they call "cybernetics." By this means, they were able to effectively control the voting behavior of their public.

The Soviet Union fit into President Wilson's policy. — He was leading the Great War to make the world safe for democracy. By "democracy" he meant Fabian socialism for the West and Communism for Russia. He was helping both Russia and America make the necessary changes. Had he been successful, these two great sister nations would have stood side–by–side with Great Britain as one overwhelming Power in a new world order. That was to be a world federated under the League of Nations, with ample enforcement powers.

The communist literature from this period is most informative. In particular, the Preamble to the Statutes of the Second Communist International, ratified in Moscow in 1920, gives a clear statement of purpose:[35] "In order to overthrow the International Bourgeoisie and to create an International Soviet Republic as a transition state to the complete abolition of the State the Communist International will use all means at its disposal including force of arms."

The idea of the State as a transitory phenomenon comes from Engles. Lenin explains it as follows:[36]

> As a matter of fact, Engles speaks here of the destruction of the bourgeois State by the proletarian revolution, while the words about it withering away refer to the remains of proletarian statehood after the Soviet revolution. The bourgeois State does not wither away according to Engles, but is put an end to by the proletariat in the course of the revolution. What withers away after the revolution is the proletarian State or Semi–State. ...
>
> ...It never enters into the head of any of the opportunists who shamelessly distort Marx that when Engles speaks here of the State "withering away" or "becoming dormant," he speaks of democracy. At first sight this seems very strange, but it is unintelligible only to the one who has not reflected on the fact that democracy is also a State and that, consequently, democracy will also disappear when the State disappears. The bourgeois State can only be "put an end to" by a revolution. The State in general, i.e. the most complete democracy, can only "wither away."

It withers away to anarchy under some larger absolute authority. The best examples are probably the Eastern bloc countries under Soviet rule. They had been overthrown by war and their local soviets had withered away. Their State and local governments should have degenerated completely into graft and corruption, but they had not yet reached that ideal.

---

[35] Quoted by Morley 1949.
[36] Lenin, 1935 quoted by Morley 1949.

That would have left families, each governed by its patriarch and their local economic and social circumstances, under only a higher authority at Moscow.

During the period of the second commintern, the internal workings of the Soviet government were transparent. However, after Stalin's takeover, in 1928, concealment became one of their objectives. And, after 1936, government became increasingly veiled, although enough remained visible to show that their practice was not what their new constitution described. For example, Stalin simply appointed whoever he wanted in the upper levels of government and secret trials and executions of all political opposition continued unabated.

With the dissolution of the Third Communist International,[37] in 1943, a red curtain was firmly drawn over whatever may have been happening. Ypsilon summarized the situation as it then appeared, in 1947, He said that no one knew the real state of affairs inside the Soviet Union, except a small circle around Stalin. This monopoly on information was was one of the most valuable assets of the dictatorship. "To eliminate [it] would mean to eliminate the dictatorship itself. To define this God is to defy him: Le dieu défini est le dieu fini." Thus, government became a living mystery and assumed the role of religion. — The idea of using democracy as both myth and tyranny comes from Sorel, who vividly argued for it.

11.5   World War I

During World War I, Germany was perilously short of food and it, therefore, was by no means certain that the war would last. Unless a food supply could be provided, they would soon have been forced to sign a peace treaty. Herbert Hoover came to the rescue, with his Belgian Relief Fund. He was one of its directors. He did the buying and shipping, while Emile Francqui arranged the distribution, mostly to Germany. Francqui's background was similar to Hoover's — He had previously been involved in slavery in the Belgian Congo and financial takings in China

America didn't enter the war until, April 2, 1917, two years after its onset on August 4, 1914. America has far more people of German origin than English and for a long time it wasn't clear which side she would come in on, if she came in at all. To influence America, England cut the transatlantic cable and set up an agency to censor every piece of mail going from England to America.[38] Then, they created an effective propaganda

---

[37] The First Communist International had been dissolved in 1876. The Second Communist International was formed in 1889 and was still in existence when World War I began in 1919 but represented the more conservative labor and socialist elements. The radicals refused to join it and began the Third Communist International under the Bolsheviks.

[38] Except, of course, for diplomatic material. Hence, President Wilson would have been fully informed.

campaign over Germany's submarine blockade of the British Isles.[39]

Once America entered the war, laws were passed which cut deeply into the American way–of–life. The war was used to strip away liberties, some of which have never been returned.[40] It was also costlier that any preceding war.[41] It was the greatest prize in history, to that date.[42] — The banks and largest corporations made those profits.

In the Spring of 1917, just after entering World War I, President Wilson directed his chief of staff, Mr. Mandell House to establish the Commission of Inquiry to develop a plan for the world order which was to follow. They originated the plan for the League of Nations.[43]

However, it wasn't accepted. Part of the problem was that government documents came to light which decreased the public's confidence. Beard and Beard wrote in 1944, p442:

> ... secret agreements, made long before 1914, between Russia, France, and Great Britain, were unearthed by historians working in the archives of Russia, Germany, and Austria thrown open to researchers by revolutions in all those countries. On the basis of clear documentary evidence scholars dissected the myth, propagated by those Powers, that Germany was wholly responsible for inaugurating the war; that on Germany must be placed all the war guilt; that the governments of Great Britain, France and Russia united by the secret agreements were administered by innocent civilians suddenly and unexpectedly attacked by a bloodthirsty villain.

---

[39] The Germans had sunk several American passenger liners and other ships, including the Lucitania, which was carrying arms and ammunition as well as passengers. The passengers had been warned by adds taken out by Germany in the New York Times, before the Lucitania sailed.

[40] A general draft was instituted; the income tax was raised in the higher brackets to as much as 65%; an inheritance tax was imposed; corporations and partnerships were taxed on "excess profits"; and the Congress conferred on the President broad powers to regulate and commandeer natural resources, industries, labor, and the sale and distribution of food. Furthermore, freedom of speech and the press were placed under the most severe restrictions to that date in American history.

[41] In 1930 the US Treasury Department estimated the following: The total cost of the war in 1919 dollars was estimated to be $180.5 billion in direct costs and $151.6 in indirect costs. The total direct cost to the US was $1 billion and total costs were estimated at $100 billion, that included $35 billion in unrepaid loans to the allies. The total direct cost to Britain was 8 billion pounds. The war left about 10 million dead and 20 million wounded.

[42] But World War II was even more costly. $240 billion was authorized by Congress for direct costs during the first year of World War II.

[43] Presumably, at least the basic outlines of that plan pre–existed, but it probably needed to be filled in and brought up to date. The commission was, also, needed to account for the plan's origins, as it would have been a political disaster had it been attributed to a British semi–secret political organization.

By reading copies of these diplomatic documents,[44] scholarly works in European history founded on them or the pub-
licity given to the findings, literate Americans in large numbers learned something of the innumerable lies, deceptions,
and frauds perpetrated by the governments of Czarist Russia,
Great Britain, and France, as well as of the Central Powers, at the expense of their own peoples and other nations.
The gleaming mirage that pictured the World War as purely
or even mainly a war for democracy and civilization dissolved
beyond recognition. Countless Americans who in 1914–18 had
yearned for a "brave new world" at the conclusion of the war
were disheartened by the proofs of sinister purposes running
against their dreams.

The overall plan for the outcome of World War I appears to have
been based on Marx's ideas: that was each national government would
gradually wither away leaving only to its own particular form of controlling
social structure at the grassroots level under a single global authority. The
specifics must have been something like this: The Soviet Union and Eastern
Bloc would have been approximately as they actually became; Germany
would be overthrown and communist, too; England and America would
have had Fabian socialism; and so on.

Mary P. Follett's, 1918, book dealt with the intended structure of
American society at the grass–roots level. She wrote: "The twentieth
century must find a new principle of association ... group organization is
to be the new method in politics ... the foundation of international order
... representative government, party organization, majority rule, with all
their excrescences, are deadwood. In their stead, ... the bringing into being of common ideas, a common purpose and a collective will." — Her
book serves as an example of the collectivist ideas which were current in
the liberal establishment at that time.

But, the exact form at the national level was not critical. The global
higher authority, the League of Nations, was the key which would make the
system work. It would have greater military power than any single nation
and control over commerce within each nation. That would give them the
power to coax or coerce each nation from whatever it was, at the end of the
war, to whatever they wanted it to be. The withering away of governments
and the molding of their peoples could, then, proceed unimpeded. — The
eventual outcome would be absolute global government under their power:
that is under a unified elite from England, America, and the Soviet Union.

According to Foster Dullas the League of Nations would have been
approved if it had been voted on right away, but opposition grew over
time.[45]

One problem was Wilson's third point, of the fourteen points which

---

[44] In January 1919 a New York newspaper published copies of several secret
treaties among Russia, Great Britain, France, and Italy.

[45] See Dullas 1954.

he pushed at the negotiations of the Versailles Treaty. That allowed the League of Nations to interfere with business and trade internal to the member nations. It was quickly dropped.

After that, the conflict swirled around Wilson's tenth point. That was the obligation of the member nations to go to war to protect the collective security. Neither Wilson nor his opponents were willing to compromise on that. So, that was why the treaty failed ratification by the Senate.

The public was, also, gradually becoming aware and growing indignant. In the end, President Wilson had a mental breakdown and was no longer capable of advancing his agenda. Apparently, he went into a depression as the result of the public's reaction to his plan for implementing worldwide communist or Fabian government. Thus, it failed and, shortly thereafter, Wilson was voted out of office.

But, it only failed ratification in America and Great Britain. The other nations passed it. So, this was a failure only in terms of the objectives of the Anglo–American establishment who intended to use it as a vehicle for global domination.

Following that failure, members of the Commission of Inquiry regrouped. They joined a monthly dinner club called the Council of Foreign Relations which met at the Metropolitan Club in New York. It had been founded by Elihu Root, in 1918. Professor Carroll Quigley, in 1960, referred to this group as "The Small New York Roundtable."[46] Similar organizations were also formed internationally. In particular, the Royal Institute of International Affairs was founded in England in 1919; and the Institute of Pacific Relations was founded in Honolulu, a few years later.

During the decade which followed, not much happened, on the surface. President Warren Harding (1921–1923) presented himself as an easy–going and honest man, and the public elected him. His campaign slogan was "back to normalcy." His goal was to return America to the cultural and economic conditions which prevailed before 1910. But, there wasn't much opportunity to see whether those were his true colors as he died, apparently of natural causes, not long after he took office. Calvin Coolidge (1923–1929) had been President Harding's Vice President. He was an honest and decent man. He continued Harding's program. In 1924, he ran against the Council of Foreign Relations' candidate, Davis, and won. — But, during his term in office, plans were being carefully laid, outside of the public sector, for the next try at a new social order.

---

[46] The Council's first president was John W. Davis a lawyer for J.P. Morgan and Company. He served as the commission's president until 1933. Mr. Davis was also the Democratic Candidate for the Presidency, in 1924. According to the Council on Foreign Relations publication *Foreign Affairs*, Herbert Hoover was another of their founding members.

Chapter 12

Nazi Germany

This chapter covers the Nazis as a cultural and religious phenomenon.

12.1 Interwar Malaise

To understand the Nazis it is necessary to know what was happening in German society, at that time.

By the late 1920's and early 1930's, Germany had sunk into meaninglessness and despair. Collectivism, Atheism, and Nihilism are usually considered to have been major contributing factors. They had grown during the Post–Hegelian period and were widespread. The German Existential philosopher, Karl Jaspers (1883–1969), wrote, in 1931, that the spirit of the age was "characterized by the unsheltered man ... There is no God, is the clamor of the masses; and hence man is worthless, slaughtered in large numbers because he is nothing."

The collectivist doctrines of German philosophy were a direct contradiction of individualism and the worth of the individual. The problem with Nihilism was similar. — By asserting the impossibility of authentic knowledge, it leads to disbelief that any personal value can be meaningful. And, true Atheism is a pathological condition in which the individual has neither personal motivations nor any system to live by.[1] — Both Freuerbach

---

[1] The leading Atheistic doctrines set up man or science as God, in the psychological sense. But this substitution was rarely effective and the destruction of an individual's religion without replacing its psychological functions could be devastating. At best, it leads to an asocial personality, who is estranged from all the motivations and bonds which form the structure of human society. For a depiction of such a person, see Albert Camus's *The Stranger*.

But, Atheism and Nihilism were, to some degree, merely a fad. For example, Camus says in *The Fall* that eighty percent of professed Atheists continued practicing their religion in private. That percentage is not to be taken as even ap-

201

and Nietzsche had been concerned about the possible loss of a religious attitude towards life and nature. Both discussed it and Nietzsche had specifically introduced his doctrines of Superman and eternal recurrence to give meaning to a Godless existence, but without success.

At that time, there was a small Kierkegaardian Renaissance in response to this problem.[2] But, it proved inadequate to meet the challenge.

The world's most respected psychiatrists were, also, working on this issue. In Switzerland, a great deal of Carl Jung's clinical practice involved reestablishing and strengthening his patient's religious beliefs to restore meaning and vitality to their lives. He was the preferred psychiatrist of the ruling elite, from before the First World War until after the Second. During that long period, when one of the upper echelon suffered a bout of remorse or, as it was called in those circles, "had a failure of nerve," they would go off to Switzerland to "take the cure" from Jung. Afterwards, they would return reinvigorated, ready to continue whatever they had been doing. Thus, Jung must have known what the big picture was. He was, also, ideally situated to understand its psychological impact. He set about crafting a religion for the people to live by in the new age which was to come into being after the First World War.

He had been the protege of Sigmund Freud. Their first recorded disagreement is said to have been over these issues. — During 1910, Sigmund Freud became enthusiastic about a new organization, the Internationaler Orden fur Ethik and Kultur, which would combine psychology and ethics to fight the authority of the State and Church,[3] but Carl Jung absolutely refused to support this. He felt that abstract ethics might suit the wise; but religions also serve a non–rational and subconscious function for the common man.

People need myths to live by. By "myth" he meant a mental image or picture, not necessarily fully rational, but which places the individual and his or her life into a larger context, especially in relation to God. He felt that the main–stream religions did this only poorly, as they were too inflexible, lacked a rich mythology, or were inconsistent with an individual's personal images. This resulted in their loss of relevance. He liked the Quaker or Unitarian approach, as it allows an individual to personalize a system of belief, but he found these denominations too austere to meet the public's needs. On the other hand, he felt that although the Roman Church has a rich and diverse mythology, it, too, was unsuitable as they prohibited any ideological flexibility. So, he helped his patients develop a living personalized mythology based on their personal images, largely drawn from their dreams.

He believed that dreams were expressing racial memories. He and many other clinical psychologists have reported insane patients who had

---

proximate, but, it indicates that the movement was both popular and superficial, in some quarters.

[2] See George J. Stack 1976.

[3] Freud strongly opposed both Christian and Judaic religions.

memories which appeared to have come from antiquity and could only be accounted for if they were inherited. — This is why they held this opinion, but it is virtually impossible to reduce this type of anecdotal evidence into a definitive proof or disproof of their existence.

Ancestral memories became part of what people, in those circles, believed, at that time. Nor was the idea completely absurd. — We can experimentally demonstrate that some memories are stored in ribo–nucleic acid (RNA), in animals such as planaria. DNA is what our genes are made of and it is transcribed to RNA in the process of making enzymes. The reverse process may, also, occur in connection with virus infections. In that case, viral RNA could code for the corresponding DNA and that can become implanted in the nucleus. There is, in fact, a lot of nuclear material whose function can't be accounted for in terms of coding for enzymes. Some of it could be ancestral memories.

This is essentially the mechanism of Lamarkian evolution, which was long promoted as an alternative to Mendelian evolution. It was particularly popular in the Soviet Union and was not abandoned until the 1950's.[4] By 1956, Carl Jung, also, had abandoned the idea of ancestral memories.[5] But, their existence has not been conclusively refuted, even today. There is just a general failure to demonstrate them. If they, infact, existed, as some people, then, believed, racial lines would evolve as the result of personal enlightenment, just as Hegel, Nietzsche, and Hitler hypothesized. These concepts got incorporated into New Age religion.

12.2   New Age Movement

The New Age Movement was one of the more important religious trends of that era. It had been founded immediately after the Franco–Prussian War. Specifically, Annie Basant and Madame Helena P. Blavatski (1831–1891)[6] were sent to America, in 1875, to spread Eastern Mysticism and the Occult.[7] According to Nesta Webster (1924), Annie Basant had previously been in the Maconnerie Mixte, which was a woman's political arm loosely associated with French Freemasonry; and Madame Blavatsky had proba-

---

[4]Soviet science was too often driven by Soviet doctrine, and ancestral memories was one of the important ideas inherited from the nineteenth century.

[5]He wrote in 1956, on his page 76, "I do not by any means assert the inheritance of ideas but only the possibility of such ideas."

[6]She was the daughter of Peter Hahn. They were Germans from Mecklenburg living in Ekaterinoslav, Russia. She married at seventeen to a much older man and divorced after only a few months. Then she traveled. In 1858, we find her a spiritualist medium. The *Encyclopedia Britannica*, 1926 edn., says that "Her jugglery was cleverly conceived, but on three occasions was exposed in the most conclusive manner."

[7]That is according to a statement by Annie Basant, but she would not say who had sent her.

bly been working with the Egyptian Brotherhood.[8] During the Franco–Prussian War, both of these groups had been strongly pro–Prussian.

They founded the Theosophical Society, in New York, in 1875. After their time, the leadership of the movement passed to Alice and Foster Bailey. Today, it is the central organization of the New Age Movement.

Anne Besant and C.W. Leadbeater promoted Yoga.[9] They stressed non–attachment as the primary technique for personal development. It lets the individual transcend the lower ego–self and, thereby, frees him or her from the bonds of personal relationships and aspirations. That also destroys the personal identity and nationalism and, thus, is generally consistent with the objectives of internationalist education which began at approximately the same time.

While Besant and Leadbeater were spreading these ideas, Blavatski was promoting an new occult doctrine, called "Neo–Gnosticism."[10] she claimed that these beliefs came from Tibetan mysticism, but the *Encyclopedia Britannica*[11] says that they are, "a mosaic of unacknowledged quotations from such books as K.R. Mackenzie's *Royal Masonic Encyclopedia*, C.W. King's *Gnostics*, Zeller's *Plato*, the works of magic by Dunlop, E. Salverte, Joseph Ennemoser, and Des Mouseaus, and the mystical writings of Eliphas Levi ...." Her works also incorporated Hindu and Buddhist beliefs, including Yoga. According to Nesta Webster, in 1921, they appeared to have been substantially influenced by cabalism. Today, the New Age Movement claims that her doctrines were inspired by the French Enlightenment. — Whatever their origins may have been, they lit a fire in many hearts. By 1891, her followers numbered approximately 100,000.[12]

Her doctrine asserts that human rights are birthrights. However, these are only held by the elect, who Blavatski identified as "Aryan," meaning the ancestral stock of the Northern long–headed peoples. She held that they originally had psychic powers, but had lost them through interbreeding with other races.[13] — She was the origin of the myth of Aryan supremacy. She was, also, the source of several other symbols and ideas which we usually associate with the Nazis.

She stated in her 1888 book, *Secret Doctrine,* that the mysteries of the

---

[8] This may indicate a line of intellectual descent from the Cabalistic Magicians, Cagliostro and Falk, and, therefore, a connection to Germany.

[9] They produced several books, both individually and jointly.

[10] Neo–Gnostic refers to a Gnostic system which has a mythology dating from recent times — usually specifically this movement.

The seminal books for this movement are Blavatski's 1877 *Isis Unveiled* and 1888 *The Secret Doctrine, the Synthesis of Science, Religion, and Philosophy.*

[11] See the article on "Blavatski" in their 1926 edition.

[12] ibid.

[13] The intellect is a very common psychological trait among the Nordic peoples, but less so among others. When it occurs in an Eastern mind, or a Western mind trained to be Eastern, where there is no place for it, it may result in those bursts of insight known as "revelations," or so we might infer from the *Cabalah.* Her idea seems to follow from this, and was one of the core concepts of her religious system.

universe and the future course of history had been revealed to her, in a crypt below a monastery in Tibet. This knowledge was contained in seven esoteric symbols. The most memorable of these was the swastika. For the Hindus, Buddhists, and Jaines it is the symbol of good fortune. But its significance in her system, as in Zoroaterism, is as the symbol for primal-fire and, therefore, the symbol for creation. According the Blavatski, it is, also, the symbol of the Aryan.

12.3 Nordic Mysticism

Blavatski's ideas were adopted by the Austrian mystic Guido von List (1848–1919), who extended them.[14] He claimed that the ancestral knowledge of the Teutonic tribes was contained in their ancient runes.

He, also, held that when the North was Christianized, the Germanic pagan religion went into hiding and their ancient knowledge was passed down by the Freemasons, Rosicrucians, Templars, and other secret societies. The mystics of the late nineteenth century reasoned that as the mythologies of many of the secret societies and mystic religions were united through some of their central concepts, they could justifiably be merged and integrated in a relatively free synthesis, as Blavatski had done.

List took from New Age and other sources whatever he wanted and filled in the gaps with his personal "ancestral memories." Between 1902 and 1908, he had a religious experience in which he claimed that a partially-new system of runes was revealed to him.[15] That was the Armanic 18–rune alphabet, which, later, was adopted and modified by the Nazis.

The body of myth which developed, during this revival of Nordic Mysticism, also incorporated some ideas from science. These included evolution and eugenics. They had caught the public's eye when Charles R. Darwin (1809–1882) published his *The Origin of Species*, in 1850, and his *The Descent of Man*, in 1871. By the end of the century, they had obtained wide popularity. His ideas dovetailed with the racial ideas of Blavatski and List.

List held that the First World War, was to unite all the Germanic peoples into an empire. It would end materialism and democracy, and put in their place an absolute theocracy led by an Aryan high–priest/king. Under him would be a council of twelve, and below them a religious order of knight–priests.[16] Only Aryan male heads of families would have the

---

[14] He was the son of a Viennese leather merchant. He worked as a newspaper reporter and writer. His major contributions were in poetry and religious thought.

[15] Beginning in 1908, List wrote eight books on runic mythology. His first and most important book was *Das Geheimnis der Runen* (The Secret of the Runes).

[16] Himmler was forming the Nazi SS to be the priest–warriors of a new Nordic religious order. — Algiz replaced the cross in their graveyards. — Their top leadership was formed in the structure of a twelve–man council. The intention appears to have been that it would eventually become the core of the world gov-

right of citizenship, and people of other races would be allowed to live only for their slave value.

One of the main publications carrying these ideas was the periodical *Ostara*, which was first published in 1905. In it you can see that, before the first World War ever began, much of the doctrine which we associate with the Nazis was already formed.

In May 1912, the German Order was founded based on these ideas. It was only open to the aristocracy and professionals who could prove their German anchestry. It soon became a wealthy and powerful organization with lodges in twelve cities. The Thule Society was their Munich Lodge. They combined List's Nordic mysticism and right–wing politics. They were the progenitors of the Nazi party.

12.4 National Socialism

World War I ended due to a revolt in Germany. Despite a series of German victories in Russia, in 1918,[17] the left–wing had undermined the German government and caused their war effort to collapse. King William II abdicated that same year and the armistice was signed shortly, thereafter.

The fledgling Weimar Republic was relatively powerless and the people felt a general revulsion for it. The opinion of historians is that their core problem was their inability to act decisively in the public interest. Under their rule, political parties formed private armies and conditions sometimes approached anarchy.

On November 8, 1918, Revolutionary Socialist Republics were declared in Munich and Berlin. The center party, the Social Democrats, took the first decisive actions against them. — They promptly killed Rosa Luxembourg and Karl Liebknecht, who had been the leaders of the communist movement in Germany.

The Thule Society was not far behind. On November 9th, at a hastily assembled meeting, the Master of the lodge, declared that:[18] "Yesterday we experienced the collapse of everything which is familiar, dear, and valuable to us. I am determined to pledge Thule to this struggle." They, then, began building a private army and on April 30, 1919, stormed Munich. This successful counter–revolution gained them wide support in German high society.

During the Autumn of 1918, the Thule society sponsored the formation of workers discussion groups. They were highly successful and Anton

---

ernment the Nazis were founding. At least, that appears to have been Himmler's intention.

[17] These were due to the Bolsheviks reducing the effectiveness of the Czar's Army.

[18] See David McWhinnie 1991. There appears to be a blackout on history from this period. But, the information is still in reference works if one is willing to ferret it out. The best source is probably books from the period, in private collections.

Drexler reformed them into the German Workers Party. Their membership was mostly not aware that they had been originated by the Thule Society. In September 1919, the Army became interested in them and sent a spy to observe what they were doing.

That spy was Adolf Hitler.[19] During the Great War, he had risen to the rank of corporal and had earned the Iron Cross, first class. But by 1919, he was back in civilian life. However, when the Army called upon him to spy on this newly formed party, he accepted. By January, 1920, he had become their head of propaganda and had drawn up a new constitution for them. During that year, much of their original leadership would be displaced, they would change their name to the National Socialist German Workers Party, and adopt the swastika as their emblem.

The Nazi's first came before the public's view when they made a triumphant entry into Coburg. In that case, they arrived in a special train and, after a scuffle, freed that city from the appointed councils which had, hitherto, been ruling them. Thus, they appeared as the popular defenders of the German people against communism. After that, they experienced a period of growth.

But, that came to an end during the Autumn of 1923. — Immediately following the Bavarian Prime Minister's declaration of an independent Bavaria, they staged a mass demonstration in opposition. But they faced German Federal troops, several of them were killed, and Hitler was sentenced to detention in a fortress.

That was when he wrote the first part of *Mein Kampf*. By then, the Nazi's fundamental orientation was essentially established: They were German nationalists, collectivists, anti–communists and obligately tied to the Neo–Gnostic beliefs of the Thule Society.[20] But, their position had to be drawn together and articulated. That was what *Mein Kampf* did.

When Hitler was released from jail, after serving less than a year of a five-year sentence, he reformed the Nazi Party. This time they had a clearly delineated set of beliefs and a leadership appointed by him.

He stated in *Mein Kampf*, that he understood the emotional content of the people's yearning to be their religious feeling, and declared his intention to provide a doctrinal faith which would transform that emotion into active service. In particular, addressing their unfocused desire for freedom he

---

[19] As a boy, Hitler, had attended a Benedictine Monastery School. Their Abbot was fascinated by the Albigensian heresy and the beliefs of the Cathers. That may have initiated Adolf's interest in Gnosticism and the Occult. Later while he was pursuing art and architecture in Vienna, he began studying the occult. He was a regular subscriber to *Ostara* and is also said to have been influenced by the teachings of Madame Blavatski. Jean–Michel Angebert examined the role the occult played in the Third Reich.

[20] Their collectivist nature and their relation to the communists were discussed by F. A. Hayek, in 1944: "... communists and Nazis or Fascists clashed more frequently with each other than with other parties. They competed for the support of the same type of mind and reserved for each other the hatred of the heretic. ......they both know that there can be no compromise between them and those who really believe in individual freedom.

wrote: "Only when the idealistic longing for independence is organized in such a way that it can fight for its ideal with military force, only then can the urgent wish of a people be transformed into a potent reality."

The system–of–belief which he formulated was based on Hegel's model in which the Transcendent Spirit is the totality of the souls of the people. Consequently he formed an Hegelian synthesis which tried to incorporate most of the aspects of what then composed Germany's heritage.[21]

The Nazi's belief differed from Hegel's in that their Image of God was determined by the Fuhrer, Hitler. He defined what the Spirit of the People would be, and he appears to have endeavored to accurately interpret their goals and beliefs in light of what would benefit the State. The rule on which social truths were incorporated may have been described by the Nazi Minister Robert Ley when he said that "Truth is whatever benefits the State; error is whatever does not benefit the State."   — As that was a time when Germany was oppressed and divided as a nation and a people, it follows that the goals of freedom and nationalism, may well have been among the principle Gods for a significant segment of the population. Hitler also recognized "people" as a racial rather than a religious concept.

His religious system drew heavily on the Nordic mysticism of List and Neo–Gnosticism. From the latter he adopted the Gnostic concept of radical dualism. Their Good principle was the totality of the Spirit of the German Race, while their Evil principle was the totality of the Spirit of the Jewish Race; and he felt that the nature of these peoples reflects their inherent psychological composition. In particular, he held that the Aryan peoples have the ability to perceive pure forms and the Laws of Nature[22] and from this comes all creativity, beauty, and civilization, but that other peoples lack that ability, and the Jews are destructive to it. He viewed mankind as being divided among these three basic types and life as the eternal struggle between these principles and races.

Hitler also incorporated Existentialism. This can be clearly seen in their adoption of the swastika. He also cast his system in the experiential world. Specifically, he took Nietzsche's myth of the Superman and gave it concrete meaning, he identified the Nazi mythology with the German and Jewish peoples, and he became their personal messianic leader.

---

[21] Alfred Rosenberg was the chief ideologist of the National Socialists, but the academic community did not consider him to be a philosopher of the first rank and the Nazi Party never accepted any academic philosophy as doctrine. They tended to be suspicious of academics and avoided making too clear a statement about their philosophical/religious position. Rosenberg's *The Myth of the Twentieth century* may be the nearest thing to a comprehensive academic philosophy for the National Socialists. The only German philosopher of the first rank who came close to providing a Nazi philosophy was Martin Heidegger, in 1933. But these fall short of the State doctrine, which was very effectively aimed at the subconscious minds of their target audience.

[22] Hitler says in *Mein Kampf*, " — If men should forget that wherever they have reached a superior level of existence, it is not the result of following the ideas of crazy visionaries, but by acknowledging and rigorously observing the iron law of Nature."

Their myths of blood and soil were also very affective. Blood in the Western mythology is identified with racial descent but, also, with soul and Spirit; whereas soil is the tie of a productive agrarian people to the land. — These myths gave the Germans the biblical characteristics of the line of Jacob, as opposed to the Jews to whom they attributed the character of the line of Esau. Thus, the Nazi myths also incorporated symbolism from the *Bible*.

When the Nazis were in power, they appointed State Agencies to develop their mythology. They tried to coalesce all the myths and symbols from the totality of their culture into a single comprehensive whole. They also developed songs, rituals, pageantry, festivals, holidays, and all the other appurtenances of a religion.

The Nazis provide an example of how a religion can be constructed to mobilize the broad lower strata of society. — It was the quintessential image of them: It was based on their myths, played upon their sensitivities and prejudices, and strove after their goals. It told them what they wanted to hear, gave meaning and interest to their lives, said that what they wanted to do was morally right, and organized them to take action.

Their ministry of propaganda and culture conducted many successful state-of-the-art programs to reach their adult population. For just one example, they were the first nation to use government controlled radio broadcasts to inundate their population.

Progressive education was one of their key programs.[23] As we saw in Hegel's philosophy, it was the German people's sacred duty to merge their personal Images of God with the Spirit of their Race: that is not merely to follow the beliefs of the Nazi Party but to incorporate them into their very souls.

The Nazis used all the modern techniques, then available, to teach their new culture. The results were impressive. About this, Hitler, said in 1939, "When an opponent declares 'I will not come over to your side,' I calmly say 'Your child belongs to us already. What are you? You will pass on. Your descendants, however, now stand in the new camp. In a short time they will know nothing else but this new community.' "

In concluding this topic, it will be useful, for future reference, to provide a general definition of a "Nazi." — A Nazi is an anti-materialistic[24]

---

[23] Their strongest supporters in the academic community were involved with progressive education. It was especially advanced by Herman Keyserling (1880–1946), the poet Stefan George (1863–1933), and the statesman Walther Rathenau (1867–1925). It was popularized as part of National Socialism by Arthur Moeller van den Bruck (1876–1925), Houston Stewart Chamberlain (1855–1927), and Alfred Rosenberg (1893–1946). Alfred Baumler, the staunchest supporter of National Socialism among the German academic philosophers, was appointed professor of pedagogy at the University of Berlin. Ernst Krieck was another German philosopher of education. He developed a philosophy of education for the master race.

[24] The Nazis allowed private ownership and supported small businesses, but they generally controlled the larger financial concerns through public–private

cameralist and extreme collectivist who follows Neo–Gnostic beliefs which include a radical dualism in which the Good and Evil principles are each a people.

---

partnerships, and all jobs became either State jobs or their wages and working conditions were set by the State. Capitalism was held in poor regard, as a "Jewish" viewpoint; the "German" viewpoint was cameralism.

Chapter 13

The New Deal

This chapter covers the new order for America which was developed at Harvard and the University of Chicago after the First World War.

13.1 Fraternal and Religious Organizations

In preparation for the new order which would follow World War I, various fraternal and religious organizations were formed in America to provide a social infrastructure at the grass roots level.

The Freemasons: After Italy was united, the Freemasons withdrew from the van of the revolutionary movement and concentrated on forming fraternal societies. This were the origin of most of today's college Sororities and Fraternities.

These fraternal organizations provided a social infrastructure, binding people together into networks at the grassroots level. That prepared the way for the new democratic order which President Woodrow Wilson would try to establish after World War I. But, he did not succeed. So, the social structures the Freemasons set up never assumed their intended role. They simply remained fraternal societies. That is how the Freemasons came to be what they are today.

During their reorganization, in the 1870's, the Freemasons also added a new top level, based on Neo–Gnosticism. That is the form of belief taught by the New Age Movement. They were discussed earlier in the section on the Nazi's, and more will be said later on, in relation to the environmental movement.

The Jehovah's Witnesses were another development of the pre–war era. They were consistent with the other preparations for the new order. They would have provided a Christian social infrastructure at the

211

grass roots level.

Specifically, they were founded by Charles Taze Russell (1852–1916) in Allegheny, Pennsylvania, in 1877, immediately after the Franco–Prussian War. He was, then, only 25 years old. He sold his interest in his father's habadashery and became a full–time preacher. Two years later he began publishing *Zion's Watch Tower* and, in 1881, he founded a non–profit *Bible* society.

Like the Unitarians he rejected the Holy Trinity and the need for clergy. His beliefs were based on Christian Fundamentalism with a focus on God's coming Kingdom on Earth. The book of *Revelation* was of particular importance to him as he saw its prophesies of the end times being fulfilled in the Fabian scheme for world domination.

He organized his "churches" as *Bible* study groups. At that time they had not yet taken the name of Jehovah's Witnesses, but referred to themselves simply as *"Bible* students."

Russell thought that 1914, which was the date of the beginning of World War I,[1] would be a major turning point in history. He did not know all the details, but he thought that God's Kingdom on Earth might be founded then: That is, he interpreted "the war to end all wars" as the general conflagration described in *Revelation* 12 and 13.[2] Consequently he and his followers felt an urgency in spreading their message. Russell died suddenly, in 1916, but his followers continued his efforts.

The failure of the League of Nations did not phase them. — They, then, noticed that Chapters 12 and 13 of *Revelation* describe several stages in the evil times near the end. Now, they expect the UN to rise to world domination before Christ's second coming.

During the 1920's, they changed their methods so that most of their members participated in house–by–house lay ministry, spreading the word; in 1931 they took the name of Jehovah's Witnesses; and in 1935, concurrent with F.D. Roosevelt's New Deal, they "came to a clearer understanding regarding the heavenly kingdom class, who will reign with Christ, and their subjects on Earth."[3] They held that Christ's second coming, was to be an invisible presence. He will, then, rule the earth for a thousand years, with the aid of 144,000 anointed persons in heaven,[4] but the remainder of mankind would remain on Earth as obedient subjects. — They regard the universal salvation of man as secondary to the vindication of Jehovah's Sovereignty. And, they point out that "a kingdom needs subjects."

---

[1] But, had it not been for Hoover, that might have been the year the war ended.

[2] Russell was by no means the first to see current events as the unfolding of the prophesies in *Revelation*. For example, Josephus reported that one night all the infants in the small town of Engaddi were slain due to concern that one of them might be the "male child who is to rule all the nations with a rod of iron." as described in *Revelation* 12:5. Later, Attila the Hun would claim to have been born there, in order to cloak himself with that character.

[3] See Watchtower Bible and Tract Society of Pennsylvania 1990.

[4] See *Revelation* 20.

In that theocratic State, of the end times, their lay ministry will play the role of Rousseau's teacher, gently instructing and guiding. That millennium will be a transitional period during which mankind learns to follow God's law. In the end, mankind will have returned to the perfection which Adam enjoyed before the fall, caused by his eating of the tree of knowledge. At the end of that millennium, Christ will hand–over the Kingdom to God, and all existence will be resorbed into Him.

Like the Anabaptists, before them, they do not participate in civil society, nor do they value man's works as they say that Jehovah will destroy all of these. They regard the multitude of man's religions as the root of all evil, identifying them with the harlot of Babylon in *Revelation*.[5] They also would erase all distinctions among nations and races.

During the 1930's, to prepare to fill their role, they increased their commitment to lay ministry. With this came a need for increased organization. So, they adopted a system of unpaid elders and ministerial servants. "Their appointments are made by a governing body of anointed elders from various lands who ... hold weekly meetings in their world headquarters in Brooklyn, New York, and send instructions to the branch committees in each country."[6]

During the Second World War, they began an aggressive international campaign and, in 1943, they founded a school to train their lay ministers. Although they were conscientious objectors and did not participate in the fighting, the Nazi's executed about a thousand of them, between 1933 and 1945. The Witnesses have continued their programs in much the same way ever since.

Although, their literature is anti–League of Nations and anti–UN, and they earnestly study the *Bible*, the structure they are building is entirely compatible with world government. They provide a "Christian" alternative to the social infrastructure at the grassroots level provided by the fraternal organizations. They are outspoken and explicit that this is their intended role under a future theocratic worldwide government.

---

[5] See Watchtower Bible and Tract Society of Pennsylvania 1990.

A more conventional interpretation of the symbolism in that prophetic allegory is that it reflects the historical events of John's times. — The protracted smoldering war which afflicted Palestine finally resolved itself into a conflict between the two great cities of the Classical world, Rome and Babylon, and their attendant cultures and religions or, to be more particular, between the Romans and the Pharisees. John symbolized the former as the "beast" and the latter as the "whore." The Christians and the followers of the older Jewish religious traditions were members of neither camp. — John was telling them to adhere to their faith, for a glorious new dawn would follow the darkest hour.

Jehovah's Witnesses can be so clearly identified with the Roman approach of an authoritarian collectivist system, that one can understand their need to provide a novel reinterpret of this allegory.

[6] See Watchtower Bible and Tract Society of Pennsylvania 1990.

13.2 Social Sciences

In America, immediately after the failure of the League of Nations, the leaders of industry realized that they still had not arrived at a satisfactory structure for society. So, they encouraged university research departments to find one.

The people working at Harvard on these issues, during 1920's and 1930's, included Lawrence J. Henderson, who towered over the others in scientific achievement; B.F. Skinner, who popularized the stimulus–response method; and Elton Mayo, who was one of the pioneers of industrial psychology. — He had begun his studies on these questions at the Warton School at the University of Pennsylvania, during the war. In 1926, with Rockefeller funding, he moved to Harvard and opened their Laboratory of Industrial Psychology.[7] But it was Vilfredo Pareto who provided the core ideas which they followed. — He was the son of a Mazzinist. His father had thought that the revolution would bring about a golden age ruled by reason. But, Vilfredo found that Italian society consisted of people who were driven by subconscious urges. He became disillusioned and virulently anti–democratic.

Harvard's Paretian orientation represented a significant change in perspective. For example, when Bernard De Voto, an English Professor at Harvard, wrote in *Saturday Review* that Pareto had superseded Marx in his description of the driving forces of society, it was not well received by the liberal establishment.[8] — The Harvard group was "conservative," in the sense that they represented moneyed interests,[9] and Henderson is quoted as having acknowledged that Pareto had been referred to among them as the "Karl Marx of the Bourgeoisie."[10]

Harvard's work on social psychology interlocked with their business school, which became dedicated to creating the managerial class who would run the system.

At the same time, there was another major effort under way at Rockefeller's University of Chicago. That was already a center for progressive education, and they had, also, been involved in the Aldrich Plan, which was the Republican equivalent of the Federal Reserve Act.[11]

During the late 1920's, Charles E. Merrium and Guy Moffett founded

---

[7] From 1924–1938 that Lab's primary work was done in collaboration with the Western Electric Company.

[8] "A Primer for Intellectuals." *Saturday Review of Literature* 9, April 22, 1933. See also the letter to the editor, by Kinsley Davis, *Saturday Review* 9, May 20, 1933. Later De Voto wrote a longer defense of Pareto, "Sentiment and the Social Order," *Harpers Monthly Magazine* 16, October 1933.

[9] At that time, J. P. Morgan was their principle supporter. He supported the Theodore Roosevelts of the world. He was "conservative" in the sense that Bismark was, rather than in the Western tradition.

[10] See Scott 1992.

[11] Professor of political economics at the University of Chicago, J. Lawrence Laughlin, was given a years leave to campaign for this Act.

the Public Administration Clearing House (PACH) there,[12] with Rockefeller funds. They concentrated on training public administrators in the
new psychological methods and assisting their professional advancement.
They concentrated particularly on producing administrators for local and
County governments. Over the years, that program had a tremendous
impact.

Chester Bernard was one of the key figures in this overall effort.[13] He
was a telephone company executive, but his importance was that from 1940
to 1952 he was a trustee of the Rockefeller Foundation, and their president
from 1948 to 1952. They funded much of this research.

After about two decades these research programs arrived at a system
which worked. In particular, the 1938 final report of Harvard's Laboratory
of Industrial Psychology showed conclusively that they had been successful
in influencing employee's subconscious attitudes about their jobs.[14] Their
approach was a form of thought–control which they felt Americans would
accept. James Burnham wrote, in 1941, about this that: "Frequently,
in the United States, it is not totalitarianism but Russian or German —
in general, 'foreign' — totalitarianism that is objected to; a 100 percent
American totalitarianism would not be objectionable."[15] These developments did not go unobserved at the time.[16]

13.3   Hoover Administration

President Hoover began the implementation of this new order, which was
still partially at the planning stages. He had been intimately associated
with it from its very beginning and seems to have moved among all the
various parties. In particular, after the war he was one of the founders of
the Council of Foreign Relations, and later he was in close contact with
the Paretian scholars at Harvard, but his primary academic association
appears to have been with the University of Chicago.

His presidential campaign was heavily financed by the German international bankers on Wall Street, including Kohn–Loeb, and J. Henry
Schroder Corp.[17] Mullin (1993) concluded that they wanted him elected to

---

[12] Their address, 1313 East 60th Street, lends them the name "1313" which you
will find attached to them and the various organizations they founded.

[13] See his biography by William G. Scott, 1992. It gives a fairly detailed account of these programs, written by a retired professor who had some first–hand
knowledge of these things.

[14] See Roethlisberger, Fritz J. and William J. Dickson 1939.

[15] See his page 153.

[16] For a small selection, see William Z. Ripley 1927, Wallace Donham 1927;
George C. Homans and Charles P. Curtis jr. 1934; James Burnham 1941,
Friedrich A. Hayek 1944, and George Orwell 1946. For recent reviews with more
references see John A. Rohr 1986 and Scott 1992.

[17] Schroder Bank was established by the Schroder family of Hamburg during
the nineteenth century. Today it is one of the largest banks in the world, in
particular, it is ranked number two in capitalization of the member banks of

suspend payment on the German war debts. This moratorium was of vital interest to them because, it would allow Germany to rearm for World War II. The Nazis political movement and their rearmament was also financed by those same parties or their affiliates.[18] — One of the first things Hoover did when he got into office was suspend their payments.

But while he was in office he also implemented several other changes. One of these was an amendment he had attached to a bill, in 1930, which specified that Presidential Executive Orders would become law in thirty days unless Congress overrode them. Hoover said that this was "putting inertia on the side of change."

However, he is best known for having ushered in the Great Depression,[19] That doomed him to a single term in office. But it also created the disruption of life and habits which is essential to get the public to accept change.

Hoover was fully aware of what were then the modern methods of psychology for molding society's views. He implemented them. In particular, during the Autumn of 1929 he appointed the six member Research Committee on Recent Social Trends.[20] Their mission was to use the depression

---

the Bank of England (Mullins 1993), and its partners have often served as the Governor of the Bank of England, for example this occurred from 1973 to 1983. During the Reagan years, several executives from Schroder Bank and Bectel Corp held important posts in his administration.

[18] The J. Henry Schroder Corp. was particular involved in the Second World War, just as Kuhn Loeb had been in the First. That firm's German subsidiary was Adolf Hitler's personal bank and provided the financial assistance for his rise to power.

Baron Kurt von Schroeder was the President of the Deutsche Reichs Bank under the Nazis and an SS group leader, while the American branch of Schroder Bank managed the German government's investments in the United States (see Victor Perlo).

J. Henry Schroder was a close associate of President Hoover and profited from grain and sugar monopolies he assisted in setting up. The Schroder Company merged with Rockefeller Inc in 1938 to become Schroder–Rockefeller and they, in turn, set up the Bechtel Corporation, then the world's largest construction firm. They did a large part of the war construction for the United States.

[19] It was caused by the Federal Reserve first decreasing the interest rate in 1927, fueling wild stock speculation, and then abruptly increasing it in 1929, causing the crash on October 1929. Thus, it was artificially induced. See Mullins 1993.

Chairman of the House Banking and Currency Committee, Congressman McFadden submitted a resolution for President Hoover's impeachment, on December 13, 1932.

[20] Chaired by economist Wesley C Mitchell and including Charles E. Merriam (a social science professor at the University of Chicago, and co–founder of PACH) Shelby M. Harrison, Alice Hamilton, Howard W. Odum, and William F. Ogburn, a professor at the University of Chicago. There were also a host of others who helped in the research. That included, Charles H. Judd, of the University of Chicago who did their education study. He had been one of the students of William Wundt. Thomas J. Woofter who did their study on race relations. If you ever wondered about the origins of racial strife in America, look here. Their head of research was Eveline Burns, an English citizen, and a member of England's

to change America's culture. William Ogburn, the editor of their publications, had published a long series of books and research articles on social psychology which leaves little doubt that the Research Committee would focus on social change.[21] They were privately funded by the Rockefeller Foundation and, therefore, were outside of legislative oversight.

They were to concentrate on social instabilities rather than stabilities. The instabilities they found include virtually every issue which has been regarded as a "problem" since then.[22] As Hoover wrote in the introduction to the Committee's comprehensive report, October 11, 1933: "It should serve to help us all to see where social stresses are occurring and where major effort should be undertaken to deal with them constructively."

They used the stimulus–response methodology pioneered by William Wendt and Ian Pavlov. This was before Skinner popularized it. It had five steps in this application:

1. They began with some ideas on what the social values of the American people were and what types of public programs might induce them to change.

2. That knowledge was used to develop public programs to change the people's values.

3. Those policies were implemented for one year;

4. At the end of the year, data were collected on the social values of the people. The committee wrote annual reports on their current status and what the changes had been in the people's values. These were analyzed using a predecessor to sensitivity analysis or shock testing[23] to determine how they had responded to the program;

---

radical movement. According to statements made to Congress by Noah Mason, she provided the connection between the London School of Economics and the University of Chicago. (See Heaton 1993.)

[21] A few of his titles include:*Social Change with Respect to Culture and Original Nature, On Culture and Social Change, Recent Social Changes Since the War and Particularly in 1927, Social Characteristics of Cities: A Basis for New Interpretations of the Role of the City in American Life*

[22] The sensitivities they identified included the environmental movement, population growth, abortion, sex education, immigration, interracial marriage, the Black revolution, loss of belief in moral standards, child care by government, religious issues ...

[23] These are from a family of related methods. The most widely known of them may be "vibration testing," which has been used in mechanical and aeronautical engineering since the late 1950's. In that method a vibrator is attached to one part of a structure, such as the wingtip of an airplane and the rest of the plane is examined to see if it sets up any sympathetic vibrations. Such a response implies that the other structure's mechanical behavior is related to the one which is being vibrated. These sympathetic vibrations may be frequency specific. Therefore, the vibrator is run through the full spectrum of frequencies.

The same approach is also used in electrical engineering. In that case the vibrator is replaced by a wave generator. However, an alternative to running through all the frequencies is to input a square–wave, because Fourier analysis

5. Go to step 2.

This cycle was repeated each year for as long as the Committee was active.

William Ogburn published the Committee's final report in 1935.[24] In it he says: "The examination shows clearly enough, however, that none of the social trends studied have been unaffected. Indeed, the economic upheaval has had profound social reverberations."

These studies were intimately related to the research which was then going on at Harvard. In particular, the Paretian Scholars believed in controlling people through their subconscious minds and these studies, conducted by the Hoover Administration, were directed at finding the keys to the public's behavior.

Harvard economics professor Alvin Hansen worked directly with the Federal Reserve to coordinate their economic policies with the committee's efforts to mold America's social values, while Harvard Economics Professor Wassily Leontief[25] examined the structure of the American economy. He introduced the use of input–output analysis and, later, linear models to describe the relationships between the major segments of the American economy. Sensitivity analysis, such as the Hoover Administration's studies represented, potentially provides the coefficients in the transition matrix, which is the heart of a linear model.[26] However, the computations involved

---

shows that square–waves contain all frequencies.

A variation on this is "shock testing," in which a single square pulse is used. That might be created by turning on a switch in an electrical system. The Hoover administration was doing shock testing by abruptly changing financial and employment conditions and then observing the responses. By the end of four years of this, they had substantially improved their understanding of how the American socio–economic system functioned.

[24] William F. Ogburn 1935.

[25] Leontief was born in Leningrad, Russia, in 1906. He attended the University of Leningrad and then the University of Berlin, where he received his PhD, in 1928. He worked at the Institute for Weltwirtschaft at the University of Keil during his doctoral program and for a short time afterwards. Next he worked briefly as an economic advisor to China and then for the National Bureau of Economic Research in New York. He joined Harvard University in 1931. From 1945–1975 he was the director of the Harvard Economic Research Project on the Structure of the American Economy. He received the Nobel Prize for Economic Analysis in 1973. In 1975, he became Professor of Economics at New York University and in 1978 was also appointed director of their Institute for Economics. His principle works are his, 1941, *Structure of American Economy, 1919–1929*; *An Empirical Application of Equilibrium Analysis (1941)*; and *Input Output Economics* (1966) He also published many articles in scientific journals.

[26] Linear models usually work reasonably well, provided there are sufficient data to estimate the large number of coefficients in the transition matrix, and provided that the model is not extrapolated beyond the data set. But data are often limited and extrapolation, to provide a basis for planning, has often been the sole purpose of the exercise. The resulting bad science has produced some infamous failures. These do not, however, invalidate the approach when it is properly applied.

usually are tedious, so Leontief's earlier methods were based on a grid–like table which contained the inputs and outputs from various segments of the economy. With the advent of the computer age, the linear modeling approach became practical. It was widely used from the 1950's through the 1970's, and it is still used today, although, in the scientific world it has been superseded by modern statistical analysis and realistic modeling.[27]

Thus, Leontief introduced modeling into economics. Today, economic studies often involve large teams of scientists and technicians. A trip to a university library will reveal thick tomes expounding on massive models which are impenetrable to the general public and take technical people considerable effort to understand.

A current economic study appears to have begun in 1998, which marks a significant advance in economic analysis. — Safeway, Rite–Aid, and possibly other large nation–wide retail companies offer their customers substantial discounts for using a "club–card." Computer technology, then, allows purchases to be recorded on an individual basis and these data can be combined with comprehensive data files to obtain information on the individual's psychological type, sex, age, marital status, income level, and so on. This allows analysis to be done at a level of detail which was previously not possible.[28]

Hoover's Research Committee on Social Trends also had a component on religion, but that was insignificant compared to a completely private program run by the Rockefeller Foundation's Institute for Social and Religious Research. Their final report was massive, in 78 volumes.[29] Their main concerns were that there should be no religious revival nor any increase in religious intolerance. According to their reports, they successfully achieved these objectives. This apparently was due to the large number of itinerant preachers, who absorbed and diffused the religious impulses of the times. The Rockefeller Foundation closed that program in 1935, after

---

[27] Realistic modeling involves the use of equations which refer explicitly to processes in the real world, whereas the statistical approach is to use the equations which are best supported by data. Combining these approaches provides a powerful technique which makes linear modeling obsolete, except in special circumstances.

[28] It overcomes the statistical difficulty of "under–specification bias." A study of the causes of chronic alcoholism gives a good example of this bias: They found that the number of habitual drunkards was highly correlated with the number of Baptist ministers, in cities across the American South. But, they had neglected to include the population size of the cities. Both the number of drunks and the number of ministers in any town were directly related to its size. Once this factor had been accounted for, there was no longer any significant relationship between drunkards and ministers. — The first estimate suffered from underspecification bias, whereas the second one did not.

Before club cards, the best which could be done was to randomize over all the factors affecting economic behavior, and estimate the aggregate behavior of the masses. But, these estimates were prone to fail whenever the composition of the public changed, which it is constantly doing.

[29] See Paul H. Douglass and Edmund S. Brunner 1935.

the crisis was over.

13.4   FDR Administration

The Depression began in October 1929, the year Hoover took office and got progressively worse each year, as the Federal Reserve progressively tightened credit. They said they did this to prevent inflation. The Depression reached its low point in the winter of 1932–1933. That was when Franklin D. Roosevelt was elected. Conditions promptly improved when he infused funds into the economy through government projects and by having the Federal Reserve relax credit. Those actions increased public confidence and drew private money back into circulation, thereby, reestablishing financial liquidity. The economy did not, however, fully recover until the war effort revived industry.

Roosevelt's approach was based on the economic theories of John Keynes (1883–1946).[30] He recognized that economic "rules" reflected the aggregate financial behavior of the people and were governed by their social psychology.[31] — His work was fully consistent with the ongoing research at Harvard and the University of Chicago.

Towards the end of his term in office, Hoover had made another important innovation. This was his misuse of the Economic Stabilization Act of 1931. It had authorized and funded the construction of structures. Congress had intended that to mean buildings, dams, and other physical structures would be built to get the economy moving. However, those funds were used to create a bureaucracy, a "control structure," the National Resources Planning Board (NRPB). It was to act as the implementation arm for the planned economy. It was set up by President Hoover and handed over to President Roosevelt, who used it.

When President Franklin. D. Roosevelt took office, one of his first acts was to appoint Charles E. Merriam as the director of the newly cre-

---

[30] John Maynard Keynes was a student of Alfred Marshall and followed him as Professor of Political Economy at Cambridge. After the First World War, he served as treasurer to the Peace Conference at Versailles, but he resigned from that post because of his passionate objection to the treaty's unreasonably harsh terms. He then wrote his (1919) *Economic Consequences of Peace*, which made him an international celebrity overnight. His principle contributions to economics were contained in his (1923) *The Tract on Monetary Reform*, (1930) *Treatise on Money*, and particularly his (1936) *General Theory of Employment, Interest, and Money*.

[31] His most important contribution was that he considered the impact which private savings and income levels have upon the economy. He also was much more effective at describing the dynamics of liquidity. One of his principle concerns was preventing the accumulation of private savings. Thus, he continued the trend back toward the position of Richardo from that of Mill and Marshall, but also continued the trend which Marshall began of incorporating social psychology. He is considered to be the father of macroeconomics: that is the study of economic systems whose structure changes in response to economic and social conditions.

ated NRPB. Its other two members were Wesley Mitchell and Frederick Delano.[32] President Roosevelt called them "the planning arm of my executive office." They had two special functions "conservation of natural resources and government planning to achieve social goals."[33] They functioned for a decade (1933-1943). Throughout that period they produced reports at least annually.

They stated their overall objective in their 1937 report. It was to so alter the government of the United States that it could be merged with a world-wide administratively controlled structure outside the realm of politics. They had been moving America towards that goal by promoting "model laws" which transferred powers delegated by the public to elected representatives to the executive branch, to bureaucrats, or to citizen's committees.

Their most important recommendation was the establishment of a permanent planning board based on the principle that "good management is local self-government under central supervision."[34] However, bills to establish that system were defeated for the next four years (1935-1938). It was finally passed and funded in 1939 as part of a reorganization plan for the executive office. By 1943 the NRPB had expanded to 150 full time employees 72 field employees and 35 consultants.

13.5 Democratic Elitism

The NRPB was the beginning of the new form of government for the United States. It marks the beginning of the Post-Constitutional era of American history.

Throughout the rest of the century, this new type of government grew and expanded as the powers of representative bodies and elected officials were progressively transferred to government agencies, appointed committees, and professional managers. That has progressed, in some cases, so far that elected officials remain only as a thin facade over an essentially administrative government whose views are determined but clites outside of the public sector.

---

[32] Frederick Delano was the president's uncle. He was an American citizen but had been born in Hong Kong, in 1863. According to Mullins (1993), his father, Warren Delano, had been active in the Chinese opium trade. Frederick Delano had been a railroad operator and took over a number of lines for Kuhn Loeb Co. He had also been a member of the first Federal Reserve Board. Later he had been chairman of the privately funded citizens study of the Joint Committee on Bases of Sound Land Policy, which in 1929 issued a 168 page report *What about the Year 2000?* That answered the questions, "Will the land area of the United States meet the demands of our future population? and How are we to determine the best use of our land resources? from an economic standpoint.

[33] See the *Global 2000 Report to the President*

[34] See their December 1934 report. That report otherwise dealt with the planning and control of land-use and water.

In general, democratic elitism functions as follows. — Policies begin in a private planning organization, as an outline of general principles. As they progress from that top elite planning group through the government process and control structures to the local governments, they gradually take form. That allows them to be adapted to regional and local conditions. The control structure's role is to oversee that process.

In particular, from 1933 until 1960, the Council of Foreign Relations is thought to have been the top American elite planning organization.[35] They were composed of the heads of industry and finance together with leading political figures. They were the source of most of the plans of national significance, throughout those three decades.

They introduced their policies into the public sector through their representatives who sat on the boards of committees, such as the NRPB. The function of these control structures was to submit those policies to the Executive or Legislative branch to get them enacted, either by executive order or by legislation. Once they were passed, their next job was to transmit those policies to State and Local Governments and induce them to implement them.

At first, the National Resources Planning Board was the only control structure, but gradually others developed in parallel to them. These came and went as the political climate changed. They have included the National Security Resources Board and the Advisory Committee on Intergovernmental Relations. The oldest control structure in existence, today, may be a council of government (COG) in the region around Eugene, Oregon. It was founded in 1947, during President Truman's Administration.

Organizations serving a similar function also developed in the State, Regional, and private sectors. The most prominent of these were the professional organizations for the new class of managers, who have taken over much of the day–to–day operation of municipal and county governments. Today, there are a plethora of such organizations, which are referred to collectively as the fifth estate.[36] The National League of Cities published a directory, in 1994, listing approximately one–hundred organizations which operated nation–wide, many of them are control structures.[37]

Professor Peter Bachrach, in 1967, coined a name for this new form of government. He called it "democratic elitism." The first description of it can be found in the last chapters of Gaetano Mosca's *Ruling Class*.[38]

---

[35] The Council on Foreign Relations declined after 1960, and was shattered by the Vietnam War. That left a power vacuum until the Trilateral Commission was formed. See Croizer et al. 1975.

[36] The first three estates are the Legislative, Executive, and Judicial Branches; the fourth estate is the press; and the fifth estate is this shadow government which operates behind the scenes.

[37] It is impossible to tell whether any specific organization is a control structure or serves a different function, without familiarity with the details of its operations. But, the assumption should generally be made that any organization which has influence and has been around for more than a few years was either founded by some Power elite of was infiltrated.

[38] The first edition was published in 1896. But, this is found in the second,

Two other important early contributors were Roberto Michels and Vilfredo Pareto. Between them they give the central concepts of this new system.[39] They were all strongly anti–democratic and elitist. However, in his later writings, Mosca recognized the utility of democracy in the context of a fundamentally elite–driven system. However, it was his bitter rival, Pareto, who the Harvard scholars adopted as their guiding light. He never relented in his contempt for the common man. His general attitude is well expressed in his statement, "We need not linger on the fiction of 'popular representation,' poppycock grinds no flour."[40]

Democratic elitism is inherently unstable, but as Mosca, Pareto, Bachrach and many others have pointed out, it obtains some balance from the conflicting interests of the many groups involved and also from their mutual interest in keeping it going. — It is in a continuous act of propping itself back up.

The ruling elites form one party in the sense that they all agree to perpetuate the system, but on other issues they form factions. The importance of this becomes clear in the context of Raymond Aron's, 1950, definitional statement that "the difference between a society of the Soviet type and one of the Western type is that the former has a unified elite and the later a divided elite." — Thus, according to him, the difference between the government structures of communist and "free" democracies is only a matter of degree, structurally, they are the same. — That would be absolutely true if America were run solely by democratic elitism. But, it is not. America still retains a remnant of its republican institutions, and they are not entirely powerless.

There is always the risk of one elite or a coalition dominating, but the largest concern is with individuals outside the system who might lead the public to rise against them. Mosca felt that as long as a place is found for all talented and ambitious people, they had nothing to fear.

Another constraint on the elites is that the people must not become aware of the true state of affairs, or must accept it. To this end, they have to temper their policies and they must also have reasonably good control over the news media. — These conditions, which are necessary for this system to operate effectively, might appear to be overly restrictive, but, in fact, this is effectively how America's government has been run since the 1930's.

The individual American citizen participates passively by voting but, in practice, is virtually powerless. They can only effectively exert influence through groups. In the nineteenth century, during the American republic, the citizens formed committees to address and resolve most every civic issue. They did, in fact, effectively determine the course of government. But, that period of direct democracy was far from ideal as it was plagued

---

enlarged, edition which was published in 1923.

[39] James Meisel, 1958 and Suzanne Keller, 1963, take a different view of the importance of these early contributors.

[40] See Pareto, translated in 1935.

by prejudice and intolerance.[41]

At times, the public still forms political organizations, today, but the experience is generally unsatisfactory. — They are naive and their organizations are quickly subverted. Thus, the common citizens can rarely hold their groups together long enough to formulate any new public policy, much less bring it to fruition. The public's choices, in practice, are mostly between the views of the various leaders of established groups, and these rarely reflect the real needs or wishes of the people.

An individual gains power by joining a established group and climbing its power structure.

By the mid–1960's the public's loss of control over government had created widespread apathy. However, that was not viewed as a disadvantage by everyone, as it is one of the necessary conditions for the continued effective functioning of this type of government.[42]

Nevertheless, the public still acts as a restraining force when things go too far astray. At those times, they rise up as a mass, get informed, and vote one or another elite out of power. But, soon the elites regain control and the public goes go back to sleep. Then, elections return to being little more than a beauty contest among competing political personalities. However, that is not always the case. Sometimes positive changes are made which have a prolonged effect. For example, California has passed regulatory reform, by initiative, making government workers accountable for their actions.

One of the key changes generally associated with democratic elitism is the centralization of control. On the local level that translates to the City or County Manager form of government. The National Municipal League and the Public Administration Service were, for many years its principle advocates. In 1940, the latter organization published a review of the manager form of government in which they explicitly stated that the intention was to produce a new form of government unhampered by the antiquities of separation of powers and checks and balances.[43] Under this form of government, elected officials make general policy decisions and hold the manager responsible for their implementation. The public employees are no longer under their direct authority and, in some cases, can not even be fired by them. These changes reduce accountability and concentrates power into the hands of a single individual, the manager. The next step, of course, is to gain that individual's loyalty or place a politically aligned person in that position.

However, the manager form of government can, also, be operated in a manner which better protects the rights and interests of the public. In particular, the City Council can appoint a City Manager in place of an elected Mayor. That is more like the structure of the original American Republic, in which the State Representatives originally appointed the Sen-

---

[41] See de Toqueville.
[42] For example see Bachrach 1967.
[43] See Heaton 1993.

ators. That avoids some of the problems of democracy by introducing an
elite element into local government. This may can give a better balancing
of powers, thus, providing better protections for all parties. But, whether
the City Manager form of government is a better or a worse thing depends
on the details of how it is set up and who is appointed.

Unfortunately, examples of where it has been an improvement are far
too rare. One reason for this may be that the advice on how to structure
the manager form of government, is often provided by control structures
and, may be directed at increasing their power and influence rather than
protecting the citizen's interests. Another is that City Managers are often
professionals trained in programs such as the one at the University of
Chicago or who are members of professional organizations which promote
various agendas.

If, as the result of this restructuring, the public employees escape accountability, some of them may be expected to draw into their hands and
abuse powers over which they have no rightful authority. This phenomenon
has been studied in prisons. For example, Zimbardo et al, in 1982, in a
study of a mock–prison, showed that slightly less than a third of the guards
were "good" and did not abuse their powers, a second third were tough–
but–fair but, "over a third of the guards were extremely hostile, arbitrary
and cruel in the forms of degradation and humiliation they invented." —
In this study, they used student volunteers as guards and prisoners. These
were healthy normal college students, so, they probably represented approximately the same population as enter public employment. Thus, this
study provides a baseline for what can be expected.

A common abuse found in local governments is that the employees act
as if they make the decisions on what a member of the public may or may
not do, rather than its being determined by a standing law. That deprives
the individual of his or her freedom. But this is done so consistently that
the public becomes accustomed to it. In fact, if you ask where the relevant
ordnances can be found, a common response is that "no one has ever
asked for that before." It may even be difficult to locate copies of them.
In many cases they may be guided by unwritten "policy." In addition,
many laws have become excessive, even draconian, so that the public is
driven to prefer the arbitrary decisions of a public employee to them. This
illustrates how far America has come from rule–by–law.

One of the reasons why democratic elitism has remained stable so long
is that, most Americans are not aware of their government's actual structure. In general, they continue to believe the myths set forth in the US
and State Constitutions about how their government functions.[44] Those
beliefs are the American political religion.[45] It was taught to them at a
tender age in school, and they took it and held it on faith. In this one

---

[44] That includes people in government. Because, their job consists of its routine
operation, they are habituated to it. They have scales before their eyes and are
not likely to recognize when their daily practice departs from the principles of
law.

[45] It developed contemporary with the Soviet political religion. The basic con-

very significant regard, the vast majority of the American public are at
the developmental stage of the infant or child. As a body, they are blind
to the truth and treat the suggestion that their myths might not be true
with the same spirit of intolerance as the people of the middle ages treated
the heresies of their times.

13.6   World War II

With the opening of hostilities in World War II, in 1939,[46] the NRPB
received a new mandate, "to collect, analyze, and collate all constructive
plans for significant public and private action in the post–defensive period
insofar as these have to do with the natural and human resources of the nation." But America did not enter the war until Pearl Harbor was bombed,
during December 1941.

The authority conferred upon President Roosevelt during World War
II was far greater than that granted to President Wilson. Roosevelt received almost unlimited power over natural resources, industry, the ra-
tioning of food, and the fixing of prices. There was a universal draft of
eligible men, many women entered the work force, and men and women
were "frozen" in their jobs in vital industries. The military took over many
of the schools and trained the children, while others, left without parental
guidance, roamed the streets. Rates of juvenile crime and prostitution
rose alarmingly. Family life was largely disrupted. In the realm of civil
liberties, the Alien Registration Act of 1940 allowed the arrest and punishment of any individual based on his or her nation of origin, religion, or
organizational membership, not for what he or she said or did. Freedom
of speech and of the press were suspended.... Many of these powers were
held, in practice, by the NRPB.

In 1943, the NRPB presented another report to Congress, outlining
their next proposal for a politically planned economy.[47] It was only then
that Congress discovered that for twelve years they had been planning a
new social and economic order without any authority whatsoever. The
agency had regional, State, and local planning agencies which developed
comprehensive plans. They undertook to get their plans implemented by
the appropriate government entities, and they used federal money to lobby
local and State governments to get them to comply with their plans.

---

cepts of constructing a religion by combining myth and tyranny come from Sorel.

[46] The Second World War began in Europe during September 1939, with Germany's invasion of Poland, but America didn't enter the war until December 1941
after the bombing of Pearl Harbor. The war in Europe ended May 1945 and the
war in the Pacific ended during August that same year.

[47] If you have ever wondered where the idea of shopping malls came from, look
in their 1943 report. As to their function, they say, "The malls are not important
in themselves. They are a means for moving existing businesses out of the way,
so the planners can have free access to the central core of the cities, to construct
the anew."

Congressman Frederick C. Smith of Ohio examined their programs, in 1945 and, as a result, they were dissolved. However, soon afterwards, the National Industrial Recovery Act recreated the NRPB's under a new name, the National Security Resources Board (NSRB). This time, expressly a part of the executive branch. It functioned under Roosevelt, but Truman (1945–1953) and Eisenhower (1953–61) both ignored its recommendations and it eventually faded out of existence.

War and Peace Study: The NRPB wasn't the only planning agency. There was a second one, working in parallel, in the private sector, outside of Congressional oversight. This was the Council of Foreign Relations' War and Peace Studies Project. The Rockefeller Foundation gave more than $300,000 to support it.[48] Before America ever entered the war, they were planning the new global order for the post–war period. They had groups planning for both the internal and external impact of the war.

According to Shoup and Minter, in 1980, this project had been initiated during September of 1939 when Hamilton F. Armstrong, the editor of *Foreign Affairs*, and Isaiah Bowman, the Council's director and president of John Hopkins University, met with the Assistant Secretary of State. They agreed that their recommendations would go to the Department and the President but would not be made public.

Bretton Woods Agreement: The July 24, 1940 recommendation from the economic and financial group of the War and Peace Studies Project was that a self–contained United States – Western Hemisphere economy is impossible without great changes in the US economic system. To that end, they recommended the formation of the International Monetary Fund and the World Bank. That apparently was the origin of these ideas. During 1942, a Cabinet Committee and the American Technical Committee worked out the details.[49]

During late 1943, the Department of State formed a special advisory committee for post–war planning. Ten of its fourteen members were members of the Council. It established the framework by which decisions on post–war policy would be made: that is, it defined what the national interest would be. Their decision was that America would emerge from the war as the single super–power in the West with the entire non–communist world enthralled in its economic hegemony.[50] According to Shoup and Minter, in 1980, that advisory committee contained a core group of 6 individuals.[51]

---

[48] See Notter 1949.

[49] Shoup and Minter, in 1980, said that these committees had strong representation from the Council.

[50] The massive transfer of funds, as the result of the war, partially accounted for the economic prosperity of America during the 1950's. During that decade, 45% – 60% of all the gold reserves in the world were in Fort Knox. Nor was money the only means of payment. England also paid with territorial possessions.

The Second World War, also, ended the preeminence of the Rothschild Banking system. They failed to make the shift from Europe to America with the center of world finance. That is why they are no longer as great a financial giant as they were throughout the nineteenth century.

[51] Cordell Hull, Politician; Sumner Welles, Government employee; Norman H

who later became known as the "Information Political Advisory Group" which President Roosevelt referred to as his postwar advisors. They were the men who guided the advisory committee. In 1944, at their recommendation, a meeting was convened in Bretton Woods to create that Post–War financial system and financial institutions. It produced the Bretton Woods Agreement, which defined the post–war economic system of the West.

13.7   Truman Administration

United Nations: During 1943 and 1944, Roosevelt's Information Political Advisory Group drafted the United Nations Charter. The United Nations is strongly influenced by the international corporations because it operates under a one–country–one–vote rule, except that the most powerful countries have a veto power, through their seat on the security council. — The important thing to realize, with regard to a general vote, is that the larger international businesses have greater economic strength than many of the smaller counties.[52] A coalition of large companies might, therefore, be in a position to exert substantial influence over enough smaller countries to affect the overall outcome.[53] The Council of Foreign Relations is just such a coalition and it was their representatives who designed the UN's structure.

When the soldiers came home after the war, they had had enough government regulation to last a life–time. Furthermore, some of them had seen too much and knew from experience that things were often not quite as government said they were. It had been just the same after the first world war. However, this time, the government took measures to control information and counteract the expected reaction. In particular, the Reece Commission found a clear statement in the 1946 report of the Rockefeller Foundation that it, together with the Council of Foreign Relations had orchestrated an "historical blackout" for that purpose.[54] As a result, the press was better controlled and President Truman was able to get the United Nations authorized, whereas, President Wilson had failed with the League of Nations.

However, the Allies from World War II soon fragmented into opposing factions. Consequently, the United Nations has served as a forum and

Davis, Banker and Roosevelt's ambassador at large; Myron C. Taylor, Corporate executive; Isaiah Bowman, president of Johns Hopkins University; and Leo Pavlovsky, economist

[52]For example, Holly Sklar, in 1980, lists companies and countries by 1976 gross national product and worldwide company sales. EXXON is 23rd on the list and General Motors is 24th. They lie between Czechoslovakia (22nd) and Austria (25th). Half of the top 130 economic entities are corporations.

[53]This was only counteracted after about 1960, when the smaller countries began acting in voting blocks for their mutual interest.

[54]See Rene Wormser 1958. p209–210. This was also described by Charles Beard and Mary Beard, in 1944, and by L. H. Shoup and W. Minter, in 1980.

international planning body rather than a super-governmental Power to enforce the Anglo-American-Soviet will globally.

The Chinese Communist Revolution had been smoldering, during the war. It broke out, in March 1946. America officially supported Nationalist China but President Truman followed the State Department's advice and adopted a noninterventionist policy. The State Department held that, "the ominous result of the civil war in China was beyond the control of the government of the United States."[55] According to the findings of the McCarren Commission, the acceptance of this viewpoint by the American public was largely due to the propaganda produced by the Institute for Pacific Relations. They had become *the* experts on the Far East and had influenced the State Department.[56] However, Congress was not swayed and voted a total of $2 billion in aid for the Nationalists. But, its delivery was delayed three years and was ineffective. The Nationalists were swept from the continent in 1949 and took refuge in Formosa.

McCarthy Era: These events caused a storm in Congress, during the early 1950's. Many Senators and Congressmen felt that the Chinese Nationalists had been betrayed and attacked the "pro-Communist policy of the Far-Eastern Division of the State Department."[57] Above this crowd of angry legislators rose Senator Joseph R. McCarthy of Wisconsin with his accusation that the State Department was "thoroughly infested" with Communists and various other accusations. Some of his accusations were seen to be absurd. This led to the formation of Congressional investigating committees, including the Cox, Reece, and Walsh Commissions.

The Reece Commission, in 1953, investigated the Rockefeller, Carnegie, and Ford Foundations.[58] They found that they had been actively involved in molding the American heritage. One of their objectives was replacing individualism with collectivist and internationalist ideas. Another was the establishment of the United Nations.

One of the great foundations had, infact, concluded that in order to influence the heritage of the nation, they would have to rewrite history. At first they had approached the best-respected historians of their day. But they turned them down, flat. — The Beards, reported the incident in one of their books. — Therefore, they formed the American Historical Association to influence the hiring of history professors. The new stable of professors produced their "history" in 1932, in seven volumes. After that, the older, traditional, historians became known as "revisionists."

The Reece Commission also found that the Carnegie Foundation for International Peace had determined that war was the best method for changing the life of the people. They had, therefore, worked to get America

---

[55] *United States Relations with China with Special Reference to the Period 1944-49.* US Department of State, Far Eastern Series, 30, Washington 1949.
[56] See Rene A Wormser 1958.
[57] See Senator Robert A. Taft 1951.
[58] See Rene A. Wormser 1958.

involved in the First World War. To that end, they formed the American Council on Learned Societies. It vetted all applicants for high official positions in the State Department, before their appointment. Thus, they acquired considerable influence over that Department and got America into the war.

These Congressional investigations provided valuable insight into American history for the period beginning slightly before the First World War up to the early 1950's. But, they only touched upon programs which were completed, such as the formation of the United Nations. They did not address things which were, then, current or in planning. In particular, they said nothing of America's elite–driven structure, nor did they give even a hint of the research in social psychology which was then going on.

13.8   Group Dynamics

During the late 1930's group processes gained recognition in psychology largely as the result of the pioneering work of Kurt Lewin , during the 1930's, at the University of Iowa and later at the Massachusetts Institute of Technology.[59] His work established group dynamics in the academic world.[60]

His most important finding was that certain methods of group discussion and decision making were superior to lecturing and individual instruction for changing ideas and social conduct.

An individual who is participating in a group discussion uses different mental processes than one who is making an individual decision or doing research. Specifically, the verbal and interactive processes are right–brain processes. We generally refer to them as "qualitative." In contrast, the rational and intellectual processes used in individual decision making and research are left–brain processes. We generally refer to them as "quantitative" or "analytical." The fact that decisions which are made in groups are obtained through different mental processes than individual decisions, explains the observation that groups often reach different types of decisions. This difference between the qualitative and the analytical is also the fundamental difference between the Eastern and Western viewpoints.

During the 1940's, several major centers were founded to study group

---

[59] It should be noted that group dynamics had been studied earlier. For example, Cooley, in 1902, was one of the first to point out that a person's role in a group can have a powerful effect on the development and behavior of that individual. Mary Follett, in 1918, recognized the importance of groups to the new order that was then being planned. She later became deeply involved in University of Chicago's activities. And, in 1915 and 1934–1943, J.L. Mareno, laid out the basics of the use of group dynamics in indoctrination and education, which he called "sociometrics." (See his 1953 book.)

[60] See for example, his *A Dynamic Theory of Personality* 1935; *Frontiers in Group Dynamics* 1947; *Group Decision and Social Change* 1947; and *Resolving Social Conflicts* 1948

processes.[61] By the end of the decade, the new methods were examined and found to provide superior performance. In particular, Coch and French, 1948, studied the reasons for resistance to change in manufacturing methods in a Virginia textile industry. They found that, "Change can be accomplished by the use of group meetings in which management effectively communicates the need for change and stimulates group participation in planning the changes."

Since that time, more than a hundred books have been published on these methods. Nor is the field static, it continues to develop. For example, one of the more recent advances is described by Thomas J. Peters and Richard H. Watermann, in 1982. They discuss how to control the values of informal groups, which has not previously been well understood. However, this general approach has been around long enough that a reasonably large counter-literature has, also, developed.[62]

The weaknesses of groups include "group think," deindividuation, and "extremity shift." The term "group think," was coined by Janis, in 1971 and 1972, to describe the tendency of group members to adhere to the group norm. The group's consensus provides its members with a sense of security and also helps them maintain self-esteem when faced with difficult decisions. To maintain their unanimity, groups will often establish "mind guards" to pressure any group member who departs from their norm. The individual who remains within their fold, obtains some anonymity from his or her group membership. But, this deindividuation, also, reduces the feeling of accountability. Group members often also have a tendency to progressively move towards more-and-more extreme positions. Consequently, group decisions tend to be more radical than ones reached by individuals.[63] Social psychologists have attributed several well-known public policies disasters, in recent history, to these weaknesses.[64]

"**Total Quality Management**" (**TQM**) is what group processes are called when they are applied in the business environment. TQM's goal is to mold the beliefs and subconscious urges of the workers

---

[61] The Research Center for Group Dynamics was founded at Massachusetts Institute of Technology in 1945; in 1947 the National Training Laboratory, Institute for Applied Behavioral Sciences, was formed at Bethel, Maine, to teach group dynamics methods; the Travistock Institute of Human Relations, in England, is another center for teaching these methods; and Lippit, in 1948, describes the program at the University of Michigan's Research Center for Group Dynamics. Similar programs have been founded or conducted at many other American Universities since then.

[62] See Baritz 1960 or Odiorne 1963 for early examples or Goldhammer 1996 for a contemporary popular treatment.

[63] Although this does not always happen, it is still fairly widespread. See Raven 1974 and Myers and Lamm 1976.

[64] These include, the appeasement of Hitler in 1937 and 1938 (See Janis, ibid.), the lack of preparedness before the bombing of Pearl Harbor (see Janis and Mann 1977), the Korean War stalemate, the Bay of Pigs invasion in 1961, the escalation of the Vietnam War, and the Watergate Scandal (See Brigham and Wrightsman 1982.)

so that they will lend their consent to administrative decisions. In TQM, workers participate in groups called "action teams." But each team's facilitator controls the social dynamics of the group, and uses psychological manipulation to control their decisions. The team members are also usually carefully selected to be individuals who have personality types which will interact well in the group and which are amenable by the process. They are also selected to be individuals who are directly impacted by the team's decisions — that increases their level of involvement and helps to open them to change.

Team decisions are reached by consensus, where "consensus" is defined as unanimous agreement. That forces each team member to accept the team's decision as his or her own. — This method was not new; its first recorded use was by the Quakers, during the seventeenth century

When action teams replace middle management in industry, that provides the illusion of the communist ideal of worker control of production; and, when the same approach is used in local government, by allowing appointed stakeholder councils to establish public policy, that provides the illusion of direct democracy. However, in both cases, it is really a system for engineering worker or public consent for decisions made by a centralized authority.

Charles Lindblom, in 1977, wrote that group processes were "singled out by the Maoists as the major form of social control to be practiced in China," from their very beginning. They have quality teams and local councils in every community and workplace, nationwide. Thus, their government is based on popular democracy, but an elite controls the majority's opinions through propaganda and group processes. At first China had some failures, but they gradually got better at using these techniques.

In 1947, contemporary with the Communist Revolution in China, General Douglas MacArthur, head of the occupation government of Japan, invited W. Edwards Deming[65] to Japan to introduce TQM as part of their reconstruction. It became how they ran their industries.

The transition from a conventional to a TQM business follows a characteristic pattern, which can be recognized as the Hegelian dialectic:

1. Thesis or tradition: The first step is to form worker groups who clearly define the current state of affairs, status quo, or tradition. This is necessary in order to formulate an appropriate antithesis, with the objective of constructive change.

2. Conflict, Chaos, or transition: Chaos is created through a dialectic conflict between the thesis and antithesis. This shows the workers the impossibility of continuing along traditional lines.

3. Synthesis — Transformation: The business then declares its intention of following the TQM system instead of traditional management

---

[65] As a young man, Dr. Deming had been influenced by Elton Mayo during a summer job he took at Western Electric. Dr. Deming later became a statistician and received his PhD from Yale. Some of his methods were used in the US Census during Roosevelt's term. However, he is best known as an expert on TQM.

techniques. Full adoption of TQM, characteristically, takes about ten years.

The business is then run by constantly reiterating the above steps for every planned change.

That is how Japanese Industry has been run since that time. TQM is often said to have been the cause of their rapid recovery, and achieving the willing cooperation of their workforce, is certainly a great advantage; but a substantial part of their remarkable success was due to the transfer of American patents and technology.

During Eisenhower's term, these methods were introduced into government. By then, they had been used successfully in Japan, in business, for five years and slightly longer in China, as the form of government; it had been tested under the conditions of war during the Chinese Revolution and the Korean War; and Levine and Butler's research, published in 1952, reconfirmed that these methods were effective in American industry. Thus, by 1952, it was complete, fully tested, and was ready for use.

The Eisenhower Administration began introducing it into American Government. One of the first places it surfaced was in military quality standard, the Mil-Q-9858, introduced in 1958.

There was also a move in the Soviet Union to adopt these new methods. In particular, from October 5–14, 1952, their Nineteenth Party Congress devoted itself to outlining the transition from State socialism to communism. But, turbulence accompanied these attempted changes.

Externally a serious breach developed between Wall Street and the Soviet Union. Up to that date, Wall Street had been financing the USSR, and also had been using them to funnel funds to North Korea. But, a rupture occurred. — Stalin held anti–Semitic show trials, in Prague. They convicted and hung fourteen Czech leaders for espionage; eleven of them were Jewish and some of them were obviously not guilty. At that time, Stalin identified Trotskyites and Zionists as enemies of the State; purges soon followed in the USSR and several Eastern bloc countries. Many of the "spies" were the agents of the Wall Street bankers. After that, Soviet propaganda became stridently anti–Semitic and they often portrayed America's foreign policy as Zionist–Imperialism. They dropped that viewpoint abruptly, when Mikhail Gorbachev took over.

Also, that year, the Soviet's UN representative, Jacob Malik, rose to suggest that they were willing to see the Korean War come to an end. The first Armistice was signed in July 1953.

On January 31, 1953, *Pravda* announced the discovery of the "doctor's plot" to kill top Soviet commanders. A purge, of Jewish doctors, followed. It ended a little over a month later with Stalin's death, on March 5.

A few short months later, leading Stalinists were purged from their government. In particular, Lavrenti Beria, who had been the head of the KGB under Stalin and was one of the great masters of mass mind control, was expelled from the party on July 10 and executed on December 23.

After Stalin's death the Soviet Union reverted to State socialism and the cold war began in earnest. Georgi M. Malenkov became Premier and Nikita Kruschev became first Secretary of the Party's Central Committee. Two years later Malenkov resigned and was replaced by Marshal Nicolai Bulganin.

13.9   Eisenhower Administration

Although, America led the West, throughout the cold war era, the lead agency which coordinated the Western system[66] was the Bilderbergers, who had their headquarters in Europe. Their members included representatives of the Western States and the leading financial Powers. Their first meeting was in 1954. Prince Bernhard of Belgium served as their head, until 1976. President Eisenhower kept abreast of their meetings, usually by sending Vice–President Richard M. Nixon. Their interests have included establishing unified Western and European positions, orchestrating the Marshal Plan, NATO, International economics, and forming the European Economic Community.[67]

Behind them, we are told that there is yet another shadowy organization, the "Committee of 300."[68] Coleman says that it represents individuals of very great wealth. Its members include the Queen of England, David Rockefeller, Aurelio Peccei, Queen Juliana the wife of Prince Bernhard, and so on. These are the individuals who own most of the national banks of the world, including the member banks of the Federal Reserve and Bank of England.

Presumably, this organization represents their interests and is the vehicle and forum through which they form plans and coordinate their actions. It would be reasonable to suppose that any major global financial plan, developed by one of the top–level planning organizations on the national level might be presented to them. — Their endorsement would facilitate any global financial program.

This committee has been around for a long time. For example, Walter Rathenau, the owner of the controlling interest in the German Electric Company, mentioned it, in 1909, when he said: "Three hundred men, all of whom know one another, direct the economic destiny of Europe and choose their successors from among themselves."[69]

On the domestic scene, in 1951, at the end of his term in office, President Truman set up a new planning board[70] according to the system of the NRPB. But it moved into the private sector when President–elect Eisenhower denounced it as a cabal of New–Dealers. However, it is reasonably

---

[66] This system included the United Nations, World Bank, International Monetary Fund, Organization for Economic Cooperation and Development, and the North Atlantic Treaty Alliance.

[67] See Peter Thompson, 1980.

[68] See Coleman 1994.

[69] See Carroll Quigley 1966, page 61.

[70] The President's Materials Policy Planning Commission.

certain that both Truman and Eisenhower supported the concept of democratic elitism.[71]

To briefly recapitulate its history up to date, Hoover had been the first to attempt to introduce it. In particular, immediately after his election he had tried to get bills through Congress allowing him to reorganize the Executive Branch. But, he had been stoutly opposed. At the end of his term he set up the NRPB, entirely without authority, and Roosevelt implemented it, also, without consulting Congress. Truman, renewed the attempt to re–organize the Executive Branch. He obtained Congressional approval for a commission to study the issue and appointed Herbert Hoover as head of it. The Hoover Commission produced a plan,[72] but Congress, again resisted authorizing the re–organization. However, in 1958, during President Eisenhower's term, they authorized the use of that approach in government.[73]

A novel feature of the Hoover plan was its budgeting and accounting system, called the "Planning, Programming, and Budgeting System," (PPBS) — After all, Federal funding is the driver which causes things to happen at the State and local levels and gives them control once the plans go into implementation. So, budgeting needs to be intimately connected to planning, if they are to provide administrative governance through organic control. Thus, the Budget Office, renamed the Office of Management and Budget, was destined to become the control center for administrative government.[74]

The very next year, that is 1959, Congress approved a new planning structure after the model of the NRPB. It was the Advisory Committee on Intergovernmental Relations, ACIR.

But, it was considered necessary that any agency or department of government which uses the PPBS be under a unified command. — The principle considerations may be contained in a quote from Thomas Jefferson (reprinted 1964):

> All powers of government, legislative, executive, and judiciary, result to the legislative body. The concentrating of these in the same hands is precisely the definition of despotic

---

[71] This first experiment with liberalism, resolved many of the problems due to the ignorance, prejudice, and intolerance of the common man, which had plagued American government since the Jacksonian revolution. On the whole, the new system worked reasonably well. One of the reasons might have been that both of these Presidents were hard–headed, traditional, Americans, and so, also, were most of the elite. In addition, they could not risk taking too extreme a course as the new system was vulnerable.

[72] See Hoover Commission 1955.

[73] See the Accrued Expenditure Bill, HR 8002. — This looks like a budget issue, but there is more to it.

[74] This system became possible when Congress transferred its control over the budget to the Executive Office in the Budget Act of 1921. The National Municipal League claimed authorship of that Act. They were closely associated with the University of Chicago

government. It will be no alleviation that these will be exercised by a plurality of hands, and not by a single one. Let
those who doubt it turn their eyes on the republic of Venice.
As little will it avail us that they are chosen by ourselves. An
elective despotism was not the government we fought for, but
one which should not only be founded on free principles, but
in which the powers of government would be so divided and
balanced among several bodies of magistracy, as that no one
could transcend their legal limits, without being effectively
checked and restrained by the others."

— So, it was necessary to reorganized each branch of government, before
the PPBS is implemented in it.

The further progress of the system was that President Kennedy implemented it in the military in 1961. That was possible because the various
branches of the Armed Forces had previously been unified into the Department of Defense.

However, he evidently did not understand its full significance at that
time. — Later he would say, in an address presented at one of the ivy
league colleges, that there was a plot to use the Office of the President
to destroy the freedoms of the American people. He went on to say that
he would not tell more about it, then, but would soon. However, he was
assassinated very shortly after he said that.[75]

The Executive Office was reorganized under President Johnson, in
1965. Then, potentially, the Office of Management and Budget could
become operational center for the White House.[76] But, it was not immediately implemented.

The next step was a pilot project for the PPBS, promoted and overseen
by George Washington University.[77] It involved five States: Specifically,
California, Michigan, New York, Vermont, and Wisconsin. It, also, involved five Counties and five Cities.

In 1966, Ronald Reagan rode into the California Statehouse, where
he would preside over the implementation of these new methods. He,
also, held a seat on ACIR; initiated direct Federal management of local
governments via councils of government; and his office even produced a
book with guidelines on how administrators could induce citizens to accept
unwanted changes.[78] Later, when he was President, he would implement
the PPBS in the Office of Management and Budget, appointing his budget
director from California at its head.

---

[75] Considering that this was the core program for the restructuring of government. His stated intention to expose it undoubtedly provided an adequate motive
for his assassination. But that does not necessarily prove that this was the actual
cause.

[76] Presumably these changes were part of what Kennedy was referring to.

[77] See George Washington University, 1969. Their program was authorized and
funded by various legislative bills, including the Public Works and Economic
Development Act of 1965.

[78] See the Institute of Local Self–Government, 1974.

There were no striking changes during Bush's years. But the Clinton Administration reorganized all the US Departments which manage natural resources under a single unified leadership. They, also, tried to implement the PPBS in Health Care and a comprehensive system to control education and the work force. More is said about this later on.

Returning to the closing years of Eisenhower's term, a year before leaving office, he appointed the President's Commission on National Goals.[79] They looked forward to determine where the country should go next. It was privately funded[80], which effectively denied Congressional oversight. About 100 persons took part in the discussion and 14 submitted essays. These were published in 1960.[81]

They developed ten goals:

1. Government takeover of many aspects of personal life, that is, the development of individual capabilities, provision of opportunities for all individuals, and "manpower development reform."

2. Eliminate discrimination against all "minorities" including, not only people of color but also women, homosexuals, etc;

3. Preserve and protect democracy;

4. Progressive education and increase the number of places in graduate schools by 50% ;

5. Promote internationalism;

6. Free trade, enterprise zones, reciprocal trade agreements, encouragement of the transfer of manufacturing to other countries, deplete America's vast accumulation of wealth, and institute local business improvement areas (federally regulated areas within states);

7. Government management of the economy;

8. Technological change and a change from a production–based economy to a service–based economy, with retraining by government;

9. Comprehensive land use planning and withholding federal funds from areas which resist this program;

10. Health and welfare programs and "identify problems ... in order that government may formulate wiser policies of regulation."

Their plan didn't receive Eisenhower's signature, but that didn't reduce its acceptance by the liberal Eastern establishment. *Goals for America* was, in practice, the parting message from that first generation of elite planners

---

[79]The commission had seven members from the Council of Foreign Relations one was a president of the AFL/CIO, and the last was a retired Judge of the US Court of Appeals.

[80]Funding agencies include the Carnegie Corp. of NY, Maurice and Laura Falk Foundation, Ford Foundation, Johnson Foundation, Richardson Foundation, Rockefeller Foundation, Alfred P Sloan Foundation, and US Steel Foundation.

[81] *Goals for America: the report of the President's Commission on National Goals.*

who had pretty much been running America since FDR's time. Most of them had entered government under Theodore Roosevelt or William Taft. So, by 1960, they were well into their 80's and 90's. That explains the strong continuity in the programs throughout their epoch, for it was the span of their lives.

    Goals for America defined much of the liberal agenda, for the period from 1960 to the present.[82]

---

[82] The earlier public goals–setting studies of comparable scope, were Hoover's Research Committee on Recent Social Trends from 1929 to 1933 and Roosevelt's National Resources Planning Board from 1933 to 1943. After 1960, the next such effort came when Nixon appointed a committee to form national goals. But, he dismissed them for being too liberal, after they produced their first report. During President Carter's administration, there was a public forum on domestic policy, the *Report to the President on the White House Public Forums on Domestic Policy* December 15, 1975. That effort culminated in the *Global 2000 Report to the President*. It more–or–less reiterated *Goals for America*. There has been no similar wide–ranging public re–evaluation of goals since then.

Chapter 14

Interdependence

This chapter begins a block of four chapters, discussing the
current political programs one–by–one from 1960 to the present.
This chapter focuses on international politics and the changing economic order.

14.1 Supremacy Clause

Treaties are serious issues because the second paragraph of Article 6 of the
US Constitution, known as the "supremacy clause," states implicitly that
the US Constitution and treaties have equal force in law:

> This constitution and the laws of the United States which
> shall be made in pursuance thereof; and all treaties made, or
> which shall be made, under the authority of the United States,
> shall be the supreme law of the land; and the judges of every
> state shall be bound thereby, any thing in the constitution or
> laws of any state to the contrary notwithstanding.

Therefore, a treaty which violates the Constitution might not necessarily be invalid.[1] Thus, they may provide a means for altering the form
of our government or withdrawing State's rights or those of the citizens.

The power of the federal government to abridge State's rights through
treaties was first established by the Supreme Court decision on the case
of Missouri vs. Holland in 1920.[2] Their decision was that a treaty could
override State law.[3] However, the court reserved the right to decide in the

---

[1] There is some variety of opinion on that among judges. So what it does is
create a conflict which the court may resolve either in the Constitution's favor or
otherwise. But, among the people, the Constitution is the supreme law, and if
the written Constitution fails, then the principles upon which it is based govern.

[2] 252 US 416, 1920

[3] The specific treaty involved dealt with the protection of birds which migrate
between the US and Canada. It abridged State hunting laws.

state's favor in other cases.

In 1951, Senator Bricker's (R, Ohio) Senate Joint Resolution[4] which began the process of amending the Constitution to close this loophole. He stated[5] "The primary purpose of [this resolution] is to prohibit the use of the treaty as an instrument of domestic legislation for surrendering national sovereignty."

Senator Bricker and many conservatives from that era were particularly concerned about the impact of the UN Charter. They were worried that the US might be surrendering part of its sovereignty to the UN and that articles in the UN Charter might supersede domestic law.

Their concerns weren't wholly unfounded: for example, the decision by the California Court of Appeals[6] overturned the California Alien Land Act[7] on the grounds that it was in conflict with the UN Charter. That decision was later overturned, but the incident showed them that Article 6 posed more than an idle threat.

Senator Bricker's proposed amendment was held to have been overly restrictive. It was replaced by a more moderate amendment introduced by Senator George. The George amendment had two key sections:

1. A provision of a treaty or other international agreement which conflicts with the constitution shall not be of any force or effect.

2. An international agreement other than a treaty shall become effective as internal law in the United States only by an act of Congress.

That amendment failed ratification by a single vote, during February, 1954.[8]

During the 1970's, a second attempt was made to alter the effect of Article 6. This time the effort was led by Senator Fulbright. The objectives were to limit the president's power to make Executive Agreements.[9] After long debate, a system was devised which allows the Senate to provide advice and consent.

14.2   Disarmament Treaty

President John F. Kennedy's short term in office (1961–1963) began with the Bay of Pigs fiasco, on April 17–20, 1961. Close behind it came the "success" in the Cuban missile crisis, October, 1962. Those events prepared America for the idea of world peace. The disarmament treaty was

---

[4] See SJR 102.

[5] See Senate Hearing May 21, 1952.

[6] Fujji vs. California (217p. 2d 481)

[7] That was a state law.

[8] Johnson, 1984, who reviewed these issues, attributed its failure to the eleventh–hour defection of Senator Warren Magnuson (D, Washington).

[9] These are like treaties, but deal with lessor issues. They were only signed by the President and never came before the Legislature.

signed, shortly thereafter. It established a schedule for the progressive disarmament of America's nuclear and conventional forces. It even mandated disarming the public. At the same time, the United Nations forces were to be armed, as an international police force, and the Soviet Union's forces would be left largely intact.[10] It is still part of the Federal Code and, therefore, can be found in many libraries.

Disarmament talks continued into Carter's years, with the SALT I (Strategic Arms Limitation Treaty) and SALT II negotiations. However, commencing the dismantling of our military wasn't seriously suggested until after the Soviet economic collapse. But, then, President Bush opposed it.

That was the context of America's first Iraq War. — Iraq and Kuwait had a contested claim over oil, but Kuwait refused to negotiate a settlement. The American Ambassador to Iraq advised them that war was the only way to obtain their rights, and that the US would not interfere. That advice was given contemporary with bills which came before the US legislature to reduce the US military to about one–tenth of its size. When Iraq invaded Kuwait, the US swiftly retaliated with overwhelming force. There was strong public support for "our boys" and the bills for disarmament came to a swift end.

The economic importance of this can hardly be exaggerated as the military–industrial complex was still, at that date, the principle structure through which the Federal Government infused tax money back into the economy and supported research and development. — Disarmament was not yet economically feasible.

The opinion expressed in some of the foreign newspapers, at that time, was that the Bush administration deliberately created the Iraq War to stop the bills to disarm the US military.

But, there is more to this. — Bush declared war without Senate approval, but with United Nations approval. He claimed that the Senate's ratification of the UN Charter was sufficient authorization. This represented a significant transfer of sovereign authority from America to the United Nations. Thus, President Bush supported one of the central tenants of the disarmament treaty while maintaining the mechanism for governmental control of the economy.

Serious disarmament did not begin until the Clinton administration. His administration's programs for the environment provided an alternative economic structure for reinvestment of Federal dollars in the American economy.

By the time of the second US–Iraqi war, in December 1998, the decrease in US military power was clearly evident, and an attack of the same magnitude was no longer possible. The US was, also, hampered by the loss of support from Arab countries, as a result of the first war.

Although the US planes shown in news broadcasts, this second time,

---

[10]Notice that this establishes much the same condition as President Wilson's tenth point of his fourteen points for the Treaty of Versailles.

bore UN insignia, and an attempt was made to present it to the American
people as a UN action, it was widely known that it was unilateral. The
foreign and American news media suggested that President Clinton had
begun the conflict to distract the public's attention from the embarrassing
consequences of his affair with an intern. Whatever the true explanation
may have been, France and China, as members of the UN Security Council,
did not find sufficient justification to support the action. Nor did Congress
issue a Declaration of War. — The foreign press did not fail to remark that
it had no legal authorization, whatsoever. And, as the American public
did not support it, and many of them had reservations about the motives
involved, it failed to develop into a major conflict. However, America
has continued periodically bombing that country over the two years which
followed, although that is not covered in the news.

14.3   Vietnam

To many Americans the Vietnam War was probably the most memorable
event of the 1960's and 1970's. Unfortunately not much is known about
it. But, most people agree that our forces were fighting under constraints
which made it impossible for them to win.

Due to John F. Kennedy, in 1961, the war effort was directed by systems analysts and computer experts, using essentially the approach recommended by the Hoover Commission. That is group dynamics and the
budgeting and accounting system.

The Secretary of Defense, Robert MacNemara, was an expert on these
techniques.[11] He had just previously been at Ford Motor Company, where
he had applied them to the design of the Edsel. He returned to oversee
their implementation in the Department of Defense. — The escalation of
the Vietnam War has been considered as an example of extremity shift.[12]

In the end, the public became highly critical and demanded that the
records on the management of the war be opened to public scrutiny. The
"Pentagon Papers" were what was finally released. Everyone agrees that
they show the depth of deception, but there was a wide variety of opinion
as to what, otherwise, they revealed, if anything. — We probably can not
expect to find out more within our lifetimes.

14.4   Social Stresses

The principle social stresses of the Johnson era (1963–1969) were racial and
gender–based. These problems had grown slowly during Eisenhower's ad-

---

[11] See, for example, "How Control is Manipulated — MacNemara's Trick with
Computers." *Tactics* February 20, 1966; Major General Perry Smith's 1987 book;
or John Walsh's article in the June 1971 issue of *Science*, 172: 1008–1011.

[12] See Janis, 1971, 1972.

ministration. Kennedy's years, saw the Martin Luther King, Black Power and, Red Power movements.

The desire to end America's caste system was, then, an idea whose time had come. It had wide support among both the Black and White communities. But, the relaxing of caste barriers resulted only in some of the previously Brown/Yellow/Red peoples being redefined as "White." Not long afterwards, the window of opportunity closed.

The Johnson administration saw serious race–riots and the second "Goal for America" was achieved when affirmative action was set in place during Nixon's term. That scheme of quotas and apportionments forced the redefined caste system back upon the public.[13]

We will now consider how caste and affirmative action combined to yield a sophisticated system of slavery.

The destruction of the Black family was one of the most serious results of affirmative action. Better employment for Black women than Black men, together with substantial welfare benefits for unmarried mothers, may have been the principle causal factors. — In a graduation address delivered at one of the Ivy League Universities during the early 1980's, Mr Gallup jr discussed the results of a survey his firm had conducted to determine the cause of the high divorce rates. They found that over 90% of all divorces in America were due to one of the following factors: the woman making more money than the man, having a better job, or having a higher social status; disputes over who is the head of the household; or disputes over whether to have children, how many children, or who should raise them. In addition they found that the divorce rate rose with the educational level of the wife but decreased with that of the husband. A woman's probability of being divorced substantially increased if she had a college education and few women with advanced degrees had not been divorced at least once, if they were ever married at all. Clearly, marriage, in America, will rarely withstand the wife's taking the dominant role in the family.

In addition, the government welfare systems since the 1960's have mostly been structured so that a single mother could not marry nor live with a man without losing her benefits. So, if a woman got pregnant outside of marriage or was divorced and was poor with young children, she came under the power of the State. Social workers would then dictate many aspects of her life and she might never escape their control. This aggravated the breakdown of the family.

Within a decade, more than half of all Black children were born out of wedlock, and the percentage continued to rise, thereafter. There was, also, a sharp rise in violence among young Black males. However, the breakup of the Black family was not the sole cause; there were several other contributing factors.[14]

---

[13] That this was done against the public's will can be seen in California's repealing affirmative action, by initiative, during the 1990's. Washington State also did that, but, in that case, their Governor, Gary Locke, said that he would ignore the initiative and continue the programs.

[14] America lost its manufacturing jobs resulting in unemployment. America's

The social consequences of these problems were very marked. — During 1998, one media report stated that, at any given time, more than half of all the young Black males in Los Angeles County are either in jail or recently released and under parole.

The effects of the changes, since the early 1960's, can clearly be seen in the meteoric climb of the rates of illegitimate births, divorces, and violent crime and the plummeting of college entrance exam scores. Each of these statistics has an upward trend, beginning around 1963, continuing into the 1990's, outstripping population growth.[15]

Although reverse–discrimination on gender combined with the social service system for unmarried mothers was known, by the early 1980's, to have devastating effects on the family, rather than remedying their defects, these programs were expanded.

One of the difficulties in applying Mosca's and Pareto's ideas to America is that Americans are traditionally a rational people, whereas, their theories were based on Italians, who are an emotional people. But, if the driving cause for Italians being as they are is matriarchy, as I have suggested, introducing it into American society, might cause Americans to be that way, too. — It does, in fact, appear that this was the case for the American Black community. So, following that pilot program it was extended to all of America.

Another argument in favor of this was enunciated at the Woman's Caucus at the 1998 Washington State Democratic Convention:[16] That is that those women to whom we may justly apply Marx's dictum that "marriage is prostitution,"[17] would usually prefer, single motherhood under the wardship of the State and "freedom," in Rousseau's sense of the word, to

---

drug problems increased the level of violence and fueled the growth of gangs. — Many people believe that the US Government has been deliberately fostering the drug trade. At the very least, they have been completely ineffective in suppressing it. For example, see *Battle Lines in the Drug Trade* in *The New American* (October 27, 1997, Vol 13 no. 22). — The religious right like to point to the banning of prayer in school and the repudiation of the biblical standard in American Jurisprudence. For example see Barton 1996. But, with the exception of Fundamentalists, these factors had little influence over people's lives. Legalization of the birth control pill and abortion probably had stronger effects on public morality.

[15] In particular, Births to unwed girls ages 15–19 rose from about 15 per 1000 in 1963 to 45 per 1000 in 1993; single family households with a female head rose from 4.6 million in 1963 to 12 million in 1993; violent crime reports rose from approximately 250,000 in 1963 to 1,900,000 in 1991; and the average SAT scores dropped from around 980 in 1963 to 890 in 1980, they stabilized after that only because the tests were made progressively easier to keep the scores up. These statistics come from the Statistical Abstracts of the US, US Dept of Commerce.

[16] Some similar sentiments can be found in Hillary Clinton's book *It Takes a Village*.

[17] The abolition of marriage appears in the text of *The Communist Manifesto* rather than in the planks.

Karl Marx was building a revolutionary doctrine, but, he did not follow it himself. He was a good husband and a loving father.

marriage. Marriage would, indeed, be prostitution if, as Marx and Engles assumed, the sole bond between husband and wife were financial. That does, in fact, appear to be the case for a segment of American society.[18]

Thus, what most people regard as a social ill is, for the radical feminist or thorough Marxist, the desired state. Specifically, at the Woman's caucus, some individuals stated that they felt that a woman's "right" to live that way should be protected at the expense of marriage and traditional values. In fact, some of them went so far as to say that marriages should be broken, if at all possible, in order to free the women and show them a better paradigm.

Today, all classes of American society have high divorce rates. For example, in 1996, a publication of the Washington Department of Education stated that over 50% of all children, then, in the State's schools came from single–parent households.

Interracial marriage was another change, dating from this period, which might be calculated to have an impact on the family. — Originally, the Western view of the family bond was that it was due to the high relatedness[19] among family members. For example, when J.S.B. Haldane, was asked if he would give his life to save his brother he answered, no, but he would give his life to save an appropriately larger number of cousins. His rule was that he would do it if the total number of genes saved which they held in common with him was larger than he alone possessed. — Now consider a child from an interracial marriage between two individuals of relatively pure descent. That child will be, on the average, less closely related to either of its parents than a child chosen at random from the parent's original nationality. Where, then, is the family bond?

According to traditional Western values, there should be none. Under those conditions, the family has become simply an arbitrary group of people who know each other well. If such a family holds together, that is only because of the views of its members.

But, many people, never think about the nature of the family bond nor whether their particular family has any validity as a social group; so,

---

[18] These are not necessarily just the liberal–minded. — One dyed–in–the–wool working–class man told how, after he had graduated from High School, he and his father shipped out as able–bodied seamen. When they reached Panama, his father took him to his first whorehouse. He elaborated and, then, proceeded onwards in like kind. That was his perspective on life, and he was a married man, too. But, when he was away from home, that is how he lived.

And, he has his female counterpart. — One day when I was helping another man unload a piece of rented equipment from a flatbed truck, up drove two women in an American muscle car. They were looking for a date and were delighted to find what they called, "two working men." That seemed to be their only criterion. They were as red–necked and all–American as they could be, but they were Communist woman for all of that. Perhaps their husbands were out of town or out of work.

This is not to suggest that the whole of the working class, are this type of people, but they form a distinct segment of it.

[19] Relatedness is the proportion of the genes held in common.

this has not had as big an impact as one might expect. The impact is more noticeable when the children come from several marriages. Then, it is forced upon the consciousness of the family members.

Were the State to step in, take all the new–born infants of mixed descent from single mothers and raise them; what objection could be raised, so long as they did a good job and the infants were taken before any attachment formed? — In fact, Washington State has quietly been doing pretty much that, for possibly as long as three decades. — Here are stories to be told. — But, let it suffice to remark that in a State Legislature hearing on foster care, the State's Attorney General, Christine Gregoire, expressed her opinion that *all* children in the State should be in group homes up to the age of five.

14.5   Criminal Justice

At roughly the same time the American criminal justice system began breaking down. Justice increasingly became available only to those who could afford it. In addition, the police only responded to violent crime; and regarded other crimes as matters to be addressed in civil court.[20] But, that was only available to the wealthy. The poor were left with no recourse but violence and seem to have known, instinctively, that when the law no longer serves the purposes for which it was created,[21] it is no longer binding nor does it hold any moral authority. Predictably, the crime rates rose.

Then, the police began using Gestapo tactics, nationwide. During the late 1990's, these became familiar to the public through the television show *Cops*. But, many unsuspecting citizens who made the mistake of calling the police for help, found out, firsthand, when instead of assistance they became the victims of a heavy–handed door–busting assault, violating their rights of person, property, and due process. In other cases, they found that the police systematically deceived, told out–right lies, and endeavored to entrap them. — Not all policemen do these things, but this involves more than just a few bad cops: It reflects a national policy.

That originated in California during Ronald Reagan's term as Governor. In particular, in response to the Omnibus Crime Control Act of 1968 and the Safe Streets and Crime Control Act of that same year, he appointed a series of Commissions to redesign California's criminal justice system.[22] The California Institute for Specialized Training located in San

---

[20] In Washington State, a law prevents the police from investigating or enforcing the law in civil matters. That removes protection from virtually all white–collar and business crimes.

[21] That is, traditionally protecting life, liberty, and property for all. But, see the discussion of legal pregressivism, later on. Under that doctrine original intent has no weight.

[22] These were the California Council on Criminal Justice, the Select Committee on Law Enforcement Problems, the Office of Criminal Justice Planning, and the

Luis Obispo, was one of the outcomes of this effort. It trains peace–keeping officers in these new methods for controlling the public and conditions them to use them.

When Reagan became President, he appointed the director of that Institute, Louis Guffrida, head of the Federal Emergency Management Agency (FEMA). — Their performance has been less than satisfactory from the public's viewpoint, but judged from the objectives taught at the Institute, they were right on track. About the same time, their methods spread to police forces across the country.

Under this new regime, the financial ability to protect oneself in court often becomes the criterion distinguishing the slave–criminal class from the free. — It was not too long before being a criminal lost its social stigma. During the 1960's, it was a shameful thing to have spent time in jail, but, by the 1990's, it had become a way–of–life for a surprisingly large segment of young working–class America.

As of 1992, the United States was incarcerating more people per capita than any other country[23] and, by 1998, that had risen to approximately one out of ever 150.

A study contracted by the US Attorney General's office examined the implications of this on international trade:[24]

> A comment on foreign-produced products and cheap labor is germane to discussion of the growth and development of prison industries. Despite tariffs and other trade barriers, countries with wages significantly lower than those in this country (e.g., Hong Kong, Mexico, the Philippines, the Caribbean countries, etc.) have been able to assemble and produce products (with U.S. components) and sell them back to American markets. Considering the emerging global economy, it is reasonable to assume that the U.S. is losing significant business opportunities to foreign competitors.
>
> The possibility of promoting prison-based labor forces as an alternative to offshore competition becomes significant. If inmate labor were perceived by U.S. corporations as a viable, cost-effective alternative to offshore labor, the number of companies which might consider domestic prison-based operations could increase significantly and therefore recapture enterprises that have gone to foreign competitors.

A prison labor system has been adopted in Washington State and several other States. The services provided by inmates are not limited to making license plates, building roads, and other traditional prison industries. By the 1990's, they were manufacturing swimming suits, camping equipment, and other retail items. They are even providing a wide range of

---

Commission on Project Safer California.

[23] Criminal Justice Digest, 1992, p. 1

[24] See Dwyer and McNally 1993.

engineering and technical services to local governments. — Although un-educated Black and Mexican–American males were originally the groups most involved, the proportion of uneducated White males has been in-creasing and, the prisoner population, also, includes some college educated people who are the victims of reverse discrimination, drugs, or the domes-tic violence laws.[25] They introduce a highly trained component, providing America with a slave–labor force which compares favorably to China's. And, it is a larger one, too, relative to the American population.

Prisons are a growth industry and they are expected to expand fur-ther during the coming years, due to several factors. — The 1996 Welfare Reform Bill, which transferred the funding of welfare from the Federal gov-ernment to the States under "local control" also limited welfare benefits to five years. That implies that there will be a sharp increase in prison populations early in the twenty–first century. Also, as the outcome based education system, which is the topic of the next chapter, becomes more fully implemented, many of those individuals who fail to get their certifi-cates of initial mastery will be added to this labor pool, together with some older individuals who were educated before outcome based education and who, for one reason or another, lost their jobs. In addition, the increasing number of young people from single–parent homes should accelerate this trend.

To deal with the expected growth in prison populations, new pris-ons have been built. And, the Federal Government has also constructed a network of transportation centers at the major airports in each state, to transport prisoners from state–to–state, wherever their labor may be needed, similar to the Gulag Archipelago in the Soviet Union.

14.6   Nixon's Economic Policy

The next major development of the post–1960 era came during Nixon's term in office (1969–1974). In 1946, Richard Nixon was a small town lawyer, but he enjoyed a meteoric rise. His first elected office was a US Congress seat representing California, replacing Jerry Voorhis who had criticized the Federal Reserve. During his first year in office, he showed his colors by introducing a bill allowing the United Nations to enact, interpret, and enforce world–law to prevent war. During 1950, he won a US Senate

---

[25] The chapter on domestic violence in the Revised Code of Washington (RCW), will come as a surprise. — It authorizes a special court to fine or jail individuals, but the accused is not provided with explicit knowledge of the charges against him, a council will not be appointed if he can not afford one, it does not allow trial–by–jury, and, furthermore, the accused may not only be subjected to double–jeopardy, but may be tried three times for the same offense: Specifically, in domestic violence court, in criminal court, and in civil court, with an not–guilty verdict in one, not affecting the others.

The domestic violence code is aimed at protecting women, preemptively. That is the justification given in the RCW for those laws.

seat, in a dirty mud–slinging campaign which earned him the nickname "Tricky Dicky." As Senator, he played a minor role in the the revelations of the McCarthy era, which he enlarged to create a reputation for himself as an anti–communist. In 1952, we find him as the vice–president–elect. He was an obvious member of the ruling elite's stable; a member of the Council on Foreign Relations; and as President Eisenhower's Vice President, he represented America at the Bilderburger's meetings. Thus, he was fully cognizant of developments in that sphere.

After his narrow defeat in the Presidential race by John F. Kennedy, in 1960, he next ran for Governor of California against Pat Brown, in 1962. He had entered that race at the request of Nelson Rockefeller. During the six years which followed, he worked for the law firm of John Mitchell, who was Nelson Rockefeller's personal attorney; he drew a $200,000 salary and lived in a Manhattan luxury apartment owned by Nelson Rockefeller; and according to Gary Allen[26] his job appeared to primarily consist of rebuilding his public image, as one of Rockefeller's prime running horses.

Before his election to the Presidency, he ingratiated himself to the more liberal members of the Eastern establishment by writing an article in the Council of Foreign Relations' publication, *Foreign Affairs* promoting the recognition of Communist China. They apparently believed that he was their man. They were deceived.

He recognized China and introduced the pro–Soviet trade policy of "detente." These are often regarded as a pay–off to the liberal Eastern establishment, but, in light of America's actual relationships with those States, they appear to have been reasonable policies.[27]

By the time of his presidency, the original members of the Council of Foreign Relations were mostly gone. It had also grown to approximately 3000 members and had fragmented into sub–groups, partly over the stresses caused by the Vietnam War. President Nixon, always retained an elitist big–business orientation, but he appears to have sided with the more conservative and nationally–based businesses rather than with the liberal internationalists.[28]

The most striking events of the Nixon administration revolved about his economic policy, which he introduced during the summer of 1971. These mark the point at which he began actively opposing the internationalists.[29]

---

[26] Gary Allen 1972.

[27] The Soviet Union had been the backer of North Vietnam, but much of the arms were manufactured in the Eastern Block countries in factories funded by Wall Street. Therefore, replacing that revenue stream probably facilitated ending the war. And, China had not been America's enemy since the Korean Conflict.

[28] He also appointed moderate or conservative Supreme Court Judges. His nominations included Warren Burger, the moderate Chief Justice who replaced Earl Warren, and William Rehnquist, a conservative, later elevated to Chief Justice by President Reagan.

[29] Two other significant developments, at that time, were 1) the publication of the President's report on the first twenty–five years of the University of Michigan's Institute for Social Research and 2) the publication of Deutsch et al.'s article in

Ever since the Second World War, America had been the economic superpower, with most of the world's money. However, by the 1970's the economies of Europe and Japan had grown to where the US was only one among equals. Consequently, the Bretton Woods Agreement and all the other treaties which were predicated upon US economic supremacy no longer reflected the real world situation.

In 1971, President Nixon openly disregarded the US obligations under the GATT treaty by imposing a 10% surcharge on most imports. At the same time he aggressively demanded that Japan, South Korea, Taiwan, and Hong Kong reduce their exports to the US. This policy of "economic nationalism" was favored by the more domestically–based and nationally–oriented industries and was opposed by the transnationalists.

The domestic industries argued that they couldn't compete with foreign–manufactured products which were made using low–paid labor or, in some cases, prisoners or slaves. They felt that tariffs are necessary to maintain domestic wages, production, employment, and the American standard–of–life.

This is diametrically opposed to the view taken by the internationalists. For example, David Rockefeller wrote that[30] "Broad national interests are being served best in economic terms where free market forces are able to transcend national boundaries"[31] "It is indeed time to lift the siege against multinational enterprises so that they might be permitted to get on with the unfinished business of developing the world economy."[32]

President Nixon's policy of imposing tariffs improved the balance of trade. As a consequence, the health of the domestic economy improved; federal revenues increased; and the federal government ran a surplus.

A second aspect of President Nixon's economic policy involved how

---

Science listing the 62 key advances in the social sciences which led to major changes in the structure of government in America during the twentieth century, although he did not explicitly say that was their significance. Those two articles blew the whistle, but, few people understood them.

Due to the timing, significance, and high profile, of these articles, if they were not part of Nixon's attack on the establishment, they were responding to it.

I remember reading Deutch's article, at the time, and finding it interesting, but irrelevant. Even though I was familiar with most of the technical aspects, I did not have a clue as to what it was about until I wrote this book.

I recommend his article as a guide to what one needs to know to get a solid technical background for contemporary politics. But, add to it Zimbardo's works, which are mentioned later on. — You will, also, see that I have covered some but not all of the developments he lists. Hopefully, I have provided enough of a framework, that the rest will fall into place.

In the mid–1970's people seem to have thought in terms of huge models. But, they have too many uncertainties and do not work so well. The current programs I know of are focused on relatively narrow issues. In particular, some of these models, applied to fisheries management, can be found among the dissertations at Universities of Washington, Simon Fraser, and British Columbia.

[30] This excellent summary, in their own words, is due to Jeff Frieden 1980.
[31] from the Constitution of the Trilateral Commission, Attachment B
[32] quoted from "The Trilateral Commission," page 4

the currency was secured. In August of 1971, he disregarded the Bretton Woods Agreement and suspended the convertibility of dollars to gold. That severed any remaining connection which the Federal Reserve Notes had with the valid US currency, which according the *US Constitution* is only gold and silver.

A third aspect of President Nixon's economic policy was that he once again allowed the private ownership of gold. That potentially re-established the US currency.

Nixon's policy illustrated to the liberal Eastern establishment that they no longer had control. It was not long before Rockefeller's clique began to act. In July 1973 David Rockefeller[33] and Zbigniew Brzezinski founded the Trilateral Commission. — Within a year President Nixon had resigned from office over the Watergate affair; and on August 19, 1994 David Rockefeller's brother, Nelson Rockefeller, was appointed Vice President in the Ford administration.

The stated purposes of the Trilateral Commission are:

1. To foster cooperation between the trilateral regions: that is Europe, Japan, and North America.

2. "To formulate and propose policies which the regions and nations within the regions could follow in their relations with one another, in their foreign relations in general, and in the solution of common domestic problems including particularly relations and problems involving 1) economic matters, 2) political and defense matters, 3) developing countries, and 4) Communist countries; and to foster understanding and support of Commission recommendations both in government and private sectors in the three regions."

3. To renovate the international monetary system. The new system should serve the interests of the countries of the trilateral regions.

It would be well to also bear in mind, the description of the goal given by their co-founder, Brzezinski. He wrote in his book *Between Two Ages*:

The technotronic era involves the gradual appearance of a more controlled society. Such a society would be dominated by an elite, unrestrained by traditional values.

The Commission was initially composed of 180 members and by 1980 had 300. They came from all three of the trilateral regions, but more come from the US than elsewhere.[34]

---

[33] David Rockefeller was also one of the directors of the Council on Foreign Relations from the mid-1940's to the mid-1980's.

[34] Holly Sklar and Ros Everdell (1980) list the members and provide brief biographies for each. The Trilateralists who appear in other parts of this book are, George Bush, James E. Carter, William Clinton, Daniel J. Evans, David Rockefeller, John D. Rockefeller IV, John C. Sawhill, and George H. Weyerhaeuser.

The Commission forms working groups to study topics which are of interest to themselves.[35] Each such working group writes a report to the Commission. These have been carefully considered scholarly works, although all of them have had an internationalist leaning. The commission discusses them and acts on them. The studies which they approve are published as *The Triangle Papers*. These reports are of substantial significance. They are generally not innovative solutions, but policy recommendations to the heads of big business. Their publication usually represents their endorsement of a program which has matured and been proven successful. Consequently, pilot projects or even full implementation may have occurred before the study is released to the public. On more than a few occasions, they have become defacto government policy.

14.7   Economic Reform

By the 1970's, the Bretton Woods Agreement was no longer appropriate but neither did the Commission like the approach taken by the Nixon Administration. They wanted to move to an international system which gave them the same control world–wide as they had enjoyed in America since the time when the Federal Reserve Act had passed.

As soon as Ford took office, Nixon's economic policy was reversed. Ford also debased the coinage, replacing silver coins with copper–cored sandwiches. The more significant change, however, was the Federal Reserve Reform Act of 1975. It allowed the Federal Reserve to purchase foreign debt and issue notes based on those debts. This created international monetary interdependence. There were, however, no noticeable impacts until the process was used to back debt–for–nature swaps a decade later.

The creation and maintenance of interdependence was one of the main concerns of the Trilateral Commission. International businesses want to create and maintain needs which can not be met locally and to control transportation. That was how Rockefeller's Standard Oil Trust and the British East India Company operated. But, the positive side is that it also can increase fluidity.

14.8   Intermodal Surface Transportation:

Interdependence can be created by changing the relative costs of local and long–distance transportation and tariffs. In particular, local or domestic industries become profitable when tariffs and long–distance transportation are expensive. Conversely, a certain way to destroy those segments of the economy is to lower tariffs or make the cost of long–distance transportation insignificant.

---

[35] The topics they have examined have stayed fairly strictly within the limits of their mission statement.

That was the role played by America's magnificent Interstate Highway system. It was completed during the 1960's under the Kennedy and Johnson Administrations. It reduced the cost and delay of interstate trucking. The highway system allowed industries to manufacture on a large scale wherever it was cheapest and then to distribute their products cost–effectively. As a result, many local businesses closed and were replaced by national businesses. The next steps were to move the manufacturing overseas and to, then, to regulate transportation.

Under President Ford, the Intermodal Surface Transportation Act of 1975, made that possible. It allowed all transportation systems to be transferred to public–private partnerships. The private contractors then set and collect the tolls, outside of public oversight, and maintain these publicly owned transportation systems. This will give big businesses monopolistic control over transportation within the United States.

The best example of how this will work is provided by the toll road concept which has been actively advocated in Washington State during the 1990's. Under this proposal, all the freeways in the Puget Sound Basin will eventually become toll roads.[36] The major Highways in Eastern Washington will also be part of this system. There will be, potentially, a different toll for each lane, each section of freeway, and different period during the day. Any individual wishing to use this system must pay into an account and then place a transponder (a radio device identifying the vehicle) in the vehicle to be used. There will be sensors in each lane and there will also be video cameras of sufficiently high resolution that individual passengers can be identified. These sensors and cameras were already in place on some highways, by 1995.[37] In Washington State, the system will be operated by two large contractors.[38]

The objective is to use "congestion pricing." That is the differential adjustment of the cost of transportation among local regions to influence the public's choices — where people choose to live, by what means they choose to get about, where they go, what businesses can be profitable, and where they will be located. As this system will allow the operators to track the movements of individuals; it will potentially allow financial pressure to be targeted at the individual or at specific companies. However, the tolls will generally impact groups of people.[39] As the setting of the tolls will be outside of public control, there is nothing to prevent the contractors from doing this. Thus, big business will be able to control the profitability of other businesses in the region.

These public–private partnership toll roads have strong grassroots op-

---

[36] That is from Everett on the North to Olympia on the South and to Highway 101 on the West.

[37] But, some of the cameras have since been removed, as the local residents have found they make excellent rifle targets.

[38] At this time, they are to be Peter Kiewit and Bechtel Corporations.

[39] But, that is no protection as the liberal establishment has a history of not scrupling at harming many innocent people to get at one opponent. In fact, some of them have regarded harming broad classes of society as a desirable end in itself.

position where pilot projects were planned. On December 25, 1995, Bob Drewel, of the Puget Sound Regional Council,[40] wrote about them:

> ...we all continue to see significant evidence of public opposition to all three of the proposed plans. These projects must now go through a quite structured and relatively inflexible process over the next year or two to get to an advisory ballot. ...we fear that [this] would inevitable resurrect the previous negative media and political attention on the subject of transportation infrastructure financing. ...Such press could come at a very poor time.

Thus, the Regional Council temporary abandoned the toll roads because they might jeopardize their proposal for a light rail system from Eugene to Vancouver BC, which is another public–private partnership. They got that authorized during the autumn of 1997 and then returned to the toll road plan.

Their next objective was to convert the Tacoma Narrows Bridge to a toll bridge operated by a public–private partnership. The public advisory vote passed in November 1998. Most people thought that it was just a toll to finance improvements to that structure. That is the way this type of project has traditionally been financed in Washington State and they were oblivious to the difference.

14.9   Indian and Energy Policy

This story begins in 1959, when Alaska became the 49th state. With statehood, the Federal Government transferred 104 million acres of land to them. Alaska, then, opened much of that land for homesteading. However, the Indians claimed that that was their land and brought suit to stop its distribution. In 1966, they were able to stop any additional land transfers.

In 1968 and 1969, Atlantic Richfield and British Petroleum discovered oil reserves at Prudhow Bay on Alaska's North Slope. There is more oil in these reserves than in Saudi Arabia and there is also enough natural gas to provide America's projected needs for two centuries. These companies, therefore, wanted to build two pipelines from the oil fields to the ice–free

---

[40] The PSRC is a control structure after the model of the NRPB. The mandate which created it was derived from President Reagan's Executive Order 12372 and from the State's Growth Management Act. They receive funding from both the Federal Government and the State. Their job is planning and implementation. That is, they adapt Federal policies to local conditions and induce local and State government to accept them.

The Regional Council has a long–term comprehensive regional plan named "Vision 2020," which incorporates the Growth Management Act, the Federal Intermodal Transportation Act, economic planning, and other issues. It is available at their information center at 1011 Western Avenue, Suite 500, Seattle. They are quite open about what they are doing as they are doing precisely what they are paid to do.

port of Valdez, one for oil and the other for natural gas. However, in 1970, several Alaskan Indian groups, together with several environmental groups, filed lawsuits to block the pipelines, saying that they crossed Indian lands. Later that year, the oil companies switched sides and assisted the Indians in their suit. With both sides agreeing, the judge ruled in their favor.

Congress, under the leadership of Speaker of the House, Scoop Jackson (D Washington), acted quickly, first to transfer all disputed lands to the Alaskan Indians, and then to terminate the Indian claims by purchasing most of it back. That was the Alaskan Native Claims Settlement Act of 1970.[41] That limited all Indian claims and left the Federal Government in possession 92% of Alaska. But, these changes did not place the Alaskan Indians on an equal footing with other Americans. They retained reserved land and their tribal councils are overseen by the Bureau of Indian Affairs, who have veto power over all tribal decisions.

Although the pipeline was authorized, the Federal Government soon placed the most extreme and unreasonable environmental restrictions on the companies developing it. That raised the cost from $2 billion to $12 billion, almost driving Atlantic Richfield into bankruptcy. Some of their corporate executives believed that the Federal Government's intention was to bankrupt and then nationalize them.[42] However, by a herculean effort, they finished the oil pipeline on schedule. The natural gas pipeline was blocked by President Carter and was never built. The gas was to be pumped to Valdez, liquefied there and then shipped to the lower 48 States.

This was the beginning of the Nixon Indian policy.

Briefly the history of US–Indian relations is as follows. — The era of Indian treaty–making ended in 1857. From then until 1934, Indian affairs were under Federal regulation and the general thrust was their assimilation. To that end, in 1866, the fourteenth amendment to the US Constitution made all Indians born off reservation US citizens and the General Allotment Act of 1887[43] allowed tribes, upon their own discretion, to divide their lands into individually owned tracts and the tribal members to, then, become US citizens. Similar provisions had also been part of many of the Indian treaties. Most of the tribes placed themselves under this act. Finally, in 1924, the Indian Citizenship Act[44] made all Indians US citizens.

This period of assimilation ended with President Roosevelt's Indian Reorganization Act of 1934, also known as the Howard–Wheeler Act. It allowed the tribes to reorganize. It also channeled large amounts of money to them and provided for the restoration of their reservations under tribal rather than personal ownership. The tribes were required to develop tribal constitutions, but, until the Indian Civil Rights Act of 1968, they were not required to grant personal liberties to tribal members.

---

[41] The Federal government purchased their claim to the state for $926.5 million and the Alaska Indians retained 45 million acres.

[42] See Lindsey Williams 1980.

[43] That is also called the Dawes Severality Act: 25 USC 331–334, 339, 341, 342, 348, 349, 354, 381.

[44] See 43 Stat. 253, 8 USC.

In 1953, President Eisenhower again reversed the direction of the Indian policy.[45] But, President Kennedy's administration changed it back again, restoring most of the tribal governments. As many of the leaders of the restored tribes had previously been the leaders of the Red Power movement and leaned far to the left, many of the Tribes effectively became small socialist States.

The condition of the tribal members under them is often less that desirable. That can be seen in their having the highest suicide rate of any group in Washington State. This speaks of depression and hopelessness. Much the same phenomenon is found among prisoner populations. For example, Zimbardo et al, in 1982, found that "counterpart of the mastery and control [exhibited by the guards] was the depression and hopelessness witnessed in the prisoners."

It should be appreciated that the problems with the Tribes described in the following chapters have very little to do with the Tribal members, except as subjects of Tribal government. The group primarily involved is the employees of Tribal Government, and they are often either predominately non–Indian or represent an elite within the Indian community. Their primary allegiance may be either to the Federal government or, in a surprising number of cases, to the UN.

In 1970, President Nixon addressed Congress on the inviolability of the trust relationship in which Congress holds the Indians. In his 1972 address to Congress, he proclaimed that it was in the national interest to enhance the status and political well being of the tribes. He adopted a policy known as "self determination" which maintains the Indian tribal authorities and treats them as sovereign states.[46] The administrations which followed continued on this same course. It was even extended by President Reagan's policy of "government–to–government" relationships between the Federal government and the Tribal Authorities, ending the role of State and local governments in providing services to Indians. That create a vehicle — small tribal governments which were independent powers

---

[45] House Concurrent Resolution 108 provided for the voluntary termination of Indian tribal governments and Public Law 280 allowed States to assume law enforcement on reservations upon request.

[46] The Commissioner of Indian Affairs under the Nixon Administration, Louis R. Bruce, filled in the general picture with his statement:

> Developing Indian economics does not mean merely locating non–Indian industry close to or on the reservations so that these corporations can enjoy a cheap labor supply. It means the development of truly Indian economic systems so that a dollar once earned by an Indian citizen can be spent and kept moving throughout the Indian economy, thus developing that economy and making a maximum impact on the community ... I want to see Indian economies where dollars move from Indian hand to Indian hand and are not drained out by those non–Indian cities that develop and grow and feed upon Indian reservations.

at the local level, but which were solely dependent on the pleasure of the Federal Government.

The Nixon, Ford, and Carter Administrations then hired an army of lawyers to transfer everything they could to the Indians.[47] During the 1970's, non–government organizations also provided substantial funding.[48] With heavy funding from both government and the private sector, the Indians rapidly obtained many favorable court decisions throughout all parts of the country. Prominent among these are the Boldt decision, in 1974, which granted the Indians half of the salmon, and Judge Gignoux's decision, in 1975, which gave them more than half of Maine.

A bill introduced by Henry (Scoop) Jackson (D Washington), more than two decades ago, would have given the Indians virtual sovereignty. They would have their own judges, courts, jail, and the right to try US citizens who violated their laws on their reservations.

A further development in that same direction occurred on August 12, 1994, when Judge James Allendoerfer of Snohomish County Superior Court ruled that two juvenile Indian offenders could be sentenced by their Tribal Court[49] for robbing a pizza delivery driver and beating him with a base-ball bat.[50] Their victim was a non–Indian and the offense occurred off–reservation. He sustained permanent injuries affecting his sight and hear-ing. The criminals' tribal "punishment" was to spend a year "banished," camping on an island. However, in practice, they didn't even stay on the island but returned to town whenever they liked. One of them even applied for a driver's license during that period. As a result, Judge Allen-doerfer gave them conventional sentences. — This case demonstrates how far Tribal authority might be extended and that there are parties trying to do so.

The energy policy of the 1960's and 1970's was where this all began. The Indians were involved because their holdings of energy resources are so large that they affect national and international policies. According to the Council of Energy Resources Tribes (CERT)[51], "its twenty–three member western Indian Nations control 33% of the low sulfur strippable coal reserves, 80% of the uranium, and 10% of the oil and gas reserves in the United States." Gaining control of these domestic energy resources prepared the way for the constructive use of the 1973 OPEC boycott of

---

[47] In 1974, the first year of Carter's administration, Congress created the Legal Services Corporation with 3300 lawyers and over 1000 para legals and a large budget which reached $238.7 million by 1978 and $300 million by 1979. Also, substantial funding for this purpose went to large Universities. For example to the University of Washington (its Law school and College of Fisheries) did much of the work developing the federal/Indian side of the Boldt case.

[48] One example is the Native American Rights Fund, NARF. In October 1971 received a $1.2 million grant from the Ford Foundation. The Ford Foundation continues to be a major donor to the Indian movement to this day.

[49] The Tlingit Tribe of South East Alaska's Prince of Wales Island.

[50] see Anon 1994.

[51] Quoted from Garitty 1980.

the United States.

The first Federal program in response to the oil embargo was President Nixon's Project Independence. It increased the use of domestic energy resources.[52] In terms of the reserves in America which were known during the 1970's, there were only modest reserves of uranium and oil, excepting the Alaskan reserves which the American public were not fully cognizant of, but vast reserves of coal, adequate to supply US power for over 200 years. A large part of those reserves are under Indian land.

Garitty (1980) says that the international oil companies began buying out the smaller coal companies, but this developing monopoly didn't go unobserved. As a result, further coal development on Federal and Indian land was banned.[53]

The Trilateral Commission was founded contemporary with these events. They produced three *Triangle Papers* on energy. Their third paper, *Triangle Paper No. 17, Energy: Managing the Transition*, came out in 1978. It became the core of the Carter energy policy and its first author, John C. Sawhill, was appointed the Assistant Secretary of Energy.

Middle Eastern oil has never been the mainstay of American energy. However, it was said, at that time that the decrease in that oil supply had caused the large increases in energy prices. But, the energy shortages were mostly contrived. — They occurred progressively first in one region of the country then another throughout the Ford and Carter years. The cause of some of these shortages can be found in Federal orders which shut down selected interstate oil pipelines, beginning in 1974.[54] The government appeared to be testing the public, seeing how far they could be pushed. — In each region, the energy shortage disappeared when public resistance grew too strong.

According to Heaton, 1993, in 1978, the Head of Carter's energy program, James Schlesinger ordered that a guide for use in his department on how to deal with "...fake emergencies around the country in the next three years as a drill to gauge ...preparedness."

President Carter's approach was to use these emergencies to control many aspects of American life. He also created the Energy Mobilization Board to "cut through the red tape, the delays and endless roadblocks to completing key energy projects." As part of that, in 1979 Secretary of the Interior, Cecil Andrus lifted the ban on mining in Indian lands. However, these fraudulent energy shortages ended abruptly, in 1981, when Ronald

---

[52] Under this plan nuclear energy output was to increase ten–fold by 1985, coal production was to double, and domestic oil production was to increase by 50%.

[53] According to Jorgensen (1978), quoted by Garrity (1980), "By 1973, the Federal government had leased 680,854 acres of public and 258,7545 acres of Indian land, containing over 20 billion tons of coal, to the corporations. Leasing halted in 1973 and did not begin again until late spring 1979, because there was criticism of the fact that 70% of the land leased was going to only 15 multinational oil companies." According to Garitty (1980) approximately 75% of the known uranium reserves also were owned by essentially the same 15 oil companies.

[54] See Williams, 1980.

Reagan was elected President.

Although these shortages were contrived in America, the oil embargo produced real hardships for Japan. They previously had imported the vast majority of their oil from the Middle East, but had little control over these international events. During the December 8, 1974, meeting of the Trilateral Commission, a commissioner from Japan[55] said "when Japan was jolted by the sudden impact of the oil crisis in the wake of the 1973 middle east war, some likened the Japanese position to that of passengers in a hijacked plane." One outcome of the embargo was that Japan switched to using Alaskan oil. That met the financial needs of British Petroleum and Atlantic Richfield and created interdependence between Japan and America.

Proposed oil ports, interstate pipelines, and liquefied natural gas ports continue to be blocked in the US, pretty much, whenever and wherever they have been proposed. Two examples from the late 1980's and early 1990's were 1) the liquefied natural gas facility proposed at Coho Landing in the lee of Point Conception in Southern California and 2) the proposed supertanker port just West of Port Angeles, Washington, which was to connect to the Northern Tier Pipeline to the Midwest.

There was also an atomic component to these energy policies. — During her campaign, Washington State Governor Dixy Lee Ray promised not to authorize atomic power plants in Washington State. However, when she became governor, she immediately authorized the sale of bonds to fund the construction of a large system of them. A total of fourteen bond series were issued during the period from 1977 through 1981, which exactly corresponds with the Carter Presidency. The total principle was $2.25 billion.

The need for all those powerplants was based on a projection which had been made by Batelle Northwest.[56] Some of those powerplants came under construction, but very few were even finished. However, the parties involved made huge profits.

As there was never anything like the demand for electrical power which had been projected, the system was not economically feasible. The last set of bonds were issued after WPPSS knew that the system must default. On August 18, 1983, they defaulted. The total value of principle plus interest was $7.25 billion, the largest default on public bonds in history. Since the citizens of Washington State hadn't authorized them, they had no obligation to repay their purchasers and the Washington State Superior Court ruled neither did WPPSS nor the power companies involved.

---

[55] Nobahiko Vshiba, see Trialog No 6 Winter 1974–1975

[56] Governor, Dixy Lee Ray had been a professor at University of Washington's College of Ocean and Fisheries Science, in their atomic energy program. The School of Fisheries had acted as cover for atomic research during World War II and it retained its connection to military research after the war. Batelle had overseen the program which generated much of the material used in the atomic bombs. This link between Batelle and UW's College of Fisheries remained close even into the 1990's.

Public disapproval of Governor Ray ran very high and she didn't run for a second term. However, President Reagan appointed her the head of the Atomic Energy Commission. Later, she publicly apologized for what she had done and wrote several books about the excesses of the environmental movement.

She was followed in office by Governor John Spellman. He did not represent the liberal establishment. But, after him, came Governor Booth Gardner, the step–son of Norton Clapp (deceased), the major owner of Weyerhauser Company and a trustee of the University of Chicago, who did. The last chapter of the WPPSS scandal, to date, occurred during 1986 when the Washington State Legislature passed a bill protecting the officials involved in it from prosecution for fraud. They made that protection retroactive to 1977 to cover all the bond sales. That bill was signed into law by Governor Booth Gardner.

Chapter 15

Outcome Based Education

Progressive education is intended to provide the central organizing structure for American Society. That was true in the system Woodrow Wilson tried to implement and it is also true, today. The name for the current version of progressive education is "Outcome Based Education" (OBE.)[1]

15.1 Formal Education under OBE

The operational framework of OBE is based on the stimulus–response methods, as refined by Skinner and others, during the 1950's and 1960's. It has seven steps in this application:

1. Externally determined goals are established;

2. A test is designed so that "success" or "failure" in reaching the goals can be determined;

3. Data is collected on the status of the student and on how the student responds to programs.

4. A program is developed to achieve the mission of getting the student to the goals;

5. The program is implemented.

6. At the end of the program a test is conducted to determine if the student has reached the goals;

7. Steps three to seven are repeated indefinitely until the student either achieves the goals are leaves the system.

---

[1] See Patrick, 1994, for extensive documentation on OBE.

Goal Setting (step 1): The clients which this education system serves are not the student nor the parents but are big business, the State, and the Federal Government. They set the goals.[2]

Data Collection (step 3): The data collected are not just on the student's academic status and response to programs. They also include his or her political views, psychological profile, learning style, medical history, and probably many other things.[3] All this information is stored in comprehensive computer files held at a central location by the State.[4] These files are intended to follow the individual life–long. They will become part of a nationwide database,[5] but that is not yet fully implemented. However, it is planned to be running by the year 2000, when it will be used to conduct the US census.[6]

According to the New York Times, Communist China has a similar system of comprehensive files, which they call a "dangan." It starts in elementary school and "shadows the person throughout life," moving directly from school to employer. "The dangan contains political evaluations that affect career prospects and permission to leave the country."

Program Design (step 4): The teaching methods used in OBE are moral persuasion. The teacher is supposed to act as a coach or

---

[2]During the first years of its implementation, industry specified their needs for types of workers, and what their qualifications should be. This can be seen in the Roundtable of Washington's reports on education. Their perspective was that the citizens of the state are their labor pool. However, their goals and standards were progressively replaced by State and, then, Federal ones.

The Federal Labor Department's manuals for schools called "SCANS" emphasized reinventing K-12 education around universally recognized standards with business as the customer. They maintained that "The Federal Government should continue to bridge the gap between school and the workplace" They also stated that student competence should include the following: "participates as a member of a team; negotiates to arrive at a decision; works with cultural diversity; mental visualization; self-esteem; decision making; integrity/honesty; and sociability."

[3]Originally, in California, the Myers–Briggs Temperament Test was used to psychologically type the students. But, it has generally been replaced by the Minnesota Multiphasic Typological Test.

[4]During 1989, under Washington Governor Booth Gardner, the Department of Information Services was mandated to develop such a statewide system. It was effectively in place by 1994, although not all the desired types of data were yet incorporated. But, the breadth of data it contained was revealed when a lawyer, Elizabeth Gallagher, expressed concern in a 1995 article in a computer magazine that the system made personal psychiatric records available to a very wide range of individuals throughout the State and also that there was no way to correct erroneous data in those files.

[5]The idea of using comprehensive files to determine how the individual responds to programs can be traced back to the University of Michigan's Institute for Social Research in the 1940's. (See their 1971 report.)

[6]The present plan is that that census will be conducted by verifying computer records rather than by the traditional methods. By that date, they expect to have records on every individual in the United States. They will use the opportunity to fill in gaps and verify whatever they are not sure of.

mentor gently guiding the student through the educational system.[7] They are also supposed to leave no fingerprints: that is, no one should know how the students were influenced, particularly the students, themselves.[8] One of the best ways to gain a student's cooperation is to make the student feel that he or she has chosen the goals, made the choices and, therefore, has a measure of control over his or her own life. This increases the student's consent to the outcome.

The contribution of Kierkegaard to these methods is the idea that all true learning is experiential. Consequently, students are not provided with education in the traditional sense of logical development of theories from first principles. Instead, they are forced to deduce the theory from applications. This may suit field–dependent people who can not comprehend theory nor have any interest in it, but only want to be an end–user of a product. But, the approach greatly impedes the transmission of understanding to the better students who have the ability and want to learn. This often makes formal education a frustrating experience for them. As a result, many do not prosper, but fall by the wayside.

The teaching program may combine the Socratic approach and control of information to lead the unsuspecting student to a desired conclusion.

Computers also open new avenues for teaching.[9] — The computer creates an educational environment, provides the student with information, requires him or her to use that information or to draw a deduction from it, and then asks for an answer. That could serve as education, as a psychological evaluation, or as both. There is no way to tell these two things apart, because the difference lies only in how the information is used.

In contrast against the traditional educational methods, which tend to develop reasoning skills, OBE tends to impinge more on the students' affective faculties and rote memory. Thus, these can be developed without developing the rational parts of their minds. As these different approaches selectively develop different mental faculties, teaching methods could be used to help the student develop a well–rounded personality.

One of the central parts of these new methods involves groups in what is called "collaborative learning." These groups can be manipulated by the methods of group dynamics and their composition can be designed to achieve an appropriate balance of psychological types or level of tension. But, their most important feature is that they operate by consensus, where consensus constitutes a tentative working agreement reached unanimously.

---

[7]The Federal Labor Department's SCANS manual recommended: "Teachers and students ... change their traditional roles" with "teachers becoming coaches"

[8]This is supposed to produce an organic totalitarian society, where everyone makes the "correct" decisions without ever being told.

[9]The Federal Labor Department's SCANS manuals recommended that technology "dispenses information" and "monitors" learning. To assist in the formation of individual lesson plans, the computer will access "biographical data, assessment criteria, [and] learning styles" for each student.

That gives each group member a sense of responsibility for the outcome. Nothing is more damaging to this process than easy choices which don't create a high level of involvement from the group members. But, few things have greater influence over individuals than their reaching a group consensus where they have a high stake in the outcome. That requires their publicly forming and asserting a position and probably will usually also require some concessions. Thus, they may become deeply involved in and committed to the outcome, the group, the process, and to having their decisions externally determined. These may be the most important lessons the students learn.

These teaching methods lead to the development of right–brain and diffuse or "holistic" thinking at the expense of the left–brain mental processes of deductive reason, concentration, and the intellect. As this is the period of their lives when they are individuating into adults, replacing myths with decisions and developing their mental faculties, this may have a profound impact, which can last the rest of their lives. Specifically, it should cause a significant reduction in the number of individuals who follow a "Western" viewpoint or ever come to understand Natural Law, and a corresponding increase in Eastern ones.

For those students which the system succeeds in depriving of reason, they teach a new method for decision–making which does not require it. It has the following steps:

1. Identify the problem;

2. Brainstorm or seek information to identify several possible courses of action. For example, these might be suggested by TV, newspapers, magazines, internet, friends, authorities, etc.);

3. Choose one;

4. Celebrate the achievement;

5. See what happens;

6. If necessary, repeat the process.

This approach is compatible with group–thinking: Specifically, they defer to the group or peers in steps 2 and 3. Once you learn to recognize this behavior, you will see young people using it.

This approach has also been introduced into natural resource management, under the name, "adaptive management." It is increasingly being used by citizens' councils and managers who lack adequate professional skills. Needless to say, it rarely leads to the best management practices. — The exception is where good and bad are a matter solely of perception. In that case, if this system is responsive to the customer's views, it can be the ideal method.

There are no safeguards against abuse and a teacher may, arbitrarily or from racial, religious, class, or other prejudice, choose to destroy an individual student. They may even do this simply because they choose to, as a whim, or for the perverted pleasures of having power over someone or causing pain. They can also put false and destructive information into the student's permanent record so that he or she will never be allowed to succeed, lifelong. In particular, a student may be cross–typed, that is miss–identified by psychological type. Thus, he or she will be routed and treated inappropriately by everyone who uses the dangon, ever afterwards. That can become a perpetual torment for them. — These things not only can happen, they do happen.

Thwarting a student's natural goals can bring forth the shadow. If the student, then, has the opportunity to act upon it, in a peer–group or gang, he or she may adopt that negative value. This seems to happen relatively often in OBE and leads to the development of negative or emotional personalities or the adoption of Gnostic, Eastern, or Destructionist beliefs. Some teachers view these as desirable outcomes.

The teachers are in a position to do something close to brainwashing. To apply this approach, a student is deliberately mismatched by psychological type and learning style to place him or her under great stress and cause him or her to fail repeatedly. Once the student's resistance, self–respect, and personality have been reduced to a nullity, his or her beliefs and personality can be reformed by peers, a teacher, or a mentor. Then he or she will publicly enunciate those beliefs and make decisions based on them in group–learning experiences, or act on them outside of school in peer groups or gangs. If this is repeated again–and–again, with different values each time, the child will become as clay, to be formed at will.

The OBE system also channels students into career pathways. Counseling guidelines suggest one for each of the psychological types.[10] The Myers–Briggs Temperament Test was the first typological system extensively used for this purpose,[11] and one study shows that during the first three decades of its use in the schools in California, they succeeded in channeling over 90% of their students into the designated careers for their types. — The types who would be expected to support societal change go to influential positions, whereas, those who would oppose it are condemned to obscure or dead–end jobs.

The OBE approach appears to aim at recreating the conditions which existed in Palestine during biblical times. In particular, a large proportion of their population were probably non–rational types or had one of the mental structures diagramed in Jacob's Ladder. In addition, under the Pharisees, their socio–religious system was progressive. They saw rapid social evolution and many new religions.

---

[10] This implies that counseling is a key profession which had to be strongly influenced early in the process. It was, to judge by the publications and flyers of their professional organizations and the guidelines provided by California State.

[11] For example, it was used in California ever since it was first developed in 1962. Its use became widespread in that State when progressive education was introduced in 1965.

It has been acknowledged in a wide range of sources that the objective of OBE is social change.[12] A statement was made by Professor Phillip Vaner Velde, in 1985, which encapsulates it nicely: "man may cling to much of the language and symbols of the old creeds ... but unless a new faith ... overcomes the old ideology, ... world government is doomed. ... Nation–states have outlived their usefulness, and a new world order is necessary. ... The task of reordering our values ... should be one of the major objectives of our schools. A new political order of control over human relationships will come into being. This clearly implies that national sovereignty, which is the basis of the current nation–state system ... can be whittled away."

15.2   The OBE System

At the end of 1989, the Commission on the Skills of the American Workforce (CSAW) of the National Center on Education and the Economy (NCEE), published a report laying out what was to become the form of the OBE educational system.[13] It was filled out in greater detail, beginning in 1990.

It contains five components:

1. **Certificate of Initial Mastery:**[14] This requires that the students meet standards of political correctness. A student who passes receives a Certificate of Initial Mastery (CIM), thereby, becoming eligible for work or more schooling.

   The "New Standards Reference Exam" is the qualifying examination for the CIM. It includes essay, extended open-ended responses, short-answer responses, and multiple-choice. Scoring must, therefore, be partially subjective.

   Harcourt Brace Educational Measurement will be given a monopoly on education testing. They will also evaluate the performance of schools and determine which will be certified to issue the CIM's.

2. **Youth Centers:** Those who do not earn their CIM by age 16 "will be condemned to dead-end jobs that leave them in poverty even if they are working." They will reside in these centers until they are 21.

---

[12] For example, there have been Federal programs to train teachers to be "responsible agents of social change." See Harold G. Drummond 1964, Cuddy 1964, Barbara Morris's *Change Agents in Schools*, and Michigan State University's Behavior Student Teacher Education Project (B–STEP), Office of Education Project OEC–0–9–320424–4042.

[13] This section is based upon the work of Shirley V. Basarab.

[14] NCEE's New Standards program developed "a system of internationally benchmarked standards," for student performance, and a testing system. This program was run by them jointly with the University of Pittsburgh.

3. **Occupational Certification:** Possession of a CIM allows additional education and training leading to an occupational certificate which permits entry into the workforce in a specific career pathway.

4. **Workforce Training by Industry:** High Performance businesses will offer occupational training, based on standards specific to the job and firm. This will be publicly financed. "At least in the beginning" these standards will not be set by the government."

5. **Labor Market Boards:** These boards impose themselves between individuals seeking work and businesses seeking employees. Some States have implemented this program. Oregon is an example.

High Performance: OBE meshes seamlessly with the TQM business world. — "High performance" programs have already been introduced in various States. They require that all government bodies and corporations working for government be certified as "high performance." That has nothing to do with the quality of their products or their methods of manufacture. It requires that the company hire only workers with certificates from OBE, and only buy from or sell to other high performance companies.

The High Performance Companies are run by TQM. These businesses set school standards, hire through school–to–work programs, and obtain, from them, the graduates' psychological profiles. These are useful to personnel managers in hiring compliant employees and also provide guidance to TQM group facilitators on how best to manipulate individuals.

TQM is already used in many government organizations and businesses throughout the country.[15] Wherever you may be, look around and you may well find it in your community, too.

TQM is not used merely here and in Japan, China, and Europe; Russia is also adopting it. During 1989, after the Soviet economic collapse, several American facilitators[16] visited Russia and participated in a nine–day intensive collaborative planning project, headed by Sergei Popov. He is the president of their Inter–Regional Methodological Association, which is a group of facilitators who do TQM–style collaborative regional planning. They also were received at the Leningrad Academy of Forestry; the Committee for the Protection of Nature, which is the Russian equivalent of the EPA; and the Urban Planning Institute, which plans large cities all over Russia. Russians at these high levels were very interested in these techniques. One of the American facilitators wrote that the "... Soviet citizens

---

[15] For example, Pensacola (Florida), created a "total quality community"; Madison (Wisconsin), Visalia (California), and Phoenix (Arizona) "reinvented government" by integrating the schools, city, and private sector under TQM; the State of Oregon implemented TQM through its "benchmarks" and ' 'human investment strategy"; and all the hospitals in Washington State operate under TQM.

[16] Including Connie Miller of the Northwest Renewable Resources Center, Seattle, Washington and Bill Lincoln of the National Center Associates. See the NRRC Newsletter Fall 1990: Vol 6 No. 1

have been taught to take direction from above. No bottom–up, grass–root activities or thinking has been tolerated." But they are introducing this new approach and were getting their first experiences with its application. At that time a Soviet team of facilitators planned to visit Washington State, during 1991, to participate in a training program in TQM run by the Washington Department of Ecology.

International Standards Organization: TQM meshes seamlessly with the ISO 9000 system of international standards.[17] As of 31 December 1992, a company must be ISO 9000 certified to sell products in the European Economic Community.[18] The ISO 9000 certification requirements are high performance. One of their requirements is that a company use TQM, a second is that a company only buy from suppliers which use TQM, a third is the adoption of a "sole supplier" strategy, eliminating competition[19]. However, it protects consumer interests by allowing the customer to interface with the TQM groups within the corporation providing the product.

This system provides the international businesses, who are the end customer, with the ability to reach down into and control all the employees of their suppliers. In Japan, which has had this system for four decades, the employees are often paid in company script rather than yen. Company script can only be used to buy products from other companies affiliated in the same network. Thus, non–TQM companies and small businesses were gradually strangled.

Although the current version of ISO 9000 was written in Europe, the team which wrote it had American representation and its origin is American. It began as the Mil-Q-9858, military quality standard in 1958, under the Eisenhower Administration.[20]

Thus, we finally see the full structure of the new system for education and work–force management. It has three parts: OBE, High Performance, and ISO9000. This fits the description of a "world–wide administratively controlled structure outside the realm of politics" referred to in the 1937 NRPB report and also found by Professor Carroll Quigley, during the early 1960's, among the records of the Council on Foreign Relations.[21]

---

[17] The International Organization of Standardization was put together in 1979. It also goes under various different names: BS 5750 in England, NFX50 in France, UNE66900 in Spain, CSAZ 299 in Canada, and ANSI/ASQC Q9000 in America,
....

[18] As of 1994, there were approximately 45 thousand ISO 9000 certified firms worldwide.

[19] This system is strongly supported by the Business Roundtables and by many of the large corporations they represent.

[20] R. Kanter says that the structure of ISO 9000 is also discernible in the quality assurance programs in the Environmental Protection Agency, Food and Drug Administration, and Nuclear Regulatory Agency. See his 1994 book.

[21] See Quigley, 1966.

15.3 Higher Education

All the above techniques from OBE are also used in higher education. The elect, of course, get good educations at private colleges and so, also, do the few individuals at the public universities who are selected by the professors. But, the objective is to channel, subordinate, or destroy everyone else.

To do this there must be a system which will allow selected individuals to succeed easily so that they come to believe that they are superior, while the others will have a hard time and, thus, will be taught that they are not of the same stuff. But, none of them should find out what was done, except for those who need to know, but only after they have been thoroughly indoctrinated.

Also, the system must have strong effects as the select few will generally have been chosen for reasons other than their ability and many of them may be of the affective or memorizing types. They are likely to have less natural ability than those who are held down.

Mathematics is a key skill which is essential to much of science and engineering, so it is one of the things which they tamper with. — The professors make sure that the selected students have an advantage.

The outsiders, the individuals who are not given key information, will think that they lack mathematical ability. But, that is absurd, because math is within the capability of any reasoning person, provided that it is taught in an appropriate progression so that the students receive everything they need before they reach the point where they have to use it. — This is, precisely what is not done, and very few will see the tricks which are played on them.

Another common practice is for the professors to misadvise the students about which courses are necessary. Some courses are prerequisites, while other are absolutely crucial for the profession. But, the students are never be told. In some cases, they are even advised not to take precisely those courses they need most.

And, of course, funding, grants, and scholarships are entirely controlled by the professors, either directly, by restricting information about them, or by networking with the granting agencies.

These are just a few of the techniques which are employed. The possibilities are endless. But, if all else fails, more direct means will be used. — Push will come to shove.

Do not suppose that students have any legal protection. There may be laws on the books, but there are virtually none in practice.

The educated intellectual should be the mainstay of the professions, and perhaps, as much as half of the American population might develop into that class of person, if they were educated to that end. As the colleges take only about ten percent of the population and only a fraction of them go to graduate school, one would expect to find intellectuals well-represented in advanced courses in math and science. But, memorizing types comprised from two–thirds to three–quarters of the PhD–candidates in the highest level courses in math and statistics, at the University of

Washington, during the 1980's, and the few intellectuals were predominately foreign students.[22] Clearly there was a selection process going on.

Engineering provides an example of where this occurs. First, the individuals who are advised to go into engineering are not predisposed towards analytic thought. — It may come as a surprise, but, at the University of Washington, during the 1980's, the Civil Engineering students had the lowest Scholastic Achievement Test scores in quantitative skills of any department, including the fine and performing arts.

In addition, Civil and Mechanical Engineering Departments characteristically teach by example and rote, requiring their students to work a seemingly endless repetition of virtually identical problems. That crushes independent thought. Many of the intellectuals among them transfer to other departments or fail from sheer exasperation.

The significance of this may be that in a contracting economy, such as Rome had and America is rapidly becoming, science poses a hazard: As John S. Mill pointed out, it produces unpredictable advances and prosperity which can allow segments of the community to escape from organic control. — However, a contracting society still needs technical people. So, if they must be trained, let them have little creativity. This educational system can be relied on to produce such people.

The quality of college education has declined sharply over the last few decades. For example, during the 1950's calculus was required for High School graduation in Washington State and many other States. Three decades later, a bachelor's degree in the natural sciences from a University characteristically required only one or two quarters of calculus. Thus, a college graduate, today, is educationally not much above a high school graduate of his or her parents' generation.

Needless to say, the professors are a different class of people then they used to be. — Duke Professor H.L. Gates jr. said that "leftists, feminists, destructionists, and Marxists" have infiltrated academia and were ready to take control as the old guard retires.[23]

To this new type of educator, education means an opportunity for indoctrination. For example, ... One day, while I was quietly reading a scientific paper, in a conference room, in a different part of the university, who should walk in but my major professor and one of my fellow graduate students. I was seated behind a partition, and they did not know I was there. But, I could hear everything as the Professor began lecturing his student. The substance of what he said was that it was the duty of minority graduate students to seduce the White girls in their classes so that they did not feel themselves superior to them. — Both were members of the same minority. — He did most of the talking, and went on for about three–quarters of an hour. I remember thinking it remarkable that throughout

---

[22] The contrast was very evident and was discussed in several of the classes. But the issue of whether they were field–dependent or had other traits of particular significance never came up.

[23] See *Atlantic Monthly* March 1991.

that whole conversation, neither of them ever mentioned that the graduate student was married, much less scrupled at it.

This comparatively innocuous example was chosen to give the general tone of what higher education means today: For undergraduates, the lessons often involve issues of sex and marriage, because for many young people, college is the narrow window of opportunity between parents and marriage during which the related social values can be changed.

The debauching of youth was long an objective of the Russian communists. For example Lavrenti Beria, head of the KGB under Stalin wrote in 1934,[24] "By attacking the character and morals of man, himself, and by bringing about through contamination of youth a general degraded feeling, command of the populace is facilitated to a very marked degree. ... This has long been demonstrated by such Russians as Pavlov, and the principles have been used in handling the recalcitrant, in training children, and in bringing about the optimum behavior on the part of a population." — What he was suggesting was, of course, inducing their regression to the level of the flesh, that is the level of the infant. Sex is a very powerful means for doing this.

The counter–example of Saint Francis Assisi provides further confirmation of this general approach. — The Gray Friars promoted reason and enlightenment through the practice of strict morality. They were highly successful and their greatest contributor to science was no less than Roger Bacon. Their approach was to raise the individual to higher reasoning and open the intellectual gateway to the interiority. That results in full individuation and provides the individual access to his motivation and goals: that is, it draws him closer to God. And love of God is the moral imparitive. These changes make the individual self–actuated and close the door to indoctrination. In contrast, vice reduces him to the level of the infant or child and does the opposite.

This principle is also stated in the twelfth Sutra: "Control of these psychic activities come from the right use of the will and from ceasing from self–indulgence."

But, the undergraduates are not subjected to the full rigor of indoctrination. That is reserved for the graduate students. — Many of them are destined for influential positions in government. So, they have to be the type of public employee who would be compatible with America's intended new form of government. H.G. Wells described them as,[25] "...a disciplined organization of officials ... appointed by representative bodies of diminishing importance, and coming at last to be the working control of the State." Thus, the particular objective of this new type of professor is to convert the graduate students into a disciplined cadre. They seem to predom-

---

[24] He wrote a textbook used in the 1934 Moscow University Summer School. Part of it was recorded in the Congressional Record. This quote was drawn from Heaton 1993.

[25] See Wells, *The Open Conspiracy*. He was one of the principle writers advancing Fabian socialism. This particular book is an outline of their plan.

inately turn out authoritarian collectivists and affective personalities.[26] Obviously, they are using the techniques of internationalist education.

Various methods are used to foster group identity. A traditional approach, which we first saw in Alchemy, is to lead the student through a series of moral offenses and crimes of increasing seriousness, in this case, with the group or network in question. Eventually, he or she becomes entirely committed to the group and under their power. That, also, progressively breaks the student's moral fiber.

15.4   Implementation of OBE

Having seen what OBE is, and what it is for, let us trace its implementation.

The first educational goal from *Goals for America* to be achieved was to increase the number of billets in Graduate Schools. This began when President Kennedy (1961–1963) introduced a program to open college education to all Americans.

This program was greatly expanded by President Johnson (1963-1969) and profoundly altered the structure of American society. Prior to this, investment in a graduate education had been the main hurdle which separated professionals from the working class. However, a massive program of government scholarships which were only available to individuals from working–class origins, women, and minorities obliterated class distinctions, reducing America to a single homogeneous mass beneath the wealthy elite.

The definitive characteristic of the masses is their view that money alone determines class status. That is the Marxist paradigm which defines the proletariat and the bourgeois. — The prominent Washington DC political analyst, Kevin P. Phillips, has in recent years, published two books which present American politics of the last few decades in this light.[27] So far as he is concerned, enlightenment and every other part of the original basis of the American form of society and government are effectively non–existent. His definition of the "middle class," by which he means "bourgeois," is a combined annual household income of more than $100,000. He feels that that is the income level necessary to achieve affluence which, to him, is the sole defining property of that class.

Similarly, Walt Meuller suggested that contemporary youth culture is materialism. He said that they are motivated by the acquisition of goods, particularly of luxury items. But, any familiarity with young people shows that the majority of them are "good" in the traditional Western sense and have all the normal goals and aspirations. These books may partly be promulgating a myth errant. — The powers in America might wish that everyone was so simple, for they would, then, be easily controlled through

---

[26] Given the nature of these types, many of them probably have little or no intellect, and may primarily be memorizers. This may be part of why we have seen such a dramatic growth in junk science over the last few decades.

[27] See, Phillips, 1990 and 1993.

economics. So, if people can be made to believe this myth, some of them will indeed follow it. And, some do.

Destruction of the middle class, as distinguished from the bourgeois, has almost universally been considered to be a necessary pre–condition for establishing an absolute or Eastern form of government. — It is necessary to destroy enlightenment, the social memory of Natural Law, and all the concepts derived from them, as these are the basis of Western society. That translates to destroying the middle class, as this is their paradigm.

In the contemporary context of total quality management, where business and public policy decisions are made by appointed quality teams or local councils, members of the middle class can be disruptive as they may be guided by truth or abstract concepts of morality. For example, the medieval concept that a person in a position of power has an obligation to consider the interests of those who are not represented or are powerless, will interfere with the team's ability to make purely socially determined and self–serving decisions and, thus, will reduce the effectiveness of organic control. The ideal team member is an obligately field–dependent holistic thinker, whose decisions are entirely situational and socially determined, and whose motivations are financial. However, a team can tolerate a few stakeholders of other types provided that they approve of the process. But, they can never be expected to participate as fully nor to achieve as high a level of commitment to the team or the outcomes.

The same also applies to appointments to government jobs. — Under this scheme, the ideal government worker sees nothing, is easily manipulated, and has a high level of commitment to the department and its policies.

This scheme is designed for proletarian or bourgeois man. The underlying problem for democracy is that the vast majority is intractable. — They will not follow their natural superiors, but respond to them with all the hatreds and prejudices of class–struggle; nor are they capable of creating a leadership of their own, for they will not read nor watch anything but popular literature or entertainments, nor is it effective to force anything else upon them as they are not motivated by abstract concepts and, in some cases, can not even comprehend them. But, this scheme selects and empowers a leadership from among their ranks and then organizes them, molds them, and gets them to work in cooperation to achieve the outcomes selected by those above them in the organizational structure.

To prepare the proletariat for this new system, their older organizations, the unions, had to be destroyed. That came about due to President Reagan's policy of not enforcing the Federal laws protecting unions and their members, a policy which was continued by Presidents Bush and Clinton.

At the same time, the higher education system has become increasingly dedicated to turning out a new middle class to fill all the higher levels of the organizational superstructure. They are that "disciplined cadre" of authoritarian collectivists.

Above them are the elite, the wealthy, the masters, the only people in society who are "free" in the Classical sense. Characteristically, they were educated at one or another of a short list of prestigious private colleges, such as Harvard, Yale, Stanford, and a few others.

This ordering of society should be recognized as resembling the tri–level system of decadent Rome or, more exactly, of the Gnostic organizations, with their libertines, strict orders, and small circle of masters.

Returning to the years of the Johnson Administration, the other significant development in education was that he appointed John Gardner to be the head of the Federal Department of Health, Education, and Welfare. He had previously been the president of the Carnegie Cooperation.

In 1965, Johnson and Gardner pushed the Elementary and Secondary Education Act through the US Legislature. It established the Federal Title I grants to fund research in education, It also provided massive funding to States which tried the new methods. It was under that program that California officially adopted progressive education, in 1965.[28] There was also, at that time, a Federal effort to train teachers in these new methods.[29]

President Nixon (1969–1974) appears to have opposed the internationalist agenda. Consequently, progressive education was not supported by government, during his years.

But, in the private sector, Zbigniew Brzezinski, the co–founder of the Trilateral Commission and later President Carter's National Security Advisor, published his book, *Between Two Ages*. In it he wrote about the future State he envisioned:

> In this technetronic society the trend seems to be toward ...effectively exploiting the latest communication techniques to manipulate emotions and control reason. ...Human beings become increasingly manipulable and malleable ...the increasing availability of biochemical means of human control ...the possibility of extensive chemical mind control ...a national information grid that will integrate existing electronic data banks is already being developed ...The projected work information grid, for which Japan, Western Europe, and the United States are most suited, could create the basis for a common educational program, for the adoption of common academic standards ...

In another place in that book he wrote that the leaders in that future State would not be governed by the traditional standards of morality.

Roughly contemporary with him, the Office of Washington's Governor, Dan Evans, who was one of the founding members of the Trilateral

---

[28] See California Assembly Bill 1865, of 1965.

[29] In particular, in 1967 the US Department of Education funded a project to develop "a new kind of elementary school teacher who ... functions as a responsible agent of social change."

Commission, published a special edition of *Washington Magazine*[30] which looked forward to an idealized future for Washington State. It took the viewpoint that the public is business's labor pool, so schools in the ideal State would train according to their needs. A worker would enter business in an apprenticeship program and advance and obtain more training whenever the business leadership thought best. It even suggested that, at those times of transition in a workers' life, he or she might find a new spouse.

— These two publications show that, as of the early–1970's, the basic concepts of the OBE system existed, in embryo, among the liberal Eastern establishment and, in particular, among the founders of the Trilateral Commission. Over the years which followed, the Business Roundtables, which were formed in response to the suggestions in Triangle paper No. 8, would be one of OBE's leading advocates.

President Ford's (1974-1977) administration supported OBE. During his term in office, the general direction of the program was set by the Institute for Chief State School Officers' (CSSO) (1974) report.[31] Vladimir Turchenko's, 1976, book on the educational methods used in the Soviet Union, also had a substantial impact.—They had more experience with the methods of progressive education, because they had used them continuously, since their inception.

Relatively little happened during President Jimmy Carter's administration (1977-1981), except further teacher training.[32] That period ended with the Global 2000 Report (1980), again recommending progressive education.

President Reagan (1981–1989) had originally been a liberal Democrat, but he presented himself as a conservative Republican. The public accepted him as such.[33]

His term in office saw a dramatic increase in funding for research on education from the institutions associated with the UN,[34] but very little directly from the United States government. The Reagan administrative's,

---

[30] The edition was printed for a meeting of business leaders and circulated only among them. A few copies still exist in private collections.

[31] Their members include the well-known personalities: George Bush, James Baker, Edmond de Rothschild, Willard Wirtz, and Alvin Toffler (he was Newt Gingrich's mentor and the author of *Future Shock*.).

[32] National Education Association (NEA) established a think tank on how "to change teachers' inflexible patterns of thinking" to politically correct methods and, in 1977, a United Nation's UNESCO study championed the use of technology in education in communist countries.

[33] In his first race for Governor of California, he was supported by conservatives. However, they shunned him in his second race — That time, he was supported by the Hollywood clique. K. M. Heaton was a member of his first campaign committee and gives fairly detailed information on his position. See Heaton 1993.

[34] First, in 1981, UNESCO, the World Bank, and the Office of Economic Cooperation and Development (OECD) began researching critical thinking skills, and later, the World Bank decided to "increase the Bank's lending for education and training to about $900 million a year."

1983, report *A Nation at Risk - The Imperative for Educational Reform* followed shortly thereafter. But, the most important development during Reagan's term came, during 1985, when the U.S. Department of State granted the Carnegie Corporation authority to negotiate with the Soviet Academy of Sciences on curriculum development and the restructuring of American education.[35] Only a few months later, Washington State published *Schools for the 21st Century.* which drew upon the Soviet's teaching methods. It became the model for the national OBE program.

After this point, things began moving rapidly as many short–lived organizations were created for specific purposes. Many of them were interrelated through interlocking directorates. It becomes a bewildering array of names and faces, a veritable alphabet soup of organizations. The central line of what transpired may have been that a Carnegie organization developed a master plan for the structure of OBE, and subcontracted parts of it to various other groups.[36] But, a great deal else was happening at the same time. Their effort culminated, at the end of 1989, with the CSAW commission's publication of the report, mentioned earlier, which defined the structure of the OBE educational system.

President George Bush (1989–1993) had previously been a member of the CSSO committee, when they had written their report, in 1974, during President Ford's term. His term began with the first-ever governor's "Education Summit." A committee which came out of that meeting, the National Educational Goals Panel, published, in 1990, six National Education Goals. The initial work on that report had been done by a committee headed by Governor Bill Clinton. Under the name, "America 2000," it was endorsed by President Bush, in 1991.

When President Bill Clinton (1993–1999) came into office, his party (D) also held a majority in both houses. Therefore, they were able get leg-

---

[35] This led to *The General Agreement of the Government of the U.S. and the Government of the USSR on Contacts, Exchanges and Cooperation in Scientific, Technical, Educational, Cultural and Other Fields.*, which signed in Geneva on November 21, 1985. Among other things, it encourages Soviets cooperation and input into designing the curriculum and teaching materials for America's schools. — They have more experience with these techniques than any other nation, as they have used them continuously since shortly after their revolution.

Dr. David Hamburg in an interview with the Los Angeles *Times*, reported June 12 1987, regarding the reason the Carnegie Corporation did the negotiation: "Privately endowed foundations can operate in areas government may prefer to avoid."

[36] Based on the Reagan Administration's *A Nation at Risk* report, a Carnegie inspired organization, the Carnegie Forum on Education and the Economy (CFEE) commissioned Marc Tucker, to develop a program to improve education. To implement this, in 1988 he formed the driving organization of today's education reform across the nation, the NCEE. This organization navigates and fuels education reform nationally. A few other notables who repeatedly reappeared on commissions and boards, include David Rockefeller Jr., Boeing's Frank Schronz, Brian Benzell, Hillary Clinton, and Bill Clinton. During 1987, we find (then Governor) Bill Clinton involved in a Study Commission on Global Education, financed by the Rockefeller, Ford and Exxon Foundations.

islation enacted. He renamed "America 2000," "Goals 2000" and pushed it through Congress as the *Goals 2000 Educate America Act*. That was followed by the *School-To-Work Opportunities Act* and the *Improving America's Schools Act*.

The juggernaut rolled on but gradually slowed. National socialized medicine went down first. It would have created the national comprehensive data base. After the 1994 election, they no longer had control of both houses. Next, in 1996, OBE ran into the backlash from parents and the Christian Right, and the *Careers Act* failed to come out of legislative conference. The people promoting OBE then switched to Charter Schools, which, in the final analysis, are very similar. However, the public doesn't seem to have recognized that yet. By 1996, 21 States passed laws authorizing them. During 1997, President Clinton while speaking on education and welfare in North Carolina, announced that the schools teaching the military's children would be the first to fully adopt the new standards. He said that that would be accomplished by 1999.

15.5 Eugenics

The OBE system constitutes a eugenic policy. Eugenics have been around for a long time.[37] Historically, one of their central concerns was decreasing dysgenesis: That is the progressive decrease of a nation's average intelligence due to the tendency of the less intelligent to have more children. Studies have estimated that the rate of decrease of IQ is 1–4 IQ points per decade during peace-time.[38] However, war tends to reverse the process by eliminating the less intelligent.

Therefore, permanent peace implies that the bulk of the population will deteriorate into stupidity. There are people, today, who feel that reducing the average IQ to somewhere around 85 would be a good thing as it would make them contented with their life as slaves.[39] Therefore, it is not surprising that permanent peace has often been one of the objectives in the liberal agenda.

Many people object to the suggestion that intelligence is heritable. Nevertheless, it appears to have a genetic component. For just one example among many, L. Erlenmeyer–Kimling and F. Jarvik showed, in 1963,

---

[37]In particular, they were discussed by prominent scientists such as Thomas Malthus (1766–1834), Charles R. Darwin's (1809–1882), Francis Galton (1822–1911), and John S. Haldane (1860–1936) one to two centuries ago.

[38]That is a little misleading. — The rate of dysgenesis is not constant. It decreases as the average intelligence approaches the mean for the more rapidly reproducing less intelligent segment. Consequently, effective convergence to that IQ level may take substantially longer than a constant rate would predict.

[39]They do not seem to notice that the American Blacks and Mexican–Americans, who as groups have average IQ's around 85 to 95, are not docilely content with their lot, but have high crime rates and, often, harbor a resentment for the system. And much the same can be said of Whites from the lower third of graduating classes, too.

that IQ is approximately 80% heritable among Caucasians. There is also a genetic component to the presence, absence, and strength of the psychological traits which determine the personality typologies.

In this context, internationalism, which promotes racial mixing, should be recognized effecting the genetics of psychological type. Specifically, it should result in increased variation.[40]   OBE, also has genetic effects: By channeling some psychological types into dead–end careers, it selectively raises the reproductive success of some typological groups relative to others. Then, it follows that combining Internationalism and OBE, does precisely what a farmer does if he wants to "improve" the breed of his stock animals.— He introduces animals from different genetic lines to increase the range of variation and, then, selects the new types he prefers from among their offspring.

We should bear in mind that the liberal Eastern establishment has promoted eugenic policies in the past. For example, the final report, of Hoover's Research Committee on Recent Social Trends contains the following statement:

> Of the two ways of improving the qualities of a people, the first, mutation, can be dismissed as our knowledge is too limited; the second, selection and breeding for desirable qualities, offers possibilities.

Internationalism also has another effect. — An isolated people, will tend to evolve a set of traits which work well together. Over time these will gradually become stabilized in the population. When two such populations mix, their offspring, after several generations, to allow full randomization, would not be expected to perform as well as either parent stock, because they have random collections of traits rather than selected ones. Populations which have histories of extensive mixing may give some idea of the magnitude of this effect. — Latin Americans are such a population. According to Herstein and Murray 1994, they have an average IQ 10 points below the peoples from which they were derived. But this is not definitive as there is confounding from other factors.

Herrnstein and Murray[41] give us a glimpse of what they consider America's future may hold. According to them, due to decreasing IQ's, America will soon need to become a custodial State. This government will assume the responsibility for raising children, providing housing, and concentrating the under–class into urban centers where they can provide strict law enforcement. Specifically they say:

> In short, by custodial state, we have in mind a high–tech and more lavish version of the Indian reservation for some substantial minority of the nation's population, while the rest of America tries to go about its business. In its less benign forms

---

[40] That is assuming that the typological composition of different nationalities differ, which it is reasonably certain they do.

[41] See Herrnstein and Murray 1994, pages 520–526.

the solution will become more and more totalitarian. Benign or otherwise 'going about its business' in the old sense will not be possible. It is difficult to imagine the United States preserving its heritage of individualism, equal rights before the law, free people running their own lives, once it is accepted that a significant part of the population must be made permanent wards of the State.

The OBE/TQM/ISO 9000 system creates a type of caste system. In this case, an individual's station in life is determined not by the caste into which he or she is born, but by the score he or she receives in a psychological evaluation. That will determine the individual's fate for the remainder of his or her life. This is based on a belief in genetic predetermination and the corresponding philosophy of culture.[42]

This general approach was tried in England, where it was known by the name of their psychological evaluation, the "eleven-plus exam." — That exam, was given at age eleven. It determined a child's future. But it did not provide a reliable measure of the children's capabilities later in life. They used this approach, during the 1950's and early 1960's. But, eventually, the supporting studies were found to have been fraudulent.

Fraud is likely to occur here, too. — The testing and certification components of OBE will be outside the public sector, where favoritism is legal. An individual with the right connections might be able to obtain any desired score for an appropriate consideration or an individual from a non-favored group may be pre-doomed. The child could, then, be molded by OBE to match whatever scores they provide.

For America to accept this new caste system, it is not even necessary that the underlying genetic concepts be true. Myths can provide the organizing principles of society, provided that the people believe them.

But, this entire scenario, is based on a genetic theory of personality which has been superseded.

15.6   Dynamic Lattice

Although, there is undeniably a genetic component to personality and, therefore, also to cultural and historical processes, their influence is grossly exaggerated in the above scheme. — The mind is flexible and people can learn and change.

The modern viewpoint is that although genetics give a predisposition, the mind develops according to which pathways are used. In some species, such as the Sea Hare, it has even been shown that brain cells grow new dendrites as learning occurs. Thus, they physically create new pathways.

---

[42] For reviews of scientific studies of the relationship between typology and culture during the early 1960's see Francis L.K. Hsu 1961, Anthony F.C. Wallace 1961, and Robert A LeVine 1974.

It is not clear whether that may happen in humans, too, but it is generally accepted that learning and practice can affect the structure of the mind.

The most striking examples may come from Christianity and Islam versus Judaism. — The basic approach in Christianity and Islam is to focus upon principles, such as truth and goodness and also on the physical world. This causes the development of the rational and actively initiated subconscious faculties such as the intellect. In contrast, the traditional Judaic approach involves strict orthodoxy, mysticism, and spirituality.[43] This develops the memorizing processes, feelings, and the passive subconscious processes. The results are the two different structures of the mind depicted in the Classical model and Jacob's Ladder.

The impact which the current approach to higher education has upon an individual of the Western type can be interpreted in terms of these two models. — First, through endless repetition and rewarding rote memorization skills, the student is driven down to the level of lower reasoning in the Classical model. They may even be debauched to the physical and emotional level. Thus, they are reduced to the lower levels in the Classical model. But, these are the higher levels in Jacob's Ladder. So, as their Western, active, and left–brained skills are destroyed, their Eastern, passive, and right–brained skills are developed.

Kurt Lewin in the 1930's began the process of shaking off the old deterministic ideas which had dominated the American philosophy of culture since the beginning of the twentieth century. But, society's change in viewpoint did not occur until the 1960's. That was largely due to Raymond Cattell (born 1905, retired 1973). In 1966, he incorporated this more flexible attitude into psychology, when he introduced the idea of the mind as a dynamic lattice.[44] This advance was why OBE shifted from the Myers–Briggs Test, which was used for about two decades, beginning when OBE was first implemented,[45] to the Minnesota Multi–Phasic Personality Inventory (MMPI).[46]

Cattell was, also, a pioneer in the use of multi–variate statistics. So, it is not surprising that the MMPI uses those techniques. That general approach does not assume any predetermined typological system, but tries to deduce one from multiple correlations, principle components, and other multivarient techniques.

The weakness of this approach is that it usually does not lead to any understandable new hypothesis. So, although the MMPI helped to break our thinking away from the older deterministic models, it has not provided a new model for the mind and probably can not be expected to do so.

---

[43] Today, there is substantial overlap between there three religions, so that some Christian and Islamic sects and denominations follow orthodoxy and spiritualism, whereas some branches of Judaism tend towards reason.

[44] See Barry D. Smith and Harold J. Vetter's, 1982, review.

[45] The Myers–Briggs Test was created in 1962, and OBE was first implemented in some States, in 1965.

[46] There are also several alternatives to the MMPI, including a second version of the MMPI. See the review by P.E. Vernon et al. 1992.

The literature from the last three decades, contains several new models and there appears to be a widespread consensus on adopting the more flexible viewpoint. But, if a single new model has emerged, it does not appear to have reached the political or religious realms.

The current orientation of OBE appears to be based on the Classical model combined with Jacob's Ladder, but recognizes the flexibility of the human mind and the possibility of reforming its structure from one typology to another. But, OBE also recognizes the genetic component, and follows the older caste or genocidal approach for those who can not be retrained.

15.7 Consequences

It is instructive to meet the products of OBE. — For example, one day I was working out in the weight–room in the apartment complex in which I, then, lived, in Olympia, Washington, when a group of young people walked in. They wanted to know how to use the weight machine. So, I showed them and advised them that, as they were obviously beginners, they should see what they could lift and, then, exercise with half that weight. — They looked confused and conferred together. It soon became apparent that none of them could divide by two. These were normal, healthy, polite, sociable, young people from middle class families; their parents were government employees; and they had just graduated from Olympia Highschool in the upper half of their class. That was, then, one of the State's pilot projects in OBE. They were not considered to need that arithmetic skill, as they might always expect to have calculators available.

Then, there was the young man, who was from the lower half of his graduating class. He had just been released from prison where he had been serving a term for ritual torture. He had used a cigar to burn a pentagram into a man's chest. He was a Satanist, a Christian Fundamentalist, a drug user, and I was told that he was, also, a member of the Neo–Nazis. If the first group represents OBE's ideal outcome for affective personality types, he represents the alternative ideal outcome, for non–affective types: specifically, a non–rational or memorizing personality which has been emotionalized. His social behavior was, also, ideal in the sense that he was adopting the contemporary evolving religions of faith and superstition and putting them into practice.

On the national level, beginning immediately after the widespread implementation of OBE there were more than a half–dozen incidents where a group of students from a highschool gunned down their fellow students together with some teachers. In the public discussion which followed the most recent such incident,[47] the statistic was given that all of the students who did the killings, over all of the incidents, had been introverted

---

[47] That was at Columbine High School in Littleton, Colorado, during April 1999.

white males from urban homes. Most of them were fairly bright students. But, they had a history of troubles and some were on prescription drugs to modify their psychological state. They seem to have had feelings of persecution, anger, frustration, hatred, hopelessness, and so on.

We are told that in Japan, when a student fails a crucial exam, he or she commits suicide. But, Americans have a more overt culture.

Given the methods and objectives of OBE, the conclusion seems unavoidable that the children who did the killing were probably essentially correct in their perceptions about what the system was doing to them. — The objective of OBE is to eliminate the type of people they appear to have been or to subject them to sufficient stress to cause change in the structure of their minds. That is done by their fellow students, orchestrated by the teachers. There is no need to look any further for the cause of these tragedies. But, that does not excuse their killing the other children.

Hopefully, we will see positive changes. But, whether that happens or not, people will be better able to cope with OBE if they understand what it is for and what its methods are.

Chapter 16

America's Changing Churches

This chapter addresses the changes in America's religions since the 1950's.

16.1   Christian Covenantors

During the 1970's, a loosely affiliated Fundamentalist Christian religion grew, which was variously referred to as the "Identity Christians," "Christian Covenant People," or the "Aryan Nations Church." Their growth was fueled by affirmative action and other policies which discriminated against Protestant males of Northern European origin. At about the same time, and probably due to the same cause, many white ultra–nationalist groups also arose. However, there appears to have been no coordination nor connection between these two movements.[1] But, there was some cross–over among them. — The Identity Christians were one of the religions of choice for many White ultra nationalists.[2]

These movements were popularized by William Pierce's novel *The Turner Diaries*, which depicted a successful White supremist insurgence

---

[1] According to Martin A Lee, 1997, the ultra–nationalist movements, in each of the European countries and America were spontaneous with only a limited exchange of individuals and information among them. In fact, the retired Major General of Nazi Germany, Otto Ernst Remer, tried to coordinate these groups internationally, but was unable to overcome their fierce independence. Thus, ultra–nationalism was and remains a polycentric movement of relatively small independent groups. — As a class, they are individualists rather than collectivists and, therefore, are not "Nazi" according to our definition.

[2] In contrast, Louis Farrakhan's Nation of Islam and Elijah Muhammad's Black Muslims provided Black ultra–nationalists with both a political organization and a religion.

in America. That became one of the important works for them.

By the early–1990's the Identity Christians had approximately thirty centers spread throughout the United States. One of the best known of these may be the one at Hayden Lake, Idaho.

They are Fundamentalist Christians who see the biblical prophesies unfolding in current events, or hold some related belief. — They are a polycentric movement encompassing a range of doctrines.

The religious doctrine of their more extreme seedline group provides a general outline of their beliefs: — Like all successful political or religious doctrines, it is woven around a kernel of truth. — They begin with the assumption that the original Israelites were a northern long–headed people and a large part of the ten lost tribes eventually migrated to Western Europe where they were reabsorbed by the Northern Europeans.

Their hypothesis can not be ruled out, as the Israeli's identity is essentially unknown. — If one takes the archeological and historical viewpoint on the origin of the peoples of the region, then, during biblical times, that is during the period from the twelfth century BC to the first century AD, the Philistines were one Northern Longheaded people in the region and there could easily have been other small groups of Peoples of the Sea and, of course, there were Persians, Greeks, and Romans, too. Thus, there indisputably were Northern Longheads there and opportunity for the original Hebrews to have been a group of them. That, is if the Hebrews existed at all, as a distinct people, which is not certain.

The biblical account generally supports this in that it is in every way consistent in its viewpoint that the Hebrews, Israelis, and Jews were a distinct people and a minority among the peoples of Palestine.

If we look at the Roman records from the first century AD to see what manner of people they might have been, we find that the few which give explicit descriptions of Jesus and his family describe them as having Nordic racial characteristics. As his family claimed to have been of pure descent from the House of David, and that seems to be universally accepted, presumably their characteristics were those of the Israelites and Hebrews. For example, the *Archko Volume*,[3] which represents itself as a copy of selected original documents from the period, now held in the Vatican Library, gives the following description of Jesus as reported by the court scribe, Gamaliel. He was a highly–respected individual and the teacher of the Apostle Paul. "He is the picture of his mother, only he has not her smooth round face. His hair is a little more golden than hers, although it is as much from sunburn as anything else. He is tall, his shoulders are a little drooped; his visage is thin and of a swarthy complexion, though this is from exposure. His eyes are large and a soft blue and rather dull and heavy. His lashes are long, his eyebrows are large. And he has the nose of a Jew.[4] He reminds

---

[3] See McIntosh and Twyman (translators).— I can not attest to the authenticity of these records, but the Identity Christians cite them and use them as evidence. There, also, several other documents which say much the same thing and an absence of contradiction.

[4] He certainly did not mean an aquiline nose, as this phrase would be inter-

me of an old–fashioned Jew in every sense of the word." He described Mary as flaxen blond and Joseph as auburn–haired with gray eyes.

Regarding the migration of the ten tribes, there is some evidence that a few of them ended up in Europe. Christian Covenant authors tend to attach great significance to this and have produced some creative histories on the migrations of peoples to support this concept.

Based on this and other evidence, the Identity Christians conclude that the old covenants between God and the nation of Israel apply to the Northern Europeans and the peoples derived from them as they are the descendants and relatives of the Israelis. They hold that many Jews, today, were descended from the Khazars and have no Semitic ancestry whatsoever, or are of mixed descent, and the few who claim Jewish ancestry probably have Edomites, Canaanites, and related non–Israelite peoples among their ancestors, if they are not their sole ancestry from Palestine. Thus, according to the *Bible*, they either never had the birthright of Israel or were specifically excluded from it.

The Identity Christians, also, do not fail to note that Christianity is the continuation of the pre–Christian Judaic religious heritage, whereas Rabbinic Judaism is indebted to the religious traditions of Babylon possibly more than to those of Palestine. In addition, the traditions of the Pharisees probably represent more a reaction to the older Jewish religious heritage rather than their continuation.

The *Bible* describes people with their racial origins and beliefs as being the hereditary enemies of Israel, hated by God, the synagogue of Satan, and a long list of other curses. The Identity Christians follow that precedent and conclude that the Jews, as a people, are Satan. They think of the Devil in the Christian sense that those who do evil are the realization of the Evil Principle on Earth,[5] and they believe that the Jews are evil by their nature.

Essentially what they are saying is that evil is an inherited personality trait. They point to biblical support for this concept (Psalm 58:3–4): "The wicked are estranged from the womb; They go astray as soon as they are born, speaking lies." But, it is fairly common knowledge that some children seem evil from birth and retain that tendency all their lives. Thus, if we regard evil as a personality trait, and as we know that some personality traits are inherited, it follows that if this particular trait exists, it probably is more prevalent in some races than in others.

To Western man evil is only the negation of good or its shadow. Its positive existence is alien to the Western mind and culture and its origin has puzzled many people.[6] However, there are other cultures which believe

---

preted today, as that trait came from Eastern Europe at a much later date.

[5] They specifically reject the concept of Satan as some kind of mythical creature.

[6] The inadequate treatment of evil in the Western religions and their attendant models for the psyche may be one of their major short–comings. It produces a cultural blindness and opens the door to the political doctrines discussed in the last chapter of this book.

in it. In particular, that is generally true of the Mediterranean race: They originated most of the major religions which have radical dualism. As was suggested earlier, this may be due to their being more right–brained, which gives them access to that peculiar mental process, the joy of destruction, which is part of berserkism.

Regarding the Jews, in particular, the *Talmud* and *Cabalah* provide an extensive demonology, the upper levels of Jacob's Ladder are filled with multitudes of angels and devils, and the cabalistic story of the cohabitation of Eve and Lucifer even provides a myth for the origin of evil as a personality trait. Thus, the scriptural evidence suggests that some of them do, indeed, have this trait.

However, even if a larger–than–average segment of their population has it, an individual may rise above his or her nature, remain as he or she is, or learn evil.[7] Thus, exhibiting this behavior pattern probably depends upon cultural influences.

The general rule–of–thumb is that thirty percent following one viewpoint achieves the critical mass needed to determine the nature of a culture. But, conversely, a smaller number is all that is needed to maintain a public perception, once it is established.

So, the conclusion is that it is possible for a race or culture to be evil, and that the Jews probably have the potential for this. However, few individuals are in a position to gain an accurate impression of them as a people. Consequently, individual beliefs regarding their nature will mostly be determined by personal experiences and perceptions. Therefore, the Covenantors may always be confident of having some followers on this point.

To sum up their doctrine, it is a literal interpretation of the *Old Testament* which follows from the key assumption that the Israelis were a Northern Longheaded people. The result is that it assigns the Jews and Gentiles wholly different roles in the world than are conventional. Their doctrine is possible and plausible from a Fundamentalist perspective. And if it has some weaknesses that may only make it more effective as a religious doctrine, for reasons which will be discussed later on.

It is hard to tell what will catch the public's fancy. Were these denominations to experience a sudden burst of popularity, that would reverse everything the Liberal Eastern Establishment has worked for in religion over almost two centuries. So, there probably were people looking for an opportunity to put an end to this movement, to eliminate that possibility.

The Jewish cultural perspective on the kind of criticism they were receiving from the Covenantors is also relevant. It comes from combining the old covenant which says that God will curse anyone who curses a

---

A similar conclusion was reached by Norman Dodd, the chief investigator of the Reece Commission: specifically, he concluded that the main challenge for American education was to teach the children to identify evil in their daily lives.

[7]The latter was illustrated by the case of Gilles de Rais.

Jew, with the belief from Reform Judaism that the Jewish people are the Messiah. That provides a divine mandate for them to curse anyone who curses them. And "curses" may be construed broadly. But, there was no need to do that in this case, as the Covenantors explicitly cursed them and could hardly have hit their sensitivities more squarely.

Consequently, it is likely that some people were looking for an opportunity to harm their movement while others had strong antipathies against them as individuals. A few of these people may have been in critical positions in government. This may have contributed to mistakes being made and a certain reluctance or slowness in taking appropriate corrective actions.

As a group, the Identity Christians are mostly non–violent separatists.[8] Robert Jay Mathews was an exception to that general rule. — During 1983, he and a band of followers, calling themselves "The Order," committed a series of bank robberies, to raise funds to support their political activities. According to reports, at the time, they viewed themselves as modern–day Robinhoods, supporting the oppressed by stealing from the Jewish–dominated Government/Banker complex, which they referred to as "ZOG," for "Zionist Occupation Government." Their crime spree ended when the FBI cornered them in a home on Whidbey Island, Washington. After they refused to surrender, the FBI lit the home on fire, and burnt them alive. For that final event, the FBI agents donned baseball caps with "ZOG" printed on them.

One of the outcomes of the Widbey Island incident, was that James A. Aho, examined the composition of the Identity Christian movement in Idaho.[9] He expected to find that they were ignorant prejudiced hicks; but he found, instead, that their average educational level was higher than that of Idahoans in general and that approximately 15% of their members held advanced degrees.

Almost a decade later, during 1992, the Identity Christians once again got national news coverage, when federal agents, killed the wife, son, and a friend of Randy Weaver at his isolated cabin on Ruby Ridge, in Idaho. Randy Weaver had been the victim of police entrapment.

In October 1992, after the Weaver siege was over, Peter Peters, a spiritual leader of the Identity Christians, convened a conference of more than 150 conservative and right–wing leaders at Estes Park, Colorado. Their purpose was to prevent future incidents like the ones which had occurred at Ruby Ridge. Two ideas came out of that meeting. The first was to establish formal paramilitary organizations. The second was to establish a leaderless resistance network based on the cell–group system.

A year later, 82 people were burnt alive by Federal agents in the religious community at Waco, Texas.[10] They were of a different sect, the

---

[8] But, separatism contradicts the religious beliefs of Reform Judaism and is diametrically opposed to internationalism, so they regard that viewpoint as being no improvement.

[9] See Aho 1990.

[10] Towards the end of 1999, evidence began coming out that incendiaries and

Branch Davidians, but they, too, were Christian Fundamentalists. They are known to have been studying *Revelation*, which can readily be construed unfavorably to the Jews and the Eastern Establishment. So, that placed them in about the same position as the Identity Christians. Otherwise, they do not seem to have had much in common with them nor to have been a concern to anyone.

Immediately after the Waco massacre, John Trochmann began organizing what became the leading paramilitary group of the militia movement, the Militia of Montana. It was formally founded in February 1994. Although they had real military capability, their most effective weapons were the video camera, printing press, and their fax, telephone, and computer networks. They and the other militias raised public awareness for two or three years.

Concurrent with these developments, Communist China flooded the United States with on the order of ten million very affordable semi–automatic military rifles and large quantities of ammunition. That was sufficient to arm America for civil war. — They appear to have consistently opposed the Clinton administration.[11]

As is always the case with extremist groups, the militias had their share of the lunatic fringe and they, also, were infiltrated by agents provocateurs. Consequently, a certain amount of creative myth was included among their information. But, the opinion most often found among those who examined them, was that they were closer to the mainstream than any right–wing movement has been in recent memory. They viewed themselves as being patriotic, supporting the American–way–of–life, and were open to all Americans. Attempts to paint them as racists or religious bigots are unsupportable.

Exactly two years after Waco, in 1995, Timothy McVeigh, who had some loose affiliations with the Identity Christians, and who had been kicked out of the Michigan Militia for his radicalism, supposedly bombed the Federal Building in Oklahoma City. The news broadcasts, at the time, contained so much conflicting evidence that many people doubt the veracity of the Federal case. But, no one can doubt their ability to obtain a conviction.

At that time, the public trust of government reached a record low. Specifically, a Gallup poll conducted in 1995, immediately after the bombing, showed that approximately 40 percent of the American public, believed the US government "poses an immediate threat to the rights and freedoms of ordinary citizens."

Conservatives took back power in the 1994 and 1996 elections and there were readjustments inside government. By that time, the militia movement

---

specially trained troops were involved.

[11] As the largest true civilization, at this time, China represents the antithesis of the multi–culturalism he is promoting. And, as a major developing industrial power, they are hardly likely to support Clinton's plan for global de–industrialization.

had been effectively vilified. In addition, the changes in government meant that there was no longer a cause for their existence. Then the movement evaporated as quickly as it had appeared.

16.2 Psychedelic New Agers:

Moving from the right–wing to the equally bazaar left–wing, consider the domestic scene, during the Vietnam years. — That was the time of the psychedelic movement. Students took lysergic acid diethylamide (LSD). That was the central drug of their culture.

It interacts with RNA, in which some memory is stored, it possibly also interacts with DNA and it, also, produces a radically altered state of consciousness. This was recognized by Timothy Leary who said[12] "LSD does not produce the transcendent experience, it merely acts as a chemical key. It opens the mind, frees the nervous system of its ordinary patterns and structures, and releases an enormous amount of awareness–energy. ...It is possible to ...become aware of the treasury of ancient racial knowledge welded into the nucleus of every cell in the body."

LSD appears to be a synthetic substitute for the chemical key in the mind which induces the intense sense of reality conveyed by a religious or psychic experience. And, it also interacts with memory. — What happens when large doses of it are administered to individuals or even to a whole population?

Mullins (1993) stated that LSD was developed by the Swiss pharmaceutical company, Sandoz A.G., a subsidiary of S.G. Warburg and Company. He stated that James P. Warburg[13] funded one of Travistock Institute's American subsidiaries, the Institute for Policy Studies, to work with the CIA on a study of LSD's effects. They tried it on a group of CIA agents. That was the "MK–Ultra" project supervised by Dr. Gottlieb. Unfortunately, some of their subjects committed suicide. Their relatives sued the US Government for damages and won.

According to *Business Week*,[14] Travistock Institute also conduced the psychological testing and group relations programs which were implemented by the University of California and the University of Michigan in association with the psychedelic counter–cultures which had developed, during the 1960's, in both Berkeley and Ann Arbor.

Marilyn Ferguson wrote, in 1980, that the historical importance of psychedelics was that they helped convert many technical people to the New Age movement. Her suggestion is probably correct, as they were widely used on college campuses.

---

[12]Quoted by Tal Brooke 1988. — Timothy Leary was a researcher whose primary contributions were in groups dynamics, but he is best known for his association with the psychedelic culture.

[13]He was the son of Paul Warburg who had participated in writing the Federal Reserve Act.

[14]October 26, 1963

The impact of psychedelics depends, in part, upon the subject's psychological type and particular beliefs. Individuals who govern their lives by intuition, feelings, or memorized rules may be very strongly affected. The drug may shatter the order which was trained into their minds releasing them to find a new one.   Individuals of the rational types may be less affected. But, they may discover that their beliefs have no foundation, if like most Americans, they never learned the basis of the Western tradition.[15]

Marijuana, also, has an important impact, although Marilyn Ferguson did not comment upon it. — It produces depersonalization, a dream–like state, and difficulty in concentrating and reasoning.[16] It strongly interferes with mathematical ability. In addition, it is retained in the body for 2–3 weeks and, throughout that period, even a light user may experience difficulty doing mathematics. It should not be mixed with math and science. On the whole, it should probably be regarded as inhibiting Western thought.

But, Marilyn Ferguson said that the direct effects of these drugs were not so important as their introducing people to transcendental meditation, Yoga, and related techniques.[17] She recognized that they could alter the structure of a person's brain towards an Eastern or right–brained typeology.[18] — Thus, the combination of LSD, marijuana, and meditation are a powerful recipe for Easternizing a person's mind.

Many of the individual's who followed this course joined the New Age Movement. The religious doctrine they learned[19] is that a new race of man is evolving through their racial memory. They say that that knowledge contains the mystic ability to reach inwards to where they believe enlightenment and the true reality resides.[20] They teach that the physical world is an illusion and that the over–development of the analytical mind prevents the individual from realizing that higher consciousness in which intuition and feelings *are* truth. For that reason, education must be subverted.[21] "Freedom," they feel, is a condition within the consciousness of the peoples wherein the individual takes pride in his or her contribution to the community and "justice" consists of implementing their new system. They feel that they have looked too much to others for achieving

---

[15] Enlightened Christianity ceased being the religion of the American majority more than a century ago, and seems to be no longer retained in the social memory.

[16] See *Science* 171: p21 et seq.

[17] Similarly, Ian Pavlov found, in his study of dogs, that drugs had an impact but were not as effective as the more traditional methods of brainwashing.

[18] The impact of meditation depends a great deal upon the specific approach taken. For example, Jnana Yoga is for the philosophically inclined and is not as orientalizing as Bhakti Yoga, which is suited to affective personalities.

[19] See the *World Goodwill Newsletter*, third quarter 1982. Lucius Press.

[20] They believe that the individual can progress through seven levels of development until, in the last and highest level they are Gods: that is, they come to recognize God's existence in their individual selves and God in their collective divinity.

[21] See Alice Bailey 1944, p. 9.

the needed changes rather than assuming their individual responsibilities. They say that they need to stimulate the people to demand the changes which will establish the New Age.

Human rights, they assert, are birthrights. However, these are only held by the elect. Blavatski identified them as the "Aryans," but that probably is no longer their thrust, although they remain a self-appointing elite.

They are an ethnicity in the same sense as Judaism is one. Some call Jews a "race," so, that probably is what the New Agers mean when they speak of themselves as a one. But, they are really a new caste. Their ultimate objective appears to be that they should become the top caste, with admission only to those who pass.

Marilyn Furguson said that the New Agers who entered government formed a leaderless polycentric network to advance each other and to make such changes as are needed to prepare society for the coming new age. In particular, she described them as being "dedicated to destruction and rebeginning."

While occupying those positions, they assist some people and harass others. Given the amazing range of information available in computer files and the wide range of government offices, companies, and organizations they are in, they have the potential to be very invasive to the individual. And they are subject to virtually no accountability.

As, they were drawn from the same population as the mock prison guards in Zimbardo et al's 1982 study, something over a third of them should be expected to act as the bad prison guards did. The New Age religious doctrine tells them that this is morally right and organizes them to take action.

The specific doctrine they act upon is often what they call "chaos theory." It is discussed later on. They may have learned it in college or graduate school, in courses on ecology, as a scientific theory. But, it is, also, a religious doctrine and you will find books on it in New Age bookstores. Their role is to apply it by using the Hegelian approach of forming an antithesis to any existing program or proposal so that nothing can be accomplished, or even to deliberately hurt individuals, without any apparent cause except, possibly, the perverted pleasure of cruelty.

You will soon notice, once you are familiar with these people, that they not only have no respect for the law, but they seem to have a positive hatred for it. — When they can do something either legally or illegally, they will often choose the latter. This is puzzling to someone of the Western outlook. But, see the discussion of Nietzsche and also consider that their goal is to return to the nomadic state, where there are no fixed laws but everything is socially determined. My impression is that not many of them fully understand that their role is to cause our traditional form of government to wither way.

Their adherence to the doctrine of chaos, undoubtedly accounts for a large part of what people see as the deliberate ill-will of government. Over the last few decades that has gradually replaced government's traditional faults of incompetence and intrusive officiousness.

Perhaps, those who designed these changes knew and understood Edmund Burke's remark that, the structure of government reaches but a little way. It is the spirit of the government which establishes the distinction between democracy and dictatorship. Likewise, this was recognized by John Adams when he pointed out that, "Our Constitution was made only for a moral and religious people and is wholly inadequate to the government of any other."[22] In this light, both the tyrannical spirit of this new religion for government employees and the changes in the religions of the public can be seen to be important public issues.

The existence of a New Age/Environmental network in Washington State is undeniable. However, it is impossible to tell its exact extent or composition without a formal investigation. Nevertheless, it appears to be interconnected to many other liberal–establishment and left–wing groups and it, also, clearly has connections across the country and even to Canada.

Marilyn Furguson went to considerable effort to present them as being leaderless.— They first appeared on the American political scene, during the 1960's. But, there was almost immediately an effort to control them. For example, in 1965, the UN formed the International Cooperation Council, which worked to coordinate them, and, in 1979, the Unity–in–Diversity–Council took over their work. According to Constance Cumbey, 1983, "the big push is through a vehicle known as Planetary Initiative for the World We Choose." She wrote that their "World Council of Wise Persons reads like a New Age Who's Who [of the liberal Eastern establishment]." Mark Satin[23] also discusses these structures, quoting Club of Rome sources.[24] But, these are only the establishment and internationalist groups who provide them with top–down leadership.

These networks are, also, subject to lateral control. — Power often lies in the ability to coordinate the workers or the lower and middle managers. And it may be expected that whenever a network is created various groups will infiltrate it and use it for their own ends. Thus, although the networks may be coordinated from the top down by international organizations, they also may serve unseen wire–pullers acting at their lower levels.

In fact, the New Agers say, themselves, that they were infiltrated, about two decades ago. William Irwin Thompson[25] remarked that they

---

[22] See his Oct 11, 1798 letter to a unit of the Militia of Massachusetts, in in C. Adams (ed.), reprinted 1971.

[23] See Mark Satin's *New Age Politics*.

[24] Aurelio Peccei, the founder of the Club of Rome, is prominent in the New Age leadership and there are other New Agers among their members and contributing authors.

[25] William Thompson is one of their more prominent writers and was one of the founders of their center at Findhorn. His position is fairly moderate. His works leave the impression of someone who has just discovered Enlightenment, but is not yet willing to abandon his Roman Catholic and Celtic roots in favor of something which is traditionally Protestant and English. And, he was not alone.

were surprised by the sudden growth of what he called "popular religion" within the New Age Movement. By that he meant all the divination, superstition, hippy–oils, crystallography, and so on, which can be found in any New Age bookstore. — That appears to have been mostly drawn from Cabalism. — Its introduction represents the occupation and desecration of alters. The revival of Nordic Mysticism, during the late 1980's, received essentially the same treatment. And, in both cases, their religious thrust was altered.

As to who did this, there are two principle groups which have the capability to coordinate the media blitz and simultaneous nationwide effort. One is the liberal establishment and the other is the Jewish organizations. As the first was already intimately connected to the New Age Movement, providing much of its leadership, they seem less likely. In contrast the techniques of occupation and desecration of alters as well as much of the popular religion which was introduced are part of the Jewish religious heritage. And if you look you will find that many of the clerks and merchants of these bookstores are Jewish. But that is not proof in itself, as they may have been best able to respond to this market, having some prior familiarity with Cabalism and probably an interest in the subject. — The Jewish community had legitimate grounds to be concerned about the growth of the New Age Movement: The last time this happened, it produced the Nazis and, under our definition of "Nazi," the same thing is happening this second time, too.[26] So, the overall appearance is that the Jewish organizations infiltrated the New Age Movement. But, appearances are often deceiving, particularly in the political and religious realms.

When this burst of popular religion reached a critical mass, the movement became truly polycentric, encompassing a wide range of beliefs. A few of these are neither Gnostic nor even Spiritualist. They even include a major world religion, Buddhism, among their ranks. What seems to unite this polycentric group of religions, is their enhanced level of religious awareness. But, they also all fall within the bounds of political correctness.

The New Age Movement, also, has another core group which is often overlooked. Mrs. Heaton pointed out, in 1993, that their history was presented in 1971, in the President's Report of the first twenty–five years of the Institute of Social Research, of the University of Michigan. — He described how they grew from a small isolated cell of dissenters, into a worldwide network of change agents.

---

[26] The networks described by Marilyn Furguson are almost entirely authoritarian collectivists and the products of higher education. They fit each particular in the definition of a "Nazi", except that they are internationalists rather than nationalists. But, the goal of their form of internationalism is world domination and imposing of their views on everyone else rather than recognizing and respecting other cultures and peoples. And their views seem to be a mixture of political correctness and the prejudices of the American working class. So, in the final analysis, they really are rather intolerantly ethnocentric, if not nationalistic in the strict sense.

During the early 1940's, the Department of Agriculture's Bureau of Economics was seeking to create a "new kind of survey research facility." This led to the founding, in 1946, of the Survey Research Center at the University of Michigan. One year earlier, Kurt Lewin had founded the Research Center for Group Dynamics at the Massachusetts Institute of Technology. Following his death, in 1947, these two centers combined to form the Institute for Social Research at the University of Michigan. That became the principle center for the study of group processes. In 1962, they headed an Inter–University Consortium for Political Research involving 145 other universities. Two years later they opened the Center for the Utilization of Scientific Knowledge, focusing on education; and, in 1970, they opened their Center for Political Research. The next year the National Science Foundation provided them with a sustained funding source.

Other universities have, since, developed similar centers. This includes Stanford Research Institute's center for Noetic science dedicated to the study of New Age psychopolitics.

Many of these social scientists are listed among the acknowledged leaders and guiding lights of the New Age movement. Their research programs and the related programs for changing our form of government appear to be the most substantive branch of the New Age movement.

16.3   Unitarians

The New Agers are not alone, the Unitarians are also involved in these changes. When we last looked at them, in the mid–nineteenth century, they were following German Idealism. They continued in much that same vein into the twentieth century. But, they appear to be one of the chosen vehicles of the liberal establishment, and have changed their views on religion as the establishment's political programs changed.[27]

In particular, in 1933, three Unitarian ministers and two professors produced the *Humanist Manifesto*.[28] It is mostly an acceptable rational doctrine, except that their eighth, ninth, and fourteenth points declare a socialist State as the ultimate goal, which they understand to be God. — This doctrine was introduced concurrently with the New Deal. But, as it never obtained much of a following, neither were they the object of universal execration to the extent that the New Deal was.

A decade later, in 1947, Corliss Lamont published a much more extensive work on the philosophy of Humanism. His views dovetailed with the

---

[27] That may be because they operate under a lodge system, with each group determining their own religious doctrines. Therefore, they can be taken over piecemeal. Alternatively, a few groups can be taken over and used as the religious voice of the liberal establishment, claiming to be an otherwise inoffensive denomination.

[28] It was originally printed in *The New Humanist* Vol VI No. 3, 1933. However, it is also reprinted as an appendix to Corliss Lamont's 1947 book on Humanism.

head of UNESCO, Sir Julian Huxley's, sentiment that UNESCO's general philosophy should be "a scientific world Humanism, global in extent and evolutionary in background."

The next change for the Unitarians was when they began drawing towards another non–conformist denomination, the Universalists. That denomination had been founded during the late 1800's. Their basic belief was that everyone achieves salvation in the afterlife. In 1961, these two denominations formally merged to form the Unitarian Universalists. — They enjoyed the full approval of the UN.

In addition to Universal salvation and no Trinity, they also believe in pluralism and rejected the existence of absolute truth. They also incorporated the consensus process: Specifically, they hold that a church member obtains "freedom" by coming into covenant with the congregation. The Church's function is to engineer that consent.

Each Unitarian "Church" is structured as a roundtable, where the congregation frankly discusses their religious beliefs. Their Church hierarchy lays out the general principles of their doctrine and also provides some leadership, but each congregation's beliefs evolve separately. However, the group–thinking which the roundtable discussions foster, combined with the gentle direction provided by their spiritual leaders, tends to funnel them into one path. Their religious service is, in fact, a group consensus process, and, according to F. Forrester Church et al., their core beliefs are in that process. Marshall H. McLuhan's quip, "The medium is the message,"[29] clearly describes that denomination.

16.4 UN Religions

During the last decade, new Unitarian meeting groups have been founded which follow a Neo–Gnostic Internationalist Environmentalism. — That appears to be the general direction of the UN's current religious orientation.

In 1985, Robert Muller, the director of the U.N.'s Economic and Social Council, published *New Genesis: Shaping a Global Spirituality*, which suggested a global New Age religion based largely on an environmental ethic and internationalism. His book was influential in the education community.[30] As a result, some of his ideas have been incorporated into curriculums and are currently being taught in public schools in America, under the guise of "environmental science."[31] According to Coffman, 1994,

---

[29] From the title of the first chapter of his 1964 book.

[30] In particular, during November, 1985, the National Education Association's curriculum organization held a 12-nation international-curriculum symposium to develop a "world core curriculum" to insure "peaceful and cooperative existence among the human species on this planet" based on "proposals put forth by Robert Muller."

[31] Thus, the required student competency in environmental issues, comes close to requiring that the students adopt the tenants of this new religion.

James E. Lovelock et al's, 1987 book, *Gaia, a New Way of Knowing*, also, was pivotal to the UN's involvement in New Age religion.

In addition, the UN supports the Baha'i World Faith. — Baha'i originated in Persia, in 1844, as an offshoot from Shite Islam. But, it is not a form of Islam.

Their leadership passed through a succession of leaders descended from their founder, the Bab, until 1963. Then, they came under the control of an elected body called the Universal House of Justice. Their head offices are in Haifa, Israel.[32]

They believe that all the great world religions are in complete harmony, differing only in non-essential details, that mankind should become one race, and they believe in social evolution. They see themselves as having the mission of the spiritual conquest of the world.

Regarding the harmony of all the great world religions, there is, indeed, a fundamental similarity in the ultimate goals of some branches of each of them. In particular, some parts of Buddhism, Christianity, Confucianism, Hinduism, Islam, Stoicism, Taoism, and Zorasterism seek the common objective of positive religions, which is raising man and his consciousness to a high level so that he or she may access the centers of motivation and, thus, achieve knowledge of God.

But, one immediately encounters a dichotomy. — On one side is what the Dalai Lama calls the "Ah ha! experience," which constitutes direct knowledge of Truth and Being; whereas, on the other side is a type of Love. The first is the quintessence of the intellect and the second, the quintessence of the intuition. And, they are the antithesis of each other, in part, for whereas the first mental process is the discriminative, the second is the holistic. So, while Truth or Being establishes boundaries, thus creating differences, order, harmony, and beauty; Love bridges all differences and crosses all boundaries. And, as these things are partial enigmas, evading definition, they make suitable Gods. Consequently, abstract religions, are of three types: 1) the discriminative or Western, including Christianity, Islam, Stoicism, and Zoroasterism, and also the Far Eastern doctrine of Confucianism, which follow the first principle and recognize but subordinate the second; 2) the holistic or Eastern, including Hinduism and Buddhism, which have the opposite emphasis; and 3) the obvious alternative of recognizing the dichotomy, as found in Alchemy and Taoism, or of considering religion more broadly by developing upon Kant's concept of the identity of quintessence and God,[33] such as the German Idealist and Jungian disciplines did. But, this last category of religions has yet to produce any successful positive doctrines, with the possible exception of the Nazi's religion. But, in that case, although their religion was undeniably successful, their use of radical dualism to justify genocide, made it less than positive for a segment of mankind.

The will is another important mental process. It was recognized in

---

[32] Their presence in Palestine predates Israel.
[33] See Kant's *Critique of Practical Reason* and Jung's *Psychological Types*.

Nordic Mysticism as the third root of the Ash Tree, Yggdrasil, and of roughly equal importance to the other two higher gateways to God. Freedom is its quintessence. But, the religions mentioned above are variable on how they regard it. On the one extreme we find Adolf Hitler explicitly recognizing it as one of the principle goals, which he understood to be the Gods;[34] likewise, it was of considerable importance in Nordic Mysticism and Stoicism, and, therefore, as Classical philosophy held that it was the principle benefit of enlightenment, it has an important place in Enlightened Christianity; but as one moves towards Fundamentalism, it occupies a progressively less favored position; and it was regarded negatively by Lao–Tze, the founder of Taoism, who felt that free will was the source of Evil.

Of course, each major religion, also, has denominations or sects which cross over. And, there are, also, a very few which rise above this to encompass the whole as well as understanding the role of "God" in the Human psyche. Nevertheless, overall, "God" means much the same thing to some branches of all these religions.

Their most important common property may be that they share the objective that their members should arrive at the highest state of personal development. And, what is more important, is that some of their members actually *do* arrive. So, by Jesus's standard of judging by the fruits, these are all good religions.[35]

But, it is unrealistic to extend this conclusion to those other branches of these religions and other religions which do not seek the same goal nor meet the same standard. Religion is not all the same thing, but several different things under a common name.

A large group of these other religions are those which push their members down to the level of the child. This occurs when the priest delivers to his congregation some statement or story which is well–known to them and which they all agree to say is true and sacred, but which, in reality, is wholly or partially false. Many religious myths of this type will be familiar: a few prime examples are the story of Abraham, the Trinity, the virginity of Mary, and the holocaust. These are living mysteries.

So, the next time you are in a church, temple, or synagogue where you can not decently object as the minister, priest, or rabbi goes on–and–on piling familiar falsehoods one–upon–another, observe the effect this has upon your mind. For myself, it produces a most uncomfortable feeling, a tearing sensation inside my brain, as the process pulls me away from reason and reality to slide down that slippery slope towards the familiar underworld of faith, the world of the infant or child. But, if that process is repeated often enough, it ceases to be painful.[36]

---

[34] See *Mein Kampf*

[35] Bear in mind that he did not say what the fruits were, but that freedom was probably prominent among them.

[36] That sensation of pain may be similar to that complained about by the nurses when they were forced to reason. They had affective personalities and

For this purpose, a truth would be ineffective: The living mystery must be a lie if it is to create conflict with truth and, thus, force the individual's locus of existence from reality, reason, or the left–brain, to the other parts of the mind. Thus, the service becomes a type of psychological group excursion which temporarily takes the individual out of his or her normal mind. There, in that subtilely altered state of consciousness, the individual may encounter the images of the subconscious or, at least, a subset of them which are related to the particular religion's paradigm. Then, the individual interacts with them by participating in the ritual of the religious service. All of this undoubtedly serves a cathartic subconscious function.

In a lecture given at the Travestock Institute in England, in 1939, Carl Jung said about this:

> There must be something in the cult, in the actual religious practice, which explains the peculiar fact that there are fewer complexes, or that these complexes manifest much less in Catholics than in other people. That something besides confession is really the cult itself. It is the Mass. For instance, the heart of the Mass contains a living mystery, and that is the thing that works ... And the Mass is by no means the only mystery in the Catholic Church. There are other mysteries as well. ... Now these mysteries have always been the expression of a fundamental psychological condition. Man expresses his most fundamental and most important psychological conditions in this ritual, this magic, or whatever you call it. And the ritual is the cultic performance of these basic psychological facts.

Superstitious religions do much the same thing. They usually involve belief in the power of a symbol or rite. To be affective it must contain some hidden meaning which is partially revealed. Consequently, many of the occult symbols turn out to be models for the psyche. What these religions seem to be doing is taking the individual back to the level of the infant, to that world dominated by symbols and larger schemes which are imposed externally and imperfectly understood. Emotionalization and vice help to take the individual down to the lowest level. There, in that state, they commit ritual acts, some of which are revolting to civilized sensibilities but, which are more affective for that same reason. This differs from the more conventional practices, only in in degree. — The same basic processes are involved.

If this is regarded as the core religious process, then other things which we do not normally consider to be religions are religion, too. One example is television. — An individual who does not watch television, more than a few programs a year, is not acclimated to it. I am one such person, and I can tell you that when I watch it, it comes as a shock; it is full of the most blatant propaganda, advertising, and other errant falsehoods;

were mentioned earlier, when Jacob's Ladder was introduced.

it is offensive. But, individuals who watch it routinely do not see that, they have grown accustomed to it. — That is essentially the same religious experience: Television should probably be regarded as the dominant contemporary religion of the American masses.

And, Americans, also, have their religion of government and political doctrines which contain an element of the absurd. The news media, also, is full of half–truths and falsehoods along conventional lines.[37] — Americans are a most religious people.

16.5 Foundation Programs in Religion

Having examined the religious activities of the right and left wings, now consider the center. — During Chester Bernard's tenure on the Board of the Rockefeller Foundation, from 1940 to 1954, they followed a moderate policy on religion. He gently promoted an atheistic religion for managers, which held that duty to the organization is the highest virtue.

After his retirement, the Rockefeller Foundation began its current involvement in religion. — They started funding the Union Theological Seminary. That was a liberal Protestant institution. Their influence on seminaries grew from there. It was primarily through this avenue that they have influenced the Protestant Churches in America.

They funded the education of ministers and provided guidance through their presence in the the World and Federal Councils of Churches and other top–level organizations.[38] They rarely had direct contact with the individual churches or their specific programs. However, the seminary students who followed their viewpoint prospered and after they graduated a network of similar–minded people assisted their advancement in later life. Every graduate who got into this network knew, without ever having been specifically told, that their continued support depended upon their following and implementing the program described in the literature. There were also meetings or conferences to keep them up–to–date. This is the same basic approach for organic control as is used throughout all the professions, whether it involves ministers, city planners, scientists, or whatever.

The best way to change a religion is to use the indirect approach of altering underlying principles or key processes. The objectives are to cut the religion loose from its foundation and, then, to subtilely move it just over a divide so that, thereafter, left to its own devices, the parishioners' will naturally gravitate in the desired direction. At the same time, the

---

[37] Jung pointed out that, in his treatment of psychoses, he often faced the same problem, and that the cure was for the patient to identify the process and the particular symbols and paradigms. Then, he or she could address them with reason rather than through right–brained or subconcious processes, and could free himself or herself from their influences. (See his *Mysterium Coniunctionis*.)

[38] The World Council of Churches is notoriously procommunist. For example, see the reports from their meeting in Upsala, Sweden in 1968.

seminaries were producing young ministers who had the desired new orientation. Over a period of three decades they progressively replaced the older ministers.

Historically, the Church of England was the home of Natural Theology, Christian Enlightenment and related viewpoints.[39] For that reason, the Episcopal Church, which is what the Church of England is called in America, was almost certainly one of the principle targets for change.

The changes introduced into that Church, during the 1960's, were: 1) that all Sunday services would be communions, instead of once per month; 2) the language of the service was made informal and sometimes wholly new observances were introduced to "personalize" the service; 3) at one point during the new service everyone stands up and introduces themselves to their neighbors, saying "Peace go with you," 4) the concepts of "grace" and Christ as a personal savior were introduced; 5) a prayer for peace was introduced into the service; and 6) women were ordained.

The first three changes tended to emotionalize, socialize, and raise the levels of participatory involvement and tension in what had previously been a quiet thoughtful service, a time for private reflection on the events of the week. The new service made a profound difference, it had no place for God, but was filled with intrusive social interactions and busy rituals.

The Anglican God was the God of reason, tempered by Christian kindness. So, adherence to the standards of Christian conduct had a more important place in their beliefs than in those of most other American Protestant denominations. But, one needs to pause for thought to follow that way–of–life. Their old service had designed for that.

T.S. Elliot recognized this when he wrote, in 1939: "The idea of a Christian society. . . . . . is one which we can accept or reject; but if we are to accept it, we must treat Christianity with a great deal more *intellectual* respect than is our wont; we must treat it as being for the individual a matter primarily of thought and not of feeling."

The new service did not allow time for this. Consequently, many church members found them devoid of meaning and attendance dropped accordingly.

The concept of Grace severed the religion from its rational and moral basis by replacing personal responsibility and the just and uniform God of absolute and immutable Truth with a personal savior who grants grace. That is one of the critical issues upon which the structure of our society is based. It represents the choice between the individualist's God of Truth and Order and the collectivist's God, who is arbitrary but can be approached through faith and spirituality.

During 1966, a second attack was leveled at these beliefs, with the introduction of situation ethics. The definitive work on these beliefs is found

---

[39] Some of the other Protestant denominations may be too, but as the traditional Christian approach is not to openly instruct about the Spirit, but to lay the grain among the chaff, it is difficult for a person who is not a long–term member of any specific denomination to determine whether it is or not.

in the two books by Professor Joseph Fletcher.[40] Their thesis expands upon a single short passage of scripture: " 'Love thy neighbor as thyself.' This is the first and greatest commandment, the others are like unto it." He suggests that this single rule should govern all personal conduct and be the sole standard of morality. By taking this very narrow focus, he discards all other parts of Christian thought. It soon becomes clear that he even discarded the assumption of the existence of truth. — He felt that it is socially determined.

For an enlightened Christian of reasonably good intelligence, that rule works reasonably well. But, applied by a field–dependent person, it becomes a justification for a purely holistic viewpoint in a world were every judgment of good and evil is determined by the conditions of the particular situation or by society.

Half–a–decade later, in 1971, Dr. James Downs,[41] the Chairman of Cross–Cultural Studies at the University of Hawaii, reported the reaction to this. — He noticed its impact on a the related point–of–view which anthropologists call "cultural relativism": that is the idea that the norms in any culture should be judged from within the context of that culture, rather than according to our values. He wrote: "This simple idea is so commonplace among anthropologists that I was surprised, in recent years, to find freshmen shifting uncomfortably in their seats during lectures in which the term was introduced. Some even appeared to exchange dark glances. A surprising number of American youth enter college with the idea that many of their professors are Communist–nudist–libertines whose corrupting influence must be resisted.[42] I hadn't regarded the idea of cultural relativism as dangerous. In fact, the more extreme members of the New Left, along with his right–wing counterpart, seems most apt to reject it. Perusing conservative–oriented magazines which I had neglected to read out of laziness and boredom revealed to me — with something of a shock — that relativism, cultural or otherwise, had indeed become a "dangerous" idea. Conservative writers regularly decried relativism because it challenged the idea of abstract and unchanging standards of good and bad"

---

[40] See Fletcher 1966, 1967. At that he was teaching at the Episcopal Theological School in Cambridge, Mass.

[41] He got his PhD at Berkeley, apparently in anthropology.

[42] During the mid–1970's I was a graduate student and had occasion to visit Berkeley, to use the library. One of my professors had close connections to that institution and, as chance would have it, also had communist leanings. He offered me the key to an apartment there. He said that he and four other professors shared the expenses, so that they would have a place to stay when they were in town. — When I got there, I let myself in. But, I soon noticed leopard–spotted exotic lingerie hung up to dry in the bathroom. A few minutes later, their owner arrived.— It seems that the professors shared her pleasures and, also, offered them to selected graduate students. — True to the spirit of the times, I resisted the corrupting influence and spent the night on the couch in a friend's home in a neighboring suburb. — Thus, Professor Downs was quite well informed. — They were not nudists, they prefer exotic lingerie.

The prayer for peace was probably the most flagrant alteration to the Episcopal service. To indiscriminately pray for peace is to pray for oppression, for people fight just wars to end the oppression of an unjust peace.

However, the ordination of women was the touchstone for many parishioners. Naomi Goldberg[43] wrote that neither Christianity nor Judaism can withstand the ordination of women. She argues that as these religions have a male God as their ultimate authority figure, a woman can't well represent "Him" in a synagogue or on a pulpit, for that identifies authority with the wrong sex. Also, as these religions are based on the male–dominated Biblical world, the *Bible, Torah, and Talmud* would cease to be relevant, let alone inspirational, to a society in which large numbers of women are religious leaders. Her position is plausible; she found it to be true for herself; and there are others who agree with her. As a feminist she adopted the course of renouncing her male God and putting female ones in their place.

Her approach conflicts with the one recommended by Carl Jung. He was a Gnostic and based his belief on negative theology. He held that the shadow of the male dominated world is female, and that religions are ideally based on the negative theology of the shadow–world. Therefore, he concluded that a male–dominated world should have a female God represented by priestesses.

The "American Anglicans", were, of course, neither Feminists nor Gnostics but adhered to a Western male–dominated system. They refused to accept the ordination of women and split off from the Episcopal Church. They took between a quarter and a third of the denomination's members with them. They eventually joined the Roman Church, which does not ordain women, but differs on many other points of doctrine.

These six changes constituted a program which fundamentally altered the Episcopal Church. But, they were not the only denomination which was affected. All the mainstream Protestant Churches had their programs for change.

Some of the people who left their churches due to these changes took up private worship while others rejected formal religion and replaced it with an Informal Scientism or Agnosticism. Some joined the New Age Movement; and Buddhism is the fastest growing religion in America today. America's Black Churches were also impacted: Many of them converted to Islam. Much of these shifts represent the response to the stifled need for religion at an abstract or intellectual level. But, there was also a rise in Fundamentalism, Spiritualism, and superstitious cults. — On the whole, these changing patterns of church attendance, show that the foundations' programs were very successful.

---

[43] She is an American feminist psychologist and was originally a member of a Jewish faith but converted to Feminist Witchcraft. Her (1979) book discusses the social psychology of religion.

16.6   Roman Church:

After Italy was unified, the next Pope, Leo XIII (1878–1903), recognized the impossibility of continuing the course of his predecessors. He accepted the republican form of government and modern learning. That lasted more–or–less until the 1960's.

When Pope Pius XII died in 1958, at the age of 82, the Roman Church had reached a peak in wealth, organizational strength, and orthodoxy. But, the next Pope, John XXIII, turned the Roman Church in a different direction with his policy of aggiornamento, or opening windows, meaning admitting people with different ways of thought and different paradigms.

That specifically included opening a dialogue with the Soviet Union. He corresponded directly with Kruschev, who had succeeded Bulganin as Premier, in 1958. The new relationship between the Roman Church and the Soviet Union can be seen in Pope John's never officially condemning the USSR, as his predecessors had done. He also opposed the United States war effort in Vietnam. One of his special concerns was the role of the Church in the countries of the Eastern Bloc. During his pontificate, the constraints on the Roman Church, there, began to loosen. The Church also played an important role in the changing conditions in Poland, as they gradually moved towards independence.

But the most important event during his years was their Vatican II Conference (1962–1965). He convened it and it was reconvened by Pope Paul VI.[44] At that conference, they agreed to replace their Latin service with the language of the country; they dropped teaching the philosophy of Thomas Aquinas and Natural Law; they replaced it with situation ethics and socially determined truth;[45] they became actively involved in ecumenical programs to draw together all the Christian denominations into a single Christian religion;[46] and they agreed to the eventual elimination of direct

---

[44] The recent Popes were Pius XII (1939–1958), John XXIII (1958–1963), Paul VI (1963–1978), John Paul I (1978), and John Paul II (1978–present).

[45] Contrast the ethics text used in Roman Catholic schools before and after that date. For example, look at Joseph F. Sullivan's from the 1940's versus Austin Fagothey's from 1975. Both were Jesuits and their books bear the imprimaturs of their bishops, but they could hardly be more different.

[46] Two such programs are particularly noteworthy.
The first is the World Council of Churches' ecumenical program. The World Council was founded in 1948 in Amsterdam and later moved to Geneva. Its ecumenical program is its primary mission. Within the United States, the National Council of Churches serves much the same function.
The second program is the UN's syncretist movement. It is trying to unite all the world's religions into one global religion. This movement was adopted by the United Nations almost immediately after they were formed. Its history is given by John Cotter in his book, *A Study of Syncretism, the Background and Apparatus of the Emerging One-World Church"*.
The Roman Church was only nominally involved from their first meeting in Chicago, in 1893, until the late 1960's. But, under Pope Paul VI they became active supporters, and at the hundredth meeting of the syncretist movement in Chicago, Aug 28–September 6, 1993, the Roman Catholic Church and the

papal power and its replacement with something resembling TQM.

By the end of his pontificate, a rift had developed in the Catholic leadership, between conservative and what Malachi Martin, 1990, calls "anti–church" elements. The next Pope, Paul VI, tried to clean up some of their internal problems. According to Martin, these included New Age beliefs among the highest ranks of their hierarchy.[47] Also, with the connivance of members of their anti–church block, the Church had splintered into many separate groups, a gay church, a woman's church, church's for each minority, and so on. Pope Paul characterized this as the church being "engaged in auto–destruct."

The Pope who followed him, John Paul I, began to act more vigorously to resolve these problems. But, he did not get very far. — Soon there was an assassination attempt on him. Although it was unsuccessful, he died shortly afterwards from an unknown cause. His pontificate began and ended in the same year, 1978.

In his first formal address, the current Pope, John Paul II, made it clear that he is a progressive.[48] In that speech he introduced the key words "collegiality" and "communio" which designated the group process which they were developing. He said that the Roman Church would do this so that it might come into consensus not only among all of its clergy but also with all of the members of its congregations, that they might become more committed to the Spirit of the Roman Church.[49]

In his closing remarks at the 1974 Bishops Synod on evangelization[50] he emphasized the importance of spreading their Gospel into local cultures, liberation theology, and their social and ethical aspects. He regarded that as fulfilling the mandate from Jesus Christ of "Going, therefore, teach all the nations ... preach the Gospel to every creature"[51] And, in his concluding remarks he, again, stressed the need to enhance unity so that every

---

Freemasons were designated the lead organizations for the amalgamation of all religions, explicitly including the New Age Religions.

[47] Martin quotes Pope Paul as saying that "the smoke has entered the sanctuary." meaning that these evil influences were affecting even the Vatican and Cardinals. Martin suggests that New Age initiations may have occurred in the Vatican itself. A very similar statement was made, at about that time, by the head of the Jesuits.

[48] See the Pope's address to the Cardinals in Naples Oct 17, 1978, "The Structure of Self–Determination as Core of the Theory of Person," Atti del Congresso Internazionale Tomasso d'Aquino nel suo centenaio settimo. v. 1 L'Huomo 37–44 Also OssRom 262. special ed Nov 12 1978.

[49] See also his comments in the 1969 Synod reprinted in Caprile 1970 p121, Ill Sinode dei Vescovi. Prima assemblea straordinaria 11–28 ottobre 1969 Rome 1970; K. Wjtyla 1976 "Bishops as Servants of the Faith" translation of the Pope's address to the Symposium of European Bishops. IrTheolQ 43 (1976) p265–266, and 269–271.

[50] Remarks on Oct 14, 1974. See *De evangelizatione mundi huius temporis. Par altera* Text in Caprile 1975, Ill Sinodo dei Vescovi. Terza assemblea generale Rome, p 991–1006, 1011–1016

[51] See Mathew 28.14.

particular and local church should express the Church's voice.

The changes in the Roman Church described above follow the characteristic pattern of an organization's initial conversion to TQM:

1. Thesis: This occurred under Pius XII and the early years of John XXIII, when the strength of the traditional church reached its peak. Martin, 1990, felt that the antithesis primarily used was the philosophy of the Sardinian communist Antonio Gramsci. Gramsci held that the enemy of communist man was Christian society and he formulated an antithesis expressly for the purpose of destroying Christianity.

2. Conflict: Chaos was created by the fragmentation of the Church. This began under John XXIII and continued under the next two popes.

3. Synthesis: The church was effectively declared a TQM organization with the election of John Paul II, in 1978. In a big business full transformation will take about ten years, but a church it will take longer before enough priests die or retire. John Paul stated during 1998 that he expects to live long enough to see the new order fully implemented. That must occur within a few years, as he is showing signs of age.

During his pontificate, some Jesuits put his words into action. They began spreading Christian–socialism in Latin America, teaching "liberation theology," and fomenting revolution. Consequently, several Latin American countries found it necessary to take action against them.

In particular, the American Jesuit, J. G. Carncy, was killed by the Honduran military, in 1983, as part of an action against a group of communist revolutionaries, of which he was an acknowledged member. His, 1985, posthumous autobiography gives an account of how the Roman Church and the Jesuits arc working to advance socialism in Latin America. This can be clearly seen in his praise of "Free Cuba," meaning communist Cuba, and becomes excruciatingly clear in his view that a "Christian" state is a communist theocracy.

In America, if Mexican–Americans do not assimilate, they may become a new underclass. In fact, that is already the status quo in the Southwest.

As a group, Mexican–American farm–workers tend to be emotional and have high rates of violent crime.[52] That they are the cause of significant social stress can be observed in the fact that other Americans do

---

[52] The Judges in Monterey County, California, during the 1970's, got a survey done to determine the rate of violent crime in this segment of the population: that is rape, murder, and armed robbery. They were hearing a disproportionate number of cases involving Mexican–Americans charged with these types of crimes. They were concerned that the law enforcement agencies might be practicing discrimination. — Three–hundred adult male Mexican Americans were surveyed at random. In every case, either the individual or his father or son had been convicted of one of these crimes. Considering that the conviction rate hovers around ten–percent, they concluded that the population they surveyed had a criminal culture. — These were predominantly Mexican–American agricultural

not patronize the same stores nor live in the same neighborhoods. — It takes more than legally reassigning them to the "White" caste to make them pass in society. — Although they are readily assimilated if they adopt American culture, as a group they strongly resist it and are often intolerant of Americans and non–Roman–Catholics.

Their position, is that, being partially of American Indian stock, America is rightfully their's and Americans should adopt *their* culture rather than visa–versa or a peaceful co–existance. Various activists encourage them in these views. There is a lack of evidence that the Roman Church does also,[53] but, neither are they actively opposing these problems.

The situation is undoubtedly aggravated by Spanish–language TV programming of the kind currently found in Central California. It provides a constant diet of sex and little else. That can only be calculated to emotionalize them and push them towards the infant level, if they are not there already. Were the Roman Church sincerely concerned with ameliorating their social condition, they should be mobilizing a public outcry against this, and its replacement with something morally uplifting and culturally reaffirming.

If their current status is maintained indefinitely, a situation will have been created in which individuals who come on hard times or routinely have contact with them will only be able to avoid significant social stresses by converting. This may prove significant, as the broad lower strata of society has often provided its foundation, later on.

16.7   Eurodollar

After the 1970's, the United States declined fairly rapidly. By the 1990's the Soviet Union had collapsed and by the end of that decade, so, also, had the Japanese and Far–Eastern economies. But, America's economy has not done likewise. However, America has become one of the greatest debtor nations instead of the world's creditor, and a grossly over–valued stock market teeters overhead, threatening from moment–to–moment to come crashing down. It appears to be maintained by easy credit[54] and also by

---

workers.

In contrast, in New Mexico the Mexican–Americans are usually from their middle–class and have a different culture. They do not have these problems. As a group, they are respected members of the community. Thus, in discussing, Mexican–Americans it is necessary to distinguish between their various social classes. The discussion in this section refers to the agricultural worker.

[53] The Roman Church in America has a reputation for being independent. In addition, since the time of the Vatican II conference, Roman Catholics are supposed to accept Christians of other denominations, as "separated brethren" and not discriminate against them. So, it seems likely that the Roman Church does not have any direct involvement in this, but that it is due primarily to political activists.

[54] During 1999, hardly a day goes by when the mail does not include an offer of a pre–approved credit card. The extent of this may be illustrated by the fact

the massive transfer of money from collapsed economies to America.

At the same time, pan–Europe is emerging as the new economic super-power.[55] Thus, as the century draws to a close, the world is making the transition to a new economic order.

The Eurodollar was established on January 1, 1999. It provides pan–Europe with a single currency. According to the head of the European central bank, a united Europe would have an economic strength and market size about equal to America.[56] It follows that the Anglo–American world economic order, in which London acts as the center of finance backed by America's wealth, which dominated the twentieth century, may be replaced by this new pan–European structure.[57]

The European Central Bank has an even more extreme form than the Federal Reserve. According to their head executive, their mandate makes them self–regulating, entirely outside of the political process. As there is no public control over them, no mechanism for accountability, nor any peaceful means for effecting change, the consequences seem unavoidable. — The 1999 New Years celebrations included serious riots in France and several other Western European countries. Europeans are not naive about issues of political economy, and the French, in particular, have a tradition of defiance.

Thus, the central event of the transition to a new economic order may not be taking place in the Americas. It is the unification of Europe into one federated country, from the Atlantic to the Urals.

According to Harvard Professor Samuel P. Huntington, the governing principles of this new order must come from religion. He quotes Francis Fukuyama of the US State Department who emphatically enunciated the position that democratic egalitarianism had gone as far as it could possibly go and can not be superseded by anything of its own kind.[58]

Earlier, Martin, 1990, had gone to some effort to show that the Roman Church is uniquely suited to be the lead organization in this new theocracy. He pointed to its having three critical features: 1) It has a top–down structure controlled by the Pope; 2) It is the product of no one nationality, ethnicity, or race; and 3) It has an effective worldwide organization. Its adoption of TQM also makes it ideally suited to drawing all the disparate peoples of the European region into consensus.

The point of commencement on this program appears to have been the Vatican II Conference in the early 1960's, and some of the hierarchy

---

that even my cat has been offered two, with a line of credit totaling $25,000.

[55] See Marvin Cetron and Owen Davies 1991 and Huntington 1996, for more detailed discussion of worldwide economic changes.

[56] News broadcast January 2, 1999.

[57] An alternative scenario is that the year–two–thousand (Y2K) computer bug will crash much of the world's economy, leaving the United States intact. In that event, much of the world's money may return to America, essentially recreating the conditions of the Bretton–Woods Agreement. — By the time this book is published, we will probably know what happened.

[58] See Huntington 1996.

of the Roman Church were clearly working on creating a pan–European theocracy as early as the 1970's. In particular, we find Polish Cardinal Stephan Wyszenski visiting Germany, to promote good relations between them and Poland, with a view to their eventual unification.[59] He gave his opinion, then, that the Roman Church was the only force capable of unifying Europe into one people.

Those statements were made before the collapse of the Soviet Union, was unforeseeable. However, there had been a trend in that direction since shortly after Stalin's death. — The USSR had granted East Germany sovereignty in 1954, although they left troops there for "security" reasons. Talks on German unification had begun in 1956, and trade pacts had been reached in 1957 and 1959, but negotiations broke down in 1960 and the border was closed in 1961. Then came the building of the Berlin Wall and the Berlin air–lift. Similarly, Soviet control of the other Eastern European nations was relaxed during the early 1950's, but abruptly retightened as those countries moved towards the West. — The Soviets wanted unification, but not under a Western model. They seem to have thought that the Eastern Europeans would prefer an Eastern form of government and way–of–life after having lived under communism for years. But, as the world saw, with the Soviet collapse, not even the Russians choose it when they were given a free choice.

The subsequent trend was a strong East–West conflict during the 1960's and 1970's. The next significant change may have been the Helsinki Accord, in 1975, in which the West recognized the existing boundaries in Eastern Europe. The next major event was the economic collapse of the Soviet Union.

The task of unification will not be easy, as the Eastern bloc has just emerged from the ethnic mixing, erasure of boundaries, and authoritarian regime which the Russians forced upon them. They are currently undergoing ethnic cleansing and the reestablishment of their demographics. — The choice pan–Europe is offering them is to lend their consent for the dissolution of precisely that which they are now fighting to reestablish. The principle benefits they would receive would be security and the new economic order, but these are not necessarily mutually exclusive of cultural and ethnic integrity, except that the leaders of pan–Europe insist upon it.

It would seem impossible to get their agreement to something they certainly do not want and for which there is no need. But, if the situation can be continued indefinitely in which there is not other way to obtain security, eventually leaders will be found who for one–reason–or–another will willingly agree.

Also, at the same time, the Roman Church is working, behind the scenes, to offer its solution of progressive change through consensus towards unity. Bear in mind that the time–scale over which the Church expects to achieve this may be on–the–order–of a century or two. — In that case, their plan is feasible.

---

[59] See Martin, 1990.

Yugoslavia, for one, is not buying the plan. So, in 1999, America began bombing them, with NATO authorization. The operation began slowly, and as the weeks passed the Clinton Administration tried one approach after another to win the support of the American public. — They accused the Yugoslav leadership of being Nazis,[60] Communists, child and woman killers, and so on, and so forth, ad nauseum . . . But, the support they were trying to foster never materialized. After six weeks of this propaganda they began pushing the envelope. Specifically, on April 27, 1999, the President called up 33,000 reservists in preparation for a ground war. But, only two days later Congress voted down a Declaration of War and required him to obtain Congressional approval before any troops could be deployed. Anti-war bumper stickers, also, began appearing.

President Clinton was fairly explicit about his goals.[61] He objects to the Yugoslavians daring to become a civilization. He feels that multi-culturalism is better.[62] To promote this, he is making war on them.[63]

On April 26, 1999, in a speech given to the American Society of News-paper Editors, in San Francisco, he outlined his "exit strategy" from the conflict. — He would place the region under a multi-national peace-keeping force. That is, in fact, what happened.

---

[60] This is Orwellian double-speak, because they are individualists, whereas the New Age–Environmental movement, Al Gore espouses, is "Nazi" according to our definition.

[61] Television news broadcast approximately April 27, 1999.

[62] Hayek's, 1944, discussion of the threat which globalism and collectivism pose to small countries is particularly germane.

[63] Presumably, this is being conducted under the PPBS, using a network on the ground to monitor the changing social attitudes produced by the bombing.

Chapter 17

Natural Resource Management

This chapter discusses natural resource regulation in the Post–Nixon era. It illustrates several innovations in law.

17.1 Closing the Gates of Opportunity

The American environmental movement dates back to the nineteenth century.[1] Presidents Cleveland, and Roosevelt withdrew huge tracts of land to create parks and the national forest. The objective of doing this was not to preserve nature so much as to better control labor.

Throughout the nineteenth century, the grist for the mills of American industry had been supplied by a constant tide of immigrants. There was a need for continuous immigration, because as Theodore Roosevelt put it:[2]

> An American workman could have saved money, gone West, and taken up a homestead ... a man who began with pick and shovel might have come to own a mine." But, Roosevelt continued, "Now the free lands were gone. ...few, if any, of the one hundred and fifty thousand mine workers could ever aspire to enter the small circle of men who held in their grasp the great anthracite industry. The majority of the men who earned wages in the coal industry, if they wished to progress at all, were compelled to progress not by ceasing to be wage earners, but by improving the conditions under which all the wage earners in all the industries of the country lived and

---

[1] For example, Yellowstone National Park was created by an Act of Congress in 1872.

[2] From his speech on the great coal strike of 1902.

311

worked, as well, of course, as improving their own individual efficiency.

However, the facts of the matter were that vast amounts of land were still available for homesteading, but they were being illegally withheld by the Federal Government and by those private parties who "owned" the railroad grant lands. Later, President Theodore Roosevelt attempted an even more sweeping withdrawal of natural resources from potential exploitation.[3] Thus, the gates of opportunity were deliberately closed.

Congressman Charles Lindbergh, the father of the famous aviator, reported in his 1923 book that he had seen an establishment document which had been distributed to insiders before the turn of the twentieth century in which their long–range plans were described. He stated that it specifically included the removal of all private property rights because, as it pointed out, "people without homes will not quarrel with their leaders." If the leaders have control of all homes, through central planning, they can decide who will have a home and who will not.[4]

After Theodore Roosevelt, environmentalism faded into the past. It did not rear its head again until 1960, when land use management appeared as one of the items in *Goals for America*. Implementation began with the founding of the World Wildlife Fund, in 1961, by Prince Phillip.[5]

In 1968, the UN Economic and Social Council called for an environmental summit and the Club of Rome was founded.[6] The Club of Rome's publications have been pivotal works for the environmental movement, ever since.[7] They may indicate establishment support for selected programs.

---

[3]For this end he formed the National Conservation Commission in 1908, headed by Gifford Pinchot, as an outgrowth of the (May 1908) White House Conference on Natural Resources. In December 1908 they issued the first inventory of the nation's natural resources, published as a Senate document of limited circulation. During February 1909, President Roosevelt held another conference, the first North American Conservation Conference in Washington DC and at it recommended the establishment of a permanent Conservation Commission and also the extension of the program internationally. However, these recommendations met intense congressional opposition, nor was the National Conservation Commission continued by President Taft. Nevertheless it was continued at private expense and evolved into a kind of private lobby for preservation.

[4]See Charles Lindbergh 1923 quoted by K.M. Heaton 1993.

[5]Ten years later, Prince Bernhard, the head of the Bilderburgers, founded the 1001 Club to provide a revenue stream for it.

[6]Their founder Aurelio Peccei is listed as a member of the Committee of 300. One of the other influential leaders of the Club of Rome was Hugo Thiemann, the head of Battelle Institute in Geneva.

[7]In particular, in 1972, Meadows et al. outlined the need for global controls on environmental problems in their *The Limits of Growth*; in 1974, *Mankind at the Turning Point/The Second Report of the Club of Rome* called for the end of the nation–State for the same justification; and, in 1991, King and Schneider's *The First Global Revolution*.

17.2 Federally Protected Waters

Throughout the second half of the 1960's, due to a media campaign, the public grew concerned about the deterioration of the environment. — There were some notorious examples of pollution, such as the river which flows through Cleveland, Ohio, which caught on fire.

As a result, public sentiment grew that something needed to be done about it. Federal Laws protecting the environment were passed during the Johnson (1963–1969) and Nixon (1969–1974) Administrations[8].

The Puget Sound Water Quality Authority provides a clear example of a State program driven by Federal environmental laws.[9] It illustrates how apparently well–intentioned but open–ended Federal laws can go astray when they are adapted to local needs at the State level. — Puget Sound was designated a National Estuary under the Coastal Zone Management Act of 1972.[10] That brought in some Federal funding but also mandated water quality standards. Later, its 1990 reauthorization would also require regulation of non–point source pollution.

During 1983, a new State Agency, the Puget Sound Water Quality Authority, was formed to oversee that new National Estuary and to form and implement a water quality plan for that drainage basin. Initially it was supported by local environmental groups. However, its State authorizing law was repealed and replaced two years later. The new law gave them a vague mandate and sweeping powers.[11]

The Water Quality Authority was restructured as a stakeholder council with representatives of government agencies and special interest groups. The public were not represented and only two seats were reserved for local government.

Their first job was to identify the sources of pollution. They did this

---

[8]These include the Clean Water Restoration Act of 1966, the National Environmental Policy Act (NEPA) of 1969, the Coastal Zone Management Act of 1972, the Endangered Species Act of 1973, and the Fisheries Management and Conservation Act (FCMA) of 1976.

Senator Henry M. Jackson (D WA) was the legislative author of the NEPA, which created the EPA.

Speaker of the House, Warren G. Magnuson (D WA) sponsored the FCMA. It filled in a gap left by the failure of the International Conferences on the Law of the Sea in 1958, 1980, and 1974 to reach an agreement which would protect fish stocks in international waters.

[9]From this point onwards, this chapter primarily discusses Washington State politics. These are of national significance, because, as US Senator Slade Gorton (R Washington) said, "Most of my colleagues have viewed the Northwest as a kind of national laboratory." (See Williams and Long 1995.)

[10]See CZMA section 6217.

[11]They have access to the powers contained in the State's Water Pollution Control Act to not only to stop actual pollution, but to stop a person who, "creates a substantial potential to violate." The Washington Department of Ecology feels that this open–ended law can be construed to grant them sufficient regulatory powers to meet the Federal Standards. (Stated at the June 20, 1995 meeting of the Lower Columbia Bi–State Steering Committee.)

by conducting a public opinion poll in which people were asked to identify the leading causes of water pollution in Puget Sound.[12] Using the public's perceptions, rather than actual measurements, the Authority developed a water quality plan for the Puget Sound Basin. But, its scope was much broader than that sounds. — It included components on transportation,[13] structures[14] agriculture, forestry, mining, and manufacturing. Thus, a relatively inoffensive Federal Law was translated into a draconian plan for the control of land use and people's activities.

They were soon busy putting farms out of business, driving people off their land, and generally making themselves unpopular.

In 1994, the Authority sponsored several bills in the legislature which would have further enlarged their powers. They wanted the right to do enforcement themselves and to retain the proceeds from any fines which were levied against any people they caught breaking their rules. That would have provided them with a sustainable funding source.

However, Washington State agencies, with only a few exceptions, have a sunset clause. — Every ten years they must either be reauthorized or they will automatically terminate. The Authority's sunset review came up in 1995.

Governor Lowry requested that they be reauthorized and he identified that as one of the principle issues to be addressed by the legislature that session. However, the Authority had created substantial public resentment and its reauthorization died in the House of Representatives. But, it was reintroduced in the budget, as a new agency with a slightly different name, only to be again killed. In the end the Speaker of the House, Dale Foreman (R), saved it in the conference committee. However, in doing this he revealed where this State's Republican leadership actually stood.

Other Marine Sanctuaries: Puget Sound is not the only National Marine Estuary in Washington State. Except for two short gaps, all of the State's marine and tidal waters are either in a sanctuary or preserve or are planned to be.[15]

---

[12] According to Steve Tillie of the Authority, during the Environmental Focus Group Meeting on the Marine Sanctuary held at Port Townsend, March 1995.

[13] That is, where roads can be built, what size and type, and what form of transportation can be used on them. This included whether people be allowed to drive in a region or whether they must walk, bicycle, or ride a bus.

[14] That is what types of buildings can be built, what size, how many, and where.

[15] The Columbia River Mouth is another sanctuary. There are currently plans to extend it northward to just south of Willapa Bay and inland to the first dam on the Columbia. Above that dam the Columbia Gorge Scenic River begins placing the river under Federal regulation. Governors Lowry of Washington and Roberts of Oregon authorized its formation as of December 1994.

Immediately to the north of the planned extension of the Lower Columbia National Estuary, lays first a marine preserve at Willapa Bay, and then a short gap at Westport. North of that there is a Marine Sanctuary extending along all the Pacific Coast of the Olympic Peninsula and then eastward into the Straits of Juan de Fuca After another short gap, just West of Port Angeles, there is another proposed marine sanctuary. It is planned to stretch from there eastwards to

The Sanctuary program includes the power to use any federal law enforcement agency to enforce Federal, State, and local laws if the local law enforcement agencies aren't doing that adequately. Nor is these enforcement powers confined to only these federally managed waters. One of the tools they use to do this is a legal doctrine known as Winters' doctrine.

17.3 Legal Doctrines

These are part of a major innovation in law based on the legal philosophy called "positivism," which is derived from Comte's beliefs. However, its origin can be traced back much further than that: The Pharisees used something similar when they assembled the body of legal decisions and discourses which eventually became part of the *Talmud*.

The Court's traditional role in reviewing laws was to examine their constitutionality and original legislative intent.[16] However, that changed as the result of Harvard Law School Dean Christopher C. Langdell (1826–1906). Beginning in the 1870's. he introduced "positivism" and the "case-law study method."

Legal Positivism is the belief that the law should evolve through directed change. Under this view, laws and rights are not fixed and ancient precedents and original legislative intent has little weight. The judge is guided by current social trends and previous judicial decisions. That is by "case–law," the body of decisions made from the bench. It was the invention of Christopher Langdell and has never been authorized by any legislative Act. In fact, the legislature could not legally do so, even if they wanted to, as the legislative power was granted to them by the US Constitution with the specific intent of separating and balancing powers. Therefore, they can not transfer that power to another branch of government.

However, they may be said to have consented to case–law by their inaction. And, indeed, a certain amount of evolution and growth is necessary if the law is to remain just: that is, if it is to remain reasonably consistent with the ever–changing standards of society.

Positivism and case law were, later, advanced by Roscoe Pound (1870–1964), the Dean of Harvard Law School and later of the University of Nebraska. Langdell and Pound were very influential and a succession of US Supreme Court Judges held this view from 1902 through 1969.[17]

Bellingham and the Canadian border and southward to where it meets the existing Puget Sound National Estuary. However, it encountered stiff public resistance and was abandoned as a Federal program. It was later quietly implemented by the counties.

[16]Both the doctrine and process were spelled out, in 1803, by Chief Justice John Marshall in the case of Mayberry v. Madison, I Cranch 137 (1803), 177.

[17]Positivitist Supreme Court Judges included Oliver Wendell Holmes jr, appointed 1902; Louis Brandeis, appointed 1916; Harlan F. Stone, previously the Dean of Columbia Law School; Benjamin Cardozo, appointed 1932; Charles

As Chief Justice of the US Supreme Court, William Taft[18] was a positivist on some issues, and used the Supreme Court as a legislative body,[19] but he also held certain rights to be inviolable. In particular, that included property rights. He led the court's conservative majority for a decade (1921–1930), holding their progressive block[20] in check. The court also maintained a slim "conservative" majority throughout the early 1930's and undermined many of the laws of the New Deal, particularly during 1935 and 1936. That led to President Roosevelt's court packing plan in 1937. After that, the positivists increasingly had their way.[21]

Positivism reached its peak during the Warren Court of the early 1960's. For example, by 1958, Chief Justice Earl Warren felt free to make the statement that a Constitutional Amendment "must draw its meaning from the evolving standards of decency that mark the progress of a maturing society."[22] and in 1962/63 the Supreme Court openly repudiated the Natural Law and Biblical standards upon which our legal system and national heritage had previously been based.[23]

Winters' doctrine comes from the landmark decision handed down by Judge McKenna in 1908.[24] That case involved water rights for the Indian reservation at Fort Belknap, Montana. The Indians had traded a large amount of range land for a smaller amount of farm land so that they could become farmers. However, their right to water came into question. The ruling of the court was that the grant of farming land to the Indians implied the grant of whatever water was needed to irrigate those lands. The general principle which was established was that when a grant of land is made to an Indian reservation for a specified purpose, all that is necessary to accomplish that purpose is also granted.

During the half–century following its pronouncement, Winter's Doctrine was applied only to Indian territory. However, in 1955 the ruling in the case of the Federal Power Authority v. Oregon was that Winter's Doctrine also applied to federal lands.[25] Specifically, water rights are limited to the water necessary to achieve the primary objective for which the federal lands were purchased.

The primary purpose of the proposed marine sanctuary in the Straits

---

Hughes, Chief Justice 1930–1942; and Earl Warren, Chief Justice 1953–1969.

[18] William Taft had been a Yale Law professor. His first major government appointment was as the Governor of the Philippines. In that position, he was effectively an absolute dictator. After that he served as the US President. However, he got the job he wanted when he was appointed the Chief Justice of the Supreme Court (1921–1930), by President Harding. (See Alpheus T. Mason 1958.)

[19] See the comment by Senator Norris, *Congressional Record* Vol 72 (1930): 3566).

[20] Brandise, Holmes, and Stone,

[21] See Mason 1958.

[22] Trop v. Dulles 356 US 86, 101 (1958).

[23] See Abington v. Schempp 374 US 203, 220–221 (1963).

[24] Winters v. United States 207 US 564, 28 S.Ct. 207, 52 L. Ed. 340).

[25] The limitations on its application were clarified in Arizona v. California (1963, 64) and US v. New Mexico (1978).

of Juan de Fuca was the preservation of wildlife. In their draft proposal that specifically included shellfish. As many shellfish are sensitive to water quality, under Winter's Doctrine the Marine Sanctuary program would mandate water quality management, and therefore, land use management, enforceable by Federal officers. It, therefore, comes as no surprise to find that that sanctuary's draft proposal lists the implementation of the Puget Sound Water Quality Plan as their first priority. — A sanctuary may look like a park, but under Winter's Doctrine it provides the basis for a broad confiscation of private property rights and the iron fist of law enforcement by officers who are not accountable to the local electorate.

On that later point, the County Sheriff is an elected official and is, thus, accountable to the public for his conduct and that of his department. Therefore, enforcement of the law by a Sheriff or one of his deputies can not be characterized as arbitrary, coercion, nor slavery. In contrast, Federal and State law officers do not enjoy that same level of legitimacy as their accountability occurs through a chain of command which is effectively beyond the reach of the local voters. Those law enforcement officers must, therefore, place themselves under the authority of the Sheriff.[26]

At present, this is done formally through revokable written agreements. The parts of the Marine Sanctuary Act which authorize direct law enforcement by State and Federal law officers contravene this institution and, therefore, may be the most significant change contained in the marine sanctuary program.

The public trust doctrine is another old legal principle from case law which is being used to confiscate private property. That doctrine states that the government has the power to protect public resources. Originally that doctrine was restricted to the protection of the navigability of waterways in order to protect the commerce which depended upon them. However, the courts have extended that doctrine to include as divergent issues as public access and protection of the environment and natural resources.

Dr. Ralph Johnson, a law professor at the University of Washington wrote, in 1991, that, "public trust isn't a sharp line which can't be crossed. It's a pressure to balance public interests along with the private. The doctrine sits atop a body of statutory law and gives an extra push to state agencies to deny permits for projects that would damage public resources. I don't think our agencies realize they have that power. In some states, such as California, public trust is considered almost a constitutional doctrine that is very difficult to get around. I predict that Washington eventually will go that far."

He feels that the doctrine could be extended to land and water rights. He goes on to state that, in his opinion, "If we always had to condemn

---

[26]That is not intended to suggest that the Deputy Sheriffs are of a higher standard than Federal Law Enforcement Officers. The opposite is probably more often be the case. But, this is the institution which America has to insure that the public holds the ultimate decision power over law enforcement.

property rights to protect resources, we couldn't afford it."

17.4   Boldt Case

One of the main drivers for the concern over the environment in the Pacific Northwest is the salmon crisis. That is an example of an artificially created environmental crisis but it also illustrates the use of legal doctrines.

During the late 1960's and early 1970's The Indians brought a succession of cases to the courts, either by their suing or by provoking arrest. Their central concern was fisheries. Since 1942, the states had had the power to regulate Indian fisheries, equally with others, for the purposes of conserving the fish stocks.[27] The first substantive change came, in 1970, when Judge Rummel ruled that the Indians had some special rights.[28] A series of court cases followed.

According to Joe de la Cruz, a Tribal leader from Washington State, the break–through came for the Indians when they contacted the National Governors' Association.[29] That helped to win them the support of Washington's Governor Dan Evans. With his help and that of his appointee, the Director of Fisheries, Mr. Tollefson, and with the technical support provided by the Schools of Fisheries and Law at the University of Washington, that the tribes got what they wanted. That was contained in the decisions on Boldt I (1974)[30] and Boldt II (1980) cases.

The Boldt I case is openly the product of the legal philosophy of positivism. In 1974, Judge Boldt re–interpreted the Tribal treaty right to fish "in common" to mean "apportioned," which it quite specifically does not mean and never meant.[31] The central issue is whether rights are held by individuals or groups: that is individualism versus collectivism. Judge Boldt explained in his decision that his interpretation of "in common," in favor of collectivism, reflected current social trends. Thus, his decision could hardly be a clearer example of positivism.

However, he was beginning to develop Aldsheimer's Disease so he and handed over the second part of the case to Judge Orrick. Part II hinges upon Winter's doctrine.

Based on that doctrine, and the questionable assumption that salmon are habitat limited, Judge Orrick decided that the government has a duty ". . . to refrain from degrading the fish habitat to an extent that will deprive

---

[27] This had been established in the case of Tulee vs. Washington (315, US 681 1942).

[28] Washington State Supreme Court, Judge Bartlett Rummel, Memorandum Decision No. 158069, based on Puyallup Case, Nov. 24, 1970)

[29] He made this statement during the Northwest Renewable Resources Center's "Tribes and Counties" conference, January 1997.

[30] US v. State of Washington 1974.384 F. Supp 312, 1974.

[31] For example the fourth edition 1891–1957, of Black's Law Dictionary states that "in common" means "shared in respect to title, use or enjoyment, without apportionment or division into individual parts, held by several for the equal advantage, use or enjoyment of all."

the tribes of their moderate living needs ... the state may not subordinate the fishing right to any other objectives or purposes it may prefer." That decision essentially gave the Indians, or the government on their behalf, regulatory powers over any activity which affects salmon habitat. It also gave this habitat right the highest priority. These were large powers, because a wide range of activities potentially affect salmon habitat. That includes anything which either directly or indirectly affects runoff or produces any substance which could get into the water. The lawyer for the State in Boldt I, Larry Coniff, pointed out that considered in its broadest sense, this includes, agriculture, mining, forestry, manufacturing, building, housing, recreation, power, water, sewage, transportation, regional growth plans, zoning, ... If this is carried to the extreme, very few activities couldn't be included.

The kind of situation which would get Judge Orrick's decision implemented was a disastrous collapse of the salmon fishery which the public attribute to the loss of habitat. — After that time, conditions were manipulated so that the salmon populations have been caused to decline and every effort has been made to perpetrate the hoax that this was caused by habitat loss.

In 1982, the US Supreme Court's final ruling[32] on the Boldt II decision overturned it in part and supported it in part. The parts overturned were the implied rights to fish habitat and water. The part supported was the mutual obligation of both the State and the Tribe to "each undertake reasonable steps commensurate with their respective resources and abilities to preserve and enhance the fishery." Furthermore, it says that the Supreme Court intended that there would be losses arising from reasonable development, and that these should be born 50–50 by the Indians. Thus, the most threatening parts of Orrick's decision were overturned.

However, the parties who liked the original decision continue to bluff the public into accepting conditions which they don't have to. That was possible because there are over 10,000 individual documents associated with the Boldt I and II cases and all its appeals and related actions. The public is generally not aware of this decision.

17.5   Post–Boldt Politics

During the period between Boldt II and the final Supreme Court decision, 26 big business interests formed a coalition, to deal with the impact of Boldt II.[33]

They hired James Waldo[34] to analyze the situation and make rec-

---

[32] See 694 R.2d 1374 (1982).

[33] That was the "Northwest Water Resources Committee." About half of their members represented timber companies. (See Monson 1982, Cohan 1986, and Fraidenburg 1989.)

[34] James C. Waldo is a well-known public figure. He first appeared in public life as an aid to Governor Dan Evans. After that, he went to law school. Follow-

ommendations. He found that the Orrick decision " ...if carried to the extreme, would appear to permit no balancing of interests and no flexibility for the State, the United States, or third parties."[35] However, he also recognized that the business community could turn the Orrick decision to their advantage by forming a coalition with the Indian tribal authorities.

They hosted a series of meetings, among the interested parties. These appear to have been the first time the methods of group dynamics were used in Washington State in a stakeholder council to develop a consensus on a political issue. The outcome was that they founded an Institution to represent their interests: That was the Northwest Renewable Resources Center.[36]

Fraidenburg (1989) devoted considerable effort to showing that the Northwest Renewable Resources Center was an "iron triangle": that is, a coalition of users, regulators, and legislators. Amy, in 1987, discussed the techniques for developing and managing an iron triangle in the context of natural resource management.[37] He concluded that when legislators, regulators, and resource users conspire together, it is a combination which is difficult to overcome.

The introduction of this type of organization was suggested in Triangle Paper Number 8.[38] Its thesis was that America had obtained too much freedom, and it recommended forming planning organizations with this structure, so that the elite could provide leadership to government.

The Trilateral Commission later refined its suggestions in *Triangle Papers numbers 18 and 28.* Then they recommended the use of TQM, along with several other things. —The Northwest Renewable Resources Center became experts in those techniques, too.

Control of the Press: During 1989 Mr Fraidenburg published an article exposing the Northwest Renewable Resources Center. Shortly

---

ing graduation he became an attorney with Gordon, Thomas, and Honeywell of Tacoma. He is the chairman of the board of directors of the Northwest Renewable Resources Center. During 1996, he ran as a Republican candidate for Governor in the primary race. He was the best funded candidate but only received about 5% of the Republican primary vote. The public characterized him as a "Dan Evans Republican:" that is a representative of the liberal establishment.

[35] Waldo 1981 quoted from Fraidenburg 1989

[36] The committee's final meeting was in 1984 in Port Ludlow. (see Larsen 1986, 1987.) The Northwest Renewable Resources Center was incorporated that year. Their stated objectives were the formation of public policy, the initiation of processes, and the mediation of natural resource disputes. They closed their doors in 1998.

[37] Amy also discussed stakeholder councils. One of the things he said was that "...usually the determining factor [of whether a seat is offered on the council] is whether a group has enough power to block or subvert a final agreement."

[38] A few years later, George Weyerhaeuser founded the Business Roundtable along these same lines. It draws together all the major businesses in Washington State to provide leadership on public policy issues. However, in *Elite Planners* I showed that it is effectively under the control of a relatively small group of large businesses which mostly have interlocking directorates with each other and with the Northwest Renewable Resources Center.

thereafter, the tribes demanded editorial privileges over the scientific journal which had carried his paper.[39] That is, *Northwest Environmental Journal.*

That journal comes from the Institute of Environmental Studies at the University of Washington. It was a conventional scientific journal and followed the usual editorial standards for scientific journals: that is, the content and accuracy of a scientific article is subject to peer review and editorial control is limited to the form or presentation and the appropriateness of the topic for the journal.

However, it was replaced by *Illahee.*[40] They, also, got a new co-editor. The *Free Press*[41] said that "*Illahee* is prospering more than its smaller, less editorially accessible predecessor."[42]

Salmon Co-management: From 1974 through 1984 the Indians were suing the State over their management policy at every opportunity. This took fisheries management out of the hands of the State and gave it to the Federal Courts. As Federal judges are political appointees, the result was management without any direct accountability to the public.

However, when a Public Initiative[43] which passed, in 1984, changed the rules of the game. It made granting special fishing privileges to the Indians illegal in Washington State. The intention was to put the responsibility for fisheries management firmly back into the hands of the Department of Fisheries, with little room for excuses.

But, when it became apparent that that initiative would pass, the Department of Fisheries contracted[44] the Northwest Renewable Resources Center to mediate an agreement between the State and the Tribes. The agreement they reached[45] was that they would jointly manage the resource. It also granted an effective veto power to the Indians over all of the Department of Fisheries' policies. That removed salmon management from the public sector and it also removed the process from public view as the Indians and the Department met in closed-door sessions to determine their joint policies. Joint management continues to this day.

In my 1995 book, *Salmon at Risk* I argued that the decline of the salmon was deliberately caused, mostly by manipulating the parts of their life-cycle which the public did not see.[46]

Over-harvest is probably the single largest problem. The Indians have been guilty of overfishing and abusive fishing practices. As they sometimes

---

[39] M. Fraidenburg, pers. comm 1994
[40] Its name, is derived from Northwest Indian words.
[41] See anon. 1995.
[42] Its early editions contain full-page advertisements for Weyerhaeuser Co., in contrast against the earlier journal which did not contain advertisements.
[43] Public Initiative 456
[44] Personal services contract 1350 (WDF 1984).
[45] The *Puget Sound Management Plan*, more widely known as the "co-management agreement"
[46] This is not the only publication on this theme. See also Williams, C.H. and W. Neubrech 1976, Lowman, B. 1978, and Fraidenburg, M.E. 1989.

do this flagrantly, many of the public think that the Indians are the whole cause of the problem. However, the all–citizen commercial and sport allocations have often been set too high for the health of the runs, and the poaching rates are astounding.[47] But, the Washington Department of Fish and Wildlife may be the largest single harvester. They catch the fish when they return to the hatcheries and sell them through a "surplusing" program. They also sell eggs to the foreign aquiculture industry. In addition, Alaska's refusal to stop catching Canadian Fish, in violation of the Law of the Sea, results in the Canadians not limited their catch of Washington's fish. The impact of this is significant enough that when Canada unilaterally curtailed their catch, during the last few years, Washington saw record returns. For many years, salmon were also taken by foreign a high–seas drift–net fishery. However, this problem ceased when the Federal Government began using military satellite technology as part of their enforcement effort. But, once they were able to control that fishery, there is some indication that they may begin licensing it. — These problems are still not under control.

Another issue is genetic contamination. — As a salmon's migration route and timing are inherited, crossing stocks reduces their survival.[48] This has been known, literally, for decades, but the Washington Department of Fish and Wildlife continues to cross some stocks and transport others between river basins.

Another cause for the decline is incompetence. It had been shown that imprecision in estimates of the harvest and number of spawning salmon results in decreased average harvests.[49] For example, Doug Eggers, in 1992, in reviewing the progress of the Bristol Bay, Alaska, sockeye fishery concluded that improvements in estimation methods had resulted in doubling the average harvest. But, instead of working to improve their estimates, in 1994, the year after the Washington Departments of Fisheries and Wildlife amalgamated, Wildlife was required to abandon their sampling method for estimating the catch of steelhead, which gave estimates at roughly plus–or–minus 30%, in favor of one used by Fisheries, which was known to be virtually unrelated the actual catch.[50] Later that year, they admitted that

---

[47] Tricking the wardens appears to be part of the heritage of being a commercial fisherman. But, I thought the sports fishermen were of a better breed, until I lived by a river. I estimated that for the reach of river I lived beside, more than two fish were poached for every one which was caught legally.

[48] See William Ricker (1972) and the symposium on hatchery–wild stock interactions presented in the October 1993 volume of *Fisheries Research..*

[49] For the proof see Crittenden 1994.

[50] To give some impression of the Department's belligerent attitude, I was at that time working as a consultant to them. My 1994 paper containing the proof that inaccuracy decreases the average harvest, had been submitted and they were aware of it, but, I was asked to work out the details for Wildlife's conversion to the new method. I demonstrated to them that the new approach would be worthless and that the change could only result in a major step backwards, but they insisted upon it, anyway. — In retrospect, I can see, now, that that was precisely what they wanted, because it would depress the runs with little risk of it being traced

if they were required to achieve statistical significance as a pre–condition to opening fishing, all fishing would be shut down.[51]

Marine mammals are another problem. As they are protected, their populations are no longer controlled. They eat a significant number of the returning salmon.

There is a fairly long list of other minor contributing factors.

Although there is, indeed, substantial habitat loss, in Eastern Washington, due to water diversion dams, there are not enough fish to utilize the habitat which is still available. In contrast, there is very little habitat loss in Western Washington. What loss there is is mostly due to a few dams which lack fish ladders. But, there is also some environmental degradation in the more heavily urbanized areas. A vast area of Western Washington remains pristine forest.[52] — Overall, there is a lack of proof that habitat is the limiting factor, and a fairly clear indication that it is not. The principle problem appears to be inadequate returns of adult fish.

But, there is a lack of will to resolve these problems, and clear evidence of a deliberate intent to depress the runs. — While I was still naive about the environmental movement, I went to the State offices of one of the largest and best–respected environmental organizations to complain that the Washington Department of Fish and Wildlife was cooperating with the Tribes to deliberately depress the Salmon stocks. — After their State Director had listened to me for a while he said, "Yes. We're doing that, but you'll never be able to prove it."

The next day, I went to the local environmental newspaper and clearing house. Seeing as I already knew about it, they told me the rest of the story. — It seems that the heads of the State Departments of Fish and Wildlife, Ecology, and Natural Resources had been meeting on a weekly basis with the heads of the Tribal Fish Commission, and the leading Environmental groups to decide how they would impact various salmon stocks to leverage environmental or land–use management programs.

I soon found that many of these people were only to eager to boast of what they had done. ... I had always thought that when the detective in a mystery story solved the crime because the criminal boasted of how he had done it, that that was just an artificial ploy to draw a faltering plot to a close. But, it is human nature. — It must be a terribly strain to have committed the perfect crime and have no one aware of your greatness.

Social Engineering: At its peak the commercial salmon fishery

---

to them. It never occurred to me that the results presented in my paper would be used this way. — When I walked out the door, that day, that was the last time I ever set foot in their building.

Later that year I wrote a bill, HB2021, to restore the salmon, at State Representative Jim Buck's request. It would have forced them to improve their methods. I found out later, from a Federal employee, that the Department had called a meeting of all the State and Federal agencies who were in any way involved to plan how to kill that bill.

[51] See the March 6, 1994, fiscal note to House Bill 2021.

[52] See Palmisano et al. 1993.

had supported on–the–order–of 10,000 fishermen. Based on this income, a substantial infrastructure developed and the coastal communities thrived. This continued until the 1970's when the Boldt decision began to roll back the process. Two decades later, almost no all–citizen commercial fishery remained and the infrastructure supporting them was gone too.

Removing that many family incomes from the small coastal communities had a large impact. So the State Legislature provided funding for displaced fishermen. It mostly went for their "re–education." Many of them were trained for jobs either out of the area or with government, but in the latter case, their actual re–employment appeared to hinge upon their adopting politically correct views.

Oregon State University studied the social impacts on fishing families. Many of them were broken and were replaced by non–family living arrangements and social values. — That University's studies provide the testing and measurement steps of the operant conditioning approach to social change. Thus, the destruction of Washington's salmon fishery appears to have been used for social engineering, to leverage the re–education of many members of these rural communities for new livelihoods and social attitudes.

Sustainable Fisheries: In 1993, the Washington Department of Fisheries and the leadership of ten commercial salmon fishermen's associations, without the knowledge of the fishermen they represented, formed a long–range business plan.[53] It proposed the introduction of industry quality standards to "improve" product quality in the marketplace;[54] re–education of fishermen in quality procedures; and a marketing board with a monopoly on the wholesaling of salmon.

Three years later, in 1996, the Sustainable Fisheries Foundation held a conference in Victoria, BC, to present their plan for the industry. It was attended by such notables as the Vice President, the Governors of Alaska, Washington, and Oregon, and the heads of various government departments. It was a strange hybrid between a scientific meeting and a political conference for the environmental community. Out of that meeting came a proposal for sustainable fisheries management, which controlled people but was open–ended with regard to preserving the resource.

17.6   Timber Industry

Let us return, now, to 1980 to examine another movement which developed during that era. Arnold and Gottlieb say that, "Defectors from the environmental movement have told us that Earth First! cofounder[55] Dave

---

[53] See Stuart, 1993.

[54] That translates to excluding out–of–state products, through the imposition of arbitrary and unreasonable standards designed to be unachievable by fishing industries in other States. — The retail prices might be expected to rise as the supply is restricted.

[55] The other founders were Michael Roselle and Howie Wolke

Foreman was approached by the Sierra Club and his employer, The Wilderness Society, in 1979 with an offer to fund a new extremist point group for the movement." This apparently was a ten–year commitment.

Earth First!'s membership was initially generated by a meeting, the Round River Rendezvous, held in Moab, Utah, in 1980. They referred to themselves as a "tribe" and had no fixed organizational structure. They were modeled after Edward Abbey's novel, *The Monkey Wrench Gang*, which glorifies environmental terrorism.

Earth First! engaged in sabotage and terrorism.[56] [57] That included the lethal practice of treespiking and they have also claimed at least one direct murder. Instructions on the techniques of ecoterrorism are given in Dave Foreman's book *Ecodefense: A Field Guide to Monkeywrenching*.

During the late 1980's Earth First! was infiltrated by a private detective, Barry Claussen, employed by the Washington Contract Loggers Association. His autobiography *Walking on the Edge* provides one of the more revealing works on their activities. Ten years after their founding, when Dave Foreman's ten year commitment expired, Earth First!'s leaders dispersed to other environmental organizations. They had helped put the loggers out of business.

Spotted Owl: Towards the end of that period, in 1987, the Ancient Forest Alliance, which is a coalition of mainstream environmental groups, including the Sierra Club and Wilderness Society, petitioned the US Fish and Wildlife Service to list the spotted owl as an endangered species.[58] That program had been slowly developing for several years. It came to a head in a 1988 conference in Portland.[59] The final result was that most of the timber industry was shut down and vast expanses of old growth forest were withdrawn from logging. That destroyed many businesses, communities, and families. Displaced workers were re–educated at government expense, mostly for jobs which were not in the region and, as a result, many of them eventually moved to other parts of the country.

The timber giant, Weyerhaeuser Co., had been one of the major sponsors of that program. The shutdown on logging produced a shortage of timber and paper and a sharp rise in prices. As a result, 1994 was the most profitable year in their entire history.

A decade later, new small logging companies began to appear, taking

---

[56] See Arnold and Gottleib (ibid.) and Barry Clausen 1994. They are also listed as a terrorist organization by the Federal government.

[57] So, also, did the Unibomber, Theodore Kaczynski. His list of targets was very similar to Earth First!'s, while his, 1995, *Manifesto* shows marked similarity to the ideas presented at the Rio Convention, which is discussed later on. — These people are all from the same school of thought.

[58] It turned out to be far more abundant than was previously thought. Apparently, it is closely related to or a variant of the common barn owl. It is also not restricted to old–growth timber, but uses a wide variety of habitats. But, the timber restrictions with respect to it remain in effect.

[59] Arnold and Gottlieb 1993 present a good overview of this program in their section of the National Audubon Society.

advantage of the opportunities the general collapse had created. Some of them introduced new technologies. These changes could not have occurred without the general collapse.

17.7   Chaos Theory

In terms of economic theory, although these collapses were created, they still represent the cycle of boom and bust. But, these are occurring in isolated segments of the economy one–at–a–time, rather than all together. They open new economic opportunities and provide a social learning experience without damaging the general prosperity of the nation.

What allows this, is that although the economic system, as a whole, is very large and complicated, it is composed of segments which are effectively isolated.

The understanding of the behavior of this type of system comes from ecosystems theory. — Ecosystems with only a few species, characteristically oscillate about a single stable point, in what is called a "stable limit cycle." The corresponding phenomenon in simple economic systems is their cycle of boom–and–bust. But, as ecosystems become more mature, more species are added to them and, their behavior becomes more complicated.[60] In particular, it characteristically acquires multiple stable points and its time–track[61] first oscillates about one stable point and, then, another. Its may also have more complicated behaviors.[62] Eventually, as the system adds more–and–more species and acquires more–and–more stable points, it reaches a state where there are so many stable points that they effectively merge into a continuum. Then, the time–track of the system no longer oscillates but moves freely throughout that continuum in a random–walk. Its behavior is, then, unpredictable, in the sense that one can not write a general equation for where it will be at any given time. This absence of a general solution is the state called "chaos" and these theories on the behavior of ecological systems are "chaos theory."[63]

---

[60] Their behavior is described by a system of differential equations, usually with one equation describing the dynamics of each species.

[61] This is the time–track in the multi–dimensional space where each dimension is the abundance of one species. Thus, this hyperspace has as many dimensions as the ecosystem has species.

[62] The system of differential equations defines a response surface in hyperspace. The time–track is the progress in the ever–changing abundances of the species. It has one precise location in hyperspace at any given time. Think of the time–track as a marble rolling on the response surface. — The shape of the surface, determines where the marble will go.

The analysis of the shapes of these hyperdimensional surfaces is the field of topology. These surfaces may have complicated features such as folds, ridges, cusps, and so on. Sensitivity analysis, which was mentioned earlier, is one of the methods for determining the shape of these surfaces. It is directly related to the stimulus–response methodology.

[63] It is related to "chaos" as a political and religious doctrine in that both create

Achieving the chaotic state of a mature ecosystem or a mature economy, requires a high connectivity among its various segments. If, on the other hand, the system can be compartmentalized, then its behavior can be treated segment–by–segment with each segment acting as a simple system with simple behavior.

Those who would like to control and manage the nation's economy might prefer this, because it produces a system which is oscillatory, predictable, and can be treated piecemeal. That makes is a manageable system and, also, one which can be collapsed segment–by–segment, thus, allowing change, modernization, and new economic opportunities without harming the overall economy.

---

unstable conditions which allow the system to move to a multitude of alternative future states.

Chapter 18

Land Use Management

This chapter discusses land–use management in the Post–
Nixon era, with a focus on the Clinton years. It shows how an
alleged environmental crisis is being used to restructure America's
government.

18.1 Environmental Organizations

Environmental organizations play an important role, but, most people do
not know who they represent. — Prior to the 1980's, they confined their
activities to conservation issues. If they addressed politics at all, they generally acted as the public's watchdog on government. They enjoyed wide
support and got incorporated into government committees and political
coalitions.

During the 1980's, big businesses interests began taking over many
of the larger national environmental organizations. These included The
Nature Conservancy, World Wildlife Fund, Sierra Club, and the Audubon
Society[1]

In 1985, the major donors to the environmental movement also became
coordinated by the Environmental Grantmakers Association. Arnold and
Gottlieb (1993) say that it is "an adjunct of the Rockefeller Family Fund
Inc. doing business as the Environmental Grantmakers Association. ... By
deciding which organizations get money, the grant makers help to set the
agenda of the environmental movement and influence the programs and

---

[1]See Morine 1994 for a brief account from the establishment press itself. For
a carefully documented review from their opposition see Arnold and Gottlieb,
1993. — These sources do not mention it, but we should not forget that the New
Age and Environmental Network come from these organizations and that they
were also infiltrated, for lateral control, by various other groups and networks.

strategies the activists carry out." It represents a consortium of 138 member corporations and foundations.[2]

The Nature Conservancy was the first major environmental organization to be taken over and is the archetype for the big–business environmental sector. It provides a good case study of how these take overs were done. — The Conservancy had originated in 1917, but the present organization was not incorporated until 1951. After that, for roughly two decades, they consisted of local chapters operated by volunteers who used funds from small donors to preserve small selective nature tracts and manage them.

However, Arnold and Gottlieb (1993) say that this changed, beginning in 1970, when their director of operations for the national office, Patrick F. Noonan, used a large grant from the Mary Flagler Cary Charitable Trust to advance one of their projects on the East Coast. It was highly successful and, as a result, he became the president of the Conservancy, in 1973. On the local level, the decade of the 1970's was also the period during which the chapters changed from local control to top–down control from the national office.[3] There was also a change in the Conservancy's policy: Specifically, they adopted a pattern of large projects based on grants from major donors. Specifically, Arnold and Gottlieb (1993) say that for more than a decade "a sizable fraction of the money behind the Nature Conservancy is the Mellon fortune." For example, in 1977, 42 percent of their total grants went to them.

The Conservancy's principle goal during the 1970's was the establishment of natural heritage programs in each state. These programs assess and document the natural resources in the state, select areas to be preserved, and present their recommendations in biennial state natural heritage plans. By 1980 they had established these programs in Oregon, Washington, and Wyoming.

The Nature Conservancy often acts as an agent, purchasing the land for the preserves from private parties and then reselling it to the State. However, The Conservancy characteristically retains a partial interest in the property so that they and the state end up as joint owners. In that case, the two parties draw up a memorandum of understanding for the co–management of the preserve.

For example, in 1991 The Nature Conservancy had collected all the land needed to form the Bone River Preserve. That preserve contains a marsh, a mudflat, a meandering river, forest land and an elk herd lives in the area. They then sold a 90% undivided interest in it to the State. It is closed to human access except to the DNR and The Nature Conservancy[4]. According to the memorandum of understanding, 90% of the preserve's op-

---

[2]For example, Arnold and Gottlieb (ibid.) list the top ten donors. They are all members of the liberal eastern establishment. That year they gave more than $100 million.

[3]For details on how this transition was worked see The Nature Conservancy 1980.

[4]However, for the purposes of research, the public can request entrance permits, although there is no guarantee that they will get them.

erating costs are born by the public. The Nature Conservancy contributes the remaining 10% and uses it as their private park.

In some areas these preserves are so extensive that they impact the local economy. For example, during 1995, Pacific County, Washington, Commissioner Pat Hamilton expressed concern[5] that these preserves had so reduced their tax base that they were having difficulty finding adequate funds to hire enough deputy sheriffs to provide basic law enforcement.

The next change came in 1987, when there was an internal conflict over The Nature Conservancy's policy. According to Peter Carlin (1990) more that 50 of their leaders quit and joined a new organization, Conservation International. However, he goes on to say that by 1990, these two organizations had resolved their differences. Both Arnold and Gottlieb (1993) and Morine (1994) say that one issue in dispute was whether to preserve small isolated properties or to preserve whole ecosystems.

However, at that time, there was also a change in The Nature Conservancy's principle donors from the Mellon Foundation to a broader base which closely resembles the composition of the Trilateral Commission. Also, in 1990, John C. Sawhill became their president. That is the same individual as authored Triangle Paper Number 17: *Energy, Managing the Transition*, which effectively became the Carter energy policy.[6] He has been their president ever since. The Nature Conservancy's programs are, now, closely linked to the environmental policies of the Trilateral Commission.

18.2 Debt–for–Nature Swaps

Conservation International, executed their first debt–for–nature swap, in July 1987. Specifically they bought some of the government of Bolivia's external debt, and traded it back for the government's commitment to preserve 2.7 million acres of tropical rainforest and grasslands (Peter Carlin 1990). A similar swap with Costa Rica followed in 1988. Since then there have been swaps in Brazil, Madagascar, Mexico, Colombia, and Peru.

These are complicated international financial transactions involving the Federal Reserve Bank. The Monetary Control Act of 1980, authorizes

---

[5] Interview 1995

[6] **John C. Sawhill:** (ref: Arnold and Gottlieb 1993) President of The (national) Nature Conservancy (1990 present); member of the Council on Foreign Relations and the Trilateral Commission; Associate Director of Energy and Natural Resources in the Office of Management and Budget (Nixon Administration, 1972–74); head administrator of the Federal Energy Administration (Ford Administration, 1973–75); president of New York University from 1975 to 1979; Deputy secretary of Energy (Carter Administration 1979–80); Member of the board of directors of RCA, Pacific Gas and Electric, Consolidated Edison, Philip Morris, Crane Corp., and General American Investors; trustee of Princeton University; chairman of the board of the Whitehead Institute of Biomedical Research at MIT, and Manville Personal Injury Settlement Trust, member of the board of advisors of the Center for Energy and Environmental Policy;

them to buy foreign debt with Federal Reserve Notes, backed by US debt, and then to issue more Federal Reserve Notes based on the foreign debt. The foreign debt is usually discounted and the transaction is made contingent on a debt–for–nature swap. That begins to tie the world's currencies together, under US control.

Washington State Senator Neil Amondson wrote a well–documented paper on debt–for–nature swaps. He traces the origin of the program to the Trilateral Commission and the World Bank. He suggests that the debt–for–nature–swaps are one of the steps in a progressive process of replacing the sovereign rights of nation–states with a single centralized global authority and of replacing small businesses and local economies with large international businesses.

That was the goal which emerged after President Nixon's term, as a result of his abrogating the Bretton Woods agreement. Finally, the new scheme solidified, in 1991, with the Trilateral Commission's publication of *Beyond Interdependence: Meshing the World's Economy and Ecology*.[7] As its title implies, it suggests an integrated approach involving interdependence in trade and interlocking monetary systems among nations, all justified and bound together by debt–for–nature–swap.

These swaps have often proved to be detrimental to the host countries. The crux of the problem is the "sustainable" management of the preserves by Non Government Organizations (NGO's). The word "sustainable" has been redefined. It's new definition explicitly does not mean harvest at a rate which can be maintained indefinitely by natural replacement. But it is not clear what exactly it does mean. The Brundtland Report began the process of redefinition, with the rather moderate statement: "...to meet the needs of the present without compromising the ability of the future generations to meet their needs."[8] The UN then created an ethics working group specifically for the purpose of formulating a "world ethic of sustainability for the transformation of human attitudes and values."[9] They defined "sustainable development" as "the kind of human activity that nourishes and perpetuates the historical fulfillment of the whole community of life on Earth." The Bundtland Commission's definition is generally used in material from the President's Council on Sustainable Development,[10]. When I asked Kathleen McGinty, their Laison to the White House, what the definition was, she answered that it was undefined and that they were working on its definition. She would not be more specific.

One concrete definition for it, which has repeatedly appeared in legislation in Washington State, is that something is "sustainable" when it can not be terminated by a public action. — That is to the point, because the critical question is not whether change can be caused, because effec-

---

[7] See Jim McNeill et al. 1991.

[8] See the World Commission on Environment and Development (The Brundtland Commission) 1987.

[9] Michel Rocard, press release at UNCED, June 1992; quoted from Dixey Lee Ray's *Environmental Overkill*.

[10] See *Sustainable America: A New Consensus.*, 1996

tive means are known, nor whether some specific change can be caused, but whether the elite can remain in control, because if they can do that indefinitely, they will eventually get wherever they want to go.[11] — Under this definition, "sustainable" management of a nature preserve means that an NGO has absolute authority and that neither government nor the people can influence what they do. — There are some instances where, once the NGO gained control over the land, they began unrestricted logging or mining operations without regard for either the environment or the local inhabitants.[12] But, there are also instances where they have made substantial improvements through good management.

These debt–for–nature programs are not necessarily limited to foreign countries. In particular, during 1990, Spencer Beebe said that Conservation International is looking into debt–for–nature swaps in the Pacific Northwest. He specifically mentioned a possible joint–venture with The Nature Conservancy in Washington State.[13]

During the mid–1990's, some people were suspicious that an attempt might be made to take the Federal Lands in a debt–for–nature swap or some similar maneuver. However, there is a flaw in this scenario. The ownership of the Federal Lands is disputed. The US Congress commissioned a study of this question during the 1950's[14] and concluded that in many cases the Federal Government was illegally withholding public lands from the States or counties.

The issue was taken up by Nye County, Nevada. They declared that the federal government owns no land in the State of Nevada except certain forts and office buildings. They asserted county ownership and authority to manage the lands claimed by the US government. In response, during the second week of March, 1995, the US Attorney General brought suits against both Nye County and Catrin County over these issues. Associate Attorney General John Schmidt said the, "Justice Department suit intended to send a signal to other rebel movements in California, Idaho, New Mexico, and Oregon.[15]

18.3 Rio Convention

President Clinton's focus on the environmental may, to some degree, have been simply a matter of timing: The related Federal Laws had been passed

---

[11] This, explains a great deal and, also, reveals their key vulnerability, which they will respond to if they can be touched there.

[12] See Collett 1989.

[13] See Peter Carlin 1990

[14] See anon. 1956.

[15] See Dawson and Woodbury 1995. — People who don't live in the West rarely appreciate why these sagebrush rebellions occur: Over 90% of Nevada and Alaska are claimed by the Federal Government and West of the Mississippi River they claim more than half of the land. The people are jammed onto a relatively tiny area but can not fail to see that vast expanse, all around them, which remains empty.

twenty years earlier and they were coming up for reauthorization. Consequently, the Clinton Administration and the parties behind him knew that the environment was going to be a major issue during his term in office, and they used it constructively.

The issue opened with the Trilateral Commission's 1991 Report, *Beyond Interdependence*. Then, Clinton's term began with the 1992 United Nations Convention on Environmental Development held in Rio de Janeiro.

The Secretary General for that meeting, Maurice Strong, had written the introduction to that Trilateral report, and it's first author, Jim MacNeil, had been the head of the United Nations's Bundtland Commission, which laid some of the groundwork.[16]

The Convention was called to propose reorganizing society around the evil of the environmental crisis.

But to find the first indication that this might be done we need to look two decades earlier, to Lewin, in 1967.[17] The thesis of his book was that, if there is permanent peace, the treat of war has to be replaced by some alternative "enemy."[18] It listed the following possibilities: 1) open–ended government spending, such as projects for the exploration of outer space or the construction of large public buildings and stadiums; 2) the development of an elaborate system of slavery; 3) an invasion of extra–terrestrial aliens; 4) an environmental crisis, although he said it would take several decades to create one; and 5) the poisoning of air, food, and water supplies.— Each of these things has since transpired, except, that attempts to foster a belief in extra–terrestrial aliens have been more entertaining than credible. Also, the first artificially created crisis of national significance was the energy crisis, which he did not list.

Maurice Strong, set the tone of the Rio meeting in his opening remarks: "It is the responsibility of every human being, today, to choose between the force of darkness and the force of light." He then went on to recommend the dismantling of Industrial civilization and its replacement with a controlled

---

[16] Another reference on the Rio convention is Jan Tinbergen's *Rio: Reshaping the International Order*.

[17] It created a furor in Washington, DC. *US News and World Report* called it "The book which shook the White House." (See *US News and World Report* Nov 20, 1967 no. 48.)

It was written as if it were exposing a government planning commission, established to study the effects of permanent world peace. In 1968, John Kenneth Galbraith admitted that he had been a member of that commission. (See the *London Times* January 5, 1968.) But, it remains doubtful whether such a commission ever existed. However, the answer to that question is largely irrelevant as the importance of the book lies in its content.

[18] In 1991, an establishment study echoed the message contained in *Iron Mountain*: Specifically, Alexander King and Bertrand Schneider in their report *to* the Club of Rome entitled, *The First Global Revolution* wrote: "In searching for a new enemy to unite us, we came up with the idea that pollution, the threat of global warming, water shortages, famine and the like would fit the bill ... All these dangers are caused by human intervention. ... The real enemy, then, is humanity itself."

world economy. That was the thrust of this convention and the treaty they produced.

His remarks were Luciferian, drawn from the New Age movement, and the overall plan from Rio, for dismantling society, is consistent with the New Age doctrine: For example, Madame Blavatski wrote,[19] "The interference of man in [Western] civilization can disrupt the life forces of nature and the occult, only in countries where there is no civilization can the power of nature be found — the world's soul." — That is not a bad summary although it was written more than a century earlier.

More recently, William Irwin Thompson wrote, in 1976: "How is it that when we try to do good we can often end up by creating greater evil? ... If evil can grow out of our efforts to do good, it also seems to be the case that good can grow out of our efforts to do evil." He goes on to discuss social progress as "evil," because it is a departure from the old tradition.[20]

But, the policies presented at Rio were not motivated by religious hocus-pocus nor some vague sweeping theory. The religious aspect is relevant, but it is the outcome of serious scholarly studies and careful planning.

The general principles of chaos theory described above for economic and ecological systems also apply to social systems and the mind.[22] — A mature society like an mature economy or mature ecological system may have so many different types, kinds, and conditions of people that one might expect its social values to no longer follow a simple stable oscillation about one or a few points, but be free to move in a continuum.

However, social systems usually have very low connectivity, with each segment oscillating about fixed values. — Even in a diverse society which suffers from chronic alienation, people still form their small circles of family and private friends. These groups are usually effectively unconnected. Mostly people live their separate lives in their separate homes and go to and from impersonal jobs in their private cars. The result is a society with high diversity but almost no connectivity. That would usually be a highly resilient structure and, of course, societies evolve through various forms until they reach a resilient state. Thus, even very diverse societies will normally be stable.

This illustrates that multi-culturalism alone is not sufficient to produce the chaotic state which would allow rapid societal change. To achieve that, one must either increase connectivity or obliterate all personal values.

There are many programs which aim at increasing connectivity. — These include getting the public into mass housing, group homes, public

---

[19] See Blavatski 1888, vol 2.

[20] But, he also expressed some reservations: "A new race of liberals is arising to seek 'The Creation of a Just World Order,'[21] but if we remain as unconscious in this second global wave of liberalism as we were in the first wave which came at the end of the Second World War, then we are likely to create untold horror on a planetary scale."

[22] There is a science of socio-politics and journals with papers on the mathematics of changing social values. — These processes are amenable to mathematical treatment and modeling.

transportation, on public assistance, or involved in civic groups, networks, or religions. Likewise there are a multitude of programs for decreasing personal values. — These include unrestricted immigration, forced integration, and other programs which create cross–cultural conditions. But, they have not been very successful.

However, techniques from prisoner psychology are more powerful. — The seminal paper on this may be Zimbardo's , 1969, address to the Kansas Symposium on Motivation. It is a contemporary restatement of Jung's *Psychological Types,* although he did not cite that work.[23] There had been two other recent related studies, but this is where these ideas were first presented in the context of their impact on the structure of society. What he said was that deindividuation involves a shift for the individual from personal identity to an anonymous state, from being a separate person to a group member, and from order, reason, and harmony to the arbitrary, irrational, and chaotic.

This polarity is timeless. — He quoted Nietzsche who, in speaking of the Greek Dionysus said:[24]

> Throughout the range of ancient civilizations ... we find evidence of Dionysaic celebrations. ... The central concern of such celebrations was, almost universally, a complete sexual promiscuity overriding every form of established tribal law; all the savage urges of the mind were unleased on those occasions until they reached that paroxysm of lust and cruelty which always struck me as the "witches' cauldron" par excellence. ... [pages 25 and 26]
>
> Schopenhauer has describe for us the tremendous awe which seizes man when he suddenly begins to doubt the cognitive modes of experience, in other words, when in a given instance the law of causation seems to suspend itself. If we add to this awe the glorious transport which arises in man, even from the very depths of nature, in a shattering of the pricipium individuationis, that we are in a position to apprehend the essence of Dionysaic rapture, whose closest analogy is furnished by physical intoxication. Dionysaic stirrings arise either through the influence of those narcotic potions of which all primitive races speak in their hymns, or through the powerful approach of spring, which penetrates with joy the whole frame of nature. So stirred, the individual forgets himself completely.... [page 22]
>
> In order to comprehend this total emancipation of all the symbolic powers, one must have reached the same measure of inner freedom those powers themselves were making manifest; which is to say that the votary of Dionysus could not be understood except by his own kind. It is not difficult to imagine

---

[23] See, in particular. Jung's chapters on the Dionysus and Prometheus.
[24] See Nietzsche's *The Birth of Tragedy.*

the awed surprise with which the Apollonian Greek must have looked at him. And the surprise would be further increased as the latter realized, with a shudder, that all this was not so alien to him after all, that his Apollonian consciousness was but a thin veil hiding him from the whole Dionysaic realm. [page 28]

In his 1982 study of a mock prison, Zimbardo showed that the arbitrary and unpredictably abuse of power by prison guards caused deindividuation among the prisoners. — In particular, they showed that cruelty and, also, its unpredictable application, caused the prisoners to deindividuate to an anonymous state, to a number and a uniform, defining group membership, but no personality inside. A second and related impact of the arbitrary abuse of power was that it emotionalized. That tends to remove the individual from his or her rational self and self–isolation and make them spontaneously reactive and interactive.[25] Thus, tyranny was demonstrated to produce all the desired effects: specifically, a loss of values, a shift to collectivism, and an increase in social connectedness.

These are the goals of internationalist education, but, in this case, they can be produced among the general public. All that is necessary to do this is for government employees to draw power into their own hands and to arbitrarily abuse it.[26]

Of course, many of the government employees who did this knew nothing about systems theory nor prisoner psychology. They just had personalities and attitudes like the "bad" guards in the mock prison study, and acted this way when accountability was removed. But, there were also others, more than a few, who fully understood what they did. They would often speak of it as "public education."

Chaos theory combined with prisoner psychology and organic control to direct change appears to have been the essence of President Clinton's policies, particularly those which grew out of the Rio Convention.[27] They recommended that the public be tyrannized primarily by the arbitrary and cruel enforcement of often senseless land–use management and environmental laws. The environmental crisis provided a justification for

---

[25] Notice that this is fully consistent with the Classical view of individuation. — The general principle is that forcing submission to decisions made by others and imposing a lack of rationality produces behaviors in the victim characteristic of that stage of individuation where those were the dominant conditions of mental life: That is, the infant stage.

[26] This has resulted in an imbalance, as a corresponding conservative institution has not yet developed. to oppose these forces of chaos and darkness.

[27] The delay between the first enunciation of the idea, by Zimbardo , in 1969, and its first major impact on public policy by the Clinton administration, in 1992, was longer than would normally be expected. — The study by Deutsch et al, in 1971, showed that a lag of 10 years between the first presentation of a major advance in the social sciences and its impact is more characteristic. — In this case the first paper was rather obscure. Its importance may not have been widely appreciated until the 1982 study. The lag between that second study and implementation in public policy, was exactly what would be expected.

pursuing individuals into their private lives, homes, and businesses. And if the public knew that the "crisis" was fraudulent, that just served to increase the psychological impact.

The Treaty which came out of the Rio Conference was first read to the US Senate on Nov 20 1993.[28] It failed ratification.[29]

In a few cases, such as the Waco massacre, evidence is emerging that the Clinton Administration may have issued directives to terrorize. But, it seems likely that they more often implemented schemes which had a tendency to disaster, thus, opening opportunities for change

18.4   Disaster Management

Let us consider a government program where you can see exactly where that tendency was built in, and how the program fits into the larger PPB System, so that the impact can be used constructively to mold the public's social values.

The central ideas of the Magnuson Act and the proposals for its re-authorization[30] came from the Universities of Washington and British Columbia. They are found in the First and Second Ralph Yorque Workshops on Fisheries Management.[31]

Fisheries have traditionally been managed to yield the largest harvest which can be taken year–after–year without depleting the resource. That is called "maximum sustainable yield." But, in the Magnuson Act it is replaced by the concept of managing the fishery to achieve an economic optimum, called "optimum sustainable yield." This new approach was developed in the Departments of Math and Ecology at the University of British Columbia.[32]

---

[28] See Treaty Doc. 103–20.

[29] The treaty focused on the United States. Although it was an international treaty, it was primarily a vehicle to alter our internal law. According to its Article 28, its implementation in the US is already entirely within the power of the existing legislation it lists in detail. But, that is not exactly true. The implementation of the treaty would have changed the limits to which those laws could be applied. In addition, there were some items which were entirely outside of any existing law. For example, it treats humans as a biological resource, and includes a guarantee that other countries would have access to our genetic resources. That could be interpreted as designating Americans as breeding stock. — This kind of flagrantly draconian item only makes sense in the context of the theories of the constructive use of chaos and terror given above. The treaty makes interesting reading.

[30] See the Fisheries Management and Conservation Act (FCMA) of 1976 and its reauthorization, HR4404.

[31] The Ralph Yorque Room is the lecture hall for the Department of Ecology at the University of British Columbia. To "Ralph and Yorque" is British or Canadian slang for vomiting. The name, Ralph Yorgue, has, also, been used as a pseudonym for various anonymous letters and short communications in fisheries journals.

[32] Clark 1985 and Larkin 1976 are pivotal works.

That approach isn't wrong when it is strictly applied. The problem is that it allows too much latitude when regulatory committees apply it in practice. One question is, "Optimum for whom?" But, the most critical issue turns out to be the discount rate. — It is conventional to discount future harvests because the future is uncertain. But, if the discount rate is set high enough, it is always best to take your harvest now, at the expense of future harvests. The Magneson Act allows that. The result is that over the last twenty years, one–after–another, fish stocks have been over-harvested and driven into economic extinction, all around the country.

When the Magnuson Act came up for reauthorization, in 1996, there were proposals, to use "risk adverse management" instead.[33] That is even more open–ended.

Many people call a method "risk adverse" if it is conservative in the sense that it is unlikely to lead to an undesirable outcome. But the exact meaning is that it is a Baysian statistical method.

Baysian methods use risk functions, which quantitatively define risk. Risk could be, for example, the long–term economic loss relative to the optimum. In that case, the "risk adverse" method will probably recommend the optimum sustainable yield. Likewise, the risk function could be defined so that the method recommends taking the maximum sustainable yield.

However, a risk function is a broader concept than merely economic or biological loss. It could be based on cultural value, aesthetic value, or whatever value tickles your fancy. When a regulatory committee applies this approach in practice, it will soon be found that they have a mandate to do whatever they please.

Another thing authorizing risk adverse management does is authorize the use of the consensus process by the regulatory committees. — That process is, in fact, risk adverse management because each seatholder on the committee sees to it that the parties he or she represents are unlikely to be seriously harmed by whatever program they select. But, consensus groups are prone to group–think and extremity shift. As a result they occasionally make horrible mistakes.

Authorizing risk adverse management also authorizes the use of the PPB system in fisheries management. In that case, the risk function could be defined in terms of some social value among the affected sector of the public which the government wishes to change. And, of course, the funding agency can control the regulatory committees by group processes and organic control to achieve whatever program they feel may be necessary for their purpose.

Another broader class of programs with a tendency for disaster are Clinton's program for the reinvention of government, which is discussed later on.[34] That plan involved transferring the powers of the traditional

---

[33] See HR4404. It was promoted by the Marine Conservation Network. That includes the National Audubon Society and Greenpeace.
[34] See President's Council on Sustainable Development, 1996.

jurisdictional authorities to local and regional councils which used the consensus process and which were appointed in a manner which removed accountability.

18.5   Wildlands

The Nature Conservancy's Wildlands Project implements the Rio Treaty.

According to Charles Mann and Mark Plummer in their article in *Science* Magazine, in 1993, That project was the brainstorm of Earth First cofounder, Dave Foreman, in 1980.[35] They say that, a decade later, just after leaving Earth First!, "Foreman met in San Francisco with a dozen other activists.[36] Out of that meeting grew the Wildlands Project." That was the year after John Sawhill became President of The Nature Conservancy.

The Wildlands Project calls for a network of preserves, interconnected by wildlife corridors. That is intended to cover as much as half of the North American Continent. Each preserve or corridor has a core area from which people are prohibited and a buffer zone in which only limited land uses are allowed.

The corridors supposedly allow some migration of animals among the network of preserves, creating some genetic exchange among what would otherwise be isolated animal populations. The reason to do this is to preserve those species which require a large home range per individual.[37] Without this interconnection, the small sizes of their isolated populations would increase their probability of extinction.

However, there is room for doubt as to how effective the program would be. In particular, the corridors have a high proportion of edge for their area. Therefore, they would tend to attract wildlife who would move down them a ways before wondering out into the surrounding countryside, thereby, increasing their contact with humans and domestic animals. Thus, the corridors are likely to pose an attractive nuisance more than effective genetic exchange among preserves.[38] The plan does not have much support in the scientific community.

Although the Wildlands Project does not make a lot of sense biologically, it makes sense in terms of its impact on people. It breaks up the United States into may semi–isolated communities: That is it increases compartmentalization. The director of the Wildlands project,

---

[35] That was contemporary with his founding Earth First!, the Monetary Control Act of 1980, and the beginning of the take–over of The Nature Conservancy. So, it is reasonable to suppose that these details of the plan existed at about that date.

[36] Meeting November 1991. That included Reed F. Noss the editor of *Conservation Biology*. He is generally given credit for the details of the plan.

[37] This accounts for the environmental movement's single–minded interest in animals such as wolves and grizzly bears, which require large areas and are incompatible with humans.

[38] This was observed by Dr. David Simberloff. See Mann and Plummer 1993.

David Johns, was, as a matter of fact, a political scientist at Portland State University.

Much the same can be said about in the Rio Treaty: it was not about preserving nature, it was about controlling people.

The process of building these preserves began, in 1990, with the conversion of 26 million acres of Maine and Upstate New York into the Northern Forest. That effort is being spearheaded by the Northern Forest Alliance. They are coalition of 26 mainstream environmental groups.[39] However, the cost of that preserve was immense as eighty percent of it was in private ownership. The approach taken was to use conservation easements.[40] In 1993 the Northern Forest project was adopted by the Environmental Grantwriters Association and doubled in size to include approximately 50 million acres stretching 1600 miles from Maine into Minnesota. It was renamed the Northern Woods Ecoregion.

The process of setting up the nature preserves in the Northwest began, in 1992, when the Greater Ecosystem Alliance was founded in Oregon. It began mapping and cataloging for the new system of preserves.[41] Their program was identified by the United Nations Environmental Program (UNEP)[42] as the model to be followed in implementing Article 8 of the Convention on Biological Diversity. However, the Wildlands project dropped out of sight for several years, as the public's attention was drawn to a much a more high–profile project.

18.6 Cascadia Project:

Mark Plummer, who wrote the *Science Magazine* Article on the Wildlands project was employed as a fellow of Seattle's Discovery Institute.[43] They had, at that time, developed a similar plan, which follows Conservation International's approach of forming huge preserves, instead. That makes more sense ecologically. Also, in contrast to the Wildlands Project, they specifically addressed the impact on people. Their project involved:

1. Growth Management: This is a comprehensive State land use plan which places all private land under restrictive regulations. It limits permissible land uses; limits growth to the urban areas; and has

---

[39] These include the Sierra Club, The Nature Conservancy, National Audubon Society, Wilderness Society, and National Wildlife Federation. As in the Northwest, one of the driving reasons to do this was to make the timber industry more profitable. See Coffman 1994.

[40] The Forest Legacy Program.

[41] Their sister organization in British Columbia is the Canadian EarthCare Society.

[42] See UNEP's publication *Global Biodiversity Assessment*

[43] The Discovery Institute appeared before the Public in 1994. It bills itself as a conservative forum addressing public policy issues and providing leadership. However, their composition shows that they represent a sample of the internationalist big–business interests in Washington State.

substantially raised real estate prices, out of the reach of the younger generation.

2. Seattle Mayor Norm Rice's Urban Villages Program: This is where the bulk of the population will be forced to live, except the wealthy who can afford to live in rural estates. This plan involves a system of publicly owned high density urban housing. Home businesses will be prohibited there and virtually impossible anyway, as the urban dwellers will have no raw materials to which to apply productive labor and, thereby, create value. Their ownership of firearms will be prohibited, and to provide effective policing, the renters in the mass housing would be required to sign a waiver, allowing warrentless entry and search by the police.

3. Intermodal transportation including a light rail from Eugene, Oregon, to Vancouver, BC. Conversion of all the State's highways into toll roads under private control and coordination with all the other transportation components: heavy rail, air traffic, ferries, and so on. There is also a statewide system of bike and pedestrian trails under development, the rail–to–trails program. That is how the common people will get from one area to another, if they must.

4. International trade: Seattle's location makes it a gateway to the Far East. International trade, of course, will only be accessible to the biggest corporations and their suppliers, because of the ISO 9000 and high–performance certification systems.

5. International Seattle: The urban area is to be remodeled into an "international city," a tourist mecca, a meeting place for international businessmen, a site for international trade.[44] We and our children will provide services to these tourists and international businessmen.

6. Internationalist Education: It was at this meeting that Carol Eastman (deceased 1997), the Vice Provost of the University of Washington, indicated that the entire graduate program of the University would soon be directed towards international education.

7. Religion in Civic Life: One of the more benign parts of their program was a study based on C.S. Lewis's form of Christianity. He followed the lines laid out by Carl Jung on religion.

   His God was a "living" God, "A God who has purposes and performs particular actions, who does one thing and not another, a concrete, choosing, commanding, prohibiting God with a determinate character."[45] He may suspend the rules of Nature or impose a supernatural force to cause events which are contrary to Nature. These actions are "miracles."

   C.S. Lewis argued that the mind's rational facilities mimic and conform to the rules of Nature. However, he allowed that as Nature

---

[44] The proceedings and reports of their *International Seattle* meeting held in Seattle on May 6, 1993. were published by Hammer and Chapman (1993).

[45] See Lewis 1947, page 81.

contains a God who creates miracles, man's mind and reason should adapt to those irrationalities. In his view, people should follow articles of faith, taken and held without reason, but malleable to the winds of change and intermingled with the subconscious and dreams.

8. Bioregions: The project called for the breaking up of the United States into new nations called "bioregions" under United Nations oversight. This balkanization of the United States would be expected to completely change its social and economic dynamics.

   They planed that the Cascadia bioregion would include Washington, Oregon, Idaho, Montana, and British Columbia.[46]

   The first indication of a plan to break–up the United States, may have been in the newsletter, *Taipan*.[47] They said that use of the techniques for splintering "people into factions and interest groups will allow the nation to splinter geographically."[48] They also discussed the creation of "enclaves of wealth and power." These will be virtual paradises, far enough away from the pollution, congestion, and crime of the cities to be protected geographically and electronically. One they say will be near Everett, Washington, which is, directly adjacent the proposed park. Others will be in Telluride, Colorado; Charlottesville, Virginia; and Durham, North Carolina.

9. International Park: The first move towards implementation was the attempted creation of a huge tran–border park, during 1994.[49]

---

[46] Their program is co–chaired by Mayer Bob Bose of Surry, BC and Mayer Ruth Bascom of Eugene, Oregon. Its director was Bruce Agnew. There have been several meetings and publications on this plan.

[47] See *Taipan* vols. 8 and 12. Baltimore, MD. cited by Don Kehoe 1995.

[48] These geographical regions presumably were the Northwest, Southwest, Heartland, Northeast, and Southeast, or possibly the ten regions defined by the IRS. In each of them, the social dialectic and demographics are significantly different:
In particular, the Northwest is divided between conservative rural and liberal urban segments, the environment is a major issue, and economically the region is controlled by a few large international companies.
In contrast, the Southwest is divided between liberal rural and conservative urban segments, the emerging Mexican–American underclass seems to be a significant part of the social dialectic and, the economy is diverse.
...Each of the regions differ.

[49] There were many news stories on this during that year. One which is widely available is Elizabeth Pennis's "Conservation's Ecocentrics" in *Science News* Sept. 11 1994.
The proposal was presented at several meetings including "Nature have No Borders: A Conference on the Protection and Management of the Northern Cascades Ecosystem" held March 25—27, 1994, at the University of Washington sponsored jointly by the Henry M. Jackson School of International Affairs and the Canadian Studies Center of the University of Washington and the National Parks and Conservation Association.
Their steering committee included such notables as the Canadian Consulate General, The Minister of Environment, Lands and Parks, representatives of the

It was to be constructed by combining the US North Cascades National Park and eleven other parks or wilderness areas, totaling 2.6 million acres together with Canada's Manning Provincial Park and three other parks totaling 3.0 million acres. It would have covered an area about the size of Switzerland, larger than any of the smallest nine US States. Around it there would, also, be a buffer zone, bringing its total area to 11.4 million acres. That proposal received the official support of many highly placed individuals including Washington's Governor, Mike Lowry, US Senator Patty Murry (D, Washington), and President Bill Clinton.

According to Ms. Sandra Davis, Acting Director of Canadian Heritage, Alberta Region, it would not be under either US or Canadian jurisdiction, but would "be under the auspices of UNESCO (United Nations Educational, Social, and Cultural Organization), this will be United Nations territory."

That is, of course, the clue to why *Taipan* said that the splintering of America into bioregions will allow the creation of the enclaves. They assumed that America would become balkanized so that no individual bioregion would have sufficient military power to resist the UN forces. Thus, they could maintain the great gulf growing between the very rich and the very poor.

However, the plan for an International park created stiff public resistance. — Following a series of well–attended public meetings hosted by grass–roots groups, the Cascadia project suddenly completely disappeared.

Some members of the Washington State Legislature were opposed to the Cascadia project and, other, similar developments. For example, House Joint Memorial 4006, in 1995, says, "...That this serve as a Notice and Demand that the federal government, as our agent, cease and desist, effectively immediately, mandates that are beyond the scope of its constitutionally delegated powers." A similar sentiment can also be found in House Joint Memorial 4022 from that same year. It specifically opposed any form of UN or global government.

There is also another set of UN parks. These include Olympic National Park, Yellowstone, and Smokey Mountains. They were UN biosphere preserves. Legally they may be under UN jurisdiction and the treaty which created them also designated buffer zones around them in which there could be only limited land use. Probably not one person in a hundred who lives in those zones are aware of them, yet. But even though they are dormant, for the time being, they continue to be a reality.[50]

US Forest Service and US National Park Service, and a Tribal leader, together with professors from Simon Fraser University and the School of Fisheries and Ocean Sciences at the University of Washington and leaders in the environmental community.

[50] For example, see Penny Eckert's, 1998, PhD dissertation in the Department of Forestry at the University of Washington. She examined land use practices in the buffer zone around the Olympic National Park.

18.7   Wildlands Continues

While these high-profile events were distracting the public's attention, on February 7, 1995 H.R. 852 was introduced into 104th US Congress.[51] It gives its purpose as: "To designate as wilderness, wild and scenic rivers, national park and preserve study areas, wild land recovery areas, and biological connecting corridors certain public lands in the States of Idaho, Montana, Oregon, Washington, and Wyoming, and for other purposes." Those lands total approximately 22 million acres. The bill directly follows the Biodiversity Treaty. Related bills were also introduced simultaneously at the State level.[52]

By 1998, we find the Washington State legislature funding the purchase of conservation easements along river corridors. This began as a pilot program run through a previously popular State Agency[53] The easements would be held by land trusts. Examination of their incorporation documents revealed that at least some of these organizations were connected to The Nature Conservancy. In addition, the easements purchased were generally consistent with earlier maps produced by the Wildlands Project. These easements were to be perpetual and excluded human access, except to the landowner, the holder of the easement, and relevant State employees.

Next came a related program for the farming community. — In 1998, the leaders of the dairy farmers in Washington State reached an agreement in which they would partner in the management of their farms with State, Federal, Local, and Tribal Governments. This would, supposedly, give them immunity from threatened endangered species and other environmental regulations. Each farmer was to produce a farm plan, which would be approved by the State. The State would also provide funding for any major improvement which might be necessary. However, the State can, without the farmer's consent, change the standards in the plan, and if the farmer does not or can not comply with the new standards, he will have to pay back all the State funding for the improvements. Thus, those funds constituted a loan which the State can call in at any time, by setting unreasonable or impossible standards. Amazingly, many farmers signed the contracts.

That program served as a pilot project for the Governor's salmon recovery plan.[54] Its primary focus is on raperian habitat restoration for the purpose of restoring salmon. The State will use Federal funds to lease 300–foot–wide easements along raperian corridors for a period of ten years. They will then restore habitat and plant trees in those areas. Because, of restrictions on cutting trees along stream corridors, that will permanently

---

[51] See the Northern Rockies Ecosystem Protection Act of 1995.

[52] For example, see SHB 5076 and SB5762 introduced in 1995 in Washington. They allow the formation of Wildlands type preserves.

[53] Specifically, the Interagency Committee on Outdoor Recreation.

[54] See *Extinction is Not an Option: A Statewide Strategy to Recover Salmon.* Washington State Joint Natural Resources Cabinet, September 25, 1998.

lock the land into greenbelts and, thus, carve an interlocking network of
nature preserves out of the farmland of the State. The farmers would be
responsible for the cost of maintenance and must meet standards set by
the State, but which the State can change unilaterally. The draft plan says
that compliance is "voluntary," but then goes on to say that all Federal,
State, and local agencies will aggressively enforce all laws on those farmers who do not join the system, and environmental groups will assist by
bringing private law suits against individual farmers.

These easements are generally to be held by land trusts, the restoration
work is to be done by the Conservation Districts, and other duties, such as
monitoring, will go to environmental groups. Massive funding was available
from the Federal Government, before the legislation was ever approved at
the State level. — This should help to remind us that this is a Federal
program and that this is intended to be the new conduit for infusing money
back into the economy.

The farming community did not follow the dairymen's lead, but opposed the plan. It also had opposition from the environmental community
who, found voluntary compliance inadequate. — However, it did eventually pass the legislature, in modified form, amid cries of "sell–out" from
both sides.

18.8   Water — The Chelan Agreement

In 1989, the Northwest Renewable Resources Center hosted a meeting, at a
resort near Lake Chelan for the purpose of restructuring how Washington
State's water resources are regulated. Their agreement restored to the
Tribes, State, environmental groups, and big business much of the power
they lost when the Boldt II decision was overturned by the Supreme Court.

It did not become public policy until 1991 when the legislature authorized two pilot projects based on it. One of these was in the Methow Valley
of Eastern Washington, while the other was in the Dungeness/Quilcene
Valleys of Western Washington. The pilot projects' mandate was 1) to
create management plans for these watersheds; and 2) to establish new
rules for water use and water rights. These were to be submitted to the
legislature by 1995.

In 1992, another law[55] allowed the use of the consensus process in pilot
projects to meet the public hearing and public input requirements for writing new rules in the Washington Administrative Code (WAC). Thus, these
pilot projects dovetailed with this new rule–making process, providing a
mechanism to establish the Chelan Agreement by rule, statewide. — This
would become one of the keystones in the "reinvention of government."
It allows government agencies and non–elected quasi–governmental bodies
to circumvent local elected officials and due process in the formation of
Administrative Code. For all practical purposes, that is law.

---

[55]RCW 34.05.310 and .313; Laws of 1993 C202

The Methow Pilot Project finished both their watershed plan and their water–rights rule making. Their study team was composed primarily of representatives of government agencies and the local citizens had little input into the process.[56]

Their water rule establishes a minimum flow in the river and a water bank. As long as anyone can remember, that river flowed entirely underground, in some reaches, during the Summer months. It is relatively likely that there never was year–around surface flow. But there is abundant underground flow and, therefore, plenty of water available for beneficial uses. However, now no new water rights can be issued in that drainage basin until the minimum surface flow is re–established in the river. When an old water right is retired, it goes into the water bank and any new claims are made against it, but surface flow has first priority. As a result new homes can't be built in the Methow Valley, because building permits require proof of water rights. Thus, water is used to control landuse.

In the other pilot project, the Dungeness/Quilcene Basins, the residents prevented this outcome as the pilot project's leaders were unable to get the relatively few public representatives on the committee to agree to all of the points they wanted. Consequently, they didn't complete their rule–making on water–rights before their sunset date of 1995.

However, they arrived at a plan which served a different objective: One of their stated goals was to create a greenway along the river corridor, clearing all the residences for a half–mile on either side. They originally planned to place the river under the Wild and Scenic Rivers Act, but they faced the difficulty that they could not afford to buy the properties as their aggregate value exceeded one–hundred million dollars. So, they followed an approach which has been widely used throughout the country. — That is to manage the river for a single–channel configuration. That increases the depth and velocity of flow in the main channel, causing it to increase the width of its meander belt. That gives it a tendency to break its dikes and clear the land on either side. They achieved this by prohibiting the removal of woody debris from the riverbed. Those loose logs and branches tend to form log–jams, plugging the mouths of the side–channels, leading to the desired single–channel configuration. To further their objective they, also, prohibited the river–front property owners from controlling woody growth in the floodway, thereby, obstructing it and, also, providing a source of woody debris.[57] In addition, they prohibited the maintenance of dikes, bank–protection, and other flood control structures. The effects

---

[56] In particular, their team's final report states that they received no input from the public; but the local populace has some strong opinions about how they were excluded.

[57] The traditional approach is to manage the woody growth to achieve a desired roughness length in the floodway, so that during high water, the water will spread out and move slowly, causing no damage. The computations of the velocity and discharge necessary for floodway design and management can be done using Manning's Roughness Formula, but in practice are usually done based on common sense and experience.

were predictable: Over the decade they followed this policy, there were many "acts of God:" More than a dozen residences were destroyed and the river–front owners were given a learning experience, but there was no loss of life, excepting the drowning of two canoeists who were trapped under a log–jam.

These two pilot projects were trials of appointed councils and the consensus process as a new structure for government.[58] Councils, such as these, are now being set up throughout the Northwest as part of President Clinton's plan for the reinvention of government.

They have seats reserved for "stakeholders." These include State and Federal Agencies, Local and Tribal governments, business interests, environmental groups, and selected members of the public who have a stake in the outcome. This violates the concept of impartiality, as every seathold has a conflict–of–interest by design.[59]

One of the councils' functions is to draw the agencies into consensus, so that they work in unison. — That contradicts the principle of the separation and balancing of powers.

Another of these council's intended functions is the formation of public policy: specifically, comprehensive watershed plans, salmon restoration plans, water use plans, and the like. They make these plans and submit them to the Department of Ecology, who either approves or rejects them. They never come before any elected body. Compliance with these plans will be a condition for government funding and also for the issuance of permits. Thus, they determine what agencies will do and what the public may do.

These committees are either self–appointing or appointed wholly or in part by individuals other than the governing elected body for the jurisdiction for which they will form public policies.[60] This violates the right of the citizens of the community to determine who will form public policy for them.

The communities' experiences with these committees have generally been ones of frustration. — Some progress can be made by bludgeoning them in the political process combined with playing to their susceptiblities.[61]

---

[58] The first such watershed council in Washington State was in Grays Harbor County. These two were formed not long afterwards.

[59] The regulatory committees set up by the Magnuson Act, in 1976, were an early example of this structure.

[60] For example, The watershed council which grew out of the Dunginess–Quilcene pilot project, is self–nominating with nominations confirmed by one County Commissioner and the Chief of the local Tribe rather than the County Commission making appointments through due process. In 1999, that particular watershed council was designated by the Washington Department of Ecology as the model for such councils.

[61] For example, there are often two groups involved among the stakeholders who will readily "steal" ideas, but can not be given them, and certainly will not pay the prevailing consulting fees for them: 1) Government employees who feel that they, and only they, should be the resolvers of problems and the providers of services. and 2) Members of the working class who are jealous of anyone with

Nevertheless, their progress is often so slow as to be barely perceptible and will quickly reverse if there is funding for that.

These appointed councils, in fact, have much the same structure of government as existed in the Soviet Union. But, they also have the added refinement of the consensus process. That makes them virtually identical to local government in Communist China.[62]

A quotation from James Madison summarizes the situation from the Western viewpoint:

> The preservation of a free government requires, not merely that the metes and bounds which separate each department of power be invariably maintained, but more especially that neither of them be suffered to overlap the great barrier which defends the rights of the people.
>
> The rulers who are guilty of such encroachment exceed the commission from which they derive their authority, and are tyrants. The people who submit to it are governed by laws made neither by themselves nor by an authority derived from them and are slaves
>
> It is proper to take alarm at the first experiment upon our liberties — we hold this prudent jealousy to be the first duty of citizens, and one of the noblest characteristics of the late Revolution. The freemen of America did not wait till usurped power had strengthened itself by exercise, and entangled the question in precedents. They saw all the consequences of the principle, and they avoided the consequences by denying the principle.

Watershed committees were set up all over the State. Next there followed attempts to coordinate them. Governor Lowry of Washington and the Governor of Oregon tried to do this through the organization, "For the Sake of the Salmon." It has representatives from the government, fishing, environmental, and big business sectors.[63] They are networked with Oregon State University,[64] the University of Washington, the Sus-

---

an education or are motivated by the spirit of class struggle.

[62] Notwithstanding, the left–wing opposed these developments during the riots in Seattle, on the occasion of the World Trade Organization's meeting, in December 1999. — It seems that they only like this scheme if they control it.

[63] Its offices are in Gladstone, Oregon, a suburb of Portland, in the building of a little–known interstate agency, the Pacific States Marine Fisheries Commission. The office of the regional director of Trout Unlimited is also in that building and they are represented in that organization.

[64] OSU's connection to Washington's salmon fishery is clearly shown in their doing the social studies associated its the collapse of the commercial fishery. In addition, their Dean of Science is a member of the Board of Directors of Burlington Northern. OSU has experience with collapses in the fishing industry. — For example, during the 1990's, they had been the principle contractor responsible for the fisheries in Oman, under the Omani–American Joint Commission. Their mismanagement led to international tension. (See Gallucci et al. 1990.)

tainable Fisheries Commission and the President's Council on Sustainable Development.[65] However, this organization did not manage to provide the necessary leadership. Next, the President's Coucil on Sustainable development tried to draw them together. But, that, too, did not to have met the challenge, and the watershed councils faded into the background.

Part of their difficulties appear to stem from a partisan conflict over how the system will be structured and who will run it. The Republicans have control of the House of Representatives on both the State and national levels.

There is, also, a second system of councils. These are the Water Resource Inventory Areas (WRIA). They were originally set up by the Department of Ecology to implement the Federal Clean Water Act. During 1998, the State Legislature passed several bills which helped to define their structure, as well as that of the Watershed Councils. They, also, gave the Fisheries Enhancement Groups control over most of their funding. That is yet another set of are pre–existing quasi–governmental organizations. They had been set up by the Department of Fish and Wildlife, who appoint their seatholders and fund them. They are composed of an assortment government employees together with stakeholders from the private sector.

All of these various committees are stakeholder councils: that is the Watershed Councils, WRIA's, and Fisheries Enhancement Groups. Their seatholders are appointed in various different ways, except that none of them are elected nor are they appointed by the jurisdictional authority through due process. However, the Governor vetoed substantial parts of the bills which set these organizations up. Consequently, the exact overall structure remains unresolved, although the intent is clear enough.

The driver behind these changes is the listing of several salmon stocks as endangered under the Federal Endangered Species Act. In the case of the spotted owl listings, the State did not have a recovery plan. So, what happened was determined by the courts. But, in 1998, the Legislature passed a recovery plan for the salmon. So that will not be the case this time. The WRIA's are being used for that plan's implementation. There had, at the time, been an attempt to, also, include water rights and land comprehensive land use management in the mix, but the Republicans avoided that.

Representative, Jim Buck (R), who sponsored these bills, said that it is preferable to control of the salmon recovery effort from the State level rather that basing it on local control and he felt that the Department of Fish and Wildlife was capable of the task. They control the local WRIA's organically through the Fisheries Enhancement Groups and the Legislature controls the Department, similarly, through control over their funding. Mr Buck said that, with the help of the Republicans in the US Legislature, they had been able to make most Federal funding of the various Departments

---

[65] Both of these have close connections to the University of Washington's College of Ocean and Fisheries Sciences.

of State government subject to approval by the State Legislature.[66] He, therefore, felt that they have sufficient control over the Department to gain their cooperation.[67] He, also, hoped that the Fisheries Enhancement Groups would play a significant controlling role.

In this scheme, the body of government employees becomes the real government of the State for those issues under their control; implementation occurs at the local level through the WRIA's, which are composed of local government employees, but which are dependent structures; the Fisheries Enhancement Groups are interposed between them and the Department, providing some opportunity for lateral control, but they are appointed and outside the public sector with no protections against favoritism; then, there is the Department, which is the principle entity involved, and over them there are an appointed commission and the Legislature.

That is the Republican plan. — It may represent an attempt to construct something which could possibly work out of the meager resources available to them. But, it provides an example of the withering away of representative government. In the final analysis, it may be doubted whether its rather tenuous system for legislative oversight lends any legitimacy to the WRIA's power to make rules and public policy decisions.[68] But, that same cumbersomeness has been presented as this system's principle merit, for, as was the case for the first Soviet Constitution, it allows some local control.

We have already seen one Democratic plan for this, but another emerged at the US House–Senate joint hearing on the salmon crisis:[69] Specifically, James Ruckelshaus[70] proposed that a single person should be jointly ap-

---

[66] But, the Department also has significant dedicated funded sources. Prior to about a decade ago, fishing and hunting licenses had been their sole source of revenue.

[67] The current Director of the Department appears to want to cooperate, but has had some difficulty with the employees. The Department of Fisheries was notorious. They are virtually the archetypical dedicated cadre. — Fishing licenses gave them sustainable funding and they had always been self–selecting, hiring only those who could be trusted to adhere loyally to the Department.

[68] According to the State Constitution, all rightful power is derived from the people. Therefore, whatever legitimacy the system has comes through the Legislature, as it is the only representative element in this scheme. And there is an absence of due process.

[69] US House–Senate Interior Appropriations Subcommittees, Northwest Salmon Recovery Field Hearing, April 8, 1999, Seatac WA.

[70] James D. Ruckelshaus was born in Indianapolis in 1932. He graduated from Princeton Cum Laude and, then, got a Law degree at Harvard. He was in private practice, was a Representative for Indiana, and then worked for the Department of Justice. He was one of the first administrators in the EPA, from when it opened in 1970 until 1973. Then he briefly became acting director of the FBI. Later that year, he became Deputy Attorney General, but was fired by President Nixon in the Saturday night massacre. After that, he returned to private practice for several years, before becoming a vice–President of Weyerhaeuser Company, until 1985. Overlapping with that, from 1983 to 1985, he was, once again, an

pointed by Governor Gary Locke and President William Clinton to oversee and coordinate all the salmon and related natural resource programs
in Washington State.[71] This position soon came to be referred to as the
"Fish Czar." Throughout the remainder of the meeting US Senator Slade
Gordon (R, Washington), who chaired the meeting, asked each speaker his
or her opinion of the proposal. However, they failed to achieve consensus
as the representatives of the National Marine Fisheries Service and the US
Fish and Wildlife Service expressed reservations.[72] So, a Fish Czar was
not created.[73] But, towards the end of 1999, while the Legislature was out
of session, the Governor appointed Mr. Ruckelshaus to head his salmon
recovery team.

Mr. Ruckelshaus's plan would have established the structure needed
for PPBS–style organic control centralized[74] in the office of the fish Czar
over purely appointed committees operated by the consensus process at
the local level.

Elected government will, of course, remain, but if the powers over
land use are construed as broadly as was done by the Puget Sound Water
Quality Authority, whatever structure we end up with will hold substantial
power over our daily lives.

Governor Gary Locke summarized the overall picture in an address
to the Seattle Area Chamber of Commerce Leadership Conference held
in Vancouver, BC, October 9, 1998:[75] "It comes back to our ability to
compromise our own narrow interests for the benefit of the common good.
And it comes back to our ability to put aside old ways of thinking and
either/or choices and focus, instead, on achieving the balance which moves
us forward.[76] . . . . . The effort to restore wild salmon runs will make history
in bigger ways than we usually realize. . . . . . The stakes are very high."

EPA administrator. Today he sits on Weyerhaeuser's board of directors. His
wife, Jill, sits on the board of directors of the Discovery Institute.

[71] See Walter Reid and William Ruckelshaus, 1999.

[72] This involved their delegated authority which they may not be entitled to
relinquish: Specifically, the marine sanctuaries, the scenic highways, and the
Endangered Species Act listings of salmon are each capable of providing statewide
coordination. Two of these would make the National Oceanic and Atmospheric
Administration the governing authority.

[73] This was just the most recent of a long series of attempts to create a Fish
Czar. The last one was Public Initiative 640. It would have done this, through
some tricky wording. The key to this is found in the word "following" in its section
6. It should have been "during." That made the initiative's literal meaning the
opposite of what it appeared to be. The final outcome would have been to grant
absolute authority over fishing to the Director of the Department. However, it
failed to obtain a majority.

[74] The way was prepared for this, during the early 1990's, by the amalgamation of the previously separate Washington State Departments of Fisheries and
Wildlife. That removed any separation and balancing of powers in the relevant
part of State government.

[75] I thank Don Kehoe, of Monroe, Washington, for a copy of a portion of the
Governor's speech.

[76] See Jung's comments regarding Kant on page 45 of his *Psychological Types*.

Literature Cited

Abbey, Edward 1975 *The Monkey Wrench Gang* Lippincott, Philadelphia 352 p.

Adams, C. (ed.) 1850–1856. *The Works of John Adams*, reprinted 1971.

Adams, James T. (ed.) *The American Historical Dictionary*, Charles Scribner and Sons, NY 345 p.

Aho, James A. 1990. *The Politics of Righteousness: Idaho Christian Patriotism.*

Allen, G. 1972. *None Dare Call it Conspiracy.* Concord Press. Rossmoor, Calif. 241 p.

Amondson, N. 1991. *Debt for Nature / Equity Swaps: How the Establishment Uses the World for Profit.* The Evergreen State College, Environmental Issues in Latin America, Spring Quarter, 1991. 19 pages.

Amy, D.J. 1987. *The Politics of Environmental Mediation.* Columbia University Press. New York.

Angebert, Jean–Michel *The Occult and the Third Reich.*

Anon. 1956 Jurisdiction Over Federal Areas Within the States. Report of the Interdepartmental Committee for the Study of Jurisdiction Over Federal Areas Within the States. Report of Federal Areas Within the States. Part 1 — Facts and Committee Jurisdiction Over Federal Areas Within the States. Report of Recommendations. Submitted April 1956 to the Attorney General and transmitted to the Pres. Part 2 — A text of the Law of Legislative Jurisdiction. Submitted June 1957 to the Attorney General and transmitted to the Pres. Also note a Resolution during 1957. Copies are in the Federal Record.

Anon. 1983. *The Law of the Sea: Official Text of the United Nations Conference on the Law of the Sea with Annexes and Index: Final Act of the Third United Nations Conference on the Law of the Sea: Introductory Material on the Convention and the Conference.* New York, St. Martin's Press. 224 pages.

Anon. 1991. "A Shameful Harvest: America's Illegal Wildlife Trade." *National Geographic.* 180 (3): 116–119.

Anon. 1994a. "Judge Allows Teens to Face Banishment." *The Olympian* Aug 13, 1994.

Arnold, R. and A. Gottlieb, 1993. *Trashing the Economy.* Free Enterprise Press, Bellevue, WA. 659 p.

Babbit, Bruce 1993. "The Public Interest in Western Water" based on an address entitled "Navigability: Who Owns Our Waterways" which he gave at Lewis and Clark University, Portland, on November 13, 1993.

Bachrach, Peter 1967 *The Theory of Democratic Elitism: A Critique.* Little, Brown and Co. Boston, 109 p.

Bacon, Francis 1555. *New Atlantis* in, *Advancement of Learning, Novum Organum, and New Atlantis.* Great Books of the Western World. Vol 30, Encyclopedia Britanicca, Chicago.

Bailey, Alice 1944. *Discipleship in the New Age* NY, Lucius, p. 9.

Bailey, Alice 1957. *The Externalization of the Hierarchy* Lucius Publ. Co.

Bailey, C. 1871. *Phases in the Religion of Ancient Rome.* Univ. Calif Press, Berkeley, Calif. 340 p.

Bailey, Foster. *Working God's Plan.* Lucius Publ. Co.

Bakunin, Michel 1869. *Study on German Jews*

Barney, Gerald O. et al. 1980. *Global 2000 Report to the Pres — Entering the Twenty First Century.* Report of the Council on Environmental Quality and the Department of State p 687. GPO 1980.

Barton, David 1996. Original Intent: The Courts, the Constitution, and Religion. Wallbuilder Press, Aledo TX 76008. 534 p.

Barruel, A. 1789 *Memoires pour Servir a l'Historie du Jacobinisme.* translated into English and reprinted by various publishing houses.

Beard, Charles A. and Mary R. Beard 1944 *A Basic History of the United States.* Doubleday, Doran, and Co. NY 554 p.

Bellamy, E. 1960. *Looking Backward.* New American Library. NY.

Beria, Laventi 1933. a textbook on psychopolitics. Moscow University 1934 Summer School. Partially recorded in the Congressional Record by Representative Usher Burdick of N. Dakota. See 1954 Hearings on Tax Exempt Foundations p274 et sec.

Blavatski, Helen P. 1877. *Isis Unveiled* Lucius Publ. Co. NY.

Blavatski, Helen P. 1888. *The Secret Doctrine, the Synthesis of Science, Religion, and Philosophy.* Lucius Press, NY.

Bowman, J.S. 1989. *Andrew Carnegie, Steel Tycoon.* Silver Burdett Press. Englewood Cliffs N.J. 128 p.

Boyce, William E. and Richard C. DiPrima 1977. *Elementary Differential Equations and Boundary Value Problems* John Wiley and Sons. 582 p.

Brooke, Tal 1988 *When the World Will be One.* Harvest House, Eugene OR.

Brzezinski, Zbigniew 1970. *Between Two Ages.*

Buchal, James L. 1997. *The Great Salmon Hoax.* Iconoclast Publ. PO 677 Portland OR. 97002–0677. 384 p.

Burnham, James 1941 *The Management Revolution: What is Happening in the World?*, John Day Co. NY

Camus, Albert 1948. it The Plague Knopf NY 278 p.

Camus, Albert 1942. *The Stranger* Knopf NY 154 p

Carlin, P. 1990. "The New Leaders: Spencer Beebe." *Pacific Northwest* June 1990 page 20.

Carlyle, A.J. 1941. *Political Liberty.* The Oxford University Press. London. 220 p.

Carlyle, Sir R.W. and A.J Carlyle 1908. *Political Theory of the West.* Vols 1–4. Barnes and Noble, N.Y.

Carlyle, Thomas 1839. *Chartism* in *Works of Thomas Carlyl: in 30 volumes.* Chapman Hall London.

Carlyle, Thomas 1843. *Past and Present.* Houghton Mifflin (1965) 294 p.

Carney, J. G. 1985. *To be a Revolutionary, an Autobiography.* Harper Row Co. San Francisco, Calif. 473 p.

Church, F. Forrester et al. *What Unitarian Universalists Believe: Living Principles for a Living Faith. Resources for Study and Worship.*

Churchill, R.S. and W.S. Churchill, 1967. *The Six Day War.* Houghton Mifflin, Boston.

Cicero, Marcus Tullius circa 54BC *On the Commonwealth.* Sabine, G.H. and D.B. Smith 1929. translated Bobbs–Merrill Co. New York 276 p.

Citizens Study of the Joint Committee on Bases of Sound Land Policy, 1929. *What about the Year 2000?* 168 p.

Clark, C.W. 1085. Bioeconomic modeling and fisheries management. John Wiley and Sons. NY 291 pages.

Clausen, Barry 1994. *Walking on the Edge* Merril Press, PO Box 1682, Bellevue WA 98009.

Clews, H. 1888. *Twenty Eight Years in Wall Street.* Irving Co., NY. 157 p.

Coch, L. and J.R.P. French 1948. "Overcoming Resistance to Change". *Human Relations.* 1: 512–32.

Coffman, M.S. 1994. *Saviors of the Earth?* Northfield Publ., Chicago. 319 p.

Cohan, F.G. 1986. *Treaties on Trial: The Continuing Controversy Over Northwest Fishing Rights.* University of Washington Press, Seattle, WA.

Coleman, J. 1994. *The Committee of 300.* Joseph Publ. Co., Carson City, NV. 397 p

Collins, James 1959. *God in Modern Philosophy* Henry Regnery Co. Chicago 467 p.

Commission on the Skills of the American Workforce 1990. *America's Choice: High Skills or Low Wages.*

Coppinger, Lorna and Raynond 1982. "Livestock–Guarding Dogs that Wear Sheep's Clothing." *Smithsonian* April 1982. 171:64–73.

Cotter, John *Study of Syncretism, the Background and Apparatus of the Emerging One–World Church".*

Creasy, E. 1876 *The Fifteen Decisive Battles of the World: from Marathon to Waterloo.* 22 edn. Richard Bentley and Son, London. 407 pages.

Crittenden, Robert N. 1994. *Salmon at Risk.* Privately printed, Last Printing, 6th edn, 1997.

Crittenden, Robert N. 1994. Optimum Escapement Computed Using Ricker's Spawner–Recruit Curve. *Fisheries Research.* 20:215–227.

Crittenden, Robert N. 1995. *Elite Planners.* Privately printed, Last Printing, 2nd edn, 1997.

Crittenden, Robert N. 1995. *Two Studies in Public Policy in Washington State: Salmon at Risk and Elite Planners.* Hargrave Publ., Carlsborg WA.

Crozier, M., S.P. Huntington, J. Watanuki, and Trilateral Comm. 1975 *The Crisis of Democracy: Report on the Governability of Democracies to the Trilateral Commission: Triangle Paper Number 8* New York University Press, NY 220 p.

Cumbey, Constance, 1983. *The Hidden Dangers of the Rainbow.* Huntington House, Inc. Lafayette LA 268 p.

Dawson, P. and O. Woodbury 1995. "The West is Wild Again." *Time.* March 20, 145(11): 46.

Deutsch, Karl W., John Platt, and Dieter Senghaas 1971. "Conditions Favoring Major Advances in Science." *Science* 171: 450–459.

Dewey, John 1910. *How We Think.* Heath Co., Boston.

Dewey, John 1916. *Democracy and Education.* MacMillan Co, NY.

Dewey, John 1928. "Progressive Education and the Science of Education." *Progressive Education* V: 197–204.

Dewey, John 1938. *Experience and Education.* MacMillan Co. NY

Dewey, John. 1899 *The School and Society.* Chicago University Press, Chicago.

Diderot, Denis 1875–1877 *Oeuveres Completes* Paris, Edition Assez-at–Tourneaux, Garnier Freres. Vol 9, pp 15–16.

Dirks, B. 1986. "'Long Live the Kings' Enhancement Project Begins." *The Trout and Salmon Leader,* May–June, 1986. Northwest steelhead and salmon council of Trout Unlimited.

Donham, Wallace B. 1929. "Social Significance of Business" *Harvard Business Review* 5 July 1929. 406–419 p.

Donan, Elizabeth 1935. *Documents Illustrative of the History of the Slave Trade in America.* Washington DC. 4 vols.

Douglass, Paul H. and Edmund S Brunner. *The Protestant Church as a Social Institution* Harper and Bros, NY 1935.

Downs, James E. 1971. *Cultures in Crisis.* Glencoe, Beverly Hills 196 p.

Drummond, Harrold G. 1964. "Leadership for Human Change" *Educational Leadership* Dec 1964. p147.

Dullas, Foster R. 1954. *America's Rise to World Power.* Harper and Row, NY. 314 p.

Dwyer, D.C. and R. B. McNally 1993. "Public Policy, Prison Industries, and Business: An Equitable Balance for the 1990's." *Federal Probation,* June 1993 pages 30-36. Under contract to the Judiciary, Administrative Office of U.S. Courts, No. Ju 10.8:57/2

Eby, Louise S. 1944. *The Quest for Moral Law*. Columbia University Press, NY 289 p.

Eggers, D.M. 1992. The Benefits and Costs of the Management Program for Natual Sockeye Salmon Stocks in Bristol Bay, Alaska. *Fisheries Research* 14: 159–178.

Eliot, Thomas S. *The Idea of Christian Society*. Brace Harcourt.

Engels, Friedrich 1844. *The Condition of the Working Class in England*.

Engles, Friedrich 1888 *Ludwig Freuerbach and the Outcomes of Classical German Philosophy*

Erlenmeyer–Kimling L. and F. Jarvik 1963. "Genetics and Intelligence: a review." *Science* 142: 1477–79.

Evans, Daniel J. and The Nature Conservancy 1976. *Skagit Eagles*.

Ferguson, Marilyn 1980, . *The Aquarian Conspiracy: Personal and Social Transformation of the 1980's*. St. Martin's Press NY, 448 p.

Festinger, Leon 1962. "Cognitive Dissonance." *Scientific American* October 1962.

Fichte, Johann *Critique of All Revelation*

Fletcher, Joseph 1966. *Situation Ethics: the New Morality* Westminster Press, Philadelphia. 176 p.

Fletcher, Joseph. 1967 *Moral Responsibility: Situation Ethics at Work*. Westminster Press, Philadelphia 256 p.

Follett, Mary P. 1918. *The New State: Group Organization — The Solution to Popular Government*. Self-published.

Foreman, Dave *Ecodefense: A Field Guide to Monkeywrenching*.

Fraidenburg, M.E. 1989. "The New Politics of Natural Resources: Negotiating a Shift Toward Privatization of Natural Resource Policy Making in Washington State." *The Northwest Environmental Journal*. 5: 211–240.

Frederick the Great *The Anti–Machiavel* Ohio University Press (1981) 174 p.

Frieden, J. 1980. "The Trilateral Commission: Economics and Politics in the 1970's." pages 61–88 in Holly Sklar (ed.), *Trilateralism: the commission and elite planning for world management*. South End Press, Boston. 604 p.

Froissart, Jean fourteenth century. *Chronicles* selected, translated, and edited by Geoffrey Bereton 1968. Penguin Books, Middlesex, England. 496 pages.

Frost, S.E. 1943. *The Sacred Writings of the Worlds Great Religions* New Home Library. NY, 410 p.

Gallucci V.F., L.G. Anderson, and R.N. Crittenden 1990. Evaluation of the stock assessment parts of a program in the Sultinate of Oman under the direction of the Omani–American Joint Commission. Final report to the Omani–American Joint Commission, Mr. Les Clark, P.O. Box 6001 Ruwi, Muscat, Sultanate of Oman. 58 p.

Garitty, Michael 1980. "The US Colonial Empire is as Close as the Nearest Reservation: The Pending Energy Wars." pp 238–268 in Holy Sklar *Trilateralism: Planning for World Management.* South End Press Boston 604 p.

George Washington University, 1969. *The 5-5-5 Project: Implementing the PPB in States, Cities, and Counties.*

Goerg, J.A. 1994 "The Editor's Creel." *The Reel News*: September. PO Box 211 Renton, WA 98057.

Goldberg, Naomi 1979. *Changing of the Gods: Feminism and the End of Traditional Religions.*

Goldhammer, J. D 1996. *Under the Influence: The Destructive Effects of Group Dynamics.* Prometheus Books, Amherst NY 354 p.

Golitsyn, Anatoliy 1984. *New Lies for Old* 412 p. Available from Citizens for Academic Excellence, PO Box 11164 Moline, Il 61265, $12.00.

Green, J.R. 1874. *A Short History of the English People.* American Book Co. NY 872 pages.

Halveri, Zev Ben Simon 1986. *Kabbalah and Psychology* Simon Weisner Inc, York Beach Me.

Hamilton, Alexander 1775. "The Farmer Refuted" Feb. 23, 1775. *The papers of Alexander Hamilton* Vol 1 page 86. Harold Syrett (ed.) Columbia University Press, NY 1961.

Hamkins, G. 1974. "Motivation and Individual Learning Styles". *Engineering education.* 64:408–411.

Hammer, J. and B. Chapman 1993. *International Seattle: Creating a Globally Competitive Community.* Discovery Institute, Seattle Washington. 101 p.

Hamill, J. 1931. *The Strange Career of Mr. Hoover Under Two Flags.* William Faro, NY

Harley, John E. 1931. *International Understanding — Agencies Educating for a New World.* for the series: Stanford Books on World Politics, G. H. Stuart (editor). Stanford University Press. Palo Alto, Calif. 604 p.

Harnack, A. von 1894 *History of Dogma.* Translated and republished in 1961. New York;

Hayek, Freidrich A. 1944. *The Road to Serfdom* Univ. of Chicago Press. 274 p.

Heaton, K.T. 1993 *The Impossible Dream.* Hart Publ. Bellingham, WA.

Hegel, Goerg W.F. *Philosophical History* in *The World's Great Philosophers: Man and the State: The Political Philosophers.* Ramdon House NY (1947) 523 p.

Heidegger, Martin 1933. *Die Selbstbehauptung der Deutschen Universitat*, Breslau 13 p.

Herbart, Johann Friedrich 1816 *A Textbook of Psychology*

Herbart, Johann Friedrich 1824 *Psychology as a Science*

Herrnstein, Richard J. and Charles Murray's 1994. *The Bell Curve: Intelligence and Class Structure in American Life.* The Free Press, NY. 845 p.

Hobbes, Thomas 1651. *Leviathan* Bobbs–Merrill Co. NY (1958) 298 p.

Hoeller, Stephen A. 1989 *Jung and the Lost Gospels* Quest Books. the Theosophical Publishing House, Wheaton Ill. 268 p.

Homans, George C. and Charles P. Curtis jr. 1934 *An Introduction to Pareto* Alfred Kompf NY

Hoover Commission on Reorganization of the Executive Branch 1955. *Final Report to Congress.*

House, Edward Mandell *Philip Dru: Administrator* Upper Saddle Rover Literary House (1969) 312 p.

Hsu, Francis L.K. 1961. *Psychological Anthropology: Approaches to Culture and Personality* Dorsey Press Inc. Homewood Ill. 520 p.

Hunter, Edward 1971. *Brainwashing in Red China: the Calculated Destruction of Mens Minds.* Vanguard Press NY.

Huntington, Samuel P. 1996. *The Clash of Civilizations and the Remaking of World Order.* Simon and Schuster.

Huxley, Aldus *The Doors to Perception*

Huxley, Sir Julian 1947. *UNESCO: Its Purpose and Its Philosophy.* Washington, Public Affairs Press p8.

Institute of Local Self–Government, 1974. *The Politics of Change.* Berkeley, Issued by the Office of the Governor of California.

Jaffe, James 1968. *The American Jews.* Random House, New York 161 p.

James, William 1918 *Principles of Psychology.* Dover Publ NY (1950).

Janis, I.L. 1971. "Groupthink." *Psychology Today.* November, 1971. p. 43 ff.

Janis, I.L. 1972. *Victems of Groupthink.* Boston. Houghton Mifflin.

Janis I.L. and L. Mann 1977. *Decision Making: A Psychological Analysis of Conflict, Choice, and Commitment.* The Free Press.

Jansenius, Cornelius 1740. *Augustinus*

Jaspers, Karl 1931 *Die Geistige Situation der Zeit*

Jefferson, Thomas reprinted 1964. *Notes on the State of Virginia.* Harper and Row, NY 1964.

Jenson, D., G. Draffan, and J. Osborn 1995. *Railroads and Clearcuts.* Inland Empire Public Lands Council, Distributed by Keokee Co. Publishing Inc., Sandpoint Idaho.

Johnson, L.K. 1984. *The Making of International Agreements: Congress Confronts the Executive.* New York University Press. New York. 206 pages.

Johnson, R. 1991. Washington Sea Grant, University of Washington, Seattle, WA.

Jung, Carl G. 1921 *Psychological Types*. Princeton University Press. 608 p.

Jung, Carl G. 1956. *Two Essays on Analytical Psychology.* World Publ. NY.

Jung, Carl G. 1963 *Memories, Dreams, Reflections*. New York, Pantheon pages 188–189.

Jung, Carl G. 1963 *Collected Works of C.G. Jung. Vol 14: Mysterium Coniunctionis.* G. Adler and R.E. Hull, eds. Princeton University Press.

Kant, Immanuel 1781. *Critique of Pure Reason.* Hackett Publ Co. (1996) 1030 p.

Kant, Immanuel 1788. *Critique of Practical Reason* MacMillan (1963) NY 171 p

Kant, Immanuel. *Critique of Judgment* Encyclopedia Britannica, Chicago (1952) 613 p

Kant, Immanuel. *What is Enlightenment?*

Kanter, R. 1994. *ISO 9000 Answer Book,* Oliver Whight Publ. Essex Junction VT.

Kaplan, Mordecai M. 1934. *Judaism as a Civilization.*

Kehoe, Don 1995. *Blowing in the Wind* Vol. 2 No. 1 June 1995. 19624 Hwy 2, No. 318, Monroe, WA 98272. 38 p.

Keller, Suzanne, 1963. *Beyond the Ruling Class.* New York.

Keynes, J. M. 1936. *The General Theory of Employment, Interest, and Money.* MacMillan, London.

Kipling, R. 1899 *From Sea to Sea and Other Sketches* Vol II. Doubleday, Garden City, NY. 389 p.

Langer, W. L. 1940. *An Encyclopedia of World History.* Houghton Mifflin Co., Boston, Mass. 1270 p.

Lansing 1921. cited in Beard and Beard

Larrabee, Harold A. 1944. "Naturalism in America." in *Naturalism and the Human Spirit,* ed Y.H. Krikorian. Columbia Univ. Press, NY, 321 p.

Larkin, P.E. 1977. An epitaph for the concept of maximum sustained yield. Trans. Am. Fish. Soc. 106:06: 1–11.

Larsen, R.W. 1986. "Cutting Conflicts: Former Foes Use Consensus Politics to Develop Policy." Seattle Times, November 2, 1986, Seattle WA.

Laszlo, V. de 1990 *The Basic Writings of Jung.* Princeton Univ. Press. 561 p.

Lee, Robert G. 1994. *Broken Trust, Broken Land: Freeing Ourselves from the War Over the Environment.* Book Partners, Wilsonville OR. 210 p.

Lenin (Vladimir Oulianoff) 1918. *The Chief Task of Our Times.* published by the Workers Socialist Federation. 12 p.

Lessing *Earnst and Falk*

Levi, Ephipas *The History of Magic, Including a Clear and Precise Exposition of its Procedure, its Rites, and its Mysteries.* Trasl. Arthur E. Waite. Rider London (1969).

Levine, Robert A. 1974. *Culture and Personality: Contemporary Readings.* Aldine Publ Co., Chicago 458 p.

Levine, J. and Butler, J. 1952. "Lecture vs. Group Discussion in Changing Behavior." *Journal of Applied Psychology.* 36: 29–33.

Lewin, K 1947. "Frontiers in Group Dynamics: Concept, Method, and Reality in Social Science: Social Equilibria and Social Change." *Human Relations* 1:5–41.

Lewin, K 1947. "Group Decision and Social Change." In *Readings in Social Psychology.* (eds.) T.M. Newcomb and E.L. Hartley. Holt, Rinehart, and Winston. NY.

Lewin, K 1948. *Resolving Social Conflicts.* (ed) Gertrude W. Lewin. Harper, NY.

Lewin, K. 1935. *A Dynamic Theory of Personality.* McGraw Hill, NY.

Lewin, L.C. 1967. *Report from Iron Mountain on the Possibility and Desirability of Peace.* Dial Press. NY.

Lewis, Clive S. 1947. *Miracles: A Preliminary Study.* MacMillan NY 192 p.

Lilienthal, Alfred M. 1965. *The Other Side of the Coin* Devon–Adair Co. 346 p.

Lillie, Arthur B. 1894. *Modern Mystics and Modern Magic.* Books for Libraries Press (1972), Freeport NY 172 p.

Lindblom, C. 1977. *Politics and Market.* Basic Books Inc. Publishers. New York 403 p.

Lippit, R. 1948. *Current Trends in Social Psychology.* Pittsburgh University of Pittsburgh Press.

Livy *History of Early Rome.* Heritage NY.

Locke, John 1772. *Two Treatise of Government.* London: J, Wishton.

Langland, William, fourteenth century. *Piers Plowman* University of Pennsylvania Press (1996), Philadelphia 262 p.

Lovelock, James E. et al. 1987. *Gaia, A Way of Knowing — Political Implications of the New Biology.* Edited by William I. Thompson. New York, Lindisfarne.

Lowman, B. 1978. *220 Million Custers.* Anacortes printing and publishing, 1020 Seventh Street, Anacortes Washington 98221.

Luft J. 1970. *Group Processes: an Introduction to Group Dynamics.* Mayfield. Palo Alto.).

Luntz, D. S. 1988. *The Origins of American Constitutionalism.* Baton Rouge, Louisiana State University Press.

Macauley, T. B. 1833–49 *Critical Historical and Miscellaneous Essays and Poems.* Vol II. Printed by John W. Lovell, New York. 841 p.

Macaulay, T.B. 1841 "Lord Clive." *Edinburgh Review*, January.

Macaulay, T.B. 1841 "Warren Hastings." *Edinburgh Review*, October.

Macaulay, T.B. 1848 *The history of England.* Penguin Classics, Middlesex, UK. 570 p.

Machiavelli, Niccolo *The Prince*

MacKay, Charles 1841. *Extraordinary Popular Delusions and the Madness of Crowds*

MacNeil, J, P. Winsemius, T. Yakushiji, and Trilateral Comm. 1991. *Beyond Interdependence: The Meshing of the World's Economy and the Earth's Ecology.* Oxford Univ. Press, NY 159 p.

Mann, Charles C. and Mark L. Plummer 1993. "The High Cost of Biodiversity" *Science* Vol 260, 25 June 1993, pp 1868–1871.

Mareno, J.L. 1953. *Who Will Survive .* Beacon Press.

Martin, Malachi 1990. *The Keys of this Blood: The Struggle for World Domination Between the Pope John Paul II, Mikhail Gorbachev, and The Capitalist West.*

Marx, Karl *Karl Marx: Early Writings* Translated and edited by T.B. Bottomore, 1964, McGraw–Hill, NY.

Marx, Karl and Friedrich Engels *The Communist Manifesto*

Marx, Karl *Toward a Critique of the Hegelian Philosophy of Right.*

Mason, Alpheus T. 1958. *The Supreme Court from Taft to Warren*, Norton Library NY 250 p.

McCarthy, B. 1980. *The Four Mat System: Teaching to Learning Styles.* Arlington Heights Ill, Excel.

McIntosh and Twyman (translators). *The Archko Volume.* Keats Publ. Caanan, Conn. 248 p.

McLuhan, Marshall H. 1964. *Understanding Media.* McGraw Hill, 359 p.

McNeill, Jim, Pieter Winsemius, and Taizo Yakushiji. *Beyond Interdependence: Meshing the World's Economy and Ecology.* Oxford U. Press, NY, 159 p.

McRae and Cairncross *Capitol City* Eyre, Methuen, London 1963.

McWhinnie, David 1991. *The Occult History of the Third Reich.* Lamancha/Castle, Troy, Mich. ISBN–55529–657–2.

Meadows, Kenneth 1996. *Rune Power: The Secret Knowledge of the Wise Ones.* Element Books, Rockport, MA. 262 p.

Meisel, James, 1958. *The Myth of the Ruling Class.* Ann Arbor.

Mendlovitz, Saul 1975. *On the Creation of a Just World Order.* Dutton, New York: Free Press.

Merwin, J. 1994 "The Sportsman's Dollar", part 3. *Field and Stream* Vol XCIX (2) June 1994. pages 60–66.

Meuller, Walt, 1999. *Understanding Today's Youth Culture.* Tyndale House, Il.

Michael Servetus, sixteenth century. *On the Errors of the Trinity*

Modlhammer *Moscow's Hand in the Far East*

Monson, P.C. 1882. "United States v. Washington (Phase II): The Indian Fishing Conflict Moves Upstream." *Environmental Law* 12(2): 469–503.

Moore, M.G. 1972. "Learning Autonomy: The Second Dimension of Independent Learning." *Convergence* 5: 76–87.

Morley, Felix 1949. *The Power in the People.* D. Van Nostrand Co., NY. 293 p.

Morris, Barbara *The Morris Report* PO 756, Upland, CA.

Mosca, 1896. *The Ruling Class: Elementi de Scienze Politica.* Translated by Arthur Livingston, 1939. NY.

Motram, Bob 1995. article in *Tacoma News Tribune*, 4/19/95.

Muller, Robert 1982. *New Genesis: Shaping a Global Spirituality.* Doubleday, Garden City NY 192 p.

Mullins, E. 1993 *The Secrets of the Federal Reserve.* Bankers Research Institute, Staunton VA 24401. 201 p.

Multinational Corporations Group, 1975. *A Study of the Weyerhaeuser Company as a Multinational Corporation.* Evergreen State College.

Munro, William B. 1938. *The Governments of Europe.* MacMillan Co. NY. 856 p.

Myers, Gustavus 1936. *The History of Great American Fortunes.* The Modern Library NY 732 p.

Myers, D.G. and H. Lamm 1976. "The Group Polarization Phenomenon." *Psychological Bulletin.* 83: 602–627.

National League of Cities, 1994. *Organizations and Associations: Resource Directory for Local Elected Officials.* NLC, PO Box 491 Annapolis Junction MD 20701. 31 p.

Nature Conservancy, The, 1980. *Ten year report to Northwest Members: The 1970's in the Pacific Northwest and the Northern Rockies*

Nietzsche Friedrich 1883–1884. *Thus Spake Zarathustra* penguin, Baltimore (1969) 342 p.

Nietzsche Friedrich. *The Birth of Tragedy.* Doubleday, New York reprinted 1956.

Nock, A.D. 1964. *Early Gentile Christianity and its Hellenistic Background.* New York.

North, S. 1986a. "Harbor Likely to Land Major Fish Project". *The Daily World.* March 14, 1986. Aberdeen WA.

North, S. 1986b. "Group May Mediate Local Pollution Debate." *The Daily World.* October 1, 1986. Aberdeen WA.

Notter, Harley 1949. *Post War Foreign Policy Preparation, 1939–1945.* Washington DC. 56 p.

Odiorne, G. 1963. "The Trouble with Sensitivity Training." *Journal of the American Society of Training Directors.* 17:9–20.

Ogburn, William F. 1934. *Social Changes During the Depression and Recovery (Social Changes in 1934)* University of Chicago Press, Reprinted from American Journal of Sociology Vol XL May 1935, 6: 711–828.

Ogburn, William F. 1937. *Social Characteristics of Cities, a Basis for New Interpretations of the Role of the City in American Life.* International City Managers Association, Chicago 70 p.

Ogburn, William F. 1966. *Social Change with Respect to Culture and Original Nature,* Dell Publ. Co., NY 393 p.

Ogburn, William F. 1964. *On Culture and Social Change,* University of Chicago Press. 360 p.

Ogburn, William F. 1929. *Recent Social Changes Since the War and Particularly in 1927,* University of Chicago Press.

Ogburn, William F. 1932. *Recent Social Trends in the United States.* McGraw Hill.

Orwell, George 1946 *James Burnham and the Managerial Revolution,* Socialist Book Center, London.

Pagels, Elaine 1979. *The Gnostic Gospels.* Random House 182 p.

Paine, Thomas Paine. *The Age of Reason* Citedel Press (1974) Secaucus NJ 190 p.

Palmisano et al. 1993.

Patrick, James R. 1994. *Research Manual: America 2000/Goals 2000 — Moving the Nation Educationally to a "New World Order".* Citizens for Academic Excellence, PO Box 1164, Moline, IL 61265.

Pareto, Vilfredo. *The Mind and Society.* translated in 1935 by Arthur Livingston, New York.

Pennis, Elizabeth 1994. "Conservation's Ecocentrics" in *Science News* Sept. 11 1994.

Perlo, Victor *The Empire of High Finance*

Peters, Peter J. 1985. *The Greatest Discovery of Our Age,* Scripture of America, PO Box 766, LaPorte, Colo. 80535.

Peters, Thomas J. and Richard H. Watermann 1982. *In Search of Excellence.* Harper and Row, NY.

Pike, Albert 1871. *Morals and Dogma of the Ancient and Accepted Scottish Rite of Freemasonry.* Charleston A.M. 5641.

President's Commission on National Goals, 1960. *Goals for America: The Report of the Presidents Commission on National Goals.* Prentice Hall 1960 372 p.

President's Council on Sustainable Development, 1996.] *Sustainable America: A New Consensus for Prosperity, Opportunity, and a Healthy Environment for the Future.* USGPO ISBN 0–16–048529–0.

Quigley, Carroll 1961. *The Evolution of Civilizations,* MacMillan, NY 281 p.

Quigley, Carroll. 1966 *Hope and Tragedy: A History of the World in Our Time.* MacMillan Co. NY.

Raven, B.H. 1974. "The Nixon Group." *Journal of Social Issues* 30(4). 297–320.

Reid, Walter and William Ruckelshaus, 1999. "Salmon Conservation in the Pacific Northwest: The Need for More Effective Coordination in the Development of Recovery Plans. Walter Reid and William Ruckelshaus. April 4, 1999. 6 pages. copies available from Water Reid (waltreid@ibm.net) Washington Salmon Coalition, 731 N 79th St. Seattle. WA 98103.

Ripley, William Z. 1927 *Main Street and Wall Street.* Little, Brown, and Co. Boston

Robison, J. 1798. *Proofs of a Conspiracy Against the Religions and Governments of Europe Carried on in the Secret Meetings of the Free Masons, Illuminati, and Reading Societies.* third edn. London.

Roberts, Benjamin C., Hideaki Okamoto, and George C. Lodge 1978. *Triangle Paper No. 18: Collective Bargaining and Employee Participation in Western Europe, North America, and Japan.*

Roethlisberger, Fritz J. and William J. Dickson 1939. *Management and the worker* Harvard U. Press, Cambridge MA.

Rohr, John A 1986 *To Run a Constitution* Univ. Press of Kansas, Lawrence.

Rosenberg, Alfred *The Myth of the Twentieth Century*

Rotberg, R. I, 1988. *The Founder — Cecil Rhodes and the Pursuit of Power.* Oxford University Press, Oxford.

Rudd, Augustine G. 1940 *Bending the Twig: The Revolution in Education and its Effects on Our Children.* Heritage Foundation, Chicago (1957) 304 p.

Ruskin, John 1864. *Sesames and Lilies* in *Two Lectures Delivered in Manchester in 1864.* Smith Elder, London. 196 p.

Ruskin, John *Seven Lamps of Architecture* Noonday Press, NY (1969) 210 p.

Sargent, William, 1957. *The Battle for the Mind* Harper Row.

Sawhill, John C. et al. 1078. *Triangle Paper No. 17: Energy, Managing the Transition*

Schulzinger, R.D. 1984. *The Wise Men of Foreign Affairs, the History of the Council on Foreign Relations.* Columbia Univ. Press, NY.

Scott, Wiliam G. 1992 *Chester I. Bernard and the Guardians of the Managerial State* University Press of Kansas. Lawrence 233 p.

Seutonius, *Lives of the Twelve Caesars* Modern Library NY (1931) 361 p

Shoup, L. H. and W. Minter 1980 "Shaping a New World Order: The Council of Foreign Relations' Blueprint for World Hegemony." pages 135–156 in Holly Sklar (ed.), *Trilateralism: the Commission and Elite Planning for World Management.* South End Press, Boston. 604 p.

Sklar, Holly (ed.) 1980. *Trilateralism: the Commission and Elite Planning for World Management.* South End Press, Boston. 604 p.

Smith, Adam 1776 *Wealth of Nations* in *The World's Great Philosophers: Man and the State: The Political Philosophers.* Ramdon House NY (1947) 523 p.

Smith Barry D. and Harold J. Vetter 1982. *Theoretical Approaches to Personality.* Prentice–Hall Englewood Cliffs, NJ 404 p.

Smith, Major–General Perry 1987. *Assignment Pentagon.*

Smith, Robert M. 1982. *Learning How to Learn: Applied Theory for Adults.* NY Cambridge. 201 p.

Spencer, Sir Walter Baldwin and Francis J. Gillen 1899. *The Northern Tribes of Central Australia.* Dover Publ. NY (1968).

Stack, George J. 1976. *On Kierkegaard: Philosophical Fragments.* Humanities Press, Atlantic Highlands, NJ. 127 p.

Stanford Research Institute (SRI) International 1982. *The Changing Image of Man.* Pergamon NY 259 p.

Stauffer, V. 1918 "New England and the Bavarian Illuminati." *in* Volume 82 of *Columbia University Studies in History, Economics, and Public Law.* Columbia University Press, NY 202 p. Reprinted in 1967 by Russell and Russell, NY. 374 p.

Still, W. 1990. *New World Order, the Ancient Plan of Secret Societies.* Huntinton House Printers, Layfayette, Louisiana. 205 p.

Stillman 1905. "Freemansonry." Encyclopedia Americana

Stricker, L.J. and J Ross 1962. "A Description and Evaluation of the Myers Briggs Type Indicator" *Educational Testing Service Res. Bull* pp 62–6 Princeton NJ.

Stuart, Donald L. 1993. *Washington Commercial Salmon Industry Long Range Business Plan: An Industry–State Partnership.* 55p. Salmon for Washington, Seattle WA.

Sutton, A. 1986 *America's Secret Establishment.* Liberty House Press. Billings Mt.

Tacitus *The Annals of Imperial Rome.* Penguin NY (1956) 455 p.

Taft, Robert A. 1951 *A Foreign Policy for Americans.*

Taimni, I.K. 1968. *The Science of Yoga.* Theosophical Publ. House, Madras India, distributed in the United States by Theosophical Publishing House, Wheaton, Ill.

Turchenko, Vladimir, 1976. *The Scientific and Technological Revolution in Education* Translated to English from Russian.

The Nature Conservancy's 1980. *Ten Year Report to Northwest Members: The 1970's in the Pacific Northwest and the Northern Rockies*

Thomson, K.A., W.J. Ingraham, M.C. Healey, P.H LeBlond, C. Groot, and C.G. Healey 1992. "The Influence of Ocean Currents on Latitude of Landfall and Migration Speed of Sockeye Salmon Returning to the Fraser River." *Fisheries Oceanography* 1: 162–179.

Tomovic, Rajko and K. Miomir Vukobratovic 1970. *General Sensitivity Theory*, Contribution No. 35 in the series entitled, "Modern Analytical and Computational Methods in Science and Mathematics." Richard Bellman (ed.) Elsevier, Amsterdam. 258 p.

Toqueville, Alexis. de 1945 transl. *Democracy in America.* Vintage Books, New York.

Trilateral Commission. *Trilateral Commission Task Force Reports 15–19: a Compilation of Reports to the Trilateral Commission Completed in 1978 and 1979.* New York University Press. NY 459 p.

Trilateral Commission. *Trilateral Commission Task Force Reports 1–7: a Compilation of Reports to the Trilateral Commission.* New York University Press. NY.

Trilateral Commission. *Trilateral Commission Task Force Reports 9–14: a Compilation of Reports to the Trilateral Commission Completed in 1976 and 1977.* New York University Press. NY 293 p.

US National Commission on Excellence in Education 1983. *A Nation at Risk — The Imperative for Educational Reform: A Report to the Nation and the Secretary of Education.* Gardiner, David P. head GPO.

Velde, Phillip V. 1985. *Global Mandate: Pedagogue for Peace.*

Vernon, P.E. 1986. *Soul and Body: Essays on the Theories of C.G. Jung.* Lapis Press, Santa Monica, CA. 242 p,

Vernon, P.E., N.C. Weed and J.M. Butcher 1992. *Advances in Psychological Assessment* Vol 8 (Ed.) J.C. Roser and P. Mc Reynolds, Plenum Press NY.

Waite, Arthur E. *The Mysteries of Magic* p221.

Waldbott, George L., A. W. Burgstahler, and H. L. McKinney 1978. *Fluoride the Great Dilemma.* Coronado Press Inc. Lawrence Kansas. 423 p.

Waldo, J.C. 1981 *U.S. v. Washington, Phase II: An Analysis and Recommendations.* Report prepared for the Northwest Water Resources Committee, September, 1981. Gordon, Thomas, Honeywell, Malanca, Peterson and O'Hern, One Union Square, Suite 2101, Seattle, WA.

Waldo, J.C. 1984. *Certificate of Incorporation,* Northwest Renewable Resources center. State of Washington, Secretary of State, Corporation Number 2–343481–4, April 18, 1984.

Wall, J. F. 1970. *Andrew Carnegie.* Oxford Univ. Press, NY 1137 p.

Wallace, Anthony F.C. 1961. *Culture and Personality* Random House, NY 270 p.

Washington State Board of Education *Schools for the 21st Century*

Washington State Board of Education 1995. *Final Report to the Legislature on the Schools for the Twenty–first Century Program.* Chapter 525 Laws of 1987. Olympia WA.

Watchtower Bible and Tract Society of Pennsyvannia 1990. Mankind's Search for God. International Bible Student's association, Brooklyn New York.

Webster, Nesta H. 1919. The French Revolution. The Noontide Press, Costa Mesa CA 519 p.

Webster, Nesta H. 1921. World Revolution: The Plot Against Civilization. Omni Publ, . Palmdale CA 374 p.

Webster, Nesta H. 1924. Secret Societies and Subversive Movement. Omni Publ, Palmdale CA 419 p.

Weiland, Ted R. 1994. God's Covenant People: Yesterday, Today, and Tomarrow. Mission to Israel Ministries, PO Box 248, Scottsbluff, Nebraska, 69363.

Weisman, Charles 1991. Who is Esau–Edom?, Weisman Publications, 11751, W. River Hills Dr. No 107. Burnsville MN 55337.

Wells, H.G. The Open Conspiracy: Blue Prints for World Revolution. Doubleday, Garden City NY. 200 p.

White, R.K. 1969. "Three Not–So–Obvious Contributions of Psychology to Peace] J. Social Issues 25(4): 23–39.

White, R.K. 1970. Nobody Wanted War. Doubleday, New York.

Williams, C.H. and W. Neubrech 1976. Indian Treaties, American Nightmare. Outdoor Empire Publ. Co., Seattle, WA. 92 p.

Williams, Lindsey 1980. The Energy Non–Crisis CLP publ. San Diego 240 p.

Williams, Maria, and Katherine Long 1995. "Vancouver Draws 3000 to Debate Species Act." The Seattle Times April 23, 1995.

Winthrop, John 1644. "Arbitrary Government Described and the Government of Massachusetts Vindicated from that Aspersion" pp90–112 in Charles W. Eliot (ed.) American Historical Documents The Harvard Classics. P.F. Collier and Son NY 491 p.

Wise, Stephen Samuel 1910. Free Synagogue Pulpit: Sermons and Addresses. Bloch Publ. Co. New York.

Woofter, Thomas J. 1933. Races and Ethnic groups in American life. McGraw Hill NY 247 p.

World Commission on Environment and Development (The Brundtland Commission) 1987. Our Common Future, Oxford University Press.

Wormser, Rene A 1958. The Foundations: Their Power and Their Influence Devin–Adair Co. New York. 412 p.

Wundt, William Max, ten volumes completed progressively during 1875–1920. Volkerpsychologie.

Wundt, William Max 1897. Outlines of Psychology. Transl. by William Max Wundt and Charles H. Judd, Scholarly Press, St Clair Shores Mich. (1969).

Ypsilon 1947. Pattern of World Revolution. Ziff–Davis Publ. Co., Chicago 479 p.

Zimbardo, P.G. 1970. "The Human Choice: Individuation, Reason, and Order Versus Deindividuation, Impulse, and Chaos." in W.J. Arnold and D. Levine (Eds.) *Nebraska Symposium on Motivation, 1969.* Univ. Nebraska Press, Lincoln, Nebraska.

Zimbardo, P.G., Craig Haney, W. Curtis Banks, and David Jaffe 1982. "The Psychology of Imprisonment. in John C. Brigham and Lawrence S. Wrightsman (Eds.) *Contemporary Issues in Social Psychology.* Brooks/Cole Publ. Co., Monterey CA. 395 p.

Index